# LOCKE'S EDUCATION
## FOR LIBERTY

# LOCKE'S EDUCATION FOR LIBERTY

*Nathan Tarcov*

THE UNIVERSITY OF
CHICAGO PRESS
*Chicago and London*

NATHAN TARCOV is associate professor of political
science and in the College at The University of Chicago.

THE UNIVERSITY OF CHICAGO PRESS, CHICAGO 60637
THE UNIVERSITY OF CHICAGO PRESS, LTD., LONDON

LIBRARY OF CONGRESS CATALOGING IN PUBLICATION DATA

Tarcov, Nathan.
Locke's education for liberty.

Bibliography: p.
Includes index.
1. Locke, John, 1632–1704. 2. Education—Philosophy.
3. Liberty. 4. Political science—Philosophy. I. Title.
LB475.L7T37 1984    370'.1    83-17991
ISBN 0-226-78972-1

# CONTENTS

To my mother
and to the memory of my father

# PREFACE

T his work is an effort to broaden and deepen our views of both Locke and liberalism by taking *Some Thoughts Concerning Education* seriously as more than a practical handbook for parents. I try to read it as the richest source for Locke's vision of human nature and moral virtue. I try to read it in the context of the place of the family and education in Locke's liberal politics.

I first became seriously aware of the importance of the themes of education and the family in political theory and of how comprehensive a vision of human life a book may communicate when I was an undergraduate at Cornell University. There I had the privilege of taking seminars from Allan Bloom on those rare total or synoptic books, Plato's *Republic* and Rousseau's *Emile,* which he has taught, translated, and interpreted so as to make their themes and visions alive and compelling. I first seriously studied Locke's *Thoughts* when, as a graduate student at Harvard University, I did a paper for the seminar on the Enlightenment taught by Judith Shklar. This work owes much to her specific suggestions and general encouragement. Her sympathy for Lockean liberalism helped me to move from an initial reading heavily influenced by Rousseau's reaction against the *Thoughts* to a more appreciative understanding. Harvey C. Mansfield, Jr., served as my dissertation adviser with his characteristic brilliance and generosity. His own interpretation and defense of the spirit of liberalism helped to inspirit my work.

A traveling fellowship from Harvard enabled me to spend 1972–73 in England, where I was able to work at the Bodleian Library and the Reading Room of the British Museum. At Harvard I also enjoyed the privilege of using Houghton Library. A Research Fellowship for Recent Recipients of the Ph.D. from the American Council of Learned Societies in 1977 enabled me to reconsider my work and explore related problems. Students at Harvard and the University of Chicago in my courses on Locke and on Politics and Education probably taught me more than either they or I was aware of. Later revisions benefited from the careful and constructive criticism and encouragement liberally provided by Robert Dawidoff and the comments of the readers for the University of

Chicago Press. My research assistants at Chicago, especially John Dister and Victoria Farrington, helped me correct many errors. I am responsible for those that remain. Dwight Allman prepared the index, with assistance from Jeff Bond. My wife Susan listened patiently for too many years to all the reflections and complaints involved in producing this work and helped me in more ways than either of us can remember. The dedication expresses my greatest debts.

# INTRODUCTION

**D**espite historical change and historical revisionism, there remains a very real sense in which Americans can say that Locke is *our* political philosopher. The document by virtue of which we Americans are an independent people, occupying our special station among the powers of the earth, derives its principles and even some of its language from the political philosophy of John Locke. Practically speaking, we can recognize in his work something like our separation of powers, our belief in representative government, our hostility to all forms of tyranny, our insistence on the rule of law, our faith in toleration, our demand for limited government, and our confidence that the common good is ultimately served by the regulated private acquisition and control of property as well as by the free development and application of science. As for fundamental political principles, it can be safely assumed that every one of us, before we ever heard of Locke, had heard that all men are created equal, that they are endowed with certain inalienable rights, that among them are life, liberty, and the pursuit of happiness, that to secure these rights governments are instituted among men, deriving their just powers from the consent of the governed, and that, whenever any form of government becomes destructive of these ends, it is the right of the people to alter or abolish it. It is true that since these principles were first proclaimed, Nature and Nature's God, and with them the natural character of these rights, have not fared well at the hands of skepticism and positivism; yet these fundamental political principles of freedom and equality, of individual rights and government by consent, and of the right of the people to revolution certainly have not perished from the earth.

Locke occupies a canonical place not only in the history of political philosophy but in the history of educational theory, as standard texts in that field reveal. In itself this coincidence should occasion no surprise, for Locke plays a part in the history of many other fields as well, including, above all, philosophy proper but also economics, theology, medicine, the popularization of science, colonial administration, and library science. Locke also is far from alone in this double honor; philosophers

1

have been able to stand out in the realms of both educational theory and political theory ever since the two fields of thought first flowed from their common fountainhead, the *Republic* of Plato.

There is, however, something properly surprising here. Locke's thought in these two fields is found in two separate works, the *Two Treatises of Government* and *Some Thoughts Concerning Education*. It is perhaps only to be expected that the two works do not refer to each other explicitly, since the political work was published strictly anonymously and the pedagogical work, beginning with the third edition, appeared with Locke's name, if not yet on the title page, at least owning the dedication.[1] What is surprising is that there is so little reference in either book to the subject matter of the other. According to tradition, when one of the early Greek philosophers, Xenophilus the Pythagorean, was asked how one's son should be best educated, he replied "if he should be born in a city with good laws."[2] More reliably, we know that Plato thought that to describe how political life should be properly ordered it is necessary to describe what education would be requisite to this end; indeed, his Socrates says that the guarding of the proper education is "the one great—or, rather than great, sufficient—thing" for the best political regime.[3] Similarly according to Plato, for the best education to be possible, the best regime had to be described.[4] For Plato, education serves also as the critical ingredient of political obligation.[5] Both politics and education were supposed to serve ultimately the same end, the formation of good men. Nor is this intimate connection peculiar to the utopian Plato; as Sir Ernest Barker has commented, for Aristotle the state is "by its very nature an educational institution," and his "theory of education is thus an integral and essential part of his theory of the polis."[6] Nor is this connection confined to the philosophers of the ancient Greek polis; Locke's great English contemporary Thomas Hobbes viewed university reform as the most necessary step toward the proper political order, and he regarded instruction and law-making as the two chief duties of the sovereign.[7]

But Locke's politics are liberal politics after all; they entail a limited government, and it is limited above all by being freed from the effort of trying to make men good except insofar as that is required to render secure their lives, liberty, and property. At any rate, in the *Two Treatises* education plays nothing like the role it does in the *Republic* or even in the *Leviathan*. This too squares with American tradition; for our other great political document, that which constitutes our polity, makes no mention of education at all, at least pending any antibusing or school-prayer amendments.

We are faced then with the fact that the *Two Treatises* make little mention of education, as if the proper institutions were sufficient, whatever kind of men were formed by the education found in a common-

2

wealth, just as the *Thoughts* makes no explicit requirements for prior political reform. In part the explanation may simply be that, for Locke, contemporary Englishmen were already of the proper character to effectuate his political principles and that the English political order, at least after the Revolution of 1688 (which he wrote to promote and published to justify), was an appropriate home for the education he recommended. In part the explanation lies in the liberal character of his thought: not only in his radical separation of private and public, and his defense of private from public, but in his understanding government as subordinate to liberty, as having "nothing to do with moral virtues and vices,"[8] as making men not necessarily good but only free and secure, guaranteeing them not happiness but, as our Declaration was to say, the pursuit of happiness. These two explanations, satisfaction with particular conditions and liberalism, placed in conjunction raise the serious question of whether those liberal politics depend on fortuitous coincidence for their effectiveness, so that their universal terms conceal a limiting particularity. The fate of some attempts to transplant Lockean institutions shows that they do not easily flourish in other soils. But that would not be the most serious result if liberal politics had nothing to do with education; one would have to wonder not only whether Lockean politics are universally transferable but whether they are self-sustaining. If the character of a people changes, then liberal institutions may no longer suit them; and since liberal institutions are not primarily character-forming, they seem to provide no guarantee against this eventuality or remedy for it if it does occur.

Locke's political teaching proper puts no emphasis on education, but he does present an educational theory, albeit a separate one. Unlike Hobbes's education project, which was to take effect through the sovereign's reform of the universities, Locke's reform was to make its way on its own—over the heads or behind the backs of the government and the universities alike—by influencing the reading public of parents of young children. It was not aimed at all parents, to be sure, for Locke sought to influence only the gentry and, of them, only those "so irregularly bold," as he says at the end of the *Thoughts*, "that they dare venture to consult their own Reason, in the Education of their Children, rather than wholly to rely upon Old Custom." That Locke directly appeals to parents, rather than to the government, as Hobbes does, parallels the difference in their politics, where Locke also appeals to the people (or, in practice, to the reading gentry and nobility), urging them to the occasional supreme political initiative of revolution and to a continual political vigilance and concern. For Locke, they, not the government, are the sovereign. Hobbes, on the contrary, appeals to the people only for obedience; his positive appeal is to the sovereign to sanction and establish Hobbes's doctrines in the universities.[9]

Locke not only appealed to parents rather than to government; he appealed to parents to educate their children at home rather than at schools. This domestication of education seems wholly consonant with his liberal politics. It may be surprising, however, when we consider that his politics are also antipatriarchal.

Once we have gotten over our first impression of the *Two Treatises*—that they are silent on education compared to Plato or Hobbes (or Rousseau or Dewey)—we must be struck by the importance in them of the relation between parents and children. The *Two Treatises* present themselves as an attack on, and an alternative to, Sir Robert Filmer's patriarchalism, a doctrine of politics explicitly based on an understanding of the relation between parents and children. Filmer claimed that by nature and by Scripture fathers have absolute and permanent power over their children. He argues not merely that paternal power is the archetype, the origin, or the analogy of political power but that it simply *is* political power. The *Second Treatise* does not simply set forth Locke's own positive doctrine, independently of his tedious refutation of Filmer in the now rarely read *First Treatise*. On the contrary, many of the crucial subjects of the *Second Treatise* and the approaches Locke takes to them are necessary parts of his refutation of Filmer.

One of the topics in the *Second Treatise* that is most clearly connected to Locke's polemic against Filmer is the relation between parents and children. Locke argues that adult children owe their parents not obedience as such but only honor, and even that only in proportion to the care and education bestowed by the parents. Any obedience beyond that is granted only on the basis of consent, though consent may be induced by the prospect of inheritance. Even children who are not yet adult turn out not to owe obedience, though they are, to be sure, under their parents' power. For, strictly speaking, not yet having attained the age of reason, they cannot owe any obligations. Parental power is a matter not of children's duties or even of parents' rights but rather of parents' duties. Even in the state of nature parental power as such is not permanent or absolute, and it most especially does not reach to the power of life and death, which distinguishes political power.

It is paradoxical, therefore, that Locke, who devotes a good portion of his political work to freeing political power from any patriarchal claims and to minimizing the extent of paternal power, should, when it comes to education, be so insistent on entrusting it completely to parents. This juxtaposition of Locke's educational and political works makes one aware of an aspect of the antipatriarchal argument in the *Two Treatises* that Locke himself does not emphasize. Filmer, in stating that the natural rights or duties of a father and a king are all one, had declared that

4

> As the Father over one family, so the King, as Father
> over many families, extends his care to preserve, feed,
> clothe, *instruct* and defend the whole commonwealth.[10]

Locke, far from identifying fatherly care with political power, like Filmer, draws a strict distinction between them and grants instruction solely to parental power, not to civil government.[11] Education is exclusively entrusted by him to the authority that lacks the power of life and death.

Separate though it may be, the gentleman's education Locke advocated is supportive of the politics he taught. It forms men of business and affairs. They are physically fit and courageous, able to be soldiers if necessary. But, much more important, they are willing and able to concern themselves with their estates, perhaps even with trade, and to be active and informed in public affairs. To this end, they know their country's history and laws and the geography, chronology, and other matters required for that purpose. They speak well and write well. Morally, they are in temper neither slavish nor tyrannical but free men, independent and self-reliant. This freedom, however, is not a freedom from concern for the opinion of others. On the contrary, they are acutely sensitive to praise and blame, to the power of public opinion. They are well formed to further the public interest by attending to private property while being at the same time vigilant observers of government, awake to the danger of tyranny while being no source of such danger themselves, and plausible representatives of the people should the need arise.

This portrait of the Lockean citizen or gentleman, with its emphasis on concern for esteem, may be surprising, contrary as it is to the views of Lockean man as either a hedonistic seeker of property or a rational perceiver of the good. It suggests an understanding of the *Two Treatises of Government* quite different from those associated with such views of Lockean morality.

In one of Locke's minor educational writings he makes an important distinction: "Politics contains two parts very different the one from the other, the one containing the original of societies and the rise and extent of political power, the other, the art of governing men in society."[12] Locke then goes on to recommend the *Two Treatises* for the study of the first part of politics (the *Second Treatise* bears as its full title "An Essay concerning the True Original, Extent, and End of Civil Government"). This is the part of politics that teaches rights and the duties resulting from them;[13] it is abstract and formal. The other part of politics—"very different," as Locke says in this minor essay—is an art, a matter of prudence, not a doctrine of rights and duties. He does not go on to recommend any books that directly teach this art of governing men; instead, he says that it is best learned from experience and history, and he accordingly recommends works of history and constitutional law, just

5

as he does in the *Thoughts*.[14] Locke himself had experience in the art of politics. As Peter Laslett writes, he got "a whiff of Machiavelli's world" in 1665–66 in the course of a diplomatic mission to Cleves,[15] and he spent much of the next fifteen years as Shaftesbury's confidant, secretary, and colleague at the very center of the first English political party, in the midst of elections, office-holding, and parliaments and, finally, plots and exile.[16] After the culminating victory of Whiggism in 1688 Locke returned to England and served in government again, this time on the Board of Trade. Apart from this experience, Locke's reading, as revealed by Harrison and Laslett's edition of his library catalogue, shows a concern with at least one of the classic authors of the art of governing men. After noting Locke's apparent lack of interest in Aristotle's philosophy, Laslett remarks that he "evidently took much greater pains with authors either more congenial to him or of greater intellectual importance to his own work," and the example Laslett gives is Locke's assiduous collection of the works of Machiavelli. Laslett goes on to remark, however, that "no literary debt to Machiavelli shows upon the surface for all his pains to collect that author." Elsewhere Laslett argues nonetheless that Locke's political thinking has "a somewhat unexpected precedent . . . Machiavelli and the writers of political advice," so that Locke "could perhaps be looked upon as Machiavelli's philosopher."[17] Locke's apparent interest in the side of Bacon represented by his *Essays* might also be noted in this context.[18]

Regardless of his apparent interest in such teachers of the art of governing men in society, one is faced with the fact that Locke divided politics into two very different parts: the doctrine of foundations, rights, and duties on the one hand and the art of governing men on the other. And though he himself appears to have become familiar with the latter from history, from experience, and from study of teachers of that art, he seems to have written only in the former part, where he classified his *Two Treatises of Government*. From this fact it is not proper to infer that he believed that politics could be reduced to the first part, "that politics may be reduced to a science"—a task that Hume proposed and his many successors have attempted. For Locke did recommend that gentlemen study both parts of politics. One might wish to say that, even if the doctrine of foundations cannot be understood to be the whole of politics, it is still a whole in itself, it possesses a substantial degree of autonomy. One could say that Locke's procedure implies that it is possible to show men all this—that civil society is founded on consent, that rulers have the duty to protect the rights of subjects to life, liberty, and property, and that subjects have the duty to obey when those rights are protected and the right to revolt when they are not—without having to show the rulers precisely how to govern men in the various contingencies and emergencies of political life, let alone advise the subjects on how to organize and conduct revolution. It is especially appropriate for liberal political doctrine, like liberal political rule itself, to be limited and legal in character. A doctrine of rights and duties is limited and legal in character even when it is a *natural* law to which those rights and duties belong. Such a doctrine, like liberal law, tells us of some things we must do or must not do and of others that we may do; but it does not tell us what it is wise or prudent or good for us to do, and it necessarily leaves open various realms of choice.[19]

But just as it is not possible to have a political doctrine without implications for education—for what kind of men are to be formed—even when that is not its direct object but only its indirect requirement,[20] so we can doubt whether it is possible to have a political doctrine consisting only in a teaching of rights and duties, unaccompanied by some account of the art of governing men. Locke's doctrine is one of consent as the source of political duties; but for Locke, consent as the source of political duties must be rational; it must be to such conditions as a free and rational creature would consent to. Where such conditions do not exist, no apparent formal or empirical consent is valid as constituting obligations. Where such conditions do exist, consent can be presumed. Locke's doctrine is in this respect less legalistic than it may sound. Even more fundamentally than it teaches rights and duties, it teaches what is reasonable. Locke's teaching on prerogative shows the importance of art rather than law, while his teaching on the exercise of the right of revolution, which serves to justify or at least defend his teaching on the right of revolution, is clearly a prudential as well as a jural one.[21]

Aside from such implications of the *Two Treatises,* I would like to put forward another suggestion: that in Locke's *Some Thoughts Concerning Education* one finds what is a presentation of the art of governing men on one level at least. As Locke says in the *Second Treatise,* parental power or education, though it "comes far short" of political power, is still a "natural government."[22]

Although one must be very careful in this regard, one can conclude that Locke's account of the art of governing children aids in the task of understanding what he might have written on the second part of politics. For example, Locke advocates that, instead of requiring children to do things under the threat of punishment or even as duties, it is better to allow them to do the desired things freely or even as a privilege, a tactic in child psychology our age is not unfamiliar with.[23] According to Locke, this principle applies also to grown men:

> Is it not so with grown Men? What they do chearfully
> of themselves, do they not presently grow sick of, and
> can no more endure, as soon as they find it is expected
> of them, as a Duty?[24]

Liberty itself can be the most powerful instrument of government; a teaching of rights can do more good than a teaching of duties. In the *Thoughts Concerning Education* we learn of the basis for this in human nature: the fact that men want above all to be free or to be thought free.

Similarly, Locke's advocacy of reasoning, or seeming to reason, with children rests on their desire to be thought rational.[25] The factual or prudential justification for liberty is not rationality but the pretension to rationality. There is a grave difficulty implicit in this insight because, according to Locke, this fundamental human desire for liberty is also primordially a desire for mastery, not only over oneself but also over others. Both are recognized as pride. The first aspect must be carefully separated, strengthened, and satisfied, while the second must be subjugated. Indeed, it is by accommodating the proud desire for liberty that the proud desire for mastery can best be controlled.

# *ONE*
# Natural Freedom
# and Patriarchal Politics

Locke founded liberal politics on the doctrine of natural freedom.[1] He teaches that all men are naturally free and equal and therefore subject to political power only by their own consent.[2] On that foundation he builds a liberal politics, teaching that *"the end of Law* is ... *to preserve and enlarge Freedom* ... from restraint and violence from others," in other words, that *"Political Power"* is to be used only for "the Regulating and Preserving of Property" and for defense from foreign injury, "only for the Publick Good," understood as "the good of every particular Member of that Society, as far as by common Rules, it can be provided for," understood in turn as the preservation of his property, "that is, his Life, Liberty and Estate."[3] In the *Two Treatises* this centrality of liberty and this limitation of government to the protection of individual rights are used by Locke to oppose tyranny and arbitrary government generally and to stress their constitutionalist and revolutionary implications. In the *Letter on Toleration* he uses them to oppose religious persecution specifically, and he emphasizes that civil government is concerned only with the body—its life, liberty, health, freedom from pain, and external possessions—not with the soul or with teaching the truth of opinions.[4] To maintain his hypothesis of natural freedom and the liberal politics he built on it, Locke argues against the alternative hypothesis of patriarchalism. Patriarchalism takes its bearings on human beings' original status as dependent children and so arrives at a government that treats grown men as children, and this, in its denial of their rationality and in the absence of parental affection, means in practice treating them as beasts.

### FILMER: PATRIARCHAL POLITICS AS PROVIDENTIAL POLITICS

Although John Locke wrote *Two Treatises of Government*, it is the *Second Treatise* for which he is celebrated. The title page declares that in the *First Treatise* "the False Principles and Foundation of Sir Robert Filmer, and His Followers are Detected and Overthrown," and Filmer's doctrines today seem irrelevant and absurd. Yet Locke devotes most of his Preface, which is to both *Treatises,* to his opposition to Filmer, opposing his own "hypothesis" to Filmer's "hypothesis." Only once in the work does Locke explicitly argue against any other hypothesis.[5] To save himself "from the Reproach of Writing against a dead Adversary," Locke points out that "the Pulpit, of late Years, publickly owned his [Filmer's] Doctrine, and made it the Currant Divinity of the Times" and that there are men who are "crying up his Books, and espousing his Doctrine." These remarks suggest that Locke had to address Filmer's doctrine solely to meet current conditions. However, Locke also claims in the Preface that "The King, and Body of the Nation, have since so thoroughly confuted his [Filmer's] Hypothesis, that, I suppose, no Body hereafter will have either the Confidence to appear against our Common Safety, and be again an Advocate for Slavery; or [have] the Weakness to be deceived" by such doctrines. Locke thus seems to say that already in his time Filmer was for practical purposes as irrelevant as he seems today.[6] Perhaps Locke was concerned with the possible effect of Filmer's sort of argument not only currently but at "all times." Perhaps the meaning of Locke's hypothesis—the natural freedom and equality of men—emerges most clearly in opposition to Filmer's sort of hypothesis. It is apparent already in the Preface to the *Two Treatises* that Locke's great principles are consent of the people as the only title to lawful government and the natural rights of men, which they may justly revolt to preserve, both depending on the natural freedom of men.[7] The natural freedom of men is as surely Locke's great political principle as its denial is Filmer's.

In the very first paragraph of the *Second Treatise* Locke presents his exposition of the true origin of civil government as a supplement to the *First Treatise*'s refutation of Filmer, or at least as a task made necessary only because of that refutation. Natural freedom is presented as a premise in the *Second Treatise;* it is presented as the conclusion of a long argument in the *First*.[8] But the clearest reason for beginning a consideration of Locke's educational thought, and particularly its relation to his politics, by considering Filmer and Locke's critique of Filmer is that Locke's great political work presents itself as an attack on the doctrine of patriarchal power, a doctrine of politics explicitly based on an understanding of the relation between parents and children. It is the requirements of Locke's polemic against Filmer that led him to present an analysis of the family and the rights and duties of parents and children.

Filmer's subtitle informs his reader that *Patriarcha* is "A Defense of the Natural Power of Kings against the Unnatural Liberty of the People."[9] It is a polemical or apologetic work designed to defend an old doctrine against a new one. It is organized not as a proof or deduction or even as an orderly exposition of the natural power of kings but very much as a defense of that power against various arguments brought to bear against it by defenders of the liberty of the people. Filmer attempts to place the burden of proof on his opponents. This strategy can be illustrated by the statement that concludes his examination of Suarez's denial of the royal power of Adam and of fathers in general: "until Suarez brings some reason for what he saith, I shall trust more to Bellarmine's proofs than to his denials."[10] But Filmer does not present any *proofs* from Bellarmine, either at this point or earlier, in the third chapter, where he first quoted the cardinal's bare "confession, that creation made man Prince of his posterity."[11] Nor does an examination of the passage in Bellarmine that Filmer here refers to reveal any proofs.[12] This method of Filmer's, if it can be called a method, makes it very difficult to expound his thought. One must try not to get bogged down in following his presentation or to falsify his views by oversystematization.[13]

Filmer refers to an ancient issue, as old as Plato's *Statesman* and the first chapter of Aristotle's *Politics*. "Aristotle," Filmer reports, "gives the lie to Plato, and those that say that political and economical societies are all one, and do not differ *specie,* but only *multitudine et paucitate,* as if there were 'no difference betwixt a great house and a little city.'" On this issue, Filmer sides with Plato as he understands him. He declares that family and kingdom differ only in size, not in kind:

> If we compare the natural duties of a Father with those of a King, we find them to be all one, without any difference at all but only in the latitude or extent of them. As the Father over one family, so the King, as Father over many families, extends his care to preserve, feed, clothe, instruct and defend the whole commonwealth . . . so that all the duties of a King are summed up in an universal fatherly care of his people.[14]

This ancient analogy, however, while perhaps the emotional heart of Filmer's appeal,[15] is not in itself the intellectual core of his argument.

The nerve of Filmer's theory is expressed more nearly by another reference to Plato. In his *Observations upon Aristotle's Politiques,* Filmer credits Plato with having taught Aristotle that "the original of government" is "from the power of the fatherhood." The basis for this discovery of classical intellectual influence is supposed to be an affirmation in the third book of Plato's *Laws* that "the true and first reason of authority is that the father and mother, and simply those that beget and ingender, do command and rule over all their children."[16] It is characteristic of Filmer's arguments that he here adduces a claim of authority for fathers *and mothers* as the basis of a deduction of political authority "from the power of the fatherhood" alone. It is equally characteristic of Locke's refutation that, while he frequently and at length contrasts Filmer's similarly truncated use of the Fifth Commandment with the original ("Honor thy father and thy mother," the last words of which Filmer has no use

11

for), he does not even mention Filmer's use of Plato, let alone point out its impropriety.[17] It is also characteristic of Filmer's use of classical sources, and of the radical monistic simplification that he achieves, that he suppresses the Platonic context. For Plato's Athenian Stranger enumerates *seven* claims to rule: the claims of parents over children, of the well-born over the low-born, of the old over the young, of masters over slaves, of the stronger over the weaker, of the knowing over the ignorant, and of divine favor as discovered by drawing lots. It is the sixth claim, sanctioning the rule of the wise, that in the *Laws* is said to be the greatest and according to nature.[18] While Filmer is able to make use of passages from the *Statesman* and the *Laws*, there seems to be nothing he can do with the *Republic*. There Filmer's "divine Plato" abolished the family, the children do not even know their own fathers, and the philosopher-kings rule the best city free of any competing claims from patriarchal power.[19]

Filmer himself, in any case, asserts not only that paternal rule and political or kingly rule are of the same kind, as Plato's Eleatic Stranger does in the *Statesman*,[20] but that political rule is derived from paternal power and, indeed, that paternal power is the basis of the only lawful claim to rule, as he interprets the *Laws* to teach. At another point in *Patriarcha* Filmer conflates the separate issues raised by Plato's equation of the household and the polis (*Statesman*), Aristotle's derivation of the origin of government from the power of fathers (*Politics*, bk. 1, chap. 2), and Plato's presentation of the paternal claim to rule (*Laws*). Filmer charges that Aristotle "quarrels with his master . . . most unjustly" when "the divine Plato concludes 'a commonweal to be nothing else but a large family.' " The ground Filmer gives for asserting the injustice of this classic quarrel is that Aristotle "contradicts his own principles, for they both [Plato and Aristotle] agree to fetch the original of civil government from the prime government of families."[21] Filmer does not recognize that for Aristotle it is possible to trace the origin of government from the family without either denying that the two differ in kind or asserting that the right or claim of political rulers is based on the right or claim of fathers or parents. For Aristotle, the origin has no paradigmatic status as divinely instituted, human improvement of the origin is not inconceivable or unnatural, and claims to rule are not immutable, transferable, or understood in terms of law. Nor does the Eleatic Stranger's assertion of the sameness in kind of the polis and the household entail a derivation of the former from the latter either chronologically or as a matter of right.

For Filmer, however, paternal and political power are not merely similar or analogous or related in chronological development; they are simply one and the same. One's only human subjection is to one's father, but one's king *is* one's father. Filmer achieves this remarkable result by combining the basic principle of paternal power as such with its inheritance by primogeniture and the universal human descent from one man, revealed by Scripture. Adam's original unique paternal power is inherited by his heirs, who thereby come to rule not only over their children but also over their mothers, brothers, uncles, and other relatives, who together make up the human race. Each man's subjection to his natural father is thereby subordinate to his natural father's subjection to his natural father or to his heir and so on. The same process occurred again after the Flood, when God returned the human race to its original condition and Noah was left as universal father; however, it was then crucially modified by Noah's supposed division of the world, and with it his patriarchal power, among his sons. From that and perhaps similar divisions made by other patriarchs, as well as from the division that God himself made at the time of the Tower of Babel, supposedly derive the monarchs of the seventeenth century.[22]

Filmer's provision against the most obvious objection to this scheme reveals the theoretical crux of his argument. The objection is twofold: not only is there a paucity of positive evidence linking present-day rulers to the sons of Noah as direct heirs through the eldest male line; there is even direct negative evidence of repeated changes in established lines of descent—clear departures from the rules of primogeniture (or usurpations, as Filmer must regard them). The fifth chapter of *Patriarcha* (entitled "Kings are either Fathers of their People, or Heirs of such Fathers, or the Usurpers of the Rights of such Fathers")[23] opens with the admission that "It may seem absurd to maintain that Kings now are the fathers of their people, since experience shows the contrary." But the only reference[24] in the body of the chapter to the question of usurpers, mentioned in the heading, appears in one delicate phrase in the next sentence:

> It is true, all Kings be not the natural parents of their subjects, yet they all either are, *or are to be reputed,* as the next heirs of those progenitors who were at first the natural parents of the whole people, and in their right succeed to the exercise of supreme jurisdiction. [My emphasis.][25]

In the next chapter the question of usurpation is faced more squarely. It is entitled "Of the Escheating of Kingdoms," and it accordingly begins with the question of what happens when there is apparently no heir. Filmer claims that in this circumstance there really is an heir, but he is not known because of the "negligence or ignorance of the people." In this situation, "the prime and independent heads of families" or of "great families or petty Princedoms" then "have power to consent in the uniting or conferring of their fatherly right of sovereign authority on whom they please." The new prince, however, is "substituted properly by God" and merely "testified by the ministry of the heads of the people."[26] This

13

last significant qualification, which suggests the approach Filmer is about to take to usurpation, reveals the fundamental premise of his thought. The basic political facts—that is, the identity of the rulers and, as we shall see, also the form of government—are not the work of men, not the fruit of human choice and responsibility, no matter how much they may look that way. They are the work of God; they are particular expressions of divine providence. Even those who can be said to have "power to consent" in the election of "whom they please" really only "testify" to one "substituted properly by God." The distance between this situation of escheat and election, on the one hand, and the divinely instituted inheritance of patriarchal power by primogeniture, on the other, is even greater than I have so far indicated. For the heads of the great families, princedoms, or provinces that constitute the kingdom may themselves no longer be the known natural heirs but only substitutes, chosen by the prince for their "merits, abilities, or fortunes," or the heirs of such substitutes, who now in turn may elect a prince. Thus no natural trace of the original paternal power is left but only the presumption of it, which circularly renovates itself by cooptation. It is more correct to say that the gap between this situation and the pure patriarchal paradigm is filled by particular providence rather than by presumption as such.

Divine providence supplements or modifies the pure system of patriarchal descent to make room not only for virtue ("merits, abilities") but also for vice. For now Filmer deals with the troublesome matter of usurpation, which threatens to sever from any relevance to contemporary politics all his arguments about Adam's or Noah's sons' patriarchal power and its descent to their heirs.

> If it please God, for the correction of the Prince or punishment of the people, to suffer Princes to be removed and others to be placed in their rooms, either by the factions of the nobility or rebellion of the people, in all such cases the judgment of God, who hath power to give and take away kingdoms, is most just. Yet the ministry of men who execute God's judgments without commission is sinful and damnable. God doth but use and turn men's unrighteous acts to the performance of His righteous decrees.[27]

In the institution of governments, even when men act sinfully and without divine commission, they are God's ministers on earth and execute his will. Unlike later, formally similar, doctrines of private vices making for public benefits, this doctrine does not ascribe the beneficial results of private vices to the "dextrous Management of a skilful Politician" but to the hand of God.[28] His providence is not limited to creation or revelation but is continual. Filmer's is not necessarily a claim that *every* human act is an expression of the will of God; it is a claim that the establishment of all political authority, by whatever means and whatever the form of government[29] and whoever the ruler, is nevertheless the expression of divine providence. Continuous political authority is too important to human life to be left to human beings to provide. Such a doctrine cannot, like a formally similar doctrine of undiscriminating naturalism, be charged with failure to provide any guidance for human conduct.[30] Although successful rebellion must afterward be seen to have been the will of God, and the authority it establishes must therefore be obeyed, yet, previously, it was, like all rebellion, sinful. Filmer's providentialist justification serves always as a warrant for obedience, never as a warrant for rebellion. In other words, *we* never receive a commission from God to rebel, though we know, after the result, that successful rebellions performed by sinful *others* are acts of particular providence, expressing divine justice, that result in obligations for us.

It must be admitted, however, that at the actual moment of rebellion, when the event is uncertain, our obligations may be doubtful; moreover, the "moment" may be as long as it was in the English Civil War rather than short, as it would prove to be in the Glorious Revolution. Hard problems are also posed by any efforts the previous ruler makes to regain his rule (even if he is only, as Filmer later said, "the first usurper").[31] These problems arose in practice for Filmer in his last years, when the matter of usurpation became pressing during the English Civil War and Commonwealth periods.[32] As for political action itself, he seems to have maintained a scrupulous neutrality or passivity.[33] But it was in this period that he was moved to publish his political tracts, and in the briefest of them, appended to his *Observations upon Aristotle's Politiques,* he attempted to provide *Directions for Obedience to Government in Dangerous or Doubtful Times.*[34]

In that little work Filmer cannot maintain the glib assurance that marks *Patriarcha,* written when such matters were only a threat on the horizon. He still grants obedience to the established usurper, but the previous ruler or "first usurper" retains some too. This anomalous situation, and Filmer's obscure presentation of it, call forth some of Locke's sharpest ridicule.[35] A recent scholar, John Dunn, calls it a "muddle" that reflects little credit on Filmer's "capacity for logical coherence."[36] Some of Filmer's language in the *Directions* suggests that the true heir's claim is so indelible that it seems to challenge the right Filmer concedes, both in this tract and in *Patriarcha,* to usurpers and their heirs: "though by humane laws, a long prescription may take away right, yet divine right never dies, nor can be lost, or taken away."[37] It must be remembered, however, that *Patriarcha* was written from a perspective in which usurpation had taken place long ago (e.g., those resulting from the depositions of Edward II or Richard II or the Norman Conquest)[38] and no known heir of the previous ruler remained. The acceptance of usurpers taught there, it is fair to presume, was based on those conditions. Even in the new situation, when Filmer was writing in the midst of a usurpation and when the heir was alive and hoping for restoration, it was possible for the conflict between the rights of the new and old rulers not to be understood as, in Dunn's words, posing "directly conflicting duties towards authority."[39] Filmer tries, rather, to limit the obedience due to the usurper by that due to the previous ruler. Commands of the usurper that can be presumed to coincide with those of the old ruler must be obeyed fully but not those that can be presumed to, or actually do, conflict with those of the old ruler.[40] It is a matter of one duty limiting another rather than a matter of directly conflicting duties.

Furthermore, even that limitation, like any limitation of political authority for Filmer, takes only the form of "passive obedience," not the form of active resistance. In this discussion of the obedience due to usurpers, he writes: "if men command things evil, obedience is due only by tolerating what they inflict: not by performing what they require."[41] To interpret Filmer's doctrine of the indelibility of the true heir's right (as Locke does) so as to bar the usurper's right to passive obedience in things contrary to the true ruler's command and to active obedience in other things would, as Filmer says of another subject, "derogate from God's providence."[42] It seems to be from his basic belief that God always provides men with political authority that he concludes in favor of these rights of usurpers.

It is possible, however, to push things even farther and to raise a difficulty that Filmer does not explicitly treat and that renders doubtful the possibility of preserving such providence on Filmer's basis. One can ask what happens if the previous ruler commands one precisely to *resist* the usurper. Just such an excruciating jural situation presumably characterized the Civil War, even though it was not mentioned by Filmer in 1652, when things were perhaps a little less "dangerous or doubtful."

Filmer's admission in the *Directions* of the Hobbesian principle that "protection and subjection are reciprocal" seems to lead to the result that assistance is owed to preserve but not necessarily to restore a government that has protected one.[43] This conclusion is more in harmony with *Patriarcha*'s easy acceptance of usurpers as "reputed" heirs than with the *Directions'* never-dying divine right; it would prevent actual resistance to an established usurper whatever the commands of the true heir. It is difficult, however, to render the Hobbesian premise, with its contractual connotations, compatible with Filmer's general position. To take protection or preservation even as a criterion for discerning God's particular providence is a step toward replacing particular providence with man's own provision for his preservation.

16

Even if the duties imposed by Filmer's doctrine concerning usurpation are not directly conflicting, they are not absolutely clear or universally applicable. They depend on circumstances, which means that they depend on judgment of the circumstances. Thereby they involve the great question of who is to judge, which Filmer forcefully and repeatedly flings at his opponents and which Locke is so concerned to answer.[44] Must each private man judge for himself whether the usurper is now settled or still rebelling or whether a particular command is one that preserves the subjects or is one that destroys the true governor?[45] This would entail all the dire anarchic implications Filmer warns of and would thereby derogate from God's providence.[46] Perhaps the limitations on the obedience due a usurper, other than that of direct contradiction by a command of the previous ruler, are not meant by Filmer as independent criteria but are only expressed effectively in such commands. Any command of the usurper is "presumed" to be the will of the true ruler, and conducive to the preservation of the subjects, unless it is specifically countermanded.[47] Thus it is the true ruler who judges for the subjects when it is not the usurper himself who in effect does so, and men are still preserved from freedom, that is, from the situation of not having political authority provided them without their judgment being required. In any case, the practical consequences of the problem of the judge are less anarchic for Filmer because only passive obedience, not resistance, is involved.

Let us leave aside the doubtful and dangerous *Directions* that Filmer felt impelled to offer in 1652[48] and return to the smoother *Patriarcha*, composed in happier times. Here too the problem of private judgment arises. Filmer places limits on obedience, and not only on obedience to a usurper whose orders are countermanded by his predecessor but on obedience to a lawful king. It is not usually mentioned that Filmer, who recognizes no right of resistance or revolution, does in one sphere permit, indeed require, disobedience to unlawful commands, along with acceptance of the resulting penalties ("passive obedience"). He writes:

> since the rule for *each man to know* in what to obey his Prince cannot be learnt without a relative knowledge of those points wherein a sovereign may command, it is necessary when the commands and pleasures of superiors come abroad and call for an obedience that *every man inform himself* how to regulate his actions or his sufferings, for according to the quality of the thing commanded an active or passive obedience is to be yielded, and this is not to limit the Prince's power, but the extent of the subject's obedience, by giving to Caesar the things that are Caesar's, etc.[49]

The duty of obedience is a matter of divine right, required by direct scriptural commands[50] as well as by the scripturally based patriarchal theory. But the duty of disobedience is also a matter of divine right, dictated by the scriptural maxim "Render unto Caesar the things that are Caesar's, and unto God the things that are God's."[51] However, every private man must judge by himself what things are Caesar's and what are God's, for Filmer does not, like Hobbes, make the sovereign the authoritative interpreter of Scripture.

Filmer's response to the problem of usurpation is worth so much examination, not only because it relates his theory to the politics of his time and because it raises so many difficulties, but also because it reveals the principle that is at the heart of his theory. The manifestation of divine providence in politics is not only a necessary supplement to his basic patriarchal theory but the key to it.[52] Scripture must be interpreted in the way Filmer does because God must have provided proper political authority for men at every point, even when it looks as if that authority is being violated. This principle is revealed less in Filmer's scriptural exegesis itself, which is delivered without argumentation against alternative exegeses, than in his rejections of the alternatives that result when his patriarchal exegesis is not presumed.

Filmer rejects Hobbes's "horrid condition of pure nature" because "it is not to be thought that God would create man in a condition worse than any beasts, as if he made men to no other end by nature but to destroy one another." Hobbes's primeval scarcity is likewise impossible, because "God was no such niggard in the creation, and there being plenty of sustenance and room for all men, there is no cause or use of war . . . in the state of pure nature."[53] Grotius's original communism is impossible because it would "derogate from the providence of God Almighty, to ordain a community which could not continue."[54]

As the work of God, not man, the original condition must have been perfect. Deviations from it, which are the work of man, must have the character of deteriorations, not improvements. Indeed, all subsequent apparent changes must be either sinful human defiance of God's will or instances of divine intervention, providing punishment or remedy for human sin, unless they can actually be interpreted as not constituting substantial changes at all. God-wrought changes in mankind's condition (the changes wrought after the Fall and the Flood) must partake of the perfection of the original condition at least to the extent that they provide perfect (monarchic) political authority and do not require human improvement. They cannot be characterized by natural freedom, by primeval scarcity, or by original communism, all of which would have to be remedied by human contrivance. Nor can they be characterized by an original democracy that is then transformed by its own (human)

18

agency into the other forms of government. Filmer objects that Bellar-mine says

> that by the law of God, power is immediately in the people; hereby he makes God the author of a demo-cratical estate; for a democracy is nothing else but the power of the multitude. If this be true, not only aris-tocracies but all monarchies are altogether unlawful, as being ordained (as he thinks) by men, when as God him-self hath chosen a democracy.[55]

Time after time the fundamental hypothesis is revealed: whatever exists originally exists by right because it exists by nature, that is, by God's will and not by human contrivance; the original condition constitutes natural law and divine right. This mode of thought lies also at the basis of Filmer's claim that, for each new individual, just as in the original condition of the species, the subjection to his father into which a child is born, being original or natural and provided by God, must be by right and therefore permanent.[56]

The guiding spirit of all of Filmer's ingenious criticisms of arguments purporting to show how natural freedom is transformed by consent into civil government—his questions about majority rule, representation, secession, tacit consent, women, children, servants, absentees, and later generations[57]—seems to be his providentialist view that man is neither competent to improve his original condition nor entitled to do so. (The problems that Filmer raises must be seriously faced by a theory of consent and individual rights even though we do not start from the hypothesis that inclined Filmer to raise them.)

Above all, this tendency of Filmer's thought takes the form of a belief that natural law, which expresses the will of its divine author, is strictly unchangeable; it cannot establish contrary conditions at different times.[58] Filmer invokes this necessity in order to oppose Grotius's doctrine that the law of nature both established original communism and sanctioned later private property; to oppose the right of the majority to alter the natural freedom of others; and to uphold the rights of true heirs versus usurpers.[59]

We can now see Filmer's solution to a major problem, alluded to in my earlier exposition. He never asserts that Charles I is the eldest heir of Adam or of one of Noah's sons.[60] (This renders half of Locke's *First Treatise* less biting, though not entirely irrelevant.)[61] Because Filmer tac-itly concedes that the present rulers are usurpers or the heirs of usurpers, he already, under Charles I, defends the usurper's title as possession "by the secret will of God."[62] One might therefore wonder why he trou-bles to propound his elaborate theory of Adam's monarchy and its de-scent to his heirs through the division among Noah's sons, the Hebrew

19

patriarchs, and the Jewish kings. This question of the need for patriarchal history, given providentialism, is similar to the question, often addressed to Hobbes and Locke, of the need for contract, given preservationism.[63] Locke says that Filmer "is fain to resolve all into present Possession, and makes Civil Obedience as due to an *Usurper* as to a lawful King" because he is not "able to make out any Princes Title to Government, as Heir to *Adam,* which therefore is of no use, and had been better let alone."[64] The use of it to Filmer is that Adam's monarchy, as the original, natural, and divinely established human condition, serves as authoritative model for the necessity and divine right of monarchy, to which the subsequent and present twistings of God's providence, manifest in human affairs, must be assimilated. God, by creating one man from whom all men are descended, sanctions monarchy and provides a paradigm of how to construe his subsequent provision for human political welfare.[65] Similarly, Filmer's account of the descent of patriarchal power in biblical times serves as the model for contemporary succession, even though the links between the two cannot be detailed. The very irregularities in the biblical account that Locke makes so much of in his polemic against primogeniture[66] serve Filmer's attempt to show a plausible continuity with the irregular successions of modern times. Similarly, the biblical Jewish monarchy serves as a model because it has a divine origin: "It were impiety, to think, that God who was careful to appoint judicial laws for his chosen people would not furnish them with the best form of government."[67]

If it were not for Filmer's secure beginning, he would not be able to present his arguments in the form he prefers: that of concluding that institutions or duties, if original or otherwise instituted by God, must be good for men and in any case must be accepted. Instead he would have to argue exclusively from the far more exposed ground that if something is good for men it must be divinely instituted. Filmer did indeed believe that there is independent reason for concluding that the political institutions God provided are good. In the beginning of *Patriarcha,* when first denouncing the principle of the natural freedom of mankind, he charges that "It contradicts the doctrine and history of the Holy Scriptures, the constant practice of all ancient monarchies, and the very principles of the law of nature. It is hard to say whether it be more erroneous in Divinity or dangerous in policy."[68] Filmer's objection stems from at least two sources: divinity and policy. Divinity seems to be the guide to truth and is based on Scripture and also on the "ancient fathers and doctors of the primitive Church." Policy is the guide to utility and is based on ancient political example and perhaps the law of nature. Filmer first presents evidence of the dangerousness of the doctrine of natural freedom: in the hands of papists and Puritans it justifies rebellion. Its dangerous consequence as policy is Filmer's "sufficient warrant" for an examination of its truth as doctrine. It is not unfair to say that his examination of its truth in terms of Scripture is carried on in the light of his initial awareness of its danger in terms of policy. But his scripturalism and providentialism excuse him from having to rest his case fully and openly on policy.

Finally, one should note the status of liberty in Filmer's patriarchal politics. For him men are of course not free by nature; there has been subjection from the beginning of the race, and each individual is born subject to his father. This subjection is no injury or curse but a benefit provided for us that we could not provide ourselves. Filmer distinguishes two kinds of desire for liberty. One desire is to be able to do what one pleases, to be impossibly free from subjection. The other is to share in ruling, which is possible in a commonwealth but is contrary to the divine model, to nature, and to human utility. Filmer even goes so far as to claim that such a condition is contrary to the nature of political society, and he uses Aristotelian language and authority to do so, even though Aristotle practically defines politics as a matter of ruling and being ruled in turn. In either sense, liberty is primarily sinful for Filmer. The doctrine of natural liberty he claims is popular because the people "magnify liberty as if the height of human felicity were only to be found in it, never remembering that the desire of liberty was the cause of the fall of Adam." Thus even the original monarch, Adam, the source of all human subjection, sinned in desiring liberty.[69]

There is much in Filmer's writings that may remind us of the modern autodidact: his obsession with his own idea; his confidence in tackling the most impressive structures of learning or reasoning and in dismantling them for his own purposes; his energetic pursuit of support for his thesis from whatever source it could be derived; his selective but eclectic learning; his unscrupulous assaults on his opponents from whatever position presented the most advantage; his sharp eye for seizing on the difficulties in his opponents' arguments, accompanied by blindness to the problems in his own; his persistent interpretation of selected and even truncated texts to fit the procrustean bed of his fixation, without reference to their contexts; and, perhaps above all, the evident enjoyment with which he engaged in all this activity. Nevertheless, the basic premises of his way of thought are common to a much broader and often more sophisticated tradition, which also shares some of his intellectual habits. His faith that God has fully provided for human needs, whether through the text of Scripture, the workings of his providence through the ministry of men, or, last and least, the power of human reason, is far from unique. It lies at the bottom of his confidence that every text will yield the necessary support, that reason must yield its assent unless it lacks the facts (which Scripture restores to it), and that the presence of the hand of God can easily be discerned in the doings

21

of men. This faith, and something of the exegetical and intellectual habits it gave to Filmer, can be said to characterize medieval thought from the Church Fathers to so late and sophisticated a thinker as Bellarmine or even Protestants versed in the philosophic tradition, like Hooker and Grotius. The problems this faith posed for a political thinker such as Locke, who maintained that man is by nature free, were immense, quite apart from the currency enjoyed by Filmer's peculiar theory of Adam's patriarchal monarchy.

## FILMER'S TARGETS AND PREDECESSORS AND THE MEANING OF NATURAL FREEDOM

One way in which the *First Treatise* seems to provide support for the natural freedom that is the foundation of the *Second Treatise* is that Locke claims in it that this doctrine was the standing opinion prior to the Filmerite challenge and can therefore be assumed to be still standing once that challenge is disposed of. Locke claims that only "In this last age a generation of men has sprung up among us, who would flatter princes with an Opinion, that they have a Divine Right to absolute Power" and that "To make way for this doctrine they have denied Mankind a Right to natural Freedom." Divine right is a doctrine that men "have not had Wit enough to find out till this latter Age."[70] Using such sarcasm, Locke seems to align himself with the conservative prejudice against novelty, the presumption that any important truth must have been found out long ago, that it is absurd or a mark of great vanity to think that men of long ago did not have fully as much wit as those of one's own age or oneself.[71] Thus, if Filmer's claim fails, "Governments must be left again to the old way of being made by contrivance, and the consent of Men."[72] By asserting his own tenet of the natural freedom of men as the long-standing position, not in need of proof, Locke attempts to place the burden of proof on Filmer.

Yet, as Locke notes, Filmer "seems to condemn the Novelty of the contrary Opinion."[73] Locke's accusation mirrors Filmer's own. *Patriarcha* indeed begins: "Since the time school divinity began to flourish many of the Schoolmen and other Divines have published and maintained an opinion that: 'Mankind is naturally endowed and born with freedom from all subjection.' "[74] Locke echoes not only Filmer's accusation of novelty but the claim of clerical origin of the offending opinion, or at least its clerical propagation. In his words, "the Pulpit, of late Years, publickly owned his [Filmer's] Doctrine, and made it the Currant Divinity of the Times"; as a result, the times "have reason to complain of the Drum Ecclesiastick."[75]

Locke thus appears to be merely picking up an old cause, entering into the middle of a battle already in progress. Filmer presents *Patriarcha* as a refutation of the doctrine of the natural liberty of mankind, and Locke presents the *Second Treatise* as based on the natural freedom of men.[76] It is especially easy to see them as engaged in an ongoing debate because Locke does not explain the meaning of his fundamental tenet in the *First Treatise* but only at the beginning of the *Second,* after his refutation of Filmer and after he has identified with his own the doctrines that Filmer has attacked.[77]

After noting that Filmer condemns the novelty of natural freedom, Locke goes on to claim that Filmer nonetheless confesses the novelty of his own principle of divine right, or at least confesses that *"Heyward, Blackwood, Barclay, and others, that have bravely vindicated the Right of Kings in most Points,* never thought of this, *but with one Consent admitted the Natural Liberty and Equality of Mankind."*[78] But Filmer's account of this notion of the natural liberty and equality of mankind by no means makes it clear that it means that each individual is by nature free from all subjection. From his account, the doctrine seems to be only that "mankind" or "the multitude" is free from subjection to any particular form of government, such as absolute monarchy in particular. The freedom seems to be only freedom to choose a form of government, such a liberty as Filmer later understood Milton to grant to the people: "a miserable liberty, which is only to choose to whom we will give our liberty, which we may not keep."[79] It is not clear whether, at the time Filmer wrote *Patriarcha,* he (1) was unfamiliar with any doctrine of individual natural freedom and equality or state of nature, (2) failed to see the difference between such a view and the claim that political society exists by nature and has a natural right to choose its form of government, or (3) preferred not to distinguish them clearly so as to stress the anarchic potential of even the most moderate doctrine that fell short of his doctrine of divine-right monarchy. An examination of some of the authors Filmer associates with natural freedom helps to clarify the meaning of that doctrine and, by contrast, the meaning of his own providentialism.

According to Filmer, "This tenet [natural freedom] was first hatched in the Schools for good Divinity, and hath been fostered by succeeding Papists. The Divines of the Reformed Churches have entertained it, and the common people everywhere tenderly embrace it." Filmer does not concern himself directly with the popular followers of this doctrine but rather with its learned papist and Puritan adherents. He gives Parsons and Buchanan as examples, respectively, of the "Jesuits and some zealous favourers of the Geneva discipline [who] have built a perilous conclusion, which is, 'that the people or multitude have power to punish or deprive the Prince if he transgress the laws of the kingdom'" on the grounds of the natural liberty of mankind. He adds that "Cardinal Bellarmine and Mr. Calvin both look asquint this way."[80]

23

Parsons argues against indefeasible hereditary right and monarchy and for the right of the commonwealth to choose its form of government originally and to change it subsequently, to limit government by laws and conditions, to establish and alter rules of succession, to punish and depose rulers, and to choose among pretenders, especially on grounds of religion.[81] These rights belong to "the commonwealth"; deposition, for example, is "by public authority of the whole body," "by consent and grave deliberation of the whole state and wealpublique," "not so much by private or particular men."[82] For the affirmation of the natural freedom of the commonwealth to choose its form of government is preceded by an even more fundamental affirmation, not only that the sociality of man but that "government in lyke maner and jurisdiction of magestrats . . . be also of nature," and here Parsons invokes the views of Aristotle, Cicero, and Plato.[83] He denies any asocial or apolitical condition of man: "ther was never yet nation found ether of ancient tyme or now in our dayes, by the discovery of the Indies, or els where, among whom men living together, had not some kind of Magestrate or superior, to governe them, which evidently declareth that this poynt of Magestrates is also of nature, and from god that created nature."[84] Parsons affirms that government is natural to men, not only because otherwise "one would consume and devour the other," but also because "nature taught man a far higher and more excellent ende in his commonwealth" than bodily preservation, namely, the felicity of the soul. Parsons joins the ancient philosophers and legislators, whose end was "to make their citizens good and vertuous, which was a higher end, then to have a bare consideration of temporal and bodily benefits only."[85] Parsons thus bases the natural freedom of the commonwealth to choose its form of government not on any natural freedom of the individual from all subjection but on the naturalness of society and government as means not only to man's preservation but to the perfection of his mind and the salvation of his soul.[86] He argues the characteristic consequences of such a view, that civil society should further the moral and religious good of its members, rather than the characteristic consequences of the natural freedom of individuals, that civil society should protect only the bodies, or the lives, liberties, and properties, of its members.

George Buchanan, Filmer's example of the "zealous favourers of the Geneva discipline," argues that the people are free to give kings their authority, to bind them with laws, and to depose or even kill them if they violate the laws and become tyrants.[87] But this freedom is not the same as the freedom of every individual from all subjection. J. W. Gough suggests that Buchanan regards "the people as already forming a *political* society before the King was elected," and J. W. Allen notes that "there is no social contract in Buchanan."[88] It is true that when the "Buchanan" interlocutor in Buchanan's dialogue asks whether solitary men originally came together from utility, the "Maitland" interlocutor replies that they did. But "Buchanan" concludes that nature rather than utility is responsible for human society.[89] As Gough notes, the lawless condition "is not called a state of nature"; for Buchanan it is indeed contrary to nature, the natural condition being not a collection of free and equal individuals but civil society.[90]

It may be hard to see how Calvin "looks asquint" toward popular resistance, since he proclaims our duty "to submit to the government, not only of those princes who discharge their duty to us with becoming integrity and fidelity, but of all who possess the sovereignty, even though they perform none of the duties of their function."[91] He seems as insistent as Filmer on nonresistance, just as, like him, he requires passive obedience to commands that violate the law of God.[92] Nevertheless, Filmer may well have had in mind Calvin's famous proviso that "magistrates appointed for the protection of the people and the moderation of the power of kings," such as the ephors in ancient times and now "perhaps" the three estates, have the duty "to oppose the violence or cruelty of kings," failing in which they would "fraudulently betray the liberty of the people."[93] That proviso still comes short of giving the right of resistance to the people or the multitude. And even Filmer himself sometimes concedes that in some places the "authority of a supreme Father" may be wielded by "some few or a multitude."[94] Filmer cannot be blamed for complaining, given the seditious use some Calvinists made of the loopholes that Calvin left.[95]

In any case, it was not "upon the grounds of this doctrine"—natural freedom—that Calvin may have winked at resistance. Calvin might seem to recognize society and government as natural by admitting that "man is naturally a creature inclined to society," that there is a "perpetual consent of all nations, as well as all individuals, to the laws, because the seeds of them are innate in all mankind," and that "man is sufficiently instructed in a right rule of life by that natural law."[96] But according to Calvin's doctrine of original sin, from birth man's "whole nature is as it were a seed of sin," so that "in vain do we seek in our nature for any thing that is good."[97] Although Calvin's remarks on natural sociality illustrate that "some sparks continue to shine in the nature of man," "this light is smothered by so much ignorance, that it cannot act with any degree of efficacy." He rejects "the opinion of all the philosophers, that the reason of the human understanding is sufficient for its proper government."[98] If the sparks of human virtue, society, and government are natural, they are ineffective; if they are effective, they are "gifts of the Divine Spirit."[99] This dissolution of nature into providence is characteristic of Calvin's understanding of God's government of the world and especially his "providence in the government of human society."[100] As Michael Walzer writes, Calvin "may be said to call into question the naturalness of nature"; or, as Leo Strauss writes, Calvin "understands what is commonly called natural as miraculous."[101] For Calvin, "the present hand of God," not any natural necessity, directs every apparently natural operation, every bolt of lightning, every full or dry breast, every wind, every birth, every thief or murderer.[102] This thoroughgoing providentialism leads Calvin to accept neither notion of natural freedom: neither that individuals are free from all subjection and establish government by their own consent nor that society exists by virtue of man's social and political nature and freely establishes its form of government.[103] He affirms instead that "the authority possessed by kings and other governors over all things upon earth is not a consequence of the perverseness of men, but of the holy ordinance of God, who has been pleased to regulate human affairs in this manner; forasmuch as he is present, and also presides among them, in making laws and in executing equitable judgments."[104]

Calvin is at one with Filmer when the latter declares that not only government "in the abstract . . . but the form of the power of governing, and the person having that power, are all the ordinance of God."[105] Calvin, however, more consistently accepts God's providence in the political realm, and instead of regarding only one form and one ruler as God's ordinance, as Filmer sometimes does, he views every established form of government and every ruler as a specific ordinance of God.[106] Divine institution of particular forms of government and even particular rulers justifies the demand for nonresistance—a demand from which only other divinely established institutions are exempt.[107] Like Filmer, Calvin had to recognize as expressions of divine providence not only all established governments but the successful revolutions or usurpations by which they had been established. Just as God raises up tyrants "to punish the iniquity of the people," so "sometimes he raises up some of his servants as public avengers, and arms them with his commission to punish unrighteous domination." The divine punishment of tyrants is achieved not only through such commissioned servants but also through those who, "though they were guided by the hand of God in such directions as he pleased, and performed his work without being conscious of it, nevertheless contemplated in their hearts nothing but evil."[108] For Calvin, "the same act displays the criminality of men and the justice of God," just as, for Filmer, God uses rebels' "unrighteous acts to the performance of His righteous decrees."[109] But whether executed by commissioned servants or by the wicked, "though the correction of tyrannical domination is the vengeance of God, we are not, therefore, to conclude that it is committed to us, who have received no other command than to obey and suffer."[110]

Since government for Calvin arises not from human provision for human needs but from divine providence, it exists not merely to minister

26

to those needs; its "first object" must be "the promotion of piety," and "all laws are preposterous which neglect the claims of God, and merely provide for the interests of men."[111] Calvin's two chief political teachings—nonresistance to even the most impious ruler and the responsibility of government for religion and morality—are both derived from understanding government as the expression of particular providence. Calvin rejects natural freedom, both as the freedom of individuals from all subjection and as the freedom of a society that exists by nature to freely choose its form of government, but he presents a more explicit and consistent exposition of the providentialist premise of Filmer's own view.

The other author besides Calvin who Filmer says "looks asquint" toward the right of the people to punish or depose their prince is Cardinal Bellarmine. Filmer objects to his statement that "if there be a lawful cause, the multitude may change the kingdom into an aristocracy or democracy."[112] This brief statement is the sole indication in *De Laicis* of this doctrine. In that work Bellarmine's explicit aim was limited to refuting the Anabaptists' antinomianism and to vindicating the right of Christians to be magistrates, make laws, execute capital punishment, and wage war.[113] In *De Summo Pontifice,* however, which Filmer also refers to, Bellarmine is chiefly concerned to show the authority of the pope, and in particular that, while he does not possess temporal power directly, he does so indirectly in some cases, up to and including the right to authorize popular deposition of temporal rulers.[114] In this work it is not clear whether popular deposition requires papal approval; in his *De Potestate Summi Pontificis* (a defense of the papal claims of *De Summo Pontifice* against William Barclay's *De Potestate Papae*) Bellarmine sometimes defends popular deposition as subject to papal approval and at other times defends it without reference to papal approval or with reference to papal approval as only one possibility.[115]

Bellarmine defends the papal right to authorize popular deposition of kings precisely on the grounds of the natural status of the political community and its natural freedom to choose its form of government and its governor.[116] Indeed, for Filmer, some passages of Bellarmine's "make evident the grounds of this question about the natural liberty of mankind" and "may best unfold the state of this controversy."[117] From Filmer's statement of the question "out of Bellarmine," together with the passages in *De Laicis* that it is drawn from, one sees that natural liberty is that of "the whole multitude," to whom by nature civil power belongs, to choose its forms of government and governors. Filmer adds to his quotation from Bellarmine that " 'Secular or civil power' (saith he) 'is instituted by men' "; but, for Bellarmine, while "individual forms of government in specific instances derive . . . not from the natural law," the natural freedom to choose them belongs to a commonwealth that exists by nature and "does not depend upon the consent of men": "authority of rulers considered thus in general is both by natural law and by Divine law, nor could the entire human race assembled together decree the opposite, that is, that there should be neither rulers nor leaders."[118] Bellarmine affirms that civil power is by nature, not only because of the reason Filmer gives in his restatement, "that God hath given or ordained power, is evident by Scripture," but because man is by nature "a social animal" and "a civil animal," requiring society not only for defense and the necessities of life but to acquire and exercise wisdom, justice, and the other virtues, "to cultivate our mind and our will."[119] Like Parsons, Bellarmine denies that an asocial condition ever existed, but he reaches that denial not "by experience" but by reference to Scripture, from which we learn that "the first men immediately built cities." The scriptural state of innocence is Bellarmine's basis for denying the existence of what Hobbes and Locke would call the state of nature: "there would have been political government even while man was in the state of innocence. And this is proved, firstly, because even then man would have been by nature a political and social animal."[120] Filmer's attribution of political power to the state of innocence renders continuous man's dependence on divine provision of political authority, but in Bellarmine it expresses the continuing political self-sufficiency of human nature.[121] Bellarmine's affirmation that civil power is by nature denies that individuals are by nature free from all subjection.

After denouncing Parsons and Buchanan for building popular sedition on the grounds of natural liberty and adding that Calvin and Bellarmine both "look asquint" that way, Filmer complains that those who "have learnedly confuted both Buchanan and Parsons, and vindicated the right of Kings in most points," still admit "the main foundation of popular sedition," namely, "the natural liberty and equality of mankind."[122] It is this complaint that Locke seizes on as Filmer's confession of the novelty of divine right and as proof of the ubiquity of Locke's own doctrine of natural freedom.[123] I have shown that the opponents of royal right attacked by Filmer were far from espousing Locke's natural freedom of the individual. It should be no surprise that these vindicators of the right of kings, however they offended Filmer, are no closer to Locke.

For instance, the first of the deficient vindicators of the right of kings listed here by Filmer, Sir John Hayward, maintains, in his *Answer* to Parsons, that society and government, and even its proper form, hereditary absolute monarchy, are all by nature.[124] Government itself is natural in that it is part of the secondary law of nature, the consequences and execution of the precepts of the primary law.[125] That monarchy is natural appears from diverse considerations, including convenience, God's monarchic rule of the world, the master's rule of the family, and the general

28

consent of nations.[126] Hereditary monarchy is natural because of the natural character of inheritance and primogeniture.[127]

In his argument that monarchy is natural, Hayward shrewdly seizes on Parsons's admission that "monarchy is the most excellent and perfect government, most resembling the government of god, and most agreeable unto nature." He objects: "How is it most agreeable to nature, and yet not natural?"[128] Parsons, however, says only that simple monarchy would be best *if* the prince could rule without passion. But since "a king or Prince is a man as others be," his rule must be bound by law and mixed with the other two forms of government.[129] Hayward nonetheless exposes a difficulty in all these theories of the natural freedom of the people to choose its form of government insofar as the authors of these theories express opinions as to the best, or even the most natural, form of government.[130] For though Parsons declares that forms of government are not determined by nature but are left to the free choice of every nation, he still argues that one kind is best; for him this is a mixed government rather than Hayward's absolute monarchy. A similar difficulty afflicts the view that forms of government are expressions of the particular providence of God rather than the products of natural civil societies. Calvin, who affirms that every actual form of government is by the ordinance, providence, and pleasure of God, expresses a preference for aristocracy or a mixture of aristocracy and democracy; yet for him Scripture corrects the heroic and noble preference for non-monarchic government by affirming the providential character of monarchies.[131] Filmer similarly vacillates between viewing all governments or only monarchies as expressions of divine providence.[132] Yet judgments about the relative merits of forms of government do more to disturb the claim that the people are left free by the law of nature to choose their form of government than they disturb the claim that all forms express divine providence.

One may wonder why Filmer should complain that Hayward is one of those who admit the natural liberty and equality of mankind to be "a principle unquestionable, not so much as once denying or opposing it."[133] It may be because Hayward is content to rest monarchy on nature rather than on divine ordinance.[134] Hayward even challenges the hint of an invocation of providence on Parsons's part, that "God doth approve that forme of government which every commonwealth doth chuse unto it selfe."[135] Hayward denies that one may say that God "approves" whatever form of government the commonwealth chooses because "sometimes entire governments; often, customes and statutes of state; and very commonly accidentall actions, are so unnaturall and unjust, that (otherwise then for a punishment and curse) wee cannot say that God doth approve them."[136] Hayward prefers to judge by nature and justice rather than by particular providence in gauging God's approval, and he sees no

29

necessity for assisting presumably divine punishments.[137] Similarly, Hayward denies Parsons's arguments against monarchy and primogeniture and for deposition based on the examples of God's particular providence in caring for his chosen people: "in those particular actions which God hath either done, or by expresse Oracle commanded, contrarie to the generall lawes which he hath given us . . . we are bound to the law, and not to the example"; such actions "are not proposed for imitation to us."[138] This deference to God's general laws rather than to his hand discerned in particular human events, even those recounted in Scripture, may seem to Filmer to fall short of a thorough rejection of the natural freedom of mankind.

Filmer's complaint may also arise because Hayward does not understand nature in terms of origins. Although Hayward regards society and government as natural, he does not claim that they have existed since the beginning and without interruption. There was no government during the time of the Judges and after the Flood until Nimrod, and there were other times of anarchy or interregnum.[139] Hayward does not regard political government as original because he distinguishes it from "oeconomical" power, contrary to Filmer's equation of kingdom and family, king and father.[140] Government arose from conquest; prescription lies at the basis of the hereditary titles claimed by usurpers' successors.[141] Hayward regards government, and monarchy in particular, as natural, not on account of the manner or time of its origin, but on grounds of convenience and general consent. For Filmer, however, to regard the people as originally free seems to be to grant them natural freedom.

It may be, finally, that Filmer was misled into thinking that Hayward actually viewed the people as by nature free to choose their form of government, because at one point Hayward grants this for the sake of argument (even though the opposite is "as obvious as that the sun shines"), to show that, even so, a later right to revolution does not follow. He argues that, even if the people once had the power to choose their form of government, they may lose it by cession, custom, or conquest.[142] In form this argument is not very different from Filmer's own in *Patriarcha* that begins: "But let us condescend for a while to the opinion of Bellarmine, Grotius and Suarez, and of all those who place supreme power in the whole people, and ask them . . . ."[143] Allen, in his account of Hayward, loses sight of the merely hypothetical character of this argument, and Filmer may have made the same mistake and thought that Hayward in fact accepts the natural liberty of the people, denying merely its seditious implications.[144] Filmer's own hypothetical argument, furthermore, though formally similar to Hayward's, is radically different in purpose; for it is intended to show that original natural liberty of the people could lead to no government whatsoever, whereas Hayward's is intended to show that it would still generate indefeasible hereditary monarchy and nonresistance.[145] Filmer may well, therefore, regard an argument such as Hayward's as an excessive concession to natural liberty and a failure to recognize human dependence on divine provision. Like Locke as opposed to Hobbes, Filmer as opposed to Hayward sees the absurdity of a popular "power to relinquish their power," "a miserable liberty, which is only to choose to whom we will give our liberty, which we may not keep."[146] Nevertheless, even the natural freedom that Hayward recognized merely hypothetically is that of the whole people to choose its form of government, not that of the individual in the state of nature.

Barclay is the last of the vindicators of the right of kings whom Filmer complains of as accepting "the natural liberty and equality of mankind . . . for a principle unquestionable."[147] This may seem surprising, for, as Locke notes, Barclay is a great asserter not only of the power but also of the sacredness of kings.[148] Allen explains that Barclay's "most essential contention" is that "Authority to command can only be derived from God: it cannot conceivably be derived from man . . . ; the people cannot take away what they did not and could not give." He adds that Barclay says that "absolute monarchy had been instituted immediately by God and was the only form of sovereignty of which God is known to approve."[149]

Barclay recognizes nature as the origin of society, government, and law. In this he admits he has "no great disagreement" with Buchanan. Although Barclay regards the social and civil condition as natural, he admits that at first men came together "having departed from that wild and uncouth manner of living."[150] Accordingly, though like Bellarmine and Filmer he quotes Saint Chrysostom's declaration that God made all mankind from one man "that He might signify kingdom to be more excellent than democracy and more pleasing to himself," Barclay understands this as a symbolic or analogical signification only and not as the establishment by God of an original monarchy in Adam to be continuously inherited among men.[151] On the contrary, Barclay, like Hayward, regards not Adam but Nimrod as "the first of all actively to govern with the civil power"; and, since Nimrod's was not a universal monarchy, civil government could also first arise at other times and places. Unlike Hayward, however, Barclay denies that Nimrod's rule was based on conquest.[152] For Barclay recognizes popular consent as the origin of government.

Barclay explicitly agrees with Buchanan that, originally, kings were established by the suffrages of the people, but he argues that the same utility that led to that original act leads to power remaining with the kings.[153] This premise of original freedom and popular consent is not merely the basis of a hypothetical argument, made to refute Buchanan's conclusions from his own premise, in the fashion of Hayward or Filmer.

31

When Barclay presents his own account of the origin of society, government, and laws, he argues that the first kings were the authors of society by gathering men together; they were also the authors of laws. Yet the first king became one only after the constitution of society and by the people's abdicating to him its authority, including the right to make laws.[154] Similarly, in presenting his own thematic account of the origin of monarchy, Barclay claims that the people constitute kings by their consent even when the kings are selected by God, come to the throne by inheritance, or gain it by conquest. God "prescribes who by name is to rule over whom" only "very rarely," and, even then, "the Lord wills that those whom He selects as kings be offered to the peoples and not thrust on them"; that is, they become kings only upon receiving popular consent.[155] More usually, when there is no divine designation, kings are only "said to have been set up by God and to receive power from Him, because He is the supreme author and approver of the power conferred by the multitude." God then uses the people as "a sort of instrument, a second cause," preferring "things to arise from things, or from second causes, in a reasoned and perennial order" than to bring them about, as in the interventions of particular providence, "with no intermediary."[156]

The people not only choose original monarchs and establish the laws of succession that thenceforth determine the kings; they even establish forms of government, whether democracy, aristocracy, or monarchy.[157] Accordingly, Barclay understands Saint Paul's injunction that every soul be subject to the higher powers to refer not only to monarchy but to all forms of government, just as he understands Saint Paul's explanation, "for there is no power but of God: the powers that be are ordained of God," to mean not that power comes exclusively from God but that it comes *also* from him and "not from the consent alone of the multitude."[158]

As Barclay points out, he consistently agrees with his adversaries that "the people transferred all their power and sovereignty into the hands of the Prince."[159] Filmer therefore does not err in complaining that Barclay admits the natural freedom of the people: their original right to establish forms of government, select monarchs, and determine the laws of succession. But the liberty Barclay writes of is that of peoples or cities, not the freedom of every individual from all subjection.[160]

Barclay's recognition of natural freedom lies at the basis of his concessions to popular resistance, which Locke makes extensive use of at the end of the *Second Treatise*.[161] Barclay argues that, since the people constitute kings and establish the laws of succession, they must decide the succession in the absence of an heir, in the presence of several claimants, or when the heir is "one that nature has rendered unfit for the power."[162] When Barclay concedes that popular resistance is permitted—or, rather, that it is not "resistance" if the king makes himself no longer a king, either by trying to destroy the kingdom or by trying to transfer the realm to a foreigner—he writes that "the people is made free in this way and superior, since that had been returned to it which it held in the inter-regnum before the inauguration of a king."[163] Thus the original freedom of the people leads, via the doctrine of interregnum, to exceptions in favor of popular resistance, and this apparently justifies Filmer's mis-givings about the premise, since it plays into Locke's hands.

Despite Barclay's recognition of the natural origin of society, govern-ment, and law and of the original freedom of the people to institute forms of government and select rulers, he is, as Locke says, an asserter of the sacredness of kings. Divine right is superimposed upon nature and popular consent. Barclay argues that resistance not only is contrary to the pact or transfer of popular sovereignty to the prince and to the utility for which the transfer is made in the first place, but also is contrary to the ordinance of God.[164] Kings have power conferred on them not only by the people but also by God, so that the people are doubly bound: by their own act and by the ordinance of God that follows it. This doctrine is in sharp contrast with Filmer's exclusively divine right, based on the inability of the people to confer authority.

Grace is added to nature by Barclay in this way, and it also colors his account of nature, particularly his account of the naturalness of mon-archy. He says that Buchanan and Cicero err in attributing the foun-dation of monarchy simply to human concern for establishing justice. Men also have an "innate propensity," a "secret force and faculty of nature," that propels them toward monarchy. This natural basis of mon-archy is tinged with divine mystery. It operates because monarchy has "a likeness in it of the divine governance," a reason "more abstruse and sanctified, referring to the unity of the divine majesty itself" and to its eternity, "a certain mystical reason . . . hidden in the secrets of nature," "a certain image and power of Almighty God." Although Barclay con-cedes that the founding of kingdoms "should be correctly attributed to the law of nations," and thereby preserves the natural freedom of nations to institute other forms of government, he adds that, "so far as men by a certain secret instinct of nature were inclined to them [monarchs], they to that extent can be said to be of the natural law."[165] For Barclay, divine right is added on to and tinges natural right and is in tension with natural freedom; for Filmer, the single providential institution of monarchy replaces all natural right and removes all natural freedom.

Filmer's predecessors in vindicating the right of kings fell short, in varying degrees, of his providentialist divine right and even entertained some version of what he considered the natural freedom of mankind. Nevertheless, it is clear that they did not recognize a natural freedom of every individual from all subjection and a consequent constituting of civil society by individual consent to serve individual purposes. Phraseological coincidence, however, permitted Locke to make it appear that his own principles were recognized, even by Filmer, as the long-standing ones. Furthermore, Filmer, by virtue of the very extremism of his providential divine right, not only views his predecessors as adherents of natural freedom but even tries to dissolve the freedom of the corporate people or commonwealth to choose a form of government into an anarchic freedom of each man, bound by no subjection of any kind to that people. This is most clear in his objection to the majority rule in the original multitude:

> For what freedom or liberty is due to any man by the law of nature, no inferior power can alter, limit or diminish. No one man, nor a multitude, can give away the natural right of another. . . . Therefore, unless it can be proved by some law of nature that the major, or some other part, have power to overrule the rest of the multitude, it must follow that the acts of multitudes not entire are not binding to all, but only to such as consent unto them.[166]

As is evident in this instance, Filmer of course intends to show not merely that a condition of natural freedom is anarchic but that there is no way by which it can be transformed into civil society of itself; that is, it requires the assistance of divine right. He renders Locke two services—the service of giving Locke's doctrine an apparent pedigree, by obscuring the difference between it and its predecessors, and, more substantively, the service of claiming that the doctrines of those predecessors ultimately dissolve into something like Locke's doctrine. He also poses this challenge to Locke: to explain how it is possible to get from natural freedom to civil society.[167]

## HOBBES: THE FAMILY AND THE STATE OF NATURE

Hobbes provides the outstanding effort, prior to Locke, to explain the family on the basis of the radical individualist doctrine of natural freedom: that all individuals are by nature free and equal and that all subjection is by consent. Although *Patriarcha* appears to have been written before its author encountered the writings of Thomas Hobbes, Filmer rushed into print as the first critic of *Leviathan;* his "Observations on Mr. Hobbes's *Leviathan:* or his Artificial Man—a Commonwealth" was published in 1652.[168] To follow Hobbes's efforts to explain the family, one must examine all three of his presentations of his political philosophy: the first, *De Corpore Politico,* which together with *Human Nature* constitutes *The Elements of Law;* the second, *De Cive;* and the third, *Leviathan.*[169]

Hobbes presents paternal dominion as an instance of one of his two kinds of bodies politic, commonwealths by acquisition, as distinguished from commonwealths by institution.[170] Hobbes distinguishes these two kinds without making any explicit reference to fathers, the family, or inheritance: in commonwealths by acquisition men submit to whoever has them in his power, whereas in commonwealths by institution men agree with one another to submit themselves to whomever the majority chooses.[171] They are not so much two kinds of bodies politic as "two ways of erecting a body politic," differing in origin, not in subsequent rights and duties.[172] The difference in origin includes both a difference in the object of the motivating fear, with men afraid of the sovereign in commonwealths by acquisition and afraid of others in commonwealths by institution, and a difference between separate, individual submissions in commonwealths by acquisition and collective agreement in commonwealths by institution. The commonwealth by acquisition is more natural, in that it depends on "natural force" rather than wit.[173] A commonwealth by institution requires more wit, because it requires concord among many men prior to their joint subjection to a power that can subsequently maintain their concord by their common fear of it;[174] the danger is less immediate and obvious than where subjection is to the menacing party, and mutual distrust must be overcome by calculation of future benefits. Most important, commonwealth by institution involves first the conception and only then the generation of a power that is not yet in existence, whereas commonwealth by acquisition involves subjection to a power already so much in existence that it threatens one's life. The process of instituting a commonwealth is also more arbitrary, because the identities of the members of the commonwealth and of the particular sovereign are not provided by the situation itself; they must choose and be chosen. The fundamental fact about paternal dominion in Hobbes's thought is that it is an instance of acquisition of dominion by force. As such, it is paired with the rule of masters over servants whom they have conquered and then trusted with their liberty in return for an expressed or presumed covenant of obedience.[175]

According to Hobbes, in the state of nature, "considering men again dissolved from all covenants one with another," dominion over a child belongs to its mother.[176] Only in Hobbes's first presentation does he give the argument that since "every man by the law of nature, hath right or propriety to his own body, the child ought rather to be the propriety of the mother, of whose body it is part, till the time of separation, than of the father."[177] Hobbes seems to have originated the recent argument that the mother's right over her own body gives her right over the life of her child, but he carries it beyond the time of birth. However, the special right to one's own body is by the natural law of equity, that "when we enter into peace one with another . . . *Whatsoever right any man requireth to retain, he allow every other man to retain the same.*"[178] As such, this special right would have effect and be recognized by others only if men could effectively covenant to make peace and give up their natural right to all things without instituting a sovereign to establish property by civil law, which, according to Hobbes, they cannot.[179] Hobbes cannot properly cite this special right when considering men "dissolved from all covenants," and accordingly he drops it in his later presentations. I am not aware of any other argument in Hobbes derived from union with the body— none, for instance, in regard to the right to food and drink—as distinguished from his usual argument for the right to means for preservation of one's body.[180] This abandoned argument may best be regarded as *ad hominem,* replying to those who argue for paternal dominion from generation by showing that such considerations would lead instead to maternal dominion. In the same way, he argues that generation would lead more clearly to maternal than to paternal dominion, since the father's identity is merely a matter of the mother's say-so prior to the institution of civil marriage.

Hobbes asserts more fundamentally that he cannot find "by what coherence" generation implies dominion.[181] Hobbes does not explicitly explain why he does not admit that men owe obedience in gratitude for their birth. It may be because, for him, gratitude is owed only to those who benefit another upon trust of obtaining "a greater, or no less benefit" for themselves, and "not for triumph or ostentation," in which case they do not need or therefore deserve the reward of gratitude, since "they have the reward in themselves."[182] (This paradoxical result, that we owe gratitude only to those who benefit us solely to secure our favor and to obtain future benefits from us, but not to those who benefit us for the pleasure of doing so without thought of further reward, follows from the Hobbesian rationale for gratitude. The reason for gratitude lies not in the intrinsic merit of the benefactor or in the value of the benefit but in the effect that gratitude has in furthering defense and peace; it operates as one of the natural laws "which declare unto us the ways of peace, where the same may be obtained, and of defence where it may not."[183] The natural law of gratitude is parallel to the natural law concerning revenge, that one consider not the past but "the benefit to come.")[184] Generation is an act the performers of which "have the reward in themselves," not only "*sensual* pleasure" but "a pleasure or joy of the mind consisting in the imagination of the power they have so much to please," a sort of glory or triumph, at having power not to generate but to please. So far is the act of generation from a deliberate intention to benefit or be benefited by its offspring that, "though issue sometimes follows, yet men seek not that, but to please, and to be pleased."[185] In the *Elements* Hobbes still presents sexual activity as directed toward generation because he there defines beauty as signs of generative power, defines lust or love as "indefinite desire of different sex," and claims that even what we call romantic love, "that *love* which is the great theme of poets," "cannot be without diversity of sex." But he goes on shortly to analyze the "merely sensual" love of Socrates for Alcibiades, and he regards it as one of the duties of a sovereign "to forbid unnatural copulation" in order to increase population, though "a private man living under the law of natural reason only" might engage in it.[186] And in *Leviathan* he defines love without reference to difference of sex and no longer explains beauty simply as signs of generative power.[187]

Hobbes may refuse to base paternal dominion on gratitude for generation also because generation of human beings is not an instance of human making at all but is rather the work of God by way of nature. For the generation that is truly the work of man by way of art is the generation of artificial man, the body politic.[188] Unlike Filmer, however, for whom "the power which God himself exerciseth over mankind is by right of fatherhood," Hobbes argues that even God's sovereignty over men is derived not from his creating them but from his irresistible power.[189] Men owe obligation neither to their parents for their generation nor to God for their creation.

The final reason why Hobbes refuses to base paternal dominion on gratitude for generation may be that generation is not a benefit. Paradoxically, the philosopher of self-preservation may not value life so much that he considers it a benefit when bestowed upon those not yet living, as distinct from when it is preserved for those in danger of losing it. Hobbes teaches not the love of life but the fear of death. Although the greatest of evils is death, there is no greatest good in this life, for "Life it selfe is but Motion, and can never be without Desire, nor without Feare."[190] Aristotle, in contrast, though his orientation is to living well rather than to mere life, teaches that human beings are obligated to their parents and to the gods for the benefit of having been brought into being, since he also teaches that mere life itself includes an element of beauty or nobility and some joy and natural sweetness.[191] The results of Hobbes's refusal to base paternal dominion on generation are clear in any case: men are born free; there is no natural dominion; all dominion is the result of human artifice.[192]

Hobbes attributes dominion over children to their mothers in the state of nature because he bases that dominion on preservation of the children. Dominion is not needed and therefore not owed to encourage generation, but it is needed to encourage preservation of offspring. The preservation from which paternal dominion is derived, as in the case of acquisition of dominion by force—of which paternal dominion is a part— depends on having another person in one's power so as to be able to destroy him. Thus the mother has the first right over the child at birth because she is the first to have it in her power. Any rights of fathers over children in the state of nature derive therefore from maternal contract or abandonment. There is no natural law of marriage: the content of such a contract is not set by nature. The mother may give the father, i.e., whomever she contracts with, right over the children but not over herself, over some of the children but not over all; the relation between the mother and the father may be permanent or temporary, for "copulation only" or for "society of all things"; even if it is for "society of all things" and one of the two must therefore govern, which of the two is also a matter of contract and is only "for the most part" the man, since it is "sometimes" the woman.[193] Hobbes rejects any derivation of fathers' rights from the supposed superiority of the male sex, since "there is not always that difference of strength or prudence between the man and the woman, as that the right can be determined without War."[194] The grounds on which Hobbes argues for natural sexual equality, as for natural equality generally, are not that there are no natural superiorities but that these are not effective in the state of nature. Indeed, the weaker may even have the practical advantage, since fear leads them to strike first.[195] Hobbes's argument for maternal dominion in the state of nature represents not any practical feminism but a rejection of the patriarchal arguments that would obviate his arguments from natural freedom and equality and for consent. Those premises of freedom, equality, and consent could, however, eventually become the premises of practical feminism.

Not only does Hobbes refuse to base paternal dominion in the state of nature on gratitude for generation; he does not base it on gratitude for parental care. He does not argue from "the naturall inclination of the Sexes . . . to their children."[196] His requirement that benefits, in order to deserve gratitude, be bestowed for benefits in return "and not for triumph" would exclude from gratitude not only generation but charity: "There can be no greater argument to a man, of his own power, than to find himself able not only to accomplish his own desires, but also to assist other men in theirs: and this is that conception wherein consisteth *charity*." Charity is thus a kind of glory or mental triumph, a pleasure at the "conception of our *own power*." As the first kind of charity that Hobbes specifies, "*natural affection* of parents to their children" would therefore not deserve gratitude.[197]

Hobbes bases paternal dominion not simply on gratitude but on covenant and on justice, which is the virtue of covenant-keeping.[198] Gratitude for Hobbes is a minimal obligation, not even explicitly requiring more than abstaining from harming one's benefactor; thus, falling far short of total subjection, it provides not peace itself—which only covenants of obedience and justice can establish—but merely the "beginning of [the] benevolence, or trust," that is prerequisite to peace.[199] In the state of nature, gratitude seems capable of fulfillment only by giving way to subjection and justice, since "each man is an enemy to that other, whom he neither obeys nor commands."[200] Finally, Hobbes may wish to avoid basing dominion on gratitude not so much as a natural law or virtue (which he has in any case reinterpreted into selfish future-oriented calculation) but as the passion or state of mind "which men call *Gratitude*," a "cheerfull acceptation" of benefits from one "whom we acknowledge for superiour"—a passion which inclines to "love."[201] Hobbes's effort to base obligation on one's own covenant rather than on gratitude for benefits received is part of an affirmation of human freedom—freedom from other men as well as from God and nature.[202]

Hobbes bases paternal dominion on the child's consent to a covenant of obedience. He derives the right over children from the right in the state of nature to prevent someone in one's power from subsequently attaining a dangerous equality of power. The simplest ways of doing this are by killing, binding, or maiming, but the way that constitutes dominion is by exacting a covenant of obedience. The reason why a conqueror or parent takes such a risky course, of performing first the act of sparing in return for later obedience, is the imperative in the state of nature "to get some fellows; that if there needs must be war, it may not yet be against all men, nor without some helps."[203] The supposition on which the child's covenant of obedience rests is that "it is to be presumed, that he which giveth sustenance to another, whereby to strengthen him, hath received a promise of obedience in consideration thereof. For else it would be wisdom in men, rather to let their children perish, while they are infants, than to live in their danger or subjection, when they are grown."[204]

That the child's covenant of obedience is merely "presumed" does not necessarily distinguish it from the covenant of servant to master, which is also "a supposed covenant"; what does distinguish it is its being, *necessarily*, merely presumed.[205] For children have "never power to make any covenant, or to understand the consequences thereof"; indeed, "wanting the free use of reason they are exempted from all duty."[206] The conquered servant may consent not by "expresse words" but by "other sufficient signes of the Will," but the child's "Consent, either expresse, or by other sufficient arguments declared," seems to be given before the age of consent.[207] Since Hobbes's arguments are generally from presumed rather than actual covenants, it is all the more necessary for him to justify the reasonableness of acting as if one were keeping covenants. He justifies justice on the grounds that in the state of nature one cannot preserve oneself "without the help of Confederates," which one cannot reasonably expect to retain if one breaks covenants.[208] Just as the conqueror's sparing and the parent's nourishing, if not the prior conquering and generating, seem to be efforts to "get fellows," so does the obedience of the servant and the child. The assumption that he who commands, not only he who obeys, is a fellow rather than an enemy is hard to defend on Hobbes's premises, since the commander promises nothing as to the future.[209] This justification of justice by appeal to the recurring character of covenants is weakest in application to filial obedience, since one never becomes a child again. Not only Hobbes's rationalization of filial obedience but his effort to reconcile it with his principles of natural freedom and equality and obligation by consent is problematic.[210]

On the basis of considerable evidence, Gordon J. Schochet emphasizes a "patriarchal element" in Hobbes's political philosophy and argues that the state of nature is not the condition of free individuals it is usually taken to be but is "composed of familial social units," which remove their individual members from the state of nature.[211] Filmer seized upon this patriarchal element in Hobbes and used it to argue against Hobbes's arguments from natural freedom, equality, and consent. Pointing out that Hobbes recognizes that fathers were originally sovereigns, Filmer remarks that, "If according to the order of nature he had handled paternal government before that by institution, there would have been little liberty left in the subjects of the family to consent to institution of government."[212] Filmer's argument is the more plausible since Hobbes not only admits paternal sovereignty but extends it to include dominion over adult children and grandchildren and continues it beyond the father's death by a natural-law doctrine of succession.[213] These patriarchal elements in combination seem to produce not Schochet's independent families but the whole Filmerian scheme—indeed, universal monarchy, if men share a common descent—thus annihilating the state of nature. To Filmer's horror, Hobbes avoids this ultimate conclusion by arguing from a hypothesis of plural creation (eschewing not only scriptural unique creation but Aristotelian eternal generation of men from men in favor of the Epicurean and pagan mythical notion of generation of many men from nonman).[214] While Schochet successfully solves one puzzle by showing that Hobbes's "historical" references to prepolitical familial life need not be understood, as they so often are, to be contrary to his "philosophical" account of the state of nature, he creates two others: he leaves us wondering, first, why so many have misunderstood Hobbes, or rather why Hobbes so often writes as if the state of nature were individualistic, without any reference to its familial character,[215] and, second, what prevents Hobbes's patriarchal concessions from constituting the whole of the Filmerian scheme.

Hobbes qualifies his statement that "a great Family" outside a commonwealth is "a little Monarchy"—a statement both Schochet and Filmer rely on—by this crucial qualification: "but yet a Family is not properly a Common-wealth; unlesse it be of that power by its own number, or by other opportunities, as not to be subdued without the hazard of war."

Otherwise, Hobbes continues, "where a number of men are manifestly too weak to defend themselves united, every one may use his own reason in time of danger, to save his own life, either by flight, or by submission to the enemy, as hee shall think best."[216] Given the character of the state of nature as a state of war—even if, as Schochet suggests, that war is a war of every family against every family rather than of "every man against every man," as Hobbes says—such a time of danger is always near, and it infects every moment.[217] As a result, the family as such is radically defective and always on the brink of dissolution.[218] It is likely to be dissolved long before it is able to grow into a "great Family," able to provide protection and elicit lasting obedience. The family as such is not a body politic and fails to remove its members effectively from the state of nature. Hobbes's discussion of the "dominion" of one single individual over another in the state of nature should not obscure the ultimate inadequacy and precariousness of such relations, any more than his discussion of the law of nature in the state of nature should obscure the fact that for the most part that law does not oblige to action in that state because of the lack of adequate security.[219] Such a statement as that the representation of children "has no place but in a State Civill, because before such estate, there is no Dominion of Persons" can cut two ways. It can be used tautologically, as it is by Schochet, to show that paternal rule "in the state of nature" is civil rule, or it can be used more meaningfully to show that fathers in the state of nature do not, strictly speaking, exercise effective dominion.[220] The precarious status of filial obligation in the state of nature emerges also from Hobbes's account of the Fifth Commandment, so dear to Filmer: although formally it "did oblige in the state of nature," nevertheless, "all things were determined by every man's own judgment, and therefore paternal respects also."[221] Similarly, the natural law of inheritance, which seems to threaten to push Hobbes's patriarchal concessions into the full-fledged Filmerian scheme, turns out to be ineffective in the state of nature: "amongst masterlesse men, there is perpetuall war, of every man against his neighbour; no inheritance, to transmit to the Son, nor to expect from the Father."[222] Hobbes has unobtrusively provided in advance against Filmer's criticism that he violated "the order of nature" in handling commonwealths by institution before paternal government and that he thereby concealed that the family left men no liberty to institute government. For Hobbes's explanation of the inability of small groups like the family to provide security and to substitute lasting obligation for liberty not only appears at the end of the discussion of paternal dominion in *Leviathan* but precedes each of the three accounts he gives of the generation of a body politic.[223] For Hobbes, the individual, not the family, is the basic natural unit of society.[224]

## HOBBES: THE FAMILY AND EDUCATION IN THE COMMONWEALTH

According to Hobbes, there is no natural law of marriage and therefore no necessity for the family as anything beyond mother and child in the state of nature; moreover, after *De Corpore Politico* Hobbes drops the sovereign's duty, in the commonwealth, "to forbid the promiscuous use of women . . . , to forbid one woman to have many husbands . . . , [and] to forbid marriages within certain degrees of kindred and affinity." The natural law against adultery receives definite content only through the civil law. In *De Cive,* Hobbes argues that in the state of nature "all things were common, and therefore all carnal copulations lawful," and he then goes on to say that in civil society, "though the law of nature forbid . . . adultery . . . , yet if the civil law command us to invade anything, that invasion is not . . . adultery"; and he says, further, that "copulations of heathen sexes, according to their laws, were lawful marriages." Accordingly, Hobbes rewrites the Seventh Commandment both as natural law and as scriptural commandment: "Thou shalt avoid all copulation forbidden by the laws." Therefore, "that copulation which in one city is matrimony, in another will be judged adultery."[225] The family takes definite shape and receives the sanction of natural law and Scripture only within and by virtue of the commonwealth. It appears that the civil sovereign might lawfully permit, for instance, the Spartan mode of what Christians might call adultery, or that he might even permit "the promiscuous use of women" and abolish the family entirely.[226] Similarly, Hobbes is as willing to add to the Fifth Commandment as Filmer is to subtract from it: "Thou shalt not refuse to give the honour defined by the laws, unto thy parents."[227]

The presentation in *Leviathan* shies away from such explicit relativism. It emphasizes, not the arbitrary character of the civil law upon which the character and existence of the family depend, but the dependence itself—and how that dependence may serve to reconstitute the family in its familiar form.[228] The family derives not only its security, and thus its internal obedience, from civil law but also its specific educational function. Hobbes writes in *Leviathan* of "those that are by Law allowed and appointed to Teach us, as our Parents [are] in their Houses."[229]

This educational function of the family, established by civil law, serves even as the basis for the civil force of the Fifth Commandment. Chapter 30 of *Leviathan* is devoted to the "office" or duty of the sovereign, which is divided into two main heads, instruction and legislation. Of these two, instruction is treated first and at greater length.[230] Hobbes sets forth the principles of that instruction so as to correspond to the Ten Commandments, apparently to guarantee their acceptance by the people, since even "supposing that these of mine are not such Principles of Reason; yet I am sure they are Principles from Authority of Scripture."[231] Some of these principles are parts of the content of instruction because they are "the grounds, and reasons," of "the Essentiall Rights (which are the Naturall, and Fundamentall Lawes) of Soveraignty," but others are requisite to the process of instruction itself. Among these is the fourth principle (corresponding to the Fourth Commandment of remembering the Sabbath), that the sovereign set apart certain times for the people to learn their duties and the laws and to "be put in mind of the Authority that maketh them Lawes." In a similar way, as requisite to the sovereign's instruction of the people in their duties, Hobbes presents the fifth principle, which "accordeth with the fifth Commandment."[232] This presentation begins: "And because the first instruction of Children, dependeth on the care of their Parents; it is necessary that they should be obedient to them, whilest they are under their tuition." Filial obedience within the commonwealth is commanded by the sovereign for the sake of the instruction of the people in their civil duties.

Filial obedience within the commonwealth, according to this passage, is necessary, and is therefore enjoined, only while the children are still "under the tuition" of their parents, because only then is it required for facilitating their instruction. Such filial obedience is, of course, only temporary; moreover, it is limited by the overriding commands of civil law.[233] But this limited obedience is not the only filial obligation taught here. Children must "also afterwards (as gratitude requireth,) . . . acknowledge the benefit of their education, by externall signes of honour." Adult children within the commonwealth, like enfranchised children in the state of nature,[234] owe their parents not obedience—not even obedience within the limits of the law—but merely honor, or the signs of honor. Hobbes does not say here, as he does earlier in the work, that a "Parent ought to have the honour *of a Soveraign,* (though he have surrendred his Power to the Civill Law,) because he had it originally by Nature."[235] Here he grants only "the honour due unto them for their education." The difference may result not only from the fact that here honor is derived from actual education rather than from any original or natural relation; it may also result from Hobbes's recognizing the implications of the relation of honor to power. These implications are frankly spelled out in *De Cive:*

> The *enfranchised son* or *released servant,* do now stand in less fear of their *lord* and *father,* being deprived of his natural and lordly power over them; and, if regard be had to true and inward honour, do honour him less than before. For *honour,* as hath been said in the section above, is nothing else but the estimation of another's power; and therefore he that hath least power, hath always least *honour.*[236]

As obedience during the period of tuition is necessary to make parental instruction possible, so, later, honor is necessary to reward such instruction and thereby render it reasonable and therefore probable. For, Hobbes explains, there would not be "any reason, why any man should desire to have children, or take the care to nourish, and instruct them, if they were afterwards to have no other benefit from them, than from other men."[237] This explanation seems to be what is meant by the parenthesis quoted above, that *gratitude* requires filial honor. There is a difficulty in saying that filial honor is required by gratitude, which is supposed to encourage future benefits to oneself by one's benefactors, since this honor is to be paid after the parents have already finished benefiting the child. Such honor serves, above all, the purpose of the sovereign in encouraging instruction. The sovereign is therefore the crucial party in encouraging the filial honor that peace and justice ultimately require and that gratitude alone would not ensure. Just as gratitude or the need to reward parenthood is inadequate to secure filial obedience in the state of nature and must be supplemented, initially by concern for peace, or at least for getting fellows as helps in war, and ultimately by covenants of obedience and justice, so gratitude or the need to reward parenthood is invoked to justify filial honor in society but must be supplemented by concern for peace, at least on the part of the sovereign, and by civil law. To encourage parenthood in the state of nature, the subjection of children to their parents is necessary so that they cannot become their parents' enemies; in the security of society, honor is sufficient encouragement. The disadvantage of that security is that the need for fellows as helps in war no longer serves as a motivation for both parenthood and filial obedience; instruction by the sovereign must replace it in the commonwealth.

In order to make children obey their parents while under their tuition and honor them afterwards, Hobbes says that

> they are to be taught, that originally the Father of every man was also his Soveraign Lord, with power over him of life and death; and that the Fathers of families, when by instituting a Common-wealth, they resigned that absolute Power, yet it was never intended, they should lose the honour due unto them for their education.[238]

Hobbes does not present this as his own justification of paternal authority within the commonwealth but as the doctrine that the sovereign ought to teach the people.[239] Hobbes may have accepted the patriarchal origin of many commonwealths, but he derived paternal authority in commonwealths not from that origin but, as the context of this very statement shows, from its being requisite to the sovereign's instruction of the people for the sake of peace. Richard Allen Chapman argues further that the

44

family in Hobbes's commonwealth contributes to stability not merely by "teaching the principles of Hobbes's political science" but by itself being a "Leviathan writ small," a miniature society based on obedience rendered in return for protection.[240]

The account Hobbes gives here of the article of instruction corresponding to the Seventh Commandment helps to explain how the will of the sovereign may well produce the family:

> Of things held in propriety, those that are dearest to a man are his own life & limbs; and in the next degree (in most men,) those that concern conjugall affection; and after them riches and means of living. Therefore the People are to be taught, to abstain from violence to one anothers person, by private revenges; from violation of conjugall honour; and from forcible rapine, and fraudulent surreption of one anothers goods.[241]

Not only must the sovereign establish property in goods "to prevent violence and rapine";[242] he must do the same for property in wives and children, for men in the state of nature "use Violence, to make themselves Masters of other mens persons, wives, children, and cattell" and would be ready to do the same in society were they not properly instructed or restrained.[243] For the sake of peace, men must be guaranteed their own families. Such matters, like most others, can still be regulated "according as they that have the Soveraignty shall think most convenient," so that "in some places of the world, men have the Liberty of many wives: in other places, such Liberty is not allowed."[244]

Hobbes does not say why property in conjugal affection is so dear to men. It may be an instance of the inclination of all men "not onely to the procuring, but also to the assuring of a contented life," or it may be peculiarly characteristic of those men who "would be glad to be at ease within modest bounds" instead of "taking pleasure in contemplating their own power in the acts of conquest." For rape and adultery are honorable actions as signs of power.[245] Concern for conjugal honor may also stem from the honor men hope for from their children, which presumably depends on being certain they are their own.[246] Whatever its ground, this concern serves as the basis for legislation and instruction against the injustice of adultery, which would threaten peace.

The "first instruction of Children," for which parents are responsible and from which function they derive their claim to civil recognition of their need for filial obedience and honor, is very powerful. Hobbes writes that little children "have no other rule of good and evill manners, but the correction they receive from their Parents, and Masters" and "are constant to their rule." Thus "the dispositions of boys towards all things are formed as their parents and masters wish by the rod."[247] As one

45

might expect from Hobbesian emphases on the utility and rationality of fear in other contexts, education by fear of punishment is not without effect. It is Hobbes's first principle that "all men, because they are born in infancy, are born unapt for society." Children "think that every thing ought to be given them which they desire." Therefore, "unless you give children all they ask for, they are peevish and cry, aye, and strike their parents sometimes." Men are "made fit for society not by nature, but by education."[248]

Early education is not only by correction and the rod but through habit:

> those things that when new offend, that is those that the nature of man resists in the beginning, most often repeated whet the same nature; and those which are endured at first, soon compel love. Which is observed especially in the regimen of the body, but secondly in the operations of the mind. Therefore those accustomed to wine from youth disaccustom themselves not at all easily; and those imbued with whatever opinions from boyhood, most retain them even in old age, especially men who, except in things pertaining to something familiar, are not solicitous very much about truth and falsehood. Therefore among all peoples religion and doctrine, which are taught in the first years, hold onto them perpetually, so that they hate and revile dissenters.[249]

Habit is so powerful that "if the minds of men were all of white paper, they would almost equally be disposed to acknowledge whatsoever should be in right method, and by right ratiocination delivered to them: but when men have once acquiesced in untrue opinions, and registered them as authentical records in their minds, it is no less impossible to speak intelligibly to such men, than to write legibly upon a paper already scribbled over." It is precisely because our minds are so scribbled over that it is necessary for Hobbes to make his fresh beginning "from the very first grounds of all our knowledge and sense."[250]

The effectiveness of early education derives not only from its use of punishment and habit but also from its reliance on example rather than precept.[251] Hobbes declares that "the dispositions of youths are not less but much more disposed to bad morals by example than to good ones by precept."[252]

When Hobbes writes that "The causes of this difference of Witts, are in the Passions: and the difference of Passions, proceedeth partly from the different Constitution of the body, and partly from different Education," it seems to be early education he has in mind.[253] Early education is education of the passions and morals as well as in doctrine.

Although families perform "the first instruction of Children," which is very powerful as an education of passions and manners by means of punishment, habit, and example, the universities are the source of doctrine. They are "the Fountains of Civill, and Morall Doctrine, from whence the Preachers, and the Gentry, drawing such water as they find, use to sprinkle the same (both from the Pulpit, and in their Conversation) upon the People."[254] Those fountains have been poisoned with seditious doctrine as a result of their papist foundation, and they are tainted with the democratic prejudices and vain philosophy of classical learning. Their purification is Hobbes's program. As F. C. Hood declares, "The reform of university teaching was the chief practical recommendation contained in *Leviathan*."[255] Hobbes hoped that *Leviathan* might "fall into the hands of a Soveraign, who will . . . by the exercise of entire Soveraignty, in protecting the Publique teaching of it, convert this Truth of Speculation, into the Utility of Practice." He thought *Leviathan* would be "profitably taught in the Universities, in case they also think so, to whom the judgment of the same belongeth."[256] Hobbes's concern is with doctrine or opinion rather than directly with passion or the habits of moral virtue. He grants the sovereign the right of judgment over opinions and doctrines because "the Actions of men proceed from their Opinions; and in the wel governing of Opinions, consisteth the well governing of mens Actions, in order to their Peace and Concord."[257] Although he recognizes that the causes of political evil include seditious passions, chief among them ambition, it is seditious doctrines that he is chiefly concerned with and that he directly attempts to counteract.[258] Passions are not amenable to formation in the way that opinion can be shaped by instruction:

> Potent men, digest hardly any thing that setteth up a Power to bridle their affections; and Learned men, any thing that discovereth their errours, and thereby lesseneth their Authority: whereas the Common-peoples minds, unless they be tainted with dependence on the Potent, or scribbled over with the opinions of their Doctors, are like clean paper, fit to receive whatsoever by Publique Authority shall be imprinted in them.[259]

Thus Hobbes expects that, as the result of his proposed purification of the universities, "most men, knowing their Duties, will be the less subject to serve the Ambition of a few discontented persons, in their purposes against the State."[260] He does not expect to eliminate ambition. He recognizes that

> because ambition and greediness of honours cannot be rooted out of the minds of men, it is not the duty of rulers to endeavour it; but by constant application of rewards and punishments they may so order it, that men

may know that the way to honour is not by contempt of the present government, nor by factions and the popular air, but by the contraries.[261]

Such passions must be channeled in useful directions.

Hobbes's concern with indoctrination rather than character formation does not by itself explain his greater concern with the universities than with the family. For Hobbes grants the sovereign a general superintendence of indoctrination, which might well include that "first instruction of Children" that "dependeth on the care of their Parents."[262] Nevertheless, he expects the sovereign not to regulate but to leave to subjects the liberty to "institute their children as they themselves think fit."[263] To be sure, that liberty is not to be without limits;[264] in particular, it clearly cannot extend to the liberty to send one's child to a seditious university or to hear seditious sermons.[265] This general liberty in the realm of domestic education may be granted not only on the basis of Hobbes's theory of opinion formation, wherein the universities are crucial, but also on the basis of his liberalism—his teaching that only necessary laws should be made and as much liberty left as possible.[266]

The sermons of the clergy, the conversation of the gentry, and the lessons of schoolmasters may all derive from university education or from books produced at the universities, but one may wonder whether the purification of the highest institutions of learning could easily overcome all these other influences, which would already be at work in the minds of university students before their matriculation. For, as shown above, Hobbes recognized the power of previous indoctrination.[267] Men are indeed taught fundamental doctrines "from their infancy."[268] Nevertheless, he confidently declares,

> There is no doubt, if the true doctrine concerning the law of nature, and the properties of a body politic, and the nature of law in general, were perspicuously set down and taught in the Universities, but that young men, *who come thither void of prejudice, and whose minds are as white paper,* capable of any instruction, would more easily receive the same, and afterward teach it to the people, both in books and otherwise, than now they do the contrary.[269]

Such apparent exaggeration of the untainted receptivity of university students, compared to Hobbes's other more realistic assessments of the power of early prejudice, may express his confidence in the clarity and power of his own political philosophy.[270] But it may well also express the view that the prejudices of university students are nullified by their freedom from "necessity or covetousnesse" and from "superfluity or sloth" and "sensuall pleasures" and by their consequent devotion to "deep

48

meditation."[271] In discussing a possible lay university to compete with clerical Oxford and Cambridge, Hobbes suggests that, "to make some learn the better, it would do very well that none should come thither sent by their parents, as to a trade to get their living by, but that it should be a place for such ingenuous men as, being free to dispose of their own time, love truth for itself."[272] He may ultimately be counting on their curiosity, their "Lust of the mind, that by a perseverance of delight in the continuall and indefatigable generation of Knowledge, exceedeth the short vehemence of any carnall Pleasure."[273] Chapman suggests that Hobbes's apparent assumption of unprejudiced university students indicates his reliance on private family education, but he admits that Hobbes "fails to consider the question directly."[274]

Hobbes does not argue from the family as a model for the commonwealth. In particular, he does not employ the traditional patriarchal arguments for the superiority of monarchy. At the beginning of his comparison of forms of government in *De Corpore Politico* he writes that he will omit the arguments

> that the world, as it was created, so also is it governed by one God Almighty; and that all the ancients have preferred monarchy before other governments, both in opinion, because they feigned a monarchical government amongst their gods, and also by their custom; for that in the most ancient times all people were so governed; and that paternal government, which is monarchy, was instituted in the beginning from the creation; and that other governments have proceeded from the dissolution thereof, caused by the rebellious nature of mankind, and be but pieces of broken monarchies cemented by human wit.[275]

Hobbes insists instead on considering only the relative inconvenience for the subjects of each form of government. He does not point out any tensions between these traditional patriarchal arguments and those he himself has presented, such as his views that the condition of "our ancestors" was far from exemplary, that maternal government predates paternal, that all government is to some degree by human wit, or that government is to be understood as if men were without subjection to one another at the creation.[276] In making a similar explicit omission in *De Cive*, he offers this explanation: "although, I say, these [arguments] do hold forth *monarchy* as the more eminent to us, yet because they do it by examples and testimonies, and not by solid reason, we will pass them over."[277] In that work, furthermore, he clearly presents his account of the "First Beginning of Civil Government" without any allowance for its being merely the human reconstitution of government originally in-

49

stituted by God and dissolved by human rebellion, even though in that work he renders more explicit that the traditional argument was that paternal government was instituted "by God himself" in the creation.[278] Finally, in *Leviathan* he makes no mention of such traditional patriarchal arguments at all but proceeds directly to considerations of convenience.[279]

In considering the place of patriarchal traces or elements in Hobbes's fundamentally nonpatriarchal politics, it is helpful above all to recall his basic method. Hobbes reconstitutes the world pretty much as we know it from those strange elements into which he resolves it. But he reconstitutes it in such a way that, while we still recognize it, we also see it differently from the way we saw it before—and presumably more clearly. In particular, we see the necessity of absolute sovereignty and the insignificance of claims made against it on behalf of justice (or Scripture for that matter). As Strauss writes, "Political philosophy analyses the existing State into its elements only in order that by a better synthesis of those elements the right State may be produced."[280] Nevertheless, even such familiar phenomena as Parliament or trial by jury, which one hardly associates with absolutism, reappear, derived on a Hobbesian basis and rendered compatible with the salient features of the Hobbesian world. Similarly, the familiar moral virtues, or most of them, are reconstituted, or qualities like them and bearing their names.[281] If his doctrine did not lead to an account of a world close enough to the familiar one, it would be simply unacceptable; if it did not lead to one that differed importantly, it would not be of practical reformist use. It is helpful to distinguish between two kinds of arguments: those designed to show how the familiar or something like it can, perhaps with some contortions, be derived on the basis of his principles and those designed to show that it cannot and how it must therefore be reordered. Often the familiar does not follow necessarily from Hobbes's principles but only as one possible result. His exposition of the possibility of deriving the familiar should not be taken as an endorsement of it. His specific interest is less in deriving the familiar than in correcting it. Derivation of the familiar often seems to be defensive, as if he were saying, "Don't worry, you can still have Parliament or gratitude or whatever on my basis, though it may be a little bit different." It is my suggestion that his derivation of primitive patriarchal power as a historical and scriptural fact and of parental honor as a familiar part of society has something of this character.

Hobbes's eagerness at times to show how the familiar family can be derived on his principles both in the state of nature and in society ought not to be mistaken for a genuinely patriarchal politics. He does not attempt to explain the family either in scriptural terms or in familial terms, such as generation, love, or gratitude. He explains parental claims in terms of preservation, not generation. He derives filial obedience and honor from consent, not gratitude, or at least he reinterprets gratitude as a calculation of future benefit, not as a sentiment based on a past benefit. Within the state of nature the family may exist, but it need not be the patriarchal family. The same concern for preservation that explains its existence also leads to its precariousness. Although Hobbes is able to use his principles to account for evidence of the patriarchal origin of society, he is able to account for society without any patriarchal hypotheses; he argues instead from the defective character of the patriarchal family and its tendency to dissolve into free individuals.[282] The family is precarious in the state of nature and requires civil law for its definition and support.

Hobbes's effort to treat the family as a part of a politics based on the natural freedom of equal individuals, obligated only by their own consent, is not unproblematic. Because filial obligation is based on a consent inferred from benefits received before the age of consent, it is hard to justify as calculation and harder to reconcile with any meaningful natural liberty and obligation by consent. This problem is similar to the ones that arise from Hobbes's defense of absolutism, his prohibition of resistance, and his basing obligation on past protection;[283] for these, too, limit calculation and diminish the meaning of natural liberty and consent. Hobbes explains the family not on a distinctive ground of its own but on the same ground as he explains society, namely, consent. He gives the family the basic educational function of forming passions and manners, though not doctrines, and it is to perform this function in an ambiguous private sphere created by and for public authority.

## FILMER'S CRITIQUE OF HOBBES

Filmer's criticism of Hobbes is of crucial importance to the study of Locke's antipatriarchal politics. This is so in part because of the light it sheds on the much-vexed question of the relation between the political thought of the two great English seventeenth-century political thinkers, Hobbes and Locke. Two facts are clear: Locke wrote explicitly against Filmer, with practically no reference to Hobbes,[284] and Filmer wrote in part explicitly against Hobbes.[285] This undeniable indirect relation between Locke's *Two Treatises of Government* and Hobbes's *De Cive* and *Leviathan* can serve to illuminate the general relationship between their political theories. As Peter Laslett writes, "The relation of Locke to Filmer is . . . complicated . . . by the perpetual presence between and above the two men of the Great Leviathan of Thomas Hobbes."[286]

Filmer's criticism of Hobbes is also important because it clarifies the ambiguity in the principle of the natural freedom of mankind, which is defended by Locke and denied by Filmer. That principle may in its most general form mean merely that government can be understood natu-

rally—that is to say, apart from any positive supernatural divine institution—in which sense it is common to Thomas Aquinas and Aristotle
as well as Hobbes and Locke. But it may also mean, more particularly,
that the people are free to establish the form of government they choose,
unrestricted by any universal specification of form of government by
either natural or divine law, as is maintained by Bellarmine, Buchanan,
and Grotius (among Filmer's targets in *Patriarcha*) as well as by Hobbes
and Locke. Finally, the principle of natural freedom may mean, as Hobbes
was perhaps the first to argue, that every individual man is by nature
free of all subjection, not only to any particular governor or form of
government but even to civil society itself, so that civil society has to be
understood as an artificial construction by men in the state of nature, a
view alien to Bellarmine, Buchanan, and Grotius. The principle of natural freedom is denied by Filmer in all of its meanings, often so cate-
gorically that it is difficult to tell precisely which of its meanings is at
stake.

If Hobbes is the first systematically to maintain the third position—
that every individual man is by nature free of all subjection—then one
must make the remarkable observation that Filmer seems to be denying
the Hobbesian version of natural freedom even before it was asserted.
For Filmer was eager to push the claim of the earlier adherents of natural
freedom to an extreme position that in some ways anticipated that of
Hobbes. This anticipation lends interest to Filmer's confrontation, in the
last years of his life, with the works of Hobbes, especially because Hobbes,
though he presented a more extreme version of the basic principles that
Filmer had long assaulted, arrived at practical conclusions so close to
Filmer's own as to leave Filmer ambivalent:

> With no small content I read Mr. Hobbes's book *De Cive,*
> and his *Leviathan,* about the rights of sovereignty, which
> no man, that I know, hath so amply and judiciously
> handled: I consent with him about the rights of exer-
> cising government, but I cannot agree to his means of
> acquiring it. It may seem strange I should praise his
> building, and yet mislike his foundation; but so it is, his
> *Jus Naturae,* and his *Regnum Institutivum,* will not down
> with me: they appear full of contradiction and impos-
> sibilities; a few short notes about them, I here offer,
> wishing he would consider whether his building would
> not stand firmer upon the principles of *Regnum Patri-
> moniale* (as he calls it) both according to scripture and
> reason.[287]

It is of especial importance to an understanding of Locke's antipatriarchal politics to note that here alone, in Filmer's criticism of Hobbes, can
one see in isolation and comparative clarity Filmer's argument against

that most radical version of the doctrine of natural freedom, which Locke adhered to.

Filmer was the first to seize on Hobbes's admission in *Leviathan* that his state of nature "was never generally so, over all the world."[288] Unlike later critics, however, Filmer uses the statement not in order to argue that Hobbes's state of nature is analytical or logical rather than historical but to "destroy his *jus naturale*."[289] For Filmer objects that "if not generally, then not at all, for one exception bars all if he mark it well." This objection presumes that Hobbes meant that the state of nature was the original condition, in which case it was then general. For Filmer, if a condition was not original, then it could not lawfully arise from whatever condition of dominion preceded it. Filmer also seems to take very strictly Hobbes's words "Warre of every one against every one" and "every man has a Right to every thing."[290] He seems to infer that, if *somewhere* there is peace and civil society, then there is not a war of *every* one against *every* one even if, somewhere else, such a war should exist. Here, as elsewhere, Filmer seems not to recognize or accept the Hobbesian sense of "right," which does not entail obligations on the part of others to respect the "right." Given that sense of "right," Hobbes can consistently maintain that a man in the state of nature somewhere has a right to everything even though elsewhere some things may have been apportioned among other men who have ended the state of nature among themselves.

More important for our purposes is Filmer's use of the remarks Hobbes makes following the admission, for in these Hobbes maintains that the state of nature does in fact exist in many places, such as America. Filmer denies this claim, for he wishes to show not merely that Hobbes's state of nature never existed "generally" but that it never exists at all. He objects that Hobbes "confesseth a government there of families, which government how small or brutish soever (as he calls it) is sufficient to destroy his *jus naturale*." Thus Filmer attempts again to refute Hobbes on the basis of Hobbes's own concessions to patriarchalism. He fails to appreciate the difference made by the smallness of the Americans' families, which leaves them unable to provide security to their members sufficient to remove them from the state of nature or to obligate them in a lasting manner.

It is precisely the implications for the family of Hobbes's state of nature and right of nature that most horrify Filmer. He writes:

> It is not to be thought that God would create man in a
> condition worse than any beasts, as if he made men to
> no other end by nature but to destroy one another, a
> right for the Father to destroy or eat his children, and

for children to do the like by their parents, is worse than
cannibals.[291]

Whereas such a right in the father seems indeed to be a part of Hobbes's
state of nature, with its "Right to every thing; even to one anothers
body,"[292] and even to be the foundation of parental dominion,[293] it is
not so clear that children can be said to have the right to do the like by
their parents. Indeed, in one of the footnotes Hobbes added to *De Cive*,
to "give some satisfaction to their differing thoughts" of those "who have
a little been staggered at the principles themselves,"[294] Hobbes writes:

> It hath been objected by some: if a son kill his father,
> doth he him no injury? I have answered, that a son
> cannot be understood to be at any time in the state of
> nature, as being under the power and command of them
> to whom he owes his protection as soon as ever he is
> born, namely, either his father's or his mother's, or his
> that nourished him . . . .[295]

Filmer, referring to this note, objects that this concession on Hobbes's
part "is all one with denying his own principle, for if men be not freeborn, it is not possible for him to assign and prove any other time for
them to claim a right of nature to liberty, if not at their birth."[296] Thus
Filmer takes the implications of this concession to be more far-reaching
than does Schochet, who takes it as merely equivalent to Hobbes's limitation of natural equality to "all men of riper years."[297] But if that were
so, then all that Hobbes would be saying in his footnote is that young
children cannot kill their parents but must wait until they are full grown
to do so. Filmer recognizes that not only young children but all men are
"sons." If a son cannot be "at any time" in the state of nature, then there
shall be "little liberty left."[298]

Hobbes's reassuring footnote, especially in conjunction with the demonstrations in the ninth chapter it refers to, hardly gives full satisfaction
to the objection he states. First, the objector, at one with Filmer's concern,
refers to the father; but Hobbes, in response, refers to the father, the
mother, or whoever else may have nourished the child. The ninth chapter reveals that he is referring indeed first, and perhaps last, to the
mother, whereas even the identity of his father may be unknown to a
son in the state of nature. Second, insofar as the son is under the "command of them to whom he owes his protection," Hobbes tacitly inserts
his qualification that such obedience is owed only so long as protection
is owed and that the protection that can be received from any one man,
or even from one man obeyed by a few others, is not much. Third, if a
son kills his father in self-defense, it is indeed "no injury," and the
judgment of the circumstances is necessarily the son's.[299] It is hard not
to conclude that, while the footnote may give "some satisfaction," it ought

not to be taken as simply and seriously affirming the patriarchal doctrine it gives the impression of baldly proclaiming.

Filmer is quite aware that, despite Hobbes's reassuring claim that no son is in the state of nature at any time and hence cannot justly kill his father, to say nothing of eating him, there are serious qualifications made elsewhere by Hobbes that render the father's position questionable. Filmer sees how Hobbes's concessions to patriarchy can, in combination with each other and with Scripture, be used to erect a full patriarchal structure and demolish Hobbes's own; but he also recognizes that at least some of the qualifications Hobbes makes serve to weaken even a minimal patriarchalism. Thus Filmer notes that Hobbes's requirement that the child give its consent to paternal dominion, "either express or by other sufficient arguments declared," is an obstacle to obedience by children before they reach the "age of discretion." It is paradoxical that Filmer should remind Hobbes of the necessity of recognizing the "age of discretion" despite his having complained that "it is not possible for him to assign and prove any other time for them to claim a right of nature to liberty, if not at their birth." Both objections, however, express Filmer's premise that the proper or lawful condition must exist originally and be neither begun nor ended by man; thus he objects both (1) that, if men are by nature free, they must be born so, and (2) that, if they are to be subject, they must be born so, which they cannot be by consent because they have not attained the age of discretion. It is the second argument that Filmer himself of course accepts; indeed, he believes that "all men grant [that] it [obedience?] is due before consent can be given."[300] He even mistakenly says that "Mr. Hobbes is of the same mind" because he speaks of the obedience children "owed" to their parents. "They owed," Filmer repeats, and adds, as a gloss, "not that they covenanted to give."[301] For Filmer, what men *owe* is, as such, owed before and apart from any act of their own, but, for Hobbes, what men owe is *precisely* what "they covenanted to give."[302] Filmer's gloss, to show that Hobbes is of the same mind with all men in recognizing that obedience is due from children from birth, is thus perfectly wrong, and he is closer to the truth in fearing that the Hobbesian requirement of consent means that men are freeborn after all, or are at least born exempt from all duty.[303]

Filmer also recognizes that Hobbes undercuts natural paternal dominion by granting the mother the original right over the child and deriving the father's right from her consent.[304] The Amazonian example used by Hobbes in the part of *De Cive* Filmer quotes from here (the example itself Filmer, with unwonted delicacy, does not mention) reveals that in at least one apparently lawful example maternal power exposes fathers to the risk of being warred on by their daughters, though not by their sons.[305] Indeed, both natural parents are exposed to such risks if the child is subject to neither of them but to some person who found or stole and then nourished and protected him.[306] Against the subversive specter of original maternal power Filmer invokes Scripture glossed with Aristotelian biology: "But we know that God at the creation gave the sovereignty to the man over the woman, as being the nobler and principal agent in generation." So eager is Filmer to regard the provision of proper (monarchic) political power as original and perfect that he here makes sovereignty coeval with creation rather than subsequent to the Fall and views it as a recognition of nobility rather than sin.[307]

Filmer further recognizes that Hobbes, as I have also suggested, threatens the position of fathers in the state of nature by the claim that knowledge of his fatherhood is not necessarily available to a person in the state of nature, since the mother alone can say who has fathered her child.[308] In his "answer" to this "objection" Filmer seems in fact to concede decisive ground without being aware of it. He begins:

> The answer is, that it is not at the will of the mother to make whom she will the Father, for if the mother be not in possession of a husband, the child is not reckoned to have any Father at all; but if she be in the possession of a man, the child not withstanding whatsoever the woman discovereth to the contrary is still reputed to be his in whose possession she is.

In his eagerness to refute the claim that paternal power derives from maternal power, Filmer seems to concede the substance of maternal power itself. He seems to concede the fatherless child to the mother. If he does not, we are faced with a violent anomaly in the Filmerian universe: the existence of a freeborn man, and that not the first man, Adam, but any ordinary bastard. At any rate, he seems to abandon his fundamental principle that "every man is born subject to the power of a Father."[309] It may be, however, that Filmer makes this concession only on the Hobbesian premise of a state of nature, which Filmer does not grant. He might argue that unwed mothers are subject to their fathers, and, if they are subject, so then would their offspring be.[310]

Filmer concludes this part of his discussion with another surprising admission:

> No child naturally and infallibly knows who are his true parents, yet he must obey those that in common reputation are so, otherwise the commandment of honour thy Father and thy mother were in vain, and no child bound to the obedience of it.

Not only has Hobbes wrung from Filmer a full quotation of the Fifth Commandment, including its maternal half, but he has forced him to rest filial obedience on common reputation rather than nature. Hobbes's point, of course, is not that infallible knowledge of natural fatherhood is necessary, or, indeed, that natural fatherhood has anything to do with filial obedience at all, but that rules for determining paternal power, available in civil society in the form of civil laws, are not available in the state of nature apart from the right of the first possessor, usually the mother, and any agreements she might make. Natural patriarchal power does serve Filmer, however, as the model and divine warrant for, though not the direct equivalent of, actual paternal power, resting on common reputation, just as natural patriarchal power must serve him only as model and divine warrant rather than as the direct equivalent of actual political power, resting on usurpation and reputation. Indeed, the account of parental power he is forced to give here to meet Hobbes serves as the model for his subsequent account of the obedience due to usurpers:

> where a usurper hath continued so long, that the knowl-
> edge of the right heir be lost by all the subjects, in such
> a case a usurper in possession is to be taken and reputed
> by such subjects for the true heir, and is to be obeyed
> by them as their Father. As no man hath an infallible
> certitude, but only a moral knowledge, which is no other
> than a probable persuasion grounded upon a peaceable
> possession, which is a warrant for subjection to parents
> and governors; for we may not say, because children
> have no infallible, or necessary certainty who are their
> true parents, that therefore they need not obey, because
> they are uncertain: it is sufficient, and as much as hu-
> mane nature is capable of, for children to rely upon a
> credible persuasion; for otherwise the commandment of
> "Honour thy Father," would be a vain commandment,
> and not possible to be observed.[311]

It might seem that resting parental and political power on common reputation, as Filmer does, is not very different from resting parental power on civil law or individual consent and political power on individual consent, as Hobbes does. But Filmer seems willing to concede to common reputation a special status, in certain circumstances, as expressing the "permission of God," whereas individual consent remains for him mere human action without binding force.[312]

## LIBERAL POLITICS AS ANTIPATRIARCHAL POLITICS: LOCKE'S CRITIQUE OF FILMER

Filmer's patriarchal politics involves much more than an understanding of the family and its relation to politics. It rests fundamentally on an understanding of the relation of God to man that dictates the proper interpretations of Scripture and of the workings of God's providence in human affairs. Locke's critique of patriarchal politics correspondingly includes not only an attack on Filmer's understanding of the family and its relation to politics, and on the particular scriptural and providential interpretations that are supposed to support it, but also a critique of the understanding of the relation of God and man that underlies them. To grasp the bold purpose of Locke's critique and the consequent character of the positive doctrine that the achievement of that critique permits, it is unnecessary to present all of the exegetical particulars of Locke's critique of Filmer's use of Scripture; the general shape of the critique and some of the premises it suggests will suffice.

Locke establishes first that Filmer's "Ground" or "great Position" is that *"no Man is Born free"* or that *"Men are not naturally free"* (I, §§ 2, 6).[313] But it is not directly against that ground—that is, it is not directly to establish his own hypothesis of natural freedom—that Locke aims the argument of the *First Treatise*. He argues directly, rather, against Filmer's "Basis . . . main Supposition . . . Fundamental Tenet . . . Foundation . . . [or] great Principle": the "Sovereignty of *Adam*" (I, §§ 10–12). First he establishes what this "Divine unalterable Right of Sovereignty" (§ 9) consists in, despite Filmer's supposed effort to conceal its "Gigantic Form" (§ 7); it is

> an Absolute, Arbitrary, Unlimited, and Unlimitable Power, over the Lives, Liberties, and Estates of his Children and Subjects; so that he may take or alienate their Estates, sell, castrate, or use their Persons as he pleases, they being all his Slaves, and he Lord or Proprietor of every Thing, and his unbounded Will their Law. [I, § 9]

Locke first uncovers the arguments for this sovereignty of Adam and then refutes them one by one, devoting a chapter to each. Adam's supposed titles to sovereignty are his creation, God's donation of the world to him and his consequent property in it, God's subjection of Eve to him, and his right as a father (I, §§ 14, 67).[314]

Locke, denying that Adam's creation implies any right to rule, reduces this title to one of the other three (I, §§ 15–20). As for God's donation of the world to Adam (Genesis 1:28), he argues that it gives dominion only over other animals, not over other men (I, §§ 24–28), and that it is addressed not exclusively to Adam but at least to Eve as well (I, § 29) and indeed to the whole human species (I, §§ 30–31). He makes the same interpretation of God's grant to Noah (Genesis 9:1–3) (I, §§ 32–39). Finally, he argues that it would be "more reasonable" of God to establish original community of property than sole proprietorship and that, in any case, property in itself does not give a right to rule over others without their consent (I, §§ 41–43). As for the subjection of Eve (Genesis 3:16), Locke finds it "hard to imagine" that God could thereby have granted Adam any privileges, let alone "Dominion and Monarchy" over anyone, at the same time as he was making him "a day labourer for his Life" (I, §§ 44–45). He also suggests that this statement of God's, unlike the donation of the world, may apply only to Adam and Eve and not to all mankind (I, §§ 45–47). He explains that in any case this is not a "Law to oblige a Woman to such a Subjection" but only a prediction cf how "the Laws of Mankind and customs of Nations" would generally order it (I, § 47). The subjection is in any case not "a Political Power of Life and Death" but merely "a Conjugal Power" (I, § 48). Finally, Locke denies that a husband's conjugal power over his wife gives him any power over her children (I, § 49).

Locke regards Filmer's supposition of *"Adam's Title to Sovereignty by Fatherhood"* as "the main Basis of all his Frame" (I, § 50).[315] Locke deals first with the father's title to sovereignty from begetting his children. He points out that giving life does not imply a right to take it (I, § 52). He argues that it is not parents who give children life but God (I, §§ 52–53). For parents do not know what life consists in or how it is made, nor do they even ordinarily intend to give life when they serve as the occasions for its being given (I, §§ 52–54). Finally, like Hobbes, Locke notes that begetting would give at least an equal title to sovereignty to the mother (I, § 55). Locke deals second with the father's title to sovereignty from "the Practice of Mankind" (I, §§ 56–59). He has recourse instead to the example of the beasts, who, far from exercising a right of life and death over their offspring, give their own lives for them (I, §§ 56, 58). He denies that "the Example of what hath been done, be the Rule of what ought to be," for that would justify paternal cannibalism as well as adultery, incest, and sodomy, all of which undermine the family (I, §§ 57, 59).[316] Third, he deals with the father's title to sovereignty from the Fifth Commandment (I, §§ 60–66). Like all passages of Scripture on this subject, the Fifth Commandment includes the mother equally and therefore imparts "no Sovereignty, no Supremacy" (I, §§ 60–63). Nor does it give a father such sovereignty as would enable him to dispense his grandchildren from the honor it requires them to pay to their parents (I, § 64).[317] Nor, as a duty commanded by God, can it be transferred to political rulers from natural parents (I, §§ 64–66).

Having disposed of all of Adam's titles to sovereignty, Locke proclaims the natural freedom of men (I, § 67). He then shows that Filmer's titles to sovereignty are contradictory. Filmer contradicts his doctrine of the absolute sovereignty of Adam by recognizing the title of children to power over grandchildren (I, §§ 68–70).[318] Filmer also recognizes the right of all fathers, which, if not distinguished from political power, would lead to anarchy (I, §§ 70–71). Similarly, Filmer's two chief foundations of sovereignty, fatherhood and property, are established by him in different persons, since one descends to fathers and the other to heirs, so that they produce "two Sovereigns" (I, §§ 73–77).[319]

Despite having disposed of all of Adam's titles to sovereignty, some of them more than once over, Locke proceeds to claim that Filmer fails to show how Adam's sovereignty is conveyed to later rulers. He complains that Filmer runs into contradictions by positing various means of conveyance of Adam's title: inheritance, grant, and usurpation, which, since it includes any means, even election, justifies Cromwell as much as any lawful prince (I, §§ 78–80). Locke promises to examine inheritance, grant, usurpation, and election, but he reaches only the first in that part of the *First Treatise* that "Fate" has provided us with (I, § 80).[320]

Locke insists on the urgent importance of determining who has sovereignty, since "Ideas of Government in the Fancy, though never so perfect, though never so right, cannot give Laws, nor prescribe Rules to the Actions of Men" (I, §§ 81–83). (This realistic premise points to the defect of natural law that makes civil society necessary.)[321] The inheritance of Adam's sovereignty must depend on its foundation, but because Filmer erects it on "a double Foundation"—of property from divine donation and of fatherhood from natural begetting—its inheritance seems dependent on two conditions (I, §§ 84–85).[322] Uncharacteristically, the *First Treatise* here breaks off from negatively following and refuting Filmer's doctrines and instead positively expounds Locke's own doctrines of the natural rights to property and to inheritance (I, §§ 86–90). Having thus explained that all children have as much right as parents to appropriate unappropriated things and a right to inherit their parents' property if their parents do not otherwise dispose of it, Locke can conclude that inheritance of property conveys no exclusive sovereignty to one child as heir more than, or over, the others (I, § 91). Succession to rule is different from succession to property because government is "for the good of the Governed," whereas property is "for the benefit and sole advantage of the Proprietor," who is presumed to leave it to his children unless he indicates otherwise (I, §§ 92–93). Succession to rule depends on having the same title to rule as one's predecessor, whether that be derived from the consent of the governed, the positive revealed declaration of God, or the "perfectly Personal" act of begetting, if that gives any right to rule (I, §§ 94–97). If begetting gives any power, it is therefore only to fathers over their children and not over mothers, brothers, or others, and it cannot be alienated to those who have not begotten them (I, §§ 98–103).

Locke insists that Adam's sovereignty must either belong only to his sole heir, undermining all present rulers' titles, or be irrelevant to the question of who rules, at most giving sovereignty to every man and again undermining all present rulers (I, §§ 104–5). After insisting again on the importance of determining who has sovereignty and complaining of

Filmer's obscurity on that point (I, §§ 106–10), Locke admits that Filmer "insinuates" that sovereignty descends by primogeniture (I, § 111). But Locke denies that there is either natural or scriptural warrant for primogeniture (I, §§ 111–18). Even more strongly, he denies that there is any natural or scriptural guidance for determining inheritance in the absence of sons, a condition equally necessary to resolve (I, §§ 119–28). Finally, Locke examines Filmer's "History out of Scripture" to see whether it explains the conveyance of Adam's sovereignty in the absence of any account of the rules of its descent (I, §§ 128, 129–69). He denies that Filmer correctly attributes sovereignty to the patriarchs (I, §§ 129–33, 135–38, 150). The sovereignty that was exercised was not always monarchical (I, §§ 146, 158, 164–65),[323] and, when it was monarchical, it was not exercised as an inheritance from Adam or passed down consistently by primogeniture from anyone else (I, §§ 148–50, 152–53, 159–63). At the conclusion of this examination the *First Treatise* ends (I, § 169).[324]

J. N. Figgis, in his study *The Divine Right of Kings,* argues that Filmer "paved the way" for Locke. For he regards Filmer "less as the most perfect exponent of the theory [of divine right], than as the herald of its decadence" (unlike J. W. Allen, for instance, who regards Filmer as not only "the best exponent" but perhaps also the first in England).[325] Figgis claims that Filmer saw "that a natural system of politics was more likely to prove well-founded than a purely theological scheme" or that he "regarded theology as pointing to nature as the teacher of political philosophy." He "surrendered the case for Divine Right" by "partially deserting" the "older mode of arguing from Scripture texts, as direct Divine injunctions."[326] Instead he marked the

> transition from the conception of government as directly established by Divine command to the notion that, since God is the author of nature, whatever is natural has His sanction. . . . For direct Divine Right has been substituted a constructive theory of Divine approval. The theological conception of politics is giving way before what may be termed the naturalistic.[327]

Although the older divine right, based on Scripture, "was impregnable to the assaults of criticism," since "neither natural law nor the principle of utility could avail aught against it," "Nothing was easier than to meet Filmer on his own ground, and Locke did so."[328]

The plausibility of Figgis's account makes it all the more striking that Locke presents the issue very differently. Despite Filmer's talk of nature, Locke claims in the Preface to the *Two Treatises* that "Scripture-proofs" are what Filmer "so much boasts of, and pretends wholly to build on." Frequently in the *First Treatise* he repeats the claim that Filmer "pretends to build wholly on Scripture" (I, §§ 32, 61, 128, 168).[329] Locke pays little attention to Filmer's reliance on nature or on classical authority. Locke's exaggeration of Filmer's reliance on Scripture serves not only to make more reprehensible Filmer's failure to build his doctrine securely on scriptural proofs but also to raise the question of the possibility or propriety of building a political doctrine wholly on Scripture. Locke himself does not seem to think it was required that he build his political doctrine in the *Second Treatise* wholly on Scripture.

Accordingly, Locke shows not only that in many points Filmer contradicts or distorts Scripture and therefore fails to build on it; he sometimes shows also that it cannot be built upon. For, shortly after writing that God, in addressing men, would not "lose his design in speaking, what thus spoken, they could not understand," Locke finds that "in a Matter of such moment, and so great and general Concernment" as the relation of husbands and wives, Scripture offers only "too doubtful an expression" for one to build on confidently (I, §§ 46, 49). Nor is that the only scriptural passage that Locke finds "doubtful and obscure" (I, §§ 112, 118). Scripture is "utterly silent" on other points, such as the nature of "the Rulers or Forms of Government" after the destruction of the Tower of Babel (I, §§ 144–45). Even when Locke makes conjectures about the form of government of the allegedly republican builders of the Tower, he prefaces his remarks with "As far as we can conclude any thing from Scripture in this matter" (I, § 146). He consistently denies that Scripture is the teacher of political philosophy. As early as the "First Tract on Government," written in 1660, he writes that "Scripture speaks very little of polities anywhere" and that "God doth nowhere by distinct and particular prescriptions set down rules of governments and bounds to the magistrate's authority."[330] As late as the "Paraphrase and Notes on the Epistle of St. Paul to the Romans" of his last years, he writes, of the power that Paul speaks of in the thirteenth chapter of the Epistle, that "[about] how men come by a rightful title to this [civil] power, or who has that title, he is wholly silent, and says nothing of it. To have meddled with that, would have been to decide of civil rights, contrary to the design and business of the Gospel."[331]

Locke drops not only Filmer's scriptural basis for obedience but also his scriptural basis for disobedience.[332] Filmer says that Jesus "divides all between God and Caesar, and allows nothing that we can find for the people."[333] While it is famous that Locke attributes Caesar's portion ultimately to the people ("no taxation without representation," as we Americans say),[334] Locke does not even refer to this scriptural basis for disobedience or to Filmer's concession to it. This is in contrast to Locke's eagerly seizing on the concessions the absolutist William Barclay made to disobedience, which are purely secular in character (II, §§ 232–39). To cite Filmer himself would, other things being equal, have been far more effective in refuting him than citing Barclay, with whom, as Locke twice notes, Filmer admits he is in fundamental disagreement (I, §§ 4, 67).[335]

Apart from the obscurity and silence of Scripture, which may prevent it from being built upon, there is the graver matter of its relation to reason. Locke presents Scripture, or "positive Revelation," as an alternative way of knowing God's will, reason or the law of nature being the other (I, § 16).[336] He says that reason is man's "only Star and compass" (I, § 58). That need not exclude revelation, but it does establish reason as the judge and interpreter of revelation.[337] Not just obscure but all passages of Scripture should be interpreted in accordance with the teachings of natural reason (I, §§ 41, 112). But Locke also claims that, when reason speaks, revelation is superfluous. If there is a natural right to something, then there is "no need of a positive Donation" by God, or, as he adds more cautiously, "at least it will never be a proof of such a Donation" (I, § 16).[338] Revelation is therefore treated as (an apparently unnecessary) "Confirmation" of the conclusions of natural reason (I, §§ 40, 63, 64). When reason is able to speak, as it is about civil government, then there is no need to build on Scripture.[339] Locke bases his own political premise of natural equality not on revealed universal descent from common parents but on rationally perceived "common Nature, Faculties and Powers" (I, § 67; II, § 4).

The most revealing passage in the *Treatise* on the relation between revelation and reason deals with that most important subject, the natural right to property (I, § 86).[340] According to this passage, God not only planted in Man "as in all other Animals, a strong desire of Self-preservation," but also

> spoke to him, (that is) directed him by his Senses and Reason, as he did the inferior Animals by their Sense, and Instinct, which he had placed in them to that purpose, to the use of those things, which were serviceable for his Subsistence, and given him as means of his *Preservation*. And therefore I doubt not, but before these words were pronounced, 1 *Gen*. 28, 29. (if they must be understood Literally to have been spoken) and without any such Verbal *Donation*, Man had a right to a use of the Creatures, by the Will and Grant of God.

Here Locke not only regards human reason as what he calls it in the *Essay*, "natural *Revelation*, whereby the eternal Father of Light, and Fountain of all Knowledge communicates to Mankind that portion of Truth, which he has laid within the reach of their natural Faculties";[341] he also questions whether even the particular revelations recounted in Scripture, such as God's donation of the world, discussed here, were "Literally"

63

spoken or were merely instances of man's natural reasoning.[342] When natural reason can speak, positive revelation appears to Locke to have been superfluous. Furthermore, the natural right to use the creatures, a right revealed by human reason, extends further than the original divine donation recounted in Scripture.[343] Contrary to Filmer's doctrine, Locke claims that human reason is sufficient to establish property in the world without revelation; that is the chief point of the chapter on property in the *Second Treatise* as well.

Locke not only challenges Filmer's premise that it is both possible and necessary to build a political doctrine on Scripture, but he questions Filmer's most fundamental premise of all, that God's particular providence continuously provides men with political authority. Locke recognizes that "whatsoever Providence orders," as well as what "the Law of Nature directs, or positive Revelation declares, may be said to be *by God's Appointment*" (I, § 16). By something's being ordered by providence, Locke means only that it is "de facto" (I, § 16). This kind of appointment by God does not involve particular providence nor does it enjoy any paradigmatic status that imposes obligations. Locke equates "the appointment of God" with his ordering "the course of nature" (I, § 89). In opposition to Filmer, he writes:

> If any one will say, that what happens in Providence to
> be preserved, God is careful to preserve as a thing there-
> fore to be esteemed by Men as necessary or useful, 'tis
> a peculiar Propriety of Speech, which every one will not
> think fit to imitate. [I, § 147]

Locke interprets the part of "the Curse of God upon the Woman" or his "Denouncing Judgment" (I, § 44) that refers to her being ruled by the man as merely foretelling "how by his Providence he would order it so, that she should be subject to her husband, as we see that generally the Laws of Mankind and customs of Nations have ordered it so" (I, § 47).[344] Even God's own prediction of the course of his providence carries with it no paradigmatic or obligatory status; it is merely a prediction.[345] Locke writes: "God, in this Text, gives not, that I see, any Authority to *Adam* over *Eve*, or to Men over their Wives" (I, § 47). It is not a "Law to oblige a Woman to such a Subjection" (I, § 47).[346]

Locke's rejection of providentially ordered "Laws of Mankind and customs of Nations" as a standard in the matter of conjugal subjection illustrates his general rejection of "common consent" as a standard, one of the most traditionally powerful forms of providentialism (I, § 47).[347] Most revealing on this point, as on so many others, is his exposition of the natural rights of property and inheritance in the *First Treatise* (I, §§ 86–90). He there rejects "common consent" as a justification of the filial right of inheritance, first of all because there is no actual universal explicit consent to that right (I, § 88).[348] Second, he asserts that common consent would establish only "a positive and not Natural Right" (I, § 88).[349] He similarly rejects the argument from "the Practice of Mankind" for parental power of life and death,[350] for to kill one's child is still a "most unnatural Murder," though "humane Nature is capable of" it (I, §§ 56–59). He will not admit that "the Example of what hath been done, be the Rule of what ought to be," because men, unlike animals, who follow their instincts, depart from nature and reason by the authority of examples that originate in "Folly or craft," as do many of the "Governments, Religions, and Manners" of men (I, §§ 57–58).[351] Locke nevertheless admits that common consent may have a "Foundation in Nature" or a natural cause.[352] But then it is that natural foundation or cause that may deserve respect, not the common consent as such.

Locke rejects Filmer's crucial and most revealing doctrine, that usurpers manifest divine providence and that their subjects must "wait upon God's Providence" (I, § 121).[353] He recognizes that the ultimate consequence of Filmer's doctrine is that "the Governments of the World are as they should be" and characterizes it as "absurd" (I, § 134). Filmer's providentialism is an open invitation to usurpation, insurrection, tyranny, and anarchy (I, §§ 3, 72, 81, 106; II, § 1), for it promises obedience to whoever can seize power, and it fails to distinguish lawful titles (I, §§ 78–79).

Even if Filmer's doctrine on usurpers, in supplementing his purely patriarchal argument with one from particular providence, cannot be said to offer no guidance at all for human conduct or be charged with offering conflicting guidance, it can still be charged with offering aid and comfort to sedition. Paradoxically, a doctrine of undiscriminating nonresistance can be said to encourage potential rebels and usurpers, because they will anticipate that those who adhere to it will not resist them once they are established. Such a doctrine thus has a serious weakness compared to a more intransigently legitimist doctrine (like that suggested by Filmer's language about never-dying divine right). Locke sometimes charges that Filmer's system threatens the established rulers by giving universal monarchy to Adam's heir, but this is not a serious practical danger (I, § 3). His more serious charge is that Filmer threatens established rulers by promising potential usurpers that they will eventually meet with obedience instead of active resistance and forceful attempts at restoration (I, §§ 72, 79; II, § 1). It is important to appreciate the character of this criticism, which Locke himself does not spell out. Locke cannot mean that followers of Filmer's doctrine of providential usurpation would themselves initiate such dangerous projects; if everyone followed Filmer's teaching of nonresistance, it is obvious that no usurpations or rebellions would ever occur. What Locke must mean is that, given that others will not follow this doctrine, those who do will fail to resist them and, by not resisting, will even encourage them in their rebellion. In form, this is the Machiavellian anti-Christian argument.[354]

Locke's doctrine of the "Appeal to Heaven" may appear to be similar to reliance on particular providence. In explaining the state of war in the *Second Treatise* he writes of Jephthah that

> he was forced to appeal to *Heaven. The Lord the Judge* (says he) *be Judge this day between the Children of* Israel, *and the Children of* Ammon, *Judg.* 11.27. and then Prosecuting, and relying on his *appeal,* he leads out his Army to Battle. [II, § 21]

It has been noted that, by applying this appeal to heaven (which he equates with an appeal to arms) not only to relations between nations but also to relations between peoples and governments, Locke was able to oppose "the traditional Christian view, which restricted the appeal to heaven of the governed to mere prayer."[355] I would add that the same phrase, "The Lord be judge," is also invoked in Scripture (1 Sam. 24:12, 15) in a relation between a subject and a ruler, David and Saul, but its meaning is precisely that the subject should *not* take arms against the ruler. Not only does Locke avoid the practical consequence of the providentialist version of the appeal to heaven; he also rejects its premise. He makes no claim that the result of the appeal will manifest the judgment of a just providence.[356]

Locke thus challenges not only Filmer's specific scriptural interpretations and invocations of particular providence but also his scripturalist and providentialist premises. Political doctrine neither can nor need be built on Scripture or on an attempt to see the hand of God in particular events. Locke would free man from the absolute and arbitrary power not only of human tyrants but also of a tyrannical God.[357] He substitutes a God who is the author of nature and who leaves it to man to provide for his own needs through the labor that appropriates the world and through the consent that establishes government.

## THE FAMILY AND NATURAL FREEDOM: THE *Two Treatises*

In the course of refuting Filmer's doctrines in the *First Treatise,* Locke presents many of his own teachings about the family. He emphatically denies that parents gain the power of life and death—that is, political power or sovereignty—over their children from begetting them (I, §§ 51–59).[358] But he often concedes that they have some power by that title. He writes that, just as writing or publishing a book makes one its author, so begetting children makes one their "Governor" (I, § 18). He writes of "that Right of Nature, be it what it will, to Govern them" that accrues from begetting children (I, § 19). He quotes scriptural injunctions of *obedience* to parents (I, §§ 61, 66),[359] though he writes only of a title to "*Honour*" that is "vested in the Parents by Nature, and is a right which accrews to them, by their having begotten their Children" (I, § 63). Further on in the *First Treatise* it becomes clearer that concessions to paternal power from begetting are merely hypothetical, made only to show that, even granting them, the consequences do not suffice for Filmer's purposes (I, §§ 96, 103). Yet Locke continues to make this concession: "That a Father may have a Natural Right to some kind of Power over his Children, is easily granted" (I, § 111). What is clearest about paternal power in the *First Treatise,* aside from its not extending to life and death, is that definitive treatment of it is postponed to the *Second Treatise* (I, §§ 66, 100). Locke does argue here, however, that a man who finds and brings up an abandoned child acquires "the greatest part of filial Duty and Subjection" or at least "Degrees of Paternal Power" proportionate to his "Paternal Care." He merely suggests that the natural father "may perhaps to some degrees forfeit it." But he explicitly postpones presenting the general principles upon which this instance is based (I, § 100).

Although he does not in the *First Treatise* explain "the Nature of Paternal *Power*" (I, § 100; emphasis added), Locke does explain parental duties and children's rights. The explanation is included in his exposition of the natural rights of property and inheritance (I, §§ 86–90). This explanation of natural rights begins with self-preservation.[360] He explains that the "Foundation" of the right to property is the "first and strongest desire God Planted in Men, and wrought into the very Principles of their Nature being that of Self-preservation" (I, § 88).[361] The right to self-preservation and therefore to property[362] therefore belongs, of course, as much to children as to parents (I, § 87). But since children are "by the course of Nature, born weak, and unable to provide for themselves, they have by the appointment of God himself, who hath thus ordered the course of nature, a Right to be nourish'd and maintained by their Parents" (I, § 89).[363] That this divinely appointed right is provided through the course of nature means that, next to the desire for self-preservation, "God Planted in Men a strong desire also of propagating their Kind, and continuing themselves in their Posterity" (I, § 88). Therefore, when Locke, in the same passage, writes that men are "by a like Obligation bound to preserve what they have begotten, as to preserve themselves," he seems to mean that they are bound by a similarly strong desire, though not an equally strong one (I, § 88). Similarly, and more generally, Locke writes of "intellectual Beings," in the *Essay Concerning Human Understanding,* that "the inclination, and tendency of their nature to happiness is an obligation, and motive to them, to take care not to mistake, or miss it."[364] Parents are "taught by Natural Love and Tenderness" to provide for their children (I, § 97). As Locke elaborates in the *Second Treatise,* God placed in parents "suitable Inclinations of Tenderness and Concern," wove "into the Principles of Humane Nature . . . a tenderness for their Off-spring," and planted "Affection and Tenderness . . . in the Breasts of Parents, towards their Children" (II, §§ 63, 67, 170). John W. Yolton explains that Locke's "doctrine about the rights of children and the duties of parents toward them" is "underlaid by a notion about the natural inclinations parents have toward the well-being of their children," and he then remarks that

> More than once in Locke's writings, natural inclinations are linked with rights. In *Two Treatises* self-preservation is both an inclination we all have and a right. The *Education* links love and duty: "They love their little ones, and 'tis their Duty" (34).[365]

These natural rights of children are rights to "Nourishment and Education," and corresponding natural duties of parents are to provide these; but the emphasis is on nourishment, as more directly demanded by preservation (I, §§ 89–90, 93). It includes "not only . . . a bare Subsistance but . . . the conveniences and comforts of Life, as far as the conditions of their Parents can afford it" (I, § 89).[366]

Gordon Schochet notes that this recognition of parental concern for propagation and tenderness toward their offspring seems contrary to Locke's argument that begetting does not justify sovereignty because parents beget only to satisfy a "present Appetite," since "God in his infinite Wisdom has put strong desires of Copulation into the Constitution of Men, thereby to continue the race of Mankind" (I, § 54).[367] Locke can employ mere appetite to account for copulation, which is presently satisfying, but he needs the desire for propagation or tenderness toward offspring to account for the provision of expensive nourishment and education. Concern for propagation or tenderness may come into play only when it is elicited by the actual presence of one's offspring, whereas only appetite is present in copulation. Besides, Locke seems to attribute chiefly to *fathers* a satisfaction in copulation that is unaccompanied by concern for propagation (I, § 54).[368]

Parental concern for their offspring raises the more general question of the place of instinct in human nature. The human species shares with the others a strong desire for self-preservation (I, §§ 56, 86). It differs from them in being created in "the *Image* of God," which means at least having "the intellectual Nature" or being rational creatures (I, § 30). Humans appear to differ from beasts not only in having reason but in lacking "Instinct" (I, § 86). Locke contrasts the two in one of the most striking and beautiful passages in the *Two Treatises.* Man is "a Creature, whose thoughts are more than the Sands, and wider than the Ocean," whose "fancy and passion must needs run him into strange courses, if reason, which is his only Star and compass, be not that he steers by"; his "imagination is always restless and suggests variety of thoughts," and his "will, reason being laid aside, is ready for every extravagant project." The beasts, "the irrational untaught Inhabitants" of "the Woods and Forests," by contrast "keep right by following Nature" (I, § 58).

Now Laslett, in a note to this last passage, interprets it very differently, declaring it to be "an important declaration of the essential rightness of 'Natural Man' " and saying that it "reads almost like Rousseau, the Rousseau of the *Discours sur l'Inégalité.*" The whole context, however, suggests that Locke, in the phrase "irrational, untaught inhabitants," is referring not to "Natural Man" but to the beasts. The whole section (I, §§ 56–59) is Locke's response to those who would derive paternal power from the "Practice of Mankind" of infanticide. Locke appeals not to the example of mankind but to that of lions and wolves: "These Savage Inhabitants of the Desert obey God and Nature in being tender and careful of their Off-spring" (I, § 56). In the paragraph immediately preceding the crucial contrast Locke gives an example of men who "begot Children on purpose to Fatten and Eat them"—an example that shows how far humans can depart from nature (I, § 57). (Laslett comments that this statement "has no particular relevance and seems to have been dragged in to make a sensation.") Accordingly, Locke begins the paragraph that contains the contrast at issue, "Thus far can the busie mind of Man carry him to a Brutality below the level of Beasts, when he quits his reason, which places him almost equal to Angels" (I, § 58).[369] Not only the context but the term "irrational" suggests that Locke is contrasting human beings with beasts. For Locke claims that all men (apart from children, lunatics, and idiots) are rational, in the sense that they are capable of reasoning or endowed with reason, though they may not "consult" it.[370] Locke therefore does not apply the term "irrational," apparently meaning "not endowed with reason," to men, however much they may ignore their endowment.[371] He frequently applies it to brute animals, as he does in a number of passages shortly before this one, in all of which he explicitly excludes human beings.[372] "Natural Man" is not an irrational creature who follows nature but a rational creature who can follow either his reason or his fancy. Read in its context, the crucial passage does read almost like the Rousseau of the *Discourse on Inequality,* since it describes man as uniquely unprovided with instinct.[373]

Man's distinctively human lack of instinct and his dependence instead on the senses and reason, in the *Two Treatises,* are the equivalent of the *Essay*'s denial of innate ideas. Animals are directed by instinct to specific foods and other means of self-preservation, whereas men must learn to find them by experience and by reasoning (I, § 86). Just as the *First Treatise* recognizes self-preservation as a natural "Principle of Action" (I, § 86) so the *Essay* recognizes "a desire of Happiness, and an aversion to

Misery" as "innate practical Principles" (not, be it noted, as innate ideas).[374] If men are distinguished by lack of instinct, the question arises whether concern for propagation or parental tenderness can be an instinct. One should note, first of all, that Locke says that in other animals self-preservation is merely "a strong desire" but that in men it is "the first and strongest desire"[375] and that in other animals "the Preservation of their Young" is "the strongest Principle in them" but that in men it is only "next to" self-preservation.[376] Other animals die for their young, but men even eat theirs for pleasure or sacrifice them to idols. Man lacks instinct and should but does not always follow reason, and it is in that sense that Locke says it is "the Priviledge of Man alone to act more contrary to Nature than the Wild and most Untamed part of Creation" (I, § 56).[377] Not only the subordination of concern for offspring to self-preservation but the highly malleable character of the concern itself suggests that it may not be an independent instinct but merely a derivative of self-preservation: a desire for "continuing themselves in their Posterity" (I, § 88).[378]

Locke also speaks of the conjugal side of the family in the *First Treatise*. He denies that divine law obliges women to be subject to their husbands. For Locke as for Hobbes, that subjection depends rather on "the Circumstances either of her Condition or Contract with her Husband." He admits that wives "ordinarily" are so subject, that it is "generally" so ordered by "the Laws of Mankind and customs of Nations," and even that there is "a Foundation in Nature for it" (I, § 47).[379] But he does not seem to regard it as a natural law. For Locke, unlike Hobbes, even *if* women were obligated to subjection to their husbands, it would be only to "Conjugal Power, not Political." The husband would have no power of life and death but only a power "to order the things of private Concernment in his Family, as Proprietor of the Goods and Land there, and to have his Will take place before that of his wife in all things of their common Concernment" (I, § 48). Conjugal power is doubly limited: it does not reach to matters of concern wider than the family or to matters concerning only the wife. Schochet reasonably infers that it includes "final authority over children" as a common concern. But even though Locke writes here of "every Wife" and "every Husband," it is not fair to conclude that "Locke does not seem to have questioned this aspect of the traditional patriarchal family."[380] For this statement of Locke's is clearly hypothetical, conceding a universal obligation to conjugal subjection that he has just explained depends on contract and does not reach to every wife (e.g., "our Queens *Mary* or *Elizabeth*").[381]

Locke also says in the *First Treatise* that a complete family, even one provided with servants or slaves, such as those of the biblical patriarchs or a "Planter in the West Indies," does not as such constitute a political society whose head exercises sovereignty; it seems rather to be an instance of "voluntary Societies for the time" (I, §§ 130–32).[382] He also says that "Election and Consent of Fathers of Families . . . will differ very little from Consent of the People" (I, § 148). Thus he comes close to eliding the difference between the foundation of government he recognizes and the sort of patriarchal origin that Hobbes favors teaching. But while he comes close, he still maintains the difference. Consent of the people means "the consent of every individual," not merely that of fathers of families (II, § 96).[383]

Most important, Locke not only strives to protect liberal politics from the authoritarian claims of the patriarchal family; he also offers a measure of protection to the privacy of the family from civil government. He not only poses as the defender of the family against Filmer, who by identifying paternal and political power and giving it to the sovereign seems to abolish the family; he also proclaims that "the most Absolute Power of Princes cannot absolve us" from our duty to our parents. Parental power "contains nothing of the Magistrates Power in it, nor is subjected to it" (I, §§ 64–66).

It is in the *Second Treatise* that Locke explains the nature of paternal, or rather parental, power (for it belongs to mothers as well as fathers) (II, §§ 52–53). From the beginning he makes clear his concern to distinguish political power from paternal power as well as from conjugal, managerial, and despotic power (II, § 2). This distinction is directed not simply against Filmer's theory of patriarchal monarchy but against any paternalistic view of politics.[384] Specifically, the chapter on paternal power—which comes after Locke's accounts of the state of nature and property but before his account of government—has two aims: to deny that the family, especially as understood by authoritarian patriarchalists, is a model for politics (II, § 53) and to show how it is possible to have something like the family as we know it on the basis of the principles of natural freedom and equality and of government by consent, the principles of Locke's liberal politics (II, §§ 54, 61).

Locke achieves the first aim in part by arguing that parental power belongs to both parents and therefore forms no monarchical paradigm (II, § 53). He also argues more extensively here that parental power derives only from the parental duty to take care of children, a duty explained more clearly in the *First Treatise* (II, §§ 58, 60, 67, 68).[385] Being so derived, parental power is limited by its end, the child's preservation, and therefore does not reach to a power of life and death (II, § 170). Being so derived, parental power is limited also by its justification, that children are not born capable of taking care of themselves; that is, it does not continue when the child becomes capable (II, §§ 58–59, 66, 170). Since it does not extend to life and death, and since it is not permanent, parental power is radically different from political power.

71

It cannot serve as a model or origin of political power; it exercises no sovereignty and leaves adults free.

Locke's emphasis is on the degree to which parental power "comes short" of political power (II, §§ 60, 65, 66, 69, 71, 74, 174). Yet he says that political power is power only to regulate and preserve property; but parental power is power to "manage" the child's property (II, §§ 173–74).[386] And especially if we recall that both Filmer and Hobbes give to the ruler the power to "instruct" the ruled, we will note with interest that Locke gives education solely to parental power and not to civil government. Education, which Locke tells us in the *Essay* and the *Thoughts* is most responsible for making men what they are and even exercises more influence over their conduct than do civil laws, he entrusts exclusively to the family, the authority that lacks the power of life and death.[387] One is tempted to say that that is the fundamental separation of powers. Similarly, in the *Letter on Toleration,* instruction and concern for the soul are withheld from the government and given, not simply and impossibly to the individual, but to the churches to which men voluntarily go and send their children—that is, they are given, in the first place, to parents, whose care it is to educate their children.[388]

This complex differentiation of parental from political power serves to achieve Locke's second aim as well, which is to show "how *natural Freedom and Subjection to Parents* may consist together" (II, § 61). The crux of this explanation is the transition from the condition of an infant, "without Knowledge or Understanding," "ignorant and without the use of *Reason*" (the condition that requires subjection to parents), to "a state of Reason . . . an Age of Discretion" (the condition that justifies natural freedom) (II, §§ 56, 57, 59). Since reason is the distinctive human faculty for self-preservation (I, § 86), their lack of reason is what requires children to be subject to their parents for their own preservation, just as coming to reason makes adults naturally free (II, §§ 57–63). A difficulty highly relevant to our subject arises here. Locke includes in the realm of parental power not only nourishment but education (II, §§ 56, 65, 67, 170).[389] The parent is empowered not only to substitute his or her reason for the child's until the child acquires it but also to "inform the Mind" of the child (II, §§ 58, 61, 64). Locke even writes that parental power proper (as distinct from the honor owed by adults to their parents) "is *Education*" (II, § 69).[390] This emphasis may give the impression that the attainment of reason, the title to natural freedom, is dependent on education, that is to say, on a proper education. Indeed, Gordon Schochet writes: "Parental control educates and prepares the child for the time when he will be the master of his own actions while simultaneously directing his life by taking the place of the private will and understanding that have not yet developed."[391] More strongly, Geraint Parry writes that

72

the child has to rely on the understanding of his parents who will on his behalf. The parent must, however, make his decisions in such a way as, at the same time, to train the child to a condition of maturity in which he will be able to take decisions for himself. The child must be brought to understand what it means to take responsibility. Without such an understanding the child would remain in the state of a beast.[392]

But Locke writes here as if reason comes of itself and is not dependent on education. "Thus we are *born Free,* as we are born Rational. . . Age that brings one, brings with it the other too" (II, § 61).[393] One comes to reason with age or by "the ordinary course of Nature," which is violated only in the extreme cases of *"Lunaticks* and *Ideots"* (II, § 60). The only apparent exception to this way of speaking refers not to the reason required to govern oneself and be free but to the reason that is required in a ruler. Locke writes that an infant absolute monarch must wait to rule "till Age and *Education* brought him Reason and Ability to govern himself *and others"* (II, § 61, emphasis added).[394] It is clear why Locke requires parents to educate their children so that they can be free yet fails to require children to have been educated in order to claim their freedom: he must do this in order to maintain natural freedom and equality. "A Man may owe *honour* and respect to an ancient, or wise Man," but this gives the wise man no authority, and it deprives the other of none of his freedom (II, § 70).[395]

Locke quotes Hooker's judgment that it is easier for sense than for learning to determine when a man has attained to reason (II, § 61). But Locke's point goes beyond that. He explains that as long as a child lacks the reason needed to know the law that must guide him, whether a positive law or the law of nature that reason is (II, § 6), "some Body else must guide him, who is presumed to know how far the Law allows a Liberty" (II, § 59). Just as the parent is merely *presumed* to know the law and its limits while the child is young, so is the child *presumed* to know them when he becomes an adult: "When he has acquired that state, he is presumed to know how far that Law is to be his Guide" (II, § 59).[396] When Locke writes that children become free when "they come to the use of Reason, or a state of Knowledge, wherein they may be supposed capable to understand that Rule, whether it be the Law of Nature, or the municipal Law of their Country they are to govern themselves by," he immediately adds "Capable, I say, to know it, as well as several others, who live, as Free-men, under that Law" (II, § 170). He seems to concede that they need not be perfectly capable, only as capable as "several others." Although Locke does not use the lowest common denominator of idiocy, he does understand the rationality requisite to freedom to be a relative quality, in much the same sense that reasonable Christianity must be "a religion suited to vulgar capacities."[397] For almost all practical political purposes, almost all adults are presumed rational by a sort of legal fiction. Although toleration is to be extended only to the tolerant,[398] liberty is not strictly restricted to the rational, the liberal, or the liberally educated. The relevance of education to preparation for liberty is not, however, completely denied. And the presumption of rationality extended to adults is a rebuttable one. Although they are presumed to have attained to the capacity to reason, they may show by their conduct that they have renounced it and therefore be deprived of liberty, as in the cases of criminals, aggressors, tyrants, and would-be tyrants (II, §§ 8, 10, 11, 16, 23, 172, 178, 181, 230).

Locke makes it clear that adult children do not owe their parents obedience, certainly not "absolute obedience" (II, § 66). What they owe instead is *"Honour,"* which contains "an inward esteem and reverence to be shewn by all outward Expressions" (II, § 66).[399] It extends as far as "compliance" but not to subjection (II, § 67). Locke first says (II, § 66) that it is owed by a child to "those, from whom he received his" life or "by whose means he entred into being," despite the arguments in the *First Treatise* (I, §§ 52–54) that it is not parents who give children life and that they rarely intend to do so. But he proceeds to explain that the honor he speaks of is owed "more or less, as the Father's care, cost and kindness in his Education, has been more or less" and is "due not to the bare Title of Father" but "may be varied, by the different care and kindness, trouble and expence, which is often imployed upon one Child, more than another" (II, §§ 67, 70). Thus parental power is not alone in being gained solely by preserving and educating a child and never from "the bare *act of begetting,*" for the same things seem to be true of parental honor as well (II, § 65).[400]

Strictly speaking—and Locke does not always speak strictly—we must say that adult children are not the only ones who do not owe obedience to their parents. For the very fact that explains why young children should be subject to their parents—their lack of reason or ability to know the law of reason—means that they are not *"under that Law"* and are therefore not bound by it to any duties (II, § 57).[401] "To speak properly" of a father's right of "temporary Government," one must speak rather of "the Priviledge of Children, and Duty of Parents, than any Prerogative of Paternal Power" (II, § 67).[402] I will turn to the *Thoughts* to see how parents can elicit an obedience that is justified by children's inability to recognize that it or other duties are owed.

Locke also discusses the conjugal side of the family in the *Second Treatise.* "*Conjugal Society* is made by a voluntary Compact between Man and Woman" (II, § 78). Its end "being not barely Procreation" but the nourishment of the child until he is "able to shift for himself," it must be "more firm and lasting" than among other animals, but it need not be permanent (II, §§ 79–81). The wife, particularly, has the right to "separate" if that right is specified in the contract, and, even if it is not specified there, it is apparently a "natural Right" (II, § 82). Although "the last Determination" in matters of common concern "naturally falls to the Man's share, as the abler and the stronger," that inequality seems to be only the foundation in nature for a matter determined by contract and apparently even "varied and regulated by that Contract" as far as is compatible with the preservation of the young (II, §§ 82–83). This variety may even include the situation "in those parts of *America* where when the Husband and Wife part, which happens frequently, the Children are all left to the Mother, follow her, and are wholly under her Care and Provision." Locke even suggests that natural law permits a condition where "one Woman hath more than one Husband at a time" (II, § 65).[403]

Locke adds two important points before concluding his account of parental power in the *Second Treatise*. He recognizes that parental power often seems to extend beyond the time that he posits, but he explains that this is due only to children's hope to inherit a more liberal share of their parents' property. This is "no small Tye on the Obedience of Children"; however, it is "no natural Tye or Engagement," and it does not detract from natural freedom or even belong peculiarly to the family (II, §§ 72–73). Locke also recognizes that "in the first Ages of the World" fathers became the rulers of their families (II, § 74),[404] but he insists this was only by consent of the governed, albeit "a tacit, and scarce avoidable consent" (II, § 75). Laslett says that this grants "considerable concessions to patriarchalism."[405] Schochet remarks that it shows that Locke recognizes that "mankind may well have casually drifted into political society with the help of acquired social habits."[406] I should like to emphasize that Locke's admission of the historical evidence for the patriarchal and monarchic origins of political society enables him, first, to maintain natural freedom and individual consent (II, §§ 105, 106, 112) and, second, to show that patriarchal origins lead only to faultily constructed governments and that only later do men "examine more carefully *the Original* and Rights of *Government*" and construct them so that men can "*think themselves in Civil Society*" (II, §§ 94, 111). A patriarchal origin of civil society is by no means Locke's model.

Locke's recognition of historical evidence for the patriarchal origins of political society has also been taken to strengthen the case for his recognition of a social state of nature.[407] It is true that Locke regards the family as a kind of society (II, §§ 77, 86). It is also true that he recognizes various kinds of families in the state of nature (II, §§ 71, 83). But it does not follow that the state of nature as such was "a society." Society as a larger unit comes into being only through the establishment of civil society. For Locke, man is naturally free from all subjection, not only to any other particular man but to any society. On the basis of that natural freedom Locke builds a liberal politics that restricts civil society to the preservation of the life, liberty, and property of the individuals who freely consent to it; it is not a politics based on natural sociality and aimed at piety or virtue. Also on the basis of that natural freedom he builds a family that is safe for liberalism.

The facts of life provide patriarchalism with a powerful argument against natural freedom. Human beings are not born free and equal individuals, subject only by their own consent; they are born as dependent and weak infants, incapable of consent yet subject to adult authority, which, within the patriarchal family, is that of the father. In the face of these facts, Hobbes tries to preserve natural freedom and equality, as well as government by consent, by analyzing the family as merely a smaller and therefore less successful version of the same absolute dominion as the sovereign exercises in a commonwealth—a dominion based on the same individual consent for the sake of preservation. This effort not only strains natural liberty and consent but deprives the family within the commonwealth of its originally defining sovereignty, making it a mere appendage of the sovereign. Locke's sharp distinction between political society and the family, between political power and the powers of parents or husbands, enables him to preserve natural freedom and equality as well as government by consent more effectively and without having to use such shocking arguments as plural creation or naturally fatherless families. He can give the family its due without danger, since doing so does not involve political power. Locke's distinction also enables him to produce a liberal politics that is more distinct from patriarchal politics than Hobbes's absolutism is. Government can stick to the task of preserving life, liberty, and property, while the family, being neither an authoritarian political model nor a mere emanation of political authority, can become, instead, the agency of Locke's education for liberty.

# TWO
# Authority and Liberty

Most discussion of Locke's moral teaching has been about its basis, to the practical exclusion of concern with its content. It is almost as if, in the study of Locke, scholars have been so eager "to supply a *rational foundation* for morality" that his "morality itself [has been] accepted as 'given.' "[1] Instead of addressing the vexed question of the rational foundation of morality in Locke's writings, I turn to his views of what morality consists in and of how to get men to practice it. An examination of the content of Lockean morality as articulated in *Some Thoughts Concerning Education* reveals his reconstruction of the model of the liberal gentleman on the basis of the hedonist principles familiar to the reader of the *Essay Concerning Human Understanding*. Locke himself is more concerned with getting men to practice morality than with establishing its rational foundation or elaborating its rules. As John Dunn remarks, most of Locke's unpublished discussions of ethics "are concerned directly with the problem of how men can be brought to *practise* the moral principles which they could perceive as rational."[2] In one of these manuscripts, which Dunn quotes on this point, Locke explains that there are "two parts of Ethics, the one is the rule[s] which men are generally in the right in though perhaps they have not deduced them as they should from their true principles. The other is the true motives to practice them and the ways to bring men to observe them and these are generally either not well known or not rightly applied." Locke dismisses moral discourses that omit the second part of ethics as "but the delight of speculation." The second part is exercised by the "prudent man," who considers an individual's "particular disease" and remedies it by establishing "a contrary pleasure" so that "Conscience, Reason and pleasure go together."[3] The best source for understanding Locke's teaching on this second part of ethics is his *Thoughts Concerning Education*.

In "Some Thoughts Concerning Reading and Study for a Gentleman" Locke makes a similar distinction respecting politics. There the two parts, "very different the one from the other," are "one, containing the original of societies, and the rise and extent of political power" and "the other, the art of governing men in society."[4] For the first part, Locke recommends his *Two Treatises of Government*. When he does present "the great art of government" in the chapter on property in the *Second Treatise* it is only "bye the bye," as a digression from "the argument in hand"—a digression added in the last edition.[5] Prudential considerations are not absent from the *Two Treatises*, especially regarding such matters as prerogative and the exercise of the right of revolution, but fundamentally that work presents a (natural) legal doctrine of rights and duties. But a thinker as concerned with practice as Locke was could not present a merely speculative political doctrine unsupported by an understanding of human nature and the art of governing men that that understanding makes possible. In the *Thoughts* Locke presents his understanding of the art of governing men on one level at least. He frequently refers to "governing" children and calls their educators their "governors" and their methods "instruments of government." He does not expound the rights or duties of parents but counsels them in the particulars of the art of governing children and reveals the premises of that art in human nature.

One cannot simply transfer Locke's account of the government of children to the level of the political art of governing men in society. That would be to commit the mistake that Locke belabored Filmer for. But Locke's account of the art of governing children is not irrelevant to his understanding of the second part of politics. For at a number of key points he explicitly states that the methods of governing children he recommends or their premises in the nature of children or both apply equally and in some cases even more to the government of men or to human nature. The great difference remains, however, that the power of life and death—so important for a thinker who recognizes self-preservation as the fundamental desire, law, or right—is absent in the family. Forms of self-love other than the immediate concern for self-preservation are necessarily more conspicuous.

I shall also explain in this chapter how Locke in the *Thoughts* meets the challenges posed by the *Second Treatise*. He must show first how parental authority can elicit a filial obedience that is justified by the child's lack of reason, even though reason is needed for recognizing obligations. Second, he must show how that authority, once established, can be employed so as to come to an end. Third, he must show how authority can help to derive from self-love a concern for others that makes liberty practical. In all these ways the *Thoughts* enables us to explore Locke's understanding of human nature, both its common elements and its infinite varieties, in far greater detail than is permitted by any other work of his. We are able to see his vision of human life in a much richer and more vivid way than is afforded by abstract debates over theology and natural law.

## PRIVATE AND PUBLIC, FAMILIAR AND CIVIL: THE CHARACTER OF *Some Thoughts Concerning Education* (EPISTLE DEDICATORY)

The *Thoughts* has the peculiar character of a *public* appeal for the general reformation of education, which, according to Locke's political doctrine, is properly a *private* concern. This character of the work first comes to sight in its origin and style. In the Epistle Dedicatory to his friend Edward Clarke, Locke immediately lets the reader know that the work has been adapted from private letters to Clarke. Even if Locke did not so inform him, the reader would "easily find, in the Familiarity and Fashion of the Style, that they were rather the private Conversation of two Friends, than a Discourse designed for publick View."[6] Locke lets us become, or assumes that we already are, familiar with him, that we know that he has studied medicine (§§ 2, 29) and is "a bookish Man" (§ 147).[7] He even shares with us his "own Experience" of having been tempted to become a college dropout in reaction to his studies of "abstract Notions of *Logick* and *Metaphysicks*" (§ 166).

Locke's calling attention to the private origin and familiar style of his work both underlines and mitigates the incongruity of publishing a writing that was designed for private reading and treats of private matters. The familiar and friendly style of the work, heightened by the reader's awareness of its origin, not only is appropriate to the homely details of domestic education but also helps to make more agreeable what might seem to be meddlesome advice.[8] As Locke explains in the work, one ought to treat grown men, as well as older children, with familiarity and friendliness, since they resent formal instructions and those who affect great formality (§§ 40–41, 96–97). This prudent recommendation rests on the fundamental principles of Locke's moral psychology: that since the "happiness that all Men so steadily pursue [consists] in pleasure," they therefore value those who make them easy and avoid those who make them uneasy (§ 143, p. 249). For the human pursuit of happiness, far from being a matter of mere sensuality, is radically complicated by *pride*. The reason why familiar and friendly advisers make us easy, whereas stern imposers of tasks and duties make us uneasy, is that human pride is a pride in having "Reason of their own to guide them" (§ 40) and a desire to "be thought Rational Creatures, and have our Freedom" (§ 41).

The *Two Treatises* are properly more formal and less familiar than the *Thoughts*. They deal primarily with public rather than private matters and consist chiefly in a doctrine of rights and duties rather than prudential advice. They discuss private matters only insofar as that is required to define public matters and to build those fences around the private sphere that it is the end of the public sphere to preserve.

Human pride requires not only *familiarity* in public or private discussion of private affairs but *civility* in almost all discourse (§ 143, p. 249). One must show respect. To "intrude our selves for Teachers," as one does by contradicting and correcting others, is an offensive sign, not merely of one's own pride, but of one's disrespect for others' pride. But yet "the greatest Advantage of Society" is the light gotten from "the opposite Arguings of Men of Parts" (§ 145). Dissent must be expressed: "The opposing the opinions, and rectifying the mistakes of others, is what truth and charity sometimes requires of us, and civility does not oppose" (§ 143, p. 248). But this should be "done with due caution and care of circumstances" and be expressed "by way of Enquiry, not Instruction," without "the Magisterial Air" and "with some civil Preface of Deference and Respect to the Opinions of others" (ibid. and § 145, p. 252; it is clear from the following paragraph of § 145 about the faults of "grown People" that this advice is not addressed to young people alone).

The *Thoughts* itself is emphatically a work of dissent. The Epistle Dedicatory mentions that the method of the work is contrary to "the ordinary Disciplining of Children." In the work Locke decries "the common Management of Children" and opposes the "Publick Testimony" (§ 37). Indeed, it is precisely because "the World commonly does otherwise" than what Locke recommends that he publishes his *Thoughts*: "I am saying what I think should be; which, if it were already in Fashion, I should not need to trouble the World with a Discourse on this Subject" (§ 39). Locke frequently explicitly opposes his recommendations to the "usual," "common," "ordinary," or "general" education.[9]

As a work opposing and correcting common opinions and practices, the *Thoughts* must have such a "civil Preface" as Locke recommends. Accordingly, he claims, in the Epistle Dedicatory, that he decided to publish only because of the importunity of friends "whose Judgment I defer much to," despite "the Meanness of these Papers, and my just Distrust of them." Moreover, he professes that he would "not be sorry . . . if some one abler and fitter for such a Task, would in a just Treatise of Education, suited to our *English* Gentry, rectifie the Mistakes I have made in this." This disclaimer is not merely a civil expression of respect for the opinions of others, prefacing Locke's extended effort to oppose and correct them, for he closes the work with a similar disavowal, that he "would not have it thought that I look on it as a just Treatise on this Subject" (§ 216). But then the reason given is not the private origin of the work or its author's mean abilities but precisely Locke's new contribution of emphasizing the importance of individuality, which renders a "just" or "compleat Treatise on this Subject" practically impossible. Given Locke's emphasis on the importance of remedying individual defects, his recognition of the limits of the malleability of individual temperament, and his stress on managing children by appealing to their own inclinations, individuality is crucial, and so a *general* treatise of education cannot be just. He warns that "Each Man's Mind has some peculiarity, as well as his Face, that distinguishes him from all others; and there are possibly scarce two Children, who can be conducted by exactly the same method." Rather than being an impossibly just treatise that covers every case, Locke's *Thoughts* is a "short Treatise of Education" (§ 139) that presents "the general Method of Educating a young Gentleman" as well as "a more particular Consideration of the several parts of his Education" (§ 133).

Education, though properly a private concern, is of enormous public importance. Education is "the Duty and Concern of Parents," but "the Welfare and Prosperity of the Nation so much depends on it, that I would have every one lay it seriously to Heart; and . . . set his Helping Hand to promote every where that Way of training youth . . . which is the easiest, shortest, and likeliest to produce vertuous, useful, and able Men in their distinct Callings." (Locke adds that what is "most to be taken Care of, is the Gentleman's Calling. For if those of that Rank are by their Education once set right, they will quickly bring all the rest into Order.") Education is of decisive *political* importance. Although, unlike Hobbes, Locke does not address his educational reform to rulers, he does address the general public, not simply parents, and he appeals to *patriotism* rather than simply to parental duty or to humane sentiments in general. Locke's friends prevailed on him to publish his thoughts by appealing, similarly, not to his general philanthropy but to his patriotism. The decisive consideration was that "I think it every Man's indispensible Duty, to do all the Service he can to his Country: And I see not what Difference he puts between himself and his Cattel, who lives without that Thought." We may recall from the *Two Treatises* that other animals "obey God and Nature in being tender and careful of their Off-spring" and "the Preservation of their Young, as the strongest Principle in them over rules the Constitution of their particular Natures." Human beings, in contrast, are naturally concerned with their offspring only "next to" their "first and strongest desire . . . , that of Self-preservation," but they are also bound "*to preserve the rest of Mankind.*" This natural obligation is "drawn closer" within civil society and becomes a patriotic concern for that society and its members.[10]

Locke makes it clear in the Epistle that the importunity of his friends was not merely a personal accident but a sign that "many . . . profess themselves at a Loss how to breed their Children; and the early Corruption of Youth is now become so general a Complaint." He writes at a time especially receptive to educational reform. But a similar passage (§ 70, pp. 169–70) somewhat dissociates Locke from this complaint. There he leaves it undetermined "if we may believe the general Complaint" of the early corruption of youth. Moreover, he leaves it to others to inquire "by what Fate Vice has so thriven amongst us these Years past; and by what hands it has been nurs'd up into so uncontroul'd a Dominion"; instead, he expresses his "wish, that those, who complain of the great Decay of Christian Piety and Vertue every where, and of Learning and acquired Improvements in the Gentry of this Generation, would consider how to retrieve them in the next." The dominion of vice may be due to those who, unlike Locke, are more concerned with past guilt than with future reform—perhaps those who from the pulpit have preached divine right and absolute power[11] and perhaps even those who complain of the great decay of Christian piety. Locke himself is sure that educating youth in "Innocence, Sobriety, and Industry," is important to the preservation of "that Vertue, Ability, and Learning, which has hitherto made *England* considerable in the World." He thus emphasizes again the political importance of education. He even adds that "Courage too, though it has been looked on as the Natural Inheritance of Englishmen," depends on education in virtue, since it is "impossible to find an instance of any Nation, however renowned for their Valour, who ever kept their Credit in Arms, or made themselves redoubtable amongst their Neighbours, after Corruption had once broke through, and dissolv'd the restraint of Discipline."

In the Epistle, Locke adduces the first of many examples of a child on whom his "Method" has had "no [merely] ordinary Effects" but very beneficial ones, and thus the *Thoughts* invites its readers not only to apply his recommendations but to let him know the good results, so that these can be included in the next edition.[12] It is thus a practical manual that produces a community of practitioners and in turn becomes, in part, their product. We are almost in the world of how-to books, advice columns, and call-in shows. Of this first example of success, Locke politely but ambiguously "will not say the good Temper of the Child did not very much contribute"; but that child's nature cannot have been altogether good, since Locke adds that the ordinary method "would not have mended that Temper." Despite the civil respect Locke shows to the contribution of nature, he indicates that with this child his method overcame a defective nature instead of being aided by a good nature. (The book's epigraph from Horace presents the triumph of bad education over good nature, not the poet's preceding paean to inherited virtue.)[13] The effects Locke's method had on this child were to bring him "to be in Love with his Book, to take a Pleasure in Learning, and to desire . . . to be taught more, than those about him think fit always to teach him." Locke's method spurs the child's love, pleasure, and desire instead of subjecting him directly to duty or to what his parents think fit for him. In the same way, patriotism is not only a public duty but the basis of the sort of private friendship than which Locke knows "no greater Pleasure in this Life."

## HAPPINESS AND EDUCATION (*Thoughts*, § 1)

The main body of Locke's *Some Thoughts Concerning Education* opens with a brief statement of the importance of education (§ 1). This statement begins with a brief description of happiness: "A Sound Mind in a Sound Body, is a short, but full Description of a Happy State in this World."[14] This description in itself does not show the importance of education; indeed, it might even be said to challenge it by requiring that education provide a sound mind and body if it is to provide happiness. Locke must argue that education, not nature or grace, is the source of mental and physical soundness. And indeed he does go right on to assert that "Men's Happiness or Misery is most part of their own making." This is not the assertion of individual responsibility that it may at first appear to be. Rather, it is an assertion only of immediate, not ultimate, individual responsibility. It *is* wise direction by one's own mind that enables one to "take the right Way," and it is one's own bodily strength that enables one "to advance in it," but those mental and physical qualities in turn usually come from education by others. Thus, when Locke asserts that "Men's Happiness or Misery is most part of their own making," he is speaking of the species, not of the individual. The educators make the happiness or misery of the educated; one generation is responsible for the next, though not for itself (see § 70, pp. 169–70). This claim is not only wholly consonant with the epistemology of Locke's *Essay Concerning Human Understanding;* it also clarifies the practical thrust of that teaching. Locke's denial of innate ideas and his emphasis on the impact of experience (as both sensation and reflection), though obviously environmentalist in a sense, put a premium on individual effort, on the labor necessary to gain knowledge from experience rather than passively to accept allegedly innate ideas, which are in fact only received opinions.[15] Beyond emphasizing the individual effort required to learn from experience, Locke makes it clear that the experience and environment that are so important are mostly of human construction or arrangement. The premise of the *Thoughts* is that the most important experience of all—education—is manmade.

Despite this general view of education, Locke prefaces it here with an interesting confession:

> there are some Men's Constitutions of Body and Mind
> so vigorous, and well framed by Nature, that they need
> not much Assistance from others, but by the Strength

> of their natural Genius, they are from their Cradles car-
> ried towards what is Excellent; . . .

Thus are the egalitarian implications of Lockean epistemology fundamentally mitigated by a recognition of natural inequality.[16] But that
mitigation in turn is limited in its practical effects, since

> Examples of this Kind are but few, and I think I may
> say, that of all the Men we meet with, Nine Parts of Ten
> are what they are, Good or Evil, useful or not, by their
> Education.

The *Thoughts* is designed for the education of the nine in ten who are
*not* so well framed by nature that they are carried by the strength of
their natural genius toward what is excellent.[17] Those who are so framed
can presumably take care of themselves and rise above their education,
whatever its character.


## THE BODY (§§ 2–30)

In his discussion of physical education, which immediately follows (§§ 2–
30), unlike the treatment of the education of the mind, which follows it
(§§ 31 ff.), Locke considers, almost at the outset (§ 4), the constitution
of the children for whom it is designed. Physical education is not for
the sickly child in need of physic but for those with a "*Healthy*, or at
least, *not sickly Constitution*," i.e., one that requires mere preservation.
Locke's silence on this point in the corresponding section on the education of the mind might be taken to suggest that with respect to the
mind it is ministration to one in need of assistance, not mere preservation
and improvement, that is involved.

The discussion of physical education touches on a number of points
that are important for the moral education that follows. Locke bows to
the superiority of nature to human artifice in forming the human body
(§§ 11–12), tries to restrict pupils to natural hunger and thirst so that
they will not develop artificial desires for more or special food or drink
(§§ 14 and 18), and is wary of medicine, preferring generally "to leave
[children] to Nature" (§ 29). Nevertheless he regards the artful introduction of habits as most important. "The great Thing to be minded in
Education is, what *Habits* you settle" (§ 18). The body should be "hard-
ened" (§§ 5 and 7) or systematically accustomed to endurance (§§ 5, 7,
9, 14, 21, and 22). This is for the sake of health, not "Stoical Principles"
or religious rituals, and it results from nature, not "Miracles" (§ 7). This
recommendation is based on the plasticity of human nature. As a certain
traveler whom Locke quotes says, "Nature can bring it self to many
things, which seem impossible, provided we accustom our selves from

our Infancy" (§ 5). In Locke's own words, "You cannot imagine of what Force Custom is" (§ 14). For by gradual habituation "we may bring our Bodies to any thing, without Pain, and without Danger" (§ 7). This plasticity is, on the one hand, exploited to permit permanent shaping of human behavior (e.g., accustoming the child to bread [§ 14], to rising early [§ 21], and to regular excretion [§§ 24–28]). On the other hand, it is preserved as permanent flexibility or indifference (e.g., accustoming the child to eat at any hour [§ 15], to sleep on any bed [§ 22], and to endure any weather [§ 9]). Locke also indicates here that this method of habituation affects not only the body but also the mind; for in connection with his remarks about teaching the child not to sit on the cold ground or to have a cold drink when hot from exercise, Locke notes that "the Custom of Forbearing grown into Habit" will remain (§ 10; cf. §§ 17–18). He recommends such mental as well as physical habituation because one's pupil will have his liberty as an adult, and then "there cannot always be a Guard upon him, except what you have put into his own mind by good Principles, and established Habits." This inner guard is

> the best and surest, and therefore most to be taken Care of. For, from repeated Cautions and Rules, never so often inculcated, you are not to expect any thing either in this, or any other Case, farther than Practice has established them into Habits.

This refrain of "habits, not rules," is frequent in Locke's discussion of moral education.[18] One might wonder whether Locke supposed that the mind, like the body, is best educated by the method of habituation because he understood mind also to be corporeal and therefore "as easily turned this or that way, as Water it self" (§ 2). This might also explain why people with loose bowels "have seldom strong Thoughts" (§ 23). However, Locke, unlike Hobbes, leaves open the question of the physical basis of his psychology and epistemology, which he presents as being independent of physics or physiology.[19]

The content of Lockean virtue, as well as the method of attaining it, is also indicated by several remarks in this part. The pupil is to be educated to be a "Man of Business," not a "Beau"; the standard is utility in "this World," not beauty (§ 9). He is also "to be so bred, as to be fitted to bear Arms, and be a Soldier" (§ 15). Locke also decries drunkenness and "Good-fellowship" (§§ 17–19) and midnight revels (§ 21), expense brought on by vanity (§ 20), and laziness and waste of time (§ 21). He also warns against the influence of fashion (§ 21). These admonitions suggest a severe morality of self-denial rather than consumption or spontaneity. But attention to the pupil's individual temper and constitution is also recommended (§ 21), and Locke warns that prohibition and over-strictness increase appetite and temptation (§ 20).

The question of proper parental motivation is also first addressed in this part. A wrong course, such as overdressing the child in winter, may be pursued by the mother "for fear of Harm; and the Father for fear of Censure" (§ 5). Both benevolence and concern for reputation can lead to error, and maternal fondness seems the more dangerous (see §§ 4, 7, and 13). This part also raises the related theme of inheritance: a parent should not educate his son "to sleep over his Life, in the Plenty and Ease of a full Fortune he intends to leave him" (§ 15), for one must rely on one's own ability, not on inherited fortune (see also §§ 70 [p. 171] and 90).[20]

Locke devotes the first part of the *Thoughts* to physical education not at all because that is most important for him; on the contrary, he notes at the outset that "our main Care should be about the Inside" (§ 2). Bodily health and strength are instrumental, as he indicates in his description of happiness at the very beginning: "He, whose Mind directs not wisely, will never take the right Way; and he, whose Body is crazy[21] and feeble, will never be able to advance in it" (§ 1). The body's good condition is necessary in order to advance in the right way to happiness chosen by the sound mind. What that right way is like is indicated when Locke turns to physical education in § 3, where he asserts:

> How necessary *Health* is to our Business and Happiness:
> And how requisite a strong Constitution, able to endure
> Hardships and Fatigue, is to one that will make any
> Figure in the World, is too obvious to need any Proof.

Happiness, or the right way, is here paired with business[22] and seems to involve making a figure in the world. But one cannot conclude that these goals constitute the whole or ultimate end of our education or of our activity generally; they may be only the most "obvious" ground Locke can rely on here. One must turn to his treatment of the education of the mind to find out more precisely what it is that physical education, strength, and health are instrumental to.

## SELF-DENIAL (§§ 31–39)

Locke's treatment of the education of the mind indeed begins on a more lofty level:

> Due care being had to keep the Body in Strength and
> Vigor, so that it may be able to obey and execute the
> Orders of the *Mind;* The next and principal Business is,
> to set the *Mind* right, that on all Occasions it may be
> disposed to consent to nothing, but what may be suitable

to the Dignity and Excellency of a rational Creature.
[§ 31]

This statement leaves open the question of what it is that "may be suitable to the Dignity and Excellency of a rational Creature."[23] Locke's use of such lofty, somewhat classical, phrases[24] and of other somewhat scriptural ones tends to remain formal, so their content must be sought elsewhere.

When Locke proceeds to treat of the soundness or virtue of the mind, the same instrumental treatment that was given to bodily health is explicitly applied:

> As the Strength of the Body lies chiefly in being able to endure Hardships, so also does that of the Mind. And the great Principle and Foundation of all Vertue and Worth, is placed in this, That a Man is able to *deny himself* his own Desires, cross his own Inclinations, and purely follow what Reason directs as best, tho' the Appetite lean the other way. [§ 33]

This ability to deny one's desires is useful, like bodily strength. Though this requirement surely indicates something of the self-denying character of Lockean virtue, the end of self-denial is left open by the formal phrase "what Reason directs as best." As a result, this passage has elicited a wide variety of interpretations. For John W. Yolton it serves as part of the basis for his statement that "Locke's attitude toward desire is almost wholly negative. Reason and desire very seldom, if ever, coincide."[25] Sterling P. Lamprecht, in contrast, points out that "even here [Locke] did not deny that what reason directs as best is only a greater future pleasure than the one on which the present inclination is bent."[26] We shall see that later passages in the *Thoughts* support Lamprecht.

As we shall also see, the ability to deny one's desires is not the only thing denominated by Locke as "the great Principle and Foundation of all Vertue and Worth" (see §§ 56, 61). It may be the "foundation" of virtue only in the sense that it is the necessary prerequisite of actual acts of virtue rather than the logical foundation from which the content of virtue and its particular acts can be deduced. It is not clear at this point whether Locke intends it also as the sufficient condition of virtue, of "taking the right way"; in other words, it is not clear whether, once the appetites are under control, reason is thereby in control and easily able to "direct the best," undisturbed by passion, or whether, on the contrary, reason requires further guidance for the attainment of virtue (see § 200). Self-control can, after all, be found among those whose minds give orders not generally considered virtuous. Perhaps Locke would say that such persons are not truly able to deny all of their desires but only some of them. This formal description of virtue could even be taken as purely instrumental and open-ended Machiavellian or Baconian advice on how to be able to seek whatever one finds best. Still another possibility is suggested by the immediately preceding remarks, an exhortation to parents to care for the education of their children's minds (§ 32), where Locke appeals not to parental duty or reason directly but to parental concern for their own reputations: "For when they [the children] do well or ill, the Praise or Blame will be laid there [on the breeding the parents have imparted]." This suggests that rational parental direction—and, eventually, self-direction—is related to a sensitivity to praise and blame.

One might say, however, that in this warning to parents Locke is again simply appealing to the lowest ground, "too obvious to need any proof" (cf. § 3), without abandoning the possibility of advance to other and higher ground. A further reason why he may take this ground here, besides its possibly greater effectiveness, is revealed immediately in his criticism of parents who indulge or spoil their children:

> Parents, being wisely ordain'd by Nature to love their Children, are very apt, if Reason watch not that natural Affection very warily, are apt, I say, to let it run into Fondness. They love their little ones, and 'tis their Duty: But they often, with them, cherish their Faults too. [§ 34]

Natural love alone, or even duty undirected by "Reason," is unreliable and in need of correction. Consideration of one's own future reputation can lead to wiser conduct, more beneficial to others than conduct that flows from the love "wisely ordain'd by Nature."

The problematic character of the self-denial that is here presented is also revealed by Locke's immediately following admonition to overly indulgent parents who have failed to make the child's mind "obedient to Discipline, and pliant to Reason, when at first it was most tender, most easy to be bowed." To distinguish self-control from mere conditioning, one must ask to whose reason the mind must be made pliant. It sounds very much as if the mind should be conditioned to deny its "own Desires" (§ 33), not at the behest of its own reason, but at the behest of "Reason," embodied in the command of others, namely, the parents.[27]

This ambiguity about the "reason" to which the appetites are to be submitted is soon clarified:

> He that is not used to submit his Will to the Reason of others, *when* he is *Young*, will scarce hearken or submit to his own Reason, when he is of an Age to make use of it. [§ 36]

This may be taken as an admission that the "Reason" so far spoken of has been that "of others." Still, one must wonder whether the young, at the age when their minds are "most tender," are, though unable to possess wisdom, already able to discern it in others and are thus indeed able to submit their desires to reason in a significant sense. The very fact that it is habit, that one is "used" (§ 36) to submit his will to the reason of others, would seem, given Locke's view of habit or custom, to indicate that one submits not to the reasonable as such but that, rather, what one becomes used to is simply the denial of one's desires or even submission to others and that it is this habit that is to be put to good use later (see § 200).[28]

In his admonition against parental indulgence (§ 34) Locke quotes "Solon"[29] about the importance of custom, which is one of the great themes of the *Thoughts*. One may ask whether the will to fulfill rather than deny one's desires is natural or is only the result of custom, as the use of the quotation from "Solon" would suggest. Locke's statement that "Parents, by humoring and cockering them when *little*, corrupt the Principles of Nature in their Children" (§ 35) suggests that the principles of nature somehow support moderation and rationality. This paragraph goes on to mention "ill Habits," "ill Humours . . . infused and fomented," and "Weeds" that parents have planted, all phrases suggesting that willfulness is the result of custom and human nurture. But it concludes that such creatures as dogs and horses are not "half so wilful and proud, or half so desirous to be Masters of themselves and others, as Man." It would seem, then, that men are by nature willful and proud and filled with desire to master themselves and others. This is not contrary to the preceding assertion about the effect of habit, because it is this natural propensity that lies at the basis of the bad habits that can be established by custom and is therefore presumably in need of being restrained by good habits of denial.

It should not be overlooked that Locke wrote that men are "desirous to be Masters of *themselves* and others" (my emphasis). The context (the willfulness of men and their consequent propensity to be corrupted by habitually having their wills indulged by others) might seem to have required, in the final sentence of the paragraph, only desire for mastery *over others*. The fact that Locke added mastery *over themselves* is not irrelevant. Men desire that others should not be their masters,[30] and, if they are used to having their own will in everything, they will not easily "of a suddain . . . be restrained and Curbed" (§ 35). Therefore, not only is a child not to be permitted to be master of others and not to be "taught to strike, and call Names," but he is not to be permitted to be his own master, to "have what he Cries for, and do what he pleases." There is no clear border between being entirely one's own master and being master of others; in this paragraph Locke seems to equate "he that has been used to have his Will in every thing" with "He [that] had the Will of his Maid before he could Speak or Go; he [that] had the Mastery of his Parents ever since he could Prattle." Accordingly, Locke unites desire for mastery over both self and others in his conclusion to the paragraph. He who is entirely master of himself, who can and does "do what he pleases," is a tyrant, just as he who is entirely mastered by others is a slave.[31] The wider context of this paragraph (as set by §§ 33 and 36) reminds us that being "master of oneself" has another, more positive, meaning: the very ability to deny one's desires, which is "the great Principle and Foundation of all Vertue and Worth" (§ 33); later it is called a "Mastery over his Inclinations" (§ 45),[32] and a special form of it is called the mind's having "Mastery over it self" (§ 75).[33] If this is not to be considered mere phraseological coincidence, it suggests that the virtue Locke is praising rests on the same natural human basis as the vice he warns against. The desire for mastery can be turned willfully outward over others and for doing what one pleases or it can be turned rationally inward against one's own passions, appetites, and inclinations.[34] The kinship between the virtue and the vice may also be seen in Locke's defining the virtue as a power, "the Power to govern, and deny our selves" (§ 36; see also §§ 38 and 107). One can also say that § 36 vindicates Harold Laski's claim that Locke's pedagogy is without any sense of original sin, as opposed to John Dunn's suggestion that it expresses the "corrupt human nature" of fallen man.[35] For Locke makes it entirely clear that "the having Desires . . . is not the Fault; but the not having them subject to the Rules and Restraints of Reason." The child's desires for grapes or sugarplums and the adult's desires for wine and women are not wicked in themselves. In this Locke agrees with Hobbes's explanation that he does not consider men as wicked by nature, "for the affections of the mind, which arise only from the lower parts of the soul, are not wicked themselves; but the actions thence proceeding may be so sometimes, as when they are either offensive or against duty."[36]

The moral teaching of the *Thoughts* is further elaborated as Locke proceeds from the general necessity of accustoming children to denial of their desires (§§ 33–36) to the importance of avoiding teaching the particular vices commonly instilled (§ 37). These are: violence, revenge, and cruelty, vain concern with fashionable clothes, lying, and intemperance in food and drink. Writing for gentlemen as he does,[37] Locke need not and should not explain why it is that these qualities are vices.[38] With the possible exception of lying,[39] they can plausibly be considered aristocratic vices or propensities, though surely neither indulgence in them nor disapprobation of them belongs exclusively to any class. They are not termed sins.[40] Only in the case of intemperance in food and drink can Locke be said to give a reason for avoiding it or for treating it as a vice, and the reason is the eminently sensible one of health. In this context he also mentions the "Expence of a fashionable Table," which suggests an additional sensible reason: economy.

After this brief admonitory catalogue of commonly inculcated vices, Locke returns to "the Principle of all Vertue and Excellency . . . a Power of denying our selves the Satisfaction of our own Desires, where Reason does not authorize them" (§ 38). This statement again gives the impression that Locke is making an antithesis between reason and desire, as may be seen in Yolton's use of it;[41] but Lamprecht apparently understands it to mean or allow that Locke "placed morality in a life devoted to a satisfaction of those desires only which reason authorizes one to follow."[42] Earlier Locke shows himself aware of the great human desire for freedom and autonomy (§ 35) and willing to flatter these human pretensions to rationality and individual freedom, even as he is aware of their limitations. For in his first and conspicuous general statement about the education of the mind (in § 33) he seems to overstate the individual rationality involved, only quietly to correct himself shortly thereafter (in § 36), just as he overstates the goodness of human nature and then quietly but quickly corrects himself (in § 35) and flatters nature only to retract that flattery (in § 34). So, here again (in § 38), the first and conspicuous general statement overstates the rationality involved and is obscure about who possesses it. For Locke continues: "This Power is to be got and improved by Custom, made easy and familiar by an *early* Practice . . . . Children should be used to submit their Desires, and go without their Longings, even *from their very Cradles*." This power is acquired by custom, which Locke so often opposes to reason;[43] it is acquired *early*, presumably before reason; and the habit is characterized as being one of submission or forbearance simply, without mention of authorization by reason. Locke quickly makes it clear that the reason that authorizes desires is, of course, not here the child's, for he says that "The first thing they should learn to know should be, that they were not to have any thing, because it pleased them, but because it was thought fit for them"—"thought fit," obviously, by their parents. Of course there is nothing strange in Locke's submission of young children to others' judgments; what is remarkable is, on the contrary, his apparent eagerness, in his striking general statements, to obscure the difference between this condition of submission and that of individual autonomy and rationality. One may attribute Locke's willingness to exaggerate human rationality in its less perfect forms, and in general to flatter human pretensions to rationality, to his belief that the "love to be treated as Rational Creatures" is "a Pride [to] be cherished" in men as in children and "as much as can be, made the greatest instrument to turn them by" (§ 81). One can also attribute this tendency of his to the problem he explicitly faced in the *Two Treatises:*[44] the problem of reconciling parental power over children with his affirmations of natural freedom and equality and his view of consent as the sole source of legitimate political power. It may be that, for fear of mistaken political inferences from parental power, such as

91

Filmer's, Locke makes his very assertion of submission sound like an affirmation of autonomy and point to the condition to which it is to give way. For the same reason, he may stress the rationality rather than the arbitrariness in the submission. The crux of the reconciliation of parental power and political freedom in the *Second Treatise* is in the transition from being an infant, "ignorant and without the use of *Reason*" (II, § 57), to "a state of Reason."[45] To determine the moment of this transition is, according to Locke's quotation from the judicious Hooker, a fine point, not susceptible to theoretical treatment (II, § 61). In the political context of the *Treatises* it is not necessary to press the point; if nothing else, Locke can defer to the legal "Age of one and twenty years."[46] In any case, according to the discussion in the *Second Treatise,* all adults, other than "*Lunaticks* and *Ideots*" (II, § 60), are supposed equal; that is, all are regarded as having made the transition to the rationality that entitles them to natural freedom, to not being subjected to the will of another without their own consent (II, § 54). The importance of that transition, the way in which it entitles men to that freedom, lies in the acquisition of the ability to know the law of nature (II, §§ 57, 59, and 63). One would expect that in the *Thoughts* Locke would explicitly describe the child's gradual discovery of the particular provisions of the law of nature; instead, that law is not even mentioned.[47] The child is habituated to submit his desires to his parents; when he is rational, his reason has this prefabricated habit at its disposal; but how and for what ends reason requires it is not elaborated in terms of the natural law of the *Treatises*.[48]

Since Locke overstates the child's rationality or assimilates the child's irrational submission to a rational one, one wonders whether he is being similarly if not equally free in calling the adult rationally autonomous. Locke is surely in the peculiar position here, as often elsewhere in the *Thoughts,* of simultaneously siding with reason against custom and advocating the use of custom rather than reason to teach the qualities that Locke's own reason favors and the world's custom rejects. The habitual submission of children's desires is itself, after all, "contrary to the ordinary way" (§ 38), and intemperance in food and drink receives the approbation of "the Publick Testimony" (§ 37, p. 142). The *Thoughts* closes with the hope that it may provide some

> small light to those, whose Concern for their dear little
> Ones makes them so irregularly bold, that they dare
> venture to consult their own Reason, in the Education
> of their Children, rather than wholly to rely upon Old
> Custom. [§ 216]

Yet it recommends custom rather than reason as the primary educational method. This, together with such features as Locke's silence on natural

law, makes one wonder whether the "small light" provided to the gentleman reader is, indeed, the full light of reason.

None of this, however, is to deny that, for Locke, the habit of submission to another can, in the best case, prepare for autonomous rational
self-control and, in other cases, lead to approximations of it.

It is important to note that, despite the generality of his first statement,
the denial that Locke advocates turns out in practice to be denial not of
whatever is desired but only of demands made on others, if only in the
form of inarticulate infantile cries (§ 38; see also §§ 106–7). That only
*demands* are denied is to some extent due to the fact that self-control is
being inculcated by others; but that explanation cannot be the whole or
even the chief one, since other people can become aware of one's desires
even when these are not expressed as demands. Indeed, and again despite the initial general formulation, the main thrust seems to be not
against desire as such but precisely and deliberately against the demand
that one's desires be fulfilled by others and against the expectation that
they will be. The moral point is not ascetic or puritan but "civil," to use
a favorite word of Locke's. Locke's advice to parents comes close to the
recommendations Rousseau makes in *Emile*.[49] But Locke's primary concern appears to be not so much to protect the child from coming to "live
outside of himself" or from becoming "alienated" but to protect others
from the child's becoming tyrannical or insolent. Locke does recommend, like Rousseau, that unsuitable desires be assimilated to impossible
ones ("If they were never suffered to obtain their Desire by the Impa-
tience they expressed for it, they would no more cry for other Things,
than they do for the Moon" [§ 38]); however, he does not, like Rousseau,
go so far as to advise that the human source of that impossibility be
disguised as a physical one,[50] for his concern is to prevent a desire for
mastery over others rather than to prevent all awareness of dependence
on others' wills. That awareness is in fact the basis of the parental authority he seeks to establish.

Locke is fully aware, not only that a sense of dependence is the basis
of authority, but that supplying children with "things suitable to their
Wants" (§ 38) is a prerequisite of the discipline of denying their demands.
In fact, assuring children of parental love through supplying their wants
is identified by him as the basis, not of authority itself, but of the reasonableness of that authority (§ 107, p. 210; see also §§ 53, 108, and 115,
p. 224).[51]

## AUTHORITY (§§ 40–42)

Locke shifts from a discussion of self-mastery (§§ 33–39), which in fact
must begin with the habit of submission to others, to an explicit discussion
of parental authority: its establishment and relaxation, the rewards and

punishments by which it operates, and their limitations and supplements (§§ 40–99). This is in part a shift from goal to means. Since the first discussion was devoted primarily to the goal of authority, it tended to describe the means in a way that assimilates them to the goal they eventually give way to. But now Locke sharply distinguishes the subjection of children to parental authority from the liberty of adults. He does this clearly in his general statement on establishment and relaxation of parental authority (§§ 40–42), which precedes his detailed treatment of "the Parts of the Discipline to be used" (§§ 43–99). Children should "perfectly comply with the Will of their Parents" (§ 40); this parental will is no longer described simply as impersonal "Reason." One must "establish the Authority of a Father" as soon as the child "is capable of Submission, and can understand in whose Power he is." Power is one of our "very few primary, and original" ideas.[52] It is the basis of authority. "Fear and Awe ought to give you the first Power over their Minds" (§ 42). Little children "should look upon their Parents as their Lords, their Absolute Governors; and, as such stand in Awe of them" (§ 41). Locke even says that "Liberty and Indulgence can do no Good to *Children*," but it appears later that Locke can here be referring only to *absolute* liberty; or perhaps he makes this remark simply for the sake of contrast and emphasis.

Locke goes on next to argue that parental severity should be relaxed as children "grow up to the Use of Reason" (§ 41). He asserts that this relaxation is proper because "Imperiousness and Severity, is but an ill Way of Treating Men, who have Reason of their own to guide them" (§ 40). But in a remark he appends here, Locke adds another motive besides a recognition of the children's presumably increasing ability to guide themselves rationally: severity ought to be relaxed "unless you have a Mind to make your Children when grown up, weary of you; and secretly to say within themselves, *When will you Die, Father?*" This point is further clarified in the explanation that

> We must look upon our Children, when grown up, to be like our selves; with the same Passions, the same Desires. We would be thought Rational Creatures, and have our Freedom; we love not to be uneasie under constant Rebukes and Brow-beatings; nor can we bear severe Humours, and great Distance in those we converse with. [§ 41]

What is practically decisive is not rationality itself but the common passion or *desire to be thought rational* and to have one's freedom. It is this passion or pretension that makes "Imperiousness and Severity" an "ill Way of Treating Men" and thereby practically justifies freedom and equality. (This suggestion reminds one of the famous proofs of natural mental equality from the fact of universal human pretension to wisdom in the beginning of chapter 13 of Hobbes's *Leviathan* and in the opening of Descartes's *Discourse on Method*.) Just as the factual justification of liberty here turns out to be not rationality itself but the pretension to it, so the goal is not directly the child's proper self-guidance but his being "obedient to you when past a Child" (§ 40), which is swiftly reduced to his being "your affectionate Friend," although no longer "your obedient Subject."[53] This goal, however, is useful not only to the parents; the children will appreciate being thus made "capable to deserve the Favour of their Parents, and the Esteem of every Body else" (§ 41). There is a harmony between the interests of parent and child in this respect; what pleases the parent—the child's not being willful or proud—will please the world and so be useful to the child in gaining general esteem. Of course this harmony assumes that true ability or happiness, the aim of education, lies in, or at least is marked by, general esteem. Again, esteem appears as the operative criterion of virtue (cf. § 32). We should not, however, presume that Locke intends an indiscriminate acceptance of esteem as a standard, for we have already observed his quarrel with common opinion when it comes to identifying the vices (§ 37). Nevertheless, he is far from averse to making use of its effective pressure. Locke's reader must bear in mind the fact that Locke manages both to condemn and to use general esteem. Already in this instance, one can note that, in invoking the support of general esteem, he expects it to operate against pride and the aristocratic expectation that others should fulfill one's demands and in favor of what he later in the work calls civility.

This suggestion of the intimate relationship between virtue and esteem is speedily confirmed. Locke argues that once children are grown, and "past the Rod, and Correction," then "he that is a good, a vertuous and able Man, must be made so within" (§ 42). But this is not the pure "within" of Rousseau. It is true that Locke finds inadequate the motivation that children will "Fear . . . having a scanty Portion if they displease you," (which in *Second Treatise*, § 73, he found to be "no small Tye on the Obedience of Children"); for he notes that "they will be never the less ill and wicked in private; and that Restraint will not last always." In the *Treatise* Locke sought to explain common filial obedience; in the *Thoughts* he attempts to improve on it. Indeed, in a general statement about education in this passage he contrasts the efficacy of fear with that of a truly internal motivation:

> what he is to receive from Education, what is to sway
> and influence his Life, must be something put into him
> betimes; Habits woven into the very Principles of his
> Nature; and not a counterfeit Carriage, and dissembled

Out-side, put on by Fear, only to avoid the present Anger
of a Father, who perhaps may dis-inherit him. [§ 42]

But what is that truly internal motivation? It is "the Love of you" and
"the Love of Vertue and Reputation"; this is the "Hold . . . you have
upon them," the "something put into him." But if reputation is paired
with virtue[54] as the object of this love, one might ask whether there is
any reason to consider it any more "within" and genuine than fear of
disinheritance. Surely, by Rousseau's standards, love of reputation is an
equally external concern. Locke's insistence on autonomy or inwardness
is far less stringent and perhaps more realistic and alive to vital distinctions. In any case, he appears willing to accept concern with reputation
as a most effective motivation for virtue, at least equal to, or mixed with,
love of virtue itself. In contrast to Hobbes, he refuses to accept fear as
the most salutary and rational motive.[55]

The phrase "Habits woven into the very Principles of his Nature," in
the passage quoted above, brings the reader back to the question of
Locke's unwillingness to depend on nature and his tendency to obscure
that unwillingness by employing what seems a flattery of human nature.
The phrase expresses beautifully the practical inseparability of nature
and habit and the vague border between them in the psychology of the
*Thoughts*. As Yolton says, in commenting on this passage, "love, virtue,
and reputation . . . are *acquired* not native motives for action."[56]

## REWARD AND PUNISHMENT (§§ 43–62)

In the next part of the *Thoughts* (§§ 43–62) Locke reconciles early severity
and a "*strict Hand*" with a later and "milder Sort of Government" (§ 43):

A Compliance, and Suppleness of their Wills, being by
a steady Hand introduced by Parents, before Children
have Memories,[57] to retain the Beginnings of it, will seem
natural to them, and work afterwards in them, as if it
were so"; . . . [§ 44]

According to Locke, it is by "*Awe* and *Respect*," by the "Submission, and
ready Obedience of their Minds," and by "*Reverence*," all early established, that children "are for the future to be governed," not by "*Beating,
Chiding*, or other *Servile Punishments*." But we should not forget, even
if the victims of this process are supposed to forget, that this awe orig-
inates in force even if that force is effectuated not by blows but by denying
the children's demands. This recommendation of government by means
of a reverence based on forgotten force, which permits one to govern
without further force, may have a Machiavellian ring. But Machiavelli,
at least in the political context, did not believe that the original force at
the root of authority could ever be safely forgotten, and he therefore

recommended that it be renewed by occasional "extraordinary" acts of terrifying force.[58] Even Locke, in the pedagogical context of the *Thoughts*, indicates (§ 52) that he too is willing to use blows on extraordinary later occasions when it is necessary to maintain the original authority and to subdue willfulness (§§ 78–79 and 83–84). But for the most part fear is to be forgotten and operate as habit, without memory or reflection. Similarly, on the political level one could say that Locke's treatment of the state of nature is based on a belief that the terrible beginnings of government, though they must occasionally be remembered, can be forgotten, for most purposes, more safely than Machiavelli or Hobbes thought.[59]

Locke insists equally on the original severity and the subsequent and consequently possible relaxation. We already know that severity is important for establishing obedience and reverence and so providing the child with a "Mastery over his Inclinations" (§ 45), but the character and value of that mastery are now clarified. Locke warns: "he that knows not how to *resist* the Importunity of *present Pleasure or Pain,* for the sake of what Reason tells him is fit to be done, wants the true Principle of Vertue and Industry" (§ 45). We wondered above what sort of thing it is that reason tells one is fit to be done; the phrase *"present Pleasure or Pain"* provides a suggestion: reason may dictate the pursuit of *future* pleasure and the avoidance of *future* pain and therefore require the ability to resist the importunity of present pleasure or pain.[60] The rhetoric of the opposition of reason to desire may clothe a subordination of present desires to future ones.[61] The value of this ability to resist desire is clarified by the new pairing of virtue with industry as the ends that resistance is to serve.[62] As a reader of the chapter on property in the *Second Treatise* might suppose, industry is an essential component of Lockean virtue. It is what provides the goods from which future pleasures can be derived and by which future pains can be avoided, just as it requires foregoing present pleasures and submitting to present pains. At the same time, it does not differ entirely from justice—traditionally presented as the essential constituent of virtue, from Plato's *Republic* through Aristotle's *Ethics* and Cicero's *Offices* to Hobbes's *Leviathan*— since it contributes to the prosperity of others without injuring them.[63] Locke's earlier remark (§ 35), that willfulness comes from a corruption of the principles of nature, with its implication that those principles support moderation, is qualified by this passage; for here Locke calls the habit of self-control "so contrary to unguided Nature."

We saw that Locke insists equally on initial severity and on its subsequent relaxation, and we can see now that he insists on them both for largely the same reason. The relaxation is dictated not simply by a humane revulsion against commonly indulged parental or tutorial brutality. As usual, Locke's characteristic humanity[64] rests also on hardheaded

97

reasoning: children must not have their spirits broken lest "they lose all their Vigor and Industry" (§ 46), for men who lack these are "in a worse State" than the willful, who may be curable and even seem to have special capacity for greatness.[65] Gentleness, too, serves industry. Industry requires control over desire, but it also requires desire itself. What is needed is not only native desire but "Spirit," by which Locke apparently means a sort of confidence or expectation that one can fulfill one's desires, though not an imperious demand that others shall fulfill them.[66] Desire, as the spur to industry, is necessary to happiness. As Locke warns later (§ 126), "For where there is no Desire, there will be no Industry."[67] Neither the willful nor the "low Spirits," neither tyrants nor slaves, but free men are to be produced by a Lockean education and belong in a Lockean polity. The avoidance of both extremes, "the *Sylla* and *Charybdis*" (§ 47) of education, is "the great Art" and "the true Secret of Education" (§ 46). The best way to get men to do what is wanted—let us say, to be useful to each other[68]—is not to terrify or force them but, in the language of our contemporary popular psychology and pedagogy, to "motivate" them, to arouse and then rely on their desires, while letting them think, not without justice, that they are acting for their own sakes and of their own free will (see §§ 72–76).

Locke now proceeds to elaborate his argument against continued reliance on corporal punishment (§§ 47–51). Such reliance risks *both* of two dangerous extremes (§ 47); not only, as is obvious, can it break the spirit (§ 51), but it does not contribute at all to the

> Mastery of our Natural Propensity to indulge Corporal
> and present Pleasure, and to avoid Pain at any rate; but
> rather encourages it; and thereby strengthens that in us,
> which is the Root from whence spring all Vitious Actions,
> and the Irregularities of Life. [§ 48]

For he who succumbs to "Fear of *whiping*" and therefore does what is wanted of him "in this only preferrs the greater *Corporal Pleasure,* or avoids the greater *Corporal Pain*" (§ 48). The adjectives modifying pleasure and pain (cf. § 45) also indicate a way in which the earlier general statements about the submission of desire to reason may be understood: only the propensity to indulge *corporal* and *present* pleasure and pain must be mastered, for it is this propensity that is the root of all evil. Indeed, it may be "Reason," precisely as the pursuit of other pleasures and the avoidance of other pain, that requires this mastery. One can now add that the rationally pursued pleasure and avoided pain are not only future (cf. § 45) but are also in some sense not corporal. There is an ambiguity about this category-by-elimination, the noncorporeal; it may refer to the spiritual pleasures and pains promised by Christian revelation,[69] or to intellectual pleasures and pains,[70] or to those associated with honor,[71] or even merely to the anticipation of bodily pains and pleasures.[72] An emphasis on honor, or appreciation of esteem, is apparent in Locke's remark here that no "Correction [is] useful to a Child, where the Shame of Suffering for having done Amiss, does not work more upon him, than the Pain" (§ 48). Though this remark does not mean that the sense of shame is the content of virtue or the final aim of education, it shows that, for Locke, it is the great method or instrument of government and education.[73]

Not only does corporal punishment rely on and strengthen the general propensity to give in to present pleasure and pain (§§ 48 and 52), but it even strengthens the particular desires that it seeks to suppress. It does this by what Locke calls a "Principle of Aversion" (§ 128), by which one dislikes what one is forced to and, as a corollary, likes what one is forced away from (§§ 49–50; see also §§ 124–29 and 149–50). This principle is an instance of the "Association of Ideas."[74] As Locke states here:

> Offensive Circumstances ordinarily infect innocent
> things, which they are joined with: And the very sight
> of a Cup, wherein any one uses to take nauseous Physick,
> turns his Stomach. [§ 49]

This principle seems especially related to human willfulness or the desire "to be Masters of themselves and others" (§ 35) or to "be thought Rational Creatures, and have our Freedom" (§ 41). There is a suggestion here of the notion that men are naturally indifferent to the objects of most of their desires,[75] at least compared to their overriding desire to have their own way. The manner in which one teaches is therefore more decisive than the content of one's teaching. One should not, however, confuse Locke's principle of aversion with the view that has led to aversion therapy on the model of conditioning the responses of dogs and rats, for he claims that, when one is dealing with the peculiarly willful human species, such punishments produce effects that are the opposite of what one intended.[76] That is to say, according to Locke the principle of association of ideas leads one to associate the unpleasant sensation of being beaten not with eating the forbidden fruit, for which one is beaten (§ 48), but with the abstinence from it that the beating enforces.

Since Locke opposes a continued reliance on corporal punishment, on the ground that it depends on the dangerous motive of "sensual Pleasure and Pain" (§ 48), he also rejects the use of rewards that cater directly to that motive (§§ 52–53). He repeats his earlier view that virtue requires the submission of appetite to reason (§ 52) and he particularly inveighs against luxury, pride, and covetousness.[77] Nevertheless, he concedes in the next section (§ 53) that children should be provided with all "the Conveniencies or Pleasures of Life, that are not injurious to their Health or Vertue." This is surely more in keeping with the Locke in whose thought a hedonist element has been observed[78] and, as I have already remarked, his argument is not ascetic. His kindly concession here indicates that what one should "subdue and stifle" is not, as it might seem in the section in which those words occur (§ 52), the "Love of Pleasure" itself but the "dangerous Propensity" to indulge that love apart from what "Reason advises" and "Duty requires." Nevertheless, it is important to note that Locke urges parents not to accustom a child "to place his Happiness" in money, the pleasures of the palate, or "a *Lace-Cravat.*" Locke is, at any rate, no vulgar hedonist.

This concession that Locke makes to pleasure is, however, limited by an important provision:

> that they have those Enjoyments, only as the Consequences of the State of Esteem and Acceptation they are in with their Parents and Governors; but they should *never* be offer'd or bestow'd on them, as the *Rewards of this or that particular Performance* that they shew an Aversion to. [§ 53]

Since Locke will proceed to recommend the use of praise and blame as proper rewards and punishments (§§ 56–63), one should remark that there is a fine line between use of sensual pleasures and pains as direct rewards and punishments, on the one hand, and their employment as the consequences of rewards and punishments meted out in praise and blame, on the other.[79] Nevertheless, though the line may be fine, the distinction is not insignificant for the spirit of Lockean education and morality. Industriousness may be motivated more by the desire for esteem, which both flows from and in turn provides material benefits, than by desires for those benefits themselves, as any alert inhabitant of bourgeois society may observe.[80]

Locke now proceeds to recommend the use of praise and blame as the proper instruments of government in education (§§ 56–63). Reward and punishment there must be, for,

> Remove Hope and Fear, and there is an end of all Discipline. I grant, that Good and Evil, *Reward* and *Punishment,* are the only Motives to a rational Creature: these are the Spur and Reins, whereby all Mankind are set on work, and guided, and therefore they are to be made use of to Children too. For I advise their Parents and Governors always to carry this in their Minds, that Children are to be treated as rational Creatures. [§ 54][81]

The subtle, progressive unfolding of the meaning of rationality in the *Thoughts* has reached a new stage. The implicit definition of rationality is that perhaps best known from modern economic theory: acting only from a calculation of reward and punishment. Therefore, to motivate someone by threats and promises, if not of beatings and "Sugar-plumbs" (§ 52) at least of esteem and disapproval, is to treat him as a rational being. This explains why Locke rejects revenge (§ 37), for example, as unworthy of a rational creature; for revenge is exacted not to gain a future reward but to avenge a past wrong.[82] This understanding of rationality should be kept in mind when one is considering Lockean statements, in the *Thoughts* and elsewhere, that refer in a formal way to reason or rationality, such as the phrase that occurs at the beginning of Locke's treatment of the education of the mind: "what may be suitable to the Dignity and Excellency of a rational Creature" (§ 31).[83]

The rewards and punishments that Locke recommends are esteem and disgrace, not only because they are "the most powerful Incentives to the Mind, when once it is brought to relish them," but also because they form "the true Principle, which will constantly work, and incline [children] to the right" (§ 56). Given Locke's disapproval of custom (as it actually is rather than as a potential method to be employed in behalf of his goals [§ 37]), one might expect him to offer some defense of the truth as well as the efficacy of the principle of esteem and disgrace. Instead he turns to a different hypothetical objection to it, one that seems to grant its truth. This objection asks how this principle can be "put into" children. For like the habit of restraint (and unlike willfulness and the concern with sensual pleasures),[84] a concern for esteem and disgrace does not seem to be natural or innate. Esteem and disgrace are "most powerful Incentives" *only* when the mind "is brought to relish them." Therefore, if one says that it is necessary to "*get into* Children a Love of Credit, and an Apprehension of Shame and Disgrace" (emphasis added), and not merely to count on it, one must answer those who ask how this is possible. Locke admits that to instill this principle appears difficult at first; he calls it "the great Secret of Education." This is not the first matter to be so denominated (cf. § 46, where, to be precise, Locke speaks of "the true Secret of Education"). The first "secret" lay in reconciling "these seeming Contradictions," i.e., making children both masters of their inclinations and "easy, active and free." It is reasonable to assume that the two "secrets" are one and the same: that establishing a love of esteem is the way to reconcile self-control with desire and vigorous activity. For a love of esteem, or credit, can spur activity and industry as well as restrain the inclinations that might interfere with its fulfillment, both the inclinations that distract from the activities necessary to gain credit and those that may actually lead to disgrace.

There is a further question, however. Does a love of esteem tend to suppress or to exacerbate the desire for mastery over others? This question poses a great problem for what might be considered Locke's modification of Hobbes: his substituting sensitivity to reputation for the Hobbesian fear of violent death as the salutary motive intended to tame the lust for domination in favor of the rational and industrious against the proud or lazy and quarrelsome.

In reply to the hypothetical question and to explain the great secret, Locke appears to argue first that a sensibility to praise and blame does not need to be "put in"; it is apparently, if not innate, at least natural. In order to assure devotées of the rod that there is a ready alternative, he says that children are sensible of praise "earlier perhaps than we think," though not, of course, immediately (§ 57). Consistent praise and blame for good and bad behavior will work "of it self." The only indication that Locke gives here that this sensibility may be in any way derivative is in the last phrase of the statement that children "find a Pleasure in being esteemed, and valued, especially by their Parents, and those whom they depend on." This suggests that concern for the esteem of others stems from a dependence on them or, more precisely, from recognition of that dependence.[85]

Locke does not rely entirely on the supposedly spontaneous development of sensitivity to praise and blame. He urges that "To make the Sense of *Esteem* or *Disgrace* sink the deeper, and be of the more Weight, other *agreeable or disagreeable Things should constantly accompany these different States*" (§ 58). These other agreeable or disagreeable things appear to be the very things whose use as rewards and punishments he earlier condemned, namely, sensual pleasures and pains (§§ 44–55). But he makes the same distinction here as he made there (§ 53): he rejects the *direct* use of these things as the rewards and punishments of particular actions; he recommends their use as the *consequences* of esteem or disgrace. There is something artificial in denying that sensual pleasures and pains are not the rewards and punishments, as well as the indirect consequences, of particular approved and disapproved actions, and there is something equally artificial, if not actually deceitful, in arranging that "Children may as much as possible be brought to conceive, that those that are commended, and in Esteem for doing well, will necessarily be beloved and cherished by every Body, and have all other good Things as a Consequence of it" while, conversely, he who is in disgrace will lack "what ever might satisfy or delight him." Locke cannot affirm that this correlation holds true in the world outside the carefully constructed environment he urges his readers to provide for their children.[86] The very elements of overstatement in the words "necessarily," "by every Body," and "all other good Things" are an indication of the falsity of the conception that children are to be brought to believe in. Yet it is precisely this exaggerated element, this "necessity," that serves to distinguish the proper use of material rewards and punishments from their corrupting use. Not only does the "necessary" connection between material goods and esteem strengthen and deepen the sense of esteem or disgrace; it may also serve to ennoble, or at least to render safer and more civil, the irrepressible concern with material pleasures and pains by mediating it through esteem.

I. A. Snook understands this element of necessity to mean that children are not even to know what particular actions of theirs lead to gains or losses in esteem.[87] This interpretation is baseless and severs not only the intimate relation between conduct and material rewards and punishments, which Locke intends to sever, but also the relation between conduct and esteem and disgrace, which Locke is concerned to establish. Locke certainly recommends that rewards of praise and punishments of blame be meted out for particular acts: parents should *"caress and commend them, when they do well; shew a cold and neglectful Countenance to them upon doing ill"* (§ 57; see also §§ 59, 60, and 62 and examples of similar rewards or punishments for particular acts in §§ 109, 110, 115 [pp. 223–25], 118, 119, and 131). The *direct* rewards and punishments consist in "a Look or a Word" (§ 63).[88] Material rewards or deprivations (*"agreeable or disagreeable Things,"* § 58) should be only *indirectly* tied to particular actions, since they should appear as "consequences" of the children's general condition of esteem or disgrace. In one instance (§ 107) Locke recommends that the material reward should come at "another time . . . as if it were a natural consequence of their Good-Behaviour, and not a Bargain about it." However, since that instance is precisely that of rewarding children for "contenting themselves now in the want of what they wish'd for," the requirement that the reward come later is both obvious and exceptional. In his most explicit statement on the subject, Locke says that material rewards are not to be offered beforehand as a temptation or bargain (§ 53). Sterling P. Lamprecht understands Locke's argument to be that parents should eschew the use of material rewards and punishments because "such pleasures and pains are not the accustomed consequences of actions in ordinary living, and hence are not effective in establishing habits which may be permanent."[89] Locke, however, as we have seen, directs that children be taught the opposite. Lamprecht may yet be right in thinking that the falsity of that teaching is precisely the reason for Locke's concern not to use material rewards and punishments directly (he does not mention Locke's indirect use of them). The point, however, is that such rewards are, all too often, the accustomed consequences not of *virtuous* actions in ordinary living but of vicious ones (see, e.g., §§ 52 and 37).

Socrates, despite his own ten-thousandfold poverty, jocularly claimed that money and all the other good things come from virtue.[90] Since Locke asserts that esteem is the true principle that constantly inclines to the right (§ 56) and that children are to learn that "all other good Things" are consequent on esteem (§ 58), one can say that he teaches that all good things come from virtue by way of esteem. Esteem comes to be valued at least in part, and perhaps decisively, for the sake of the good things that flow from it. But that is so only originally; for "by these Means you can come once to shame them out of their Faults . . . and make them in Love with the Pleasure of being well thought on" (§ 58). It appears that the love of esteem is inculcated by carefully arranged side effects (a process that later is, as it were, forgotten) *and* that it then comes by habit to be valued in itself.[91] This is not the only time, in Locke's teaching, that something that originally is pursued only as a means to an end comes to be pursued as if it were an end.[92]

Insofar as virtue is understood as industry, it need not be its own reward, for it provides the fruits of industry. Civility and justice are similarly best taught by reward (§§ 109–10). Virtue stands in need of assistance more efficacious than it is in itself: "In this way the Objects of their Desires are made assisting to Vertue" (§ 58). This argument reminds one of Locke's claim, in the *Reasonableness of Christianity*, that the ancient philosophers' arguments from "the excellency of virtue" and "the exalting of human nature, whose perfection lay in virtue," were "airy commendations" that "showed the beauty of virtue" but left her "unendowed," so that it was still necessary to make her "the most enriching purchase, and by much the best bargain." It was necessary to find "another relish and efficacy to persuade men" and "something solid and powerful to move them."[93] Of course, the "something" found there was the Christian promise of eternal life and bliss and the threat of damnation. But this may have been necessary only because virtue then dictated, or was thought to dictate, rules "which appeared so little to consist of their [mankind's] chief end, happiness, while they kept them from the enjoyments of this life," that "Virtue and prosperity [did] not often accompany one another."[94] In this passage in the *Thoughts* (§ 58) Locke's remedy for the inefficacy of unassisted virtue is not the Christian one he describes in the *Reasonableness;* here he is apparently attempting to make virtue consistent with happiness—compatible with the enjoyments of this life and accompanied by prosperity. For indeed, Locke did not always adhere to the assessment quoted from the *Reasonableness of Christianity.* His notion of virtue permitted him at times to say not only that virtue and industry are "as constant companions" as vice and idleness but also that "virtue and honesty always thrive, though perhaps but slowly."[95]

The notion that, by making children in love with the pleasure of being well thought of, "you may turn them as you please" (§ 58) may, like several other phrases in the *Thoughts* that have a manipulative ring to them, suggest to twentieth-century readers the frightening possibilities opened up by Lockean psychology, with its tabula rasa notion of human malleability and the suggestion that artful or scientific uses may be made of it. Before and apart from any Kantian criticism of empiricism, Locke's statement that by parental arrangement "a settled Experience from the beginning teaches Children, that the Things they delight in belong to, and are to be enjoyed by those only, who are in a State of Reputation" indicates that experience, which plays such a decisive role in the *Essay* as well as in the *Thoughts,* can be a human construction rather than a gift of nature. The difference between the results of human contrivance and the products of nature is obscured here, however, by Locke's statement that an orchestrated disapproval by parents and servants (§ 59) causes children to "come to have a natural Abhorrence for that, which they found, made them slighted and neglected by every Body." It may be argued, however, that while the choice of the particular objects of abhorrence is contrived, the basic abhorrence of whatever leads to disgrace is natural. But Locke does not make that argument here, and he has already suggested that the abhorrence itself is inculcated by use of the truly natural (§§ 48 and 50) love of sensual pleasure (§ 58), from which the abhorrence is derived. Even the words used here, "slighted and neglected by every Body," may refer not to the disgrace alone but to the incidental deprivation of "all other good Things," which may lie at the root of the "natural Abhorrence."[96]

Nevertheless, Locke writes that when whipped, for instance, children may have "the Sense that they have done amiss, and the Apprehension that they have drawn on themselves the just Displeasure of their best Friends" (§ 60). The terms "amiss" and "just" seem to suggest an independent moral sensibility. The notion of a "just" displeasure would seem to be an addition to the bare notion of displeasure, or, more generally, of punishment, and not in any way derivative from it. But no ground is indicated here on the basis of which the child is to see his friends' displeasure as *just.* One could infer that for Locke the notion of justice gains its meaning within the framework of reward and punishment, particularly when the latter take the form of praise and blame.[97] Hedonist empiricist psychology has a hard time when it attempts to produce a consistent account of our moral sentiments. This may account for such interpretations as Snook's, that pleasure cannot be the criterion of virtue because "Locke felt, as we feel . . . that a life lived in accordance with this principle is a prudent rather than a moral life."[98] Locke himself sometimes distinguishes between prudence and morality, but the end pursued by both is happiness, and he regarded "the happiness that all Men so steadily pursue [as] consisting in pleasure" (§ 143).[99]

Although Locke writes here that "Ingenuous *Shame,* and the Apprehension of Displeasure [no longer restricted to "just" displeasure], are the only true Restraint" (§ 60), and though he earlier called them "the true Principle, which will constantly work, and incline [children] to the right" (§ 56), in the next section (§ 61) he parenthetically acknowledges another moral basis:

105

> ... though [reputation] be not the true Principle and
> Measure of Vertue, (for that is the Knowledge of a Man's
> Duty, and the Satisfaction it is to obey his Maker, in
> following the Dictates of that Light God has given him,
> with the Hopes of Acceptation and Reward) yet it is that,
> which comes nearest to it: And being the Testimony and
> Applause that other People's Reason, as it were by a
> common Consent, gives to vertuous and well-ordered
> Actions, it is the proper Guide and Encouragement of
> Children, till they grow able to judge for themselves,
> and to find what is right by their own Reason.

According to this passage, reputation is the proper provisional standard for children, while adults are to be guided by their own reason. To make this view consistent with the reference to shame as the true principle (§ 56), one could interpret the broadly stated earlier passage as intended to apply only to children. But there are several difficulties with this view of the present passage. One might say that the "Satisfaction" that constitutes the adult standard lies simply in obedience to God or in obedience to the dictates of reason (the "Light"). But the better reading, especially in view of Locke's teaching that reward and punishment are the only motives of a rational creature, is that this satisfaction lies in proceeding "with the Hopes of Acceptation and Reward." Given the mention of man's Maker and the reference to reason as the gift of God, the acceptation and reward seem to be those provided by God in the next life. This would not be the only passage of Locke's suggesting that reason finds the obligation of morality to lie in the prospect of divine reward and punishment.[100] This passage, by speaking of virtue as following the dictates of reason, seems to require that the reward of virtue be known by reason.[101] But according to Locke, unassisted reason knows nothing either of divine reward and punishment or of the next life.[102] When Locke writes here merely of the "Hopes" of acceptation and reward, he may be acknowledging that such acceptation and reward are not known with certainty by unassisted reason. But the impression this passage is likely to convey is that one who *hopes* personally to gain that reward does so with certain knowledge of its existence. It may be, however, that Locke deliberately left unspecified the "acceptation" and reward mentioned here, in order to leave open the possibility that the rewards of virtue are worldly rather than the otherworldly ones promised in Christian revelation. Then, however, the distinction he makes here between reputation and the true principle would seem less radical.

If it is difficult to say that these hopes of acceptation and reward are attested by one's "own Reason," it is even more difficult to call reputation the testimony of "other People's Reason," given Locke's assertion that reason speaks against "the Publick Testimony" (§ 37). This difficulty is heightened here when Locke shifts from the parental esteem he had suggested previously (§§ 57–60) to reputation in general—i.e., to the applause of other people and even "common Consent."[103] This shift is necessary because in the next section (§ 62) Locke tells parents how, by praising them publicly and blaming them privately, they are to attach their children to "the good Opinion of others." This heightens the difficulty, because parents, in praising and blaming their children, are likely to express a concern for them beyond any concern that the public would have for a particular individual, and these parents, after all, may even be entitled, as readers of Locke, to a special presumption of rationality or freedom from custom (see § 216). This peculiar bestowal of the rank of reason on the reputation that serves as the basis of the child's provisional morality may stimulate one to ask whether all children are truly to become "able to judge for themselves, and to find what is right by their own Reason." Locke, who claimed that he was unable to write a demonstrative morality,[104] could hardly have expected all or most men "to find what is right by their own Reason" alone, though he may have thought it possible that they were "able" to do so.[105] A few men need no assistance even from the cradle (§ 1); others may need it far beyond.

## PUNISHMENT: ITS LIMITS, ALTERNATIVES, AND ADMINISTRATION (§§ 63–87)

The next part of the *Thoughts* (§§ 63–87) alternates between considerations of the limitations on, the alternatives to, and the administration of "the common Rewards and Punishments" (§ 63). Locke first of all exempts from punishment all "innocent Folly, Playing, and *Childish Actions*" (§ 63; this applies even when such activity results in "considerable Damage," § 116). In this realm the children are to be given their liberty not because they are employing it rationally but because their playfulness is "wisely adapted by Nature to their Age and Temper." Playfulness serves not only to improve their strength and health but "to keep up their Spirits," which would be spoiled if they were punished for innocent follies (cf. § 46).

Locke's second restriction on punishment emerges in his injunction to parents not to overburden their children with rules, which he admits runs contrary to "the ordinary Method of Education" (§ 64). One should not teach by "*Rules* and Precepts," which depend on thought, but by practice, which depends on habit.[106] Here again the line between nature and nurture is erased: "by repeating the same Action, till it be grown habitual in them, the Performance will not depend on Memory or Reflection, the Concomitant of Prudence and Age, and not of Childhood; but will be natural in them." Similarly, Locke says here that an action can become "by constant Use as natural to a well-bred Man, as breathing;

it requires no Thought, no Reflection." Like the dependence on repu- tation, the dependence on habit seems at first to be merely provisional, awaiting the coming of prudence and age. But the example Locke gives is that of a well-bred *man*. Similarly, he says that through habit children can be cured *forever* of their faults. It may therefore be the reader's first impression, not the recommended dependence, that proves to be provisional.

The attack on rules and precepts in the *Thoughts* is one of the clearest links between it and the *Essay*.[107] The practical effect of the doctrine of innate ideas, which Locke attacks in the *Essay,* is to protect the inculcation of supposedly innate maxims and opinions that are often, in fact, mere prejudices.[108] The doctrine leads to the view that the imposition of pre- cepts is sufficient because children already know them or at least are innately disposed to accept them. Its adherents are therefore overwilling to punish for the supposedly willful violations of these known precepts. This link is contrary to the claim of Yolton that "the effects of his [Locke's] general philosophy upon his *Education* are slight."[109] Yolton thinks that the pedagogical effect of innatism is to "make the teaching of religion and morals redundant."[110] Despite Yolton's expertise on innatism,[111] Locke's view of the matter is better expressed by de Bartolomeis, who says that "innatism is denounced [by Locke] as the fruit of an education founded on authority and superstition."[112]

The method of rules and precepts and its innatist basis, which Locke rejects, might at least have held out the reassurance that the rules that memory will retain or that reflection will support tend somehow to be in harmony with human nature. But, according to Locke, men can be taught almost anything by custom and habit. In deploring the fact that the method of habituation is "so much neglected," Locke parenthetically wonders if "ill Customs" are to "be wonder'd at in any thing" (§ 66, p. 159). If that is so, it is hard to assume that the customs the pupils are to be accustomed to are other than ill. The method of habituation must serve peculiarly Lockean aims, for otherwise it will serve only the better to engraft the ill customs of the world, unless the world is changed to permit or encourage good education. This last possibility suggests an interdependence between the projects of the *Thoughts* and the *Two Treatises*.

For Locke, another advantage of teaching by habit rather than by precept, besides its superior effectiveness, is that it permits paying more attention to "the Child's natural Genius and Constitution" (§ 66, p. 159). This respect for individuality on the part of the philosopher of liberty has been much noted, especially as presaging later theories of education. This respect does pave the way for later developments, but there is still an enormous distance between this Lockean attitude and worshipful rapture over the supposed individuality and creativity of children. Locke bows realistically to necessity; while recognizing that the possibilities of transforming temperament are limited, he does not reject the desirability of attempts at transformation or improvement. He simply warns that "We must not hope *wholly* to change their Original Tempers . . . without spoiling them" (§ 66, p. 159; my emphasis). He asserts that "God has stampt certain Characters upon Men's Minds," but he is not overcome by reverence for the divine handiwork, for, while it "can hardly be totally alter'd, and transform'd into the contrary," it "may perhaps be a little mended."[113] One studies a child's nature not merely to adjust to it but to see "how it may be improved." Human "Industry" (§ 66, p. 159) is to be applied to the improvement even of human nature, at least in its individual forms. At the same time, one should not fail to observe how far Locke is from the other allegedly Lockean extreme of asserting a total human malleability and equality, which emerged in Helvétius and Condillac and continues into our own time. The tabula rasa applies absolutely only to knowledge, not to abilities, temperaments, or desires.[114] As always, Locke is sensible.

Locke's concession to the individual's nature is also a part of his effort to appeal to the passions of individuals, to make the objects of their desires "assisting to virtue" (§ 58). If one is to depend on men's desires (as well as on habit) to motivate them, rather than on fear or autonomous reason, then one must make some accommodation to the natures of individuals and to the particular objects they desire, though the most effectual desires are common enough.

This point highlights the peculiar combination that constitutes Locke's attitude toward nature. Though he finds that much less is natural than is generally thought to be, he realistically accepts what is. He is unwilling to rely on nature to provide the highest things but is willing to accept it as a low yet effective basis. One should not, therefore, depend on natural rationality or benevolence but should prudently accommodate natural desire and willfulness.

The admonition "to make the best of what Nature has given" leads reasonably enough to an attack on affectation, the result of vainly attempting a total transformation. Affectation is of peculiar importance, being not "the Product of untaught Nature" but "the proper Fault of Education" (§ 66, p. 160). As such, it might be said to be the special target of the *Thoughts Concerning Education*. Affectation "has always the Laudable Aim of Pleasing, though it always misses it." Given that esteem is "the true Principle, which will constantly work, and incline them to the right" (§ 56), even if it is not "the true Principle and Measure of Vertue" but only that "which comes nearest to it" (§ 61), it is not surprising that the aim of pleasing is laudable. We also learn here something of the particular character dictated by this aim:

> We cannot but be pleased with an Humane, Friendly,
> civil Temper, wherever we meet with it. A Mind free,
> and Master of it self and all its Actions, not low and
> narrow, not haughty and insolent, not blemished with
> any great Defect, is what every one is taken with.

Locke beautifully expresses how this pleasing character expresses itself:
"All those little Expressions of Civility and Respect, which Nature or
Custom has established in Conversation" constitute, when performed
with ease, "that Beauty, which shines through some Men's Actions, sets
off all that they do, and takes all they come near."

Affectation, on the other hand, is said to lack "the Beauty that Ac-
companies what is Natural." But, like some other Lockean references to
nature or to what is natural, this one may be somewhat misleading. It
may seem to mean that in affectation actions are performed by artifice
that should properly be performed by nature. Affectation is unnatural
and displeasing, for it presents "a Disagreement between the outward
Action, and the Mind within," while "Gracefulness . . . arises from that
Natural Coherence, which appears between the Thing done, and such
a Temper of Mind, as cannot but be approved of, as suitable to the
Occasion." Gracefulness differs from affectation not because its outward
actions are strictly natural expressions of what is naturally within. Though
its actions are indeed "easy and unconstrain'd," they are said to be "natural Emanations from the Spirit and Disposition within" only "as it were."
They are achieved only when men "by a constant Practice" have made
them "so easy to themselves, that they seem not Artificial or Studied,
but naturally to flow from a Sweetness of Mind, and a well turn'd Disposition." Locke also leaves it undetermined whether "Nature or Custom
has established in Conversation" these expressions. Gracefulness is an
apparent though artificial naturalness, "an habitual and becoming Easiness." Locke cooperates gracefully with this illusion by lending it the
mantle of the vocabulary of naturalness. Gracefulness is natural only in
the sense that it does not depend on memory or reflection (cf. § 64), and
is therefore above suspicion of being deliberately deceptive, since deliberate deception requires reflection. If true gracefulness springs from a
congruence between the outward action and the mind within, it is less
because both are strictly natural than because both are habitual and
therefore "free" and "easy," not "awkward and forced."

Not only does Locke praise the sincerity of a graceful congruence
between outward expressions of civility and a civil temper within, but
he even praises "Plain and rough Nature left to it self" as being, if second
best, still "much better than an Artificial Ungracefulness" (§ 66, p. 161).
Although he gives this degree of preference to plain and rough nature,
he does not by any means, like others in a later epoch, assign it to the

highest rank. He surely did not share the Rousseauian view of the goodness of nature, and the education he designed was therefore not negative but decidedly and openly formative. Nevertheless, his argument against affectation has some relation to later attacks on inauthenticity and hypocrisy. This relation lies in the argument's direct connection to his immediately preceding and frequently repeated attack on teaching by precept (§§ 64–66). For Locke adds at the end of his discussion of affectation that it "has often its rise" in the mistaken method of teaching by precept instead of by practice and habit (§ 66, p. 161). Traditional education teaches precepts that their addressees are often incapable of performing or of performing sincerely.

The requirement of practice means that we must aim at what is practicable and even at what is frequently practicable. It is better to practice a lower but practicable action than to remember but transgress a loftier but less practicable rule. We are better off with some "want of an Accomplishment, or some Defect in our Behaviour" than in affectation of "the utmost Gracefulness." Locke's requirement of practice therefore affects not only the number of rules, as he points out (§ 65), but also their content. There is also a peculiar difficulty in practicing prohibitions, the characteristic thou-shalt-nots of scriptural morality, and Locke recommends against issuing prohibitions until and unless the behavior they forbid has already appeared (§§ 85, 89, and 128). It might be remarked that God did not follow this rule of Lockean pedagogy in educating the first man and woman.[115]

The attack on precepts is reminiscent of the moral realism in the political sphere of Machiavelli, Bacon, and Hobbes. The old education has told men to follow rules and examples that are ill suited to any but the most extraordinary natures; in the effort to follow them, men fail or fall into insincerity or worse (cf. § 65). Men should do what is "easy and natural" to them or what can be made so by practice. Transgressions should be treated rather as forgetfulness than as willful wrongdoing (§ 66, p. 158), though it would seem that, insofar as the role of memory is successfully minimized, they are not even that but mere failure of habit.

Despite the importance of a pleasing manner, civility in the mind is more important and can act as its source. This is not because of a general sufficiency of every internal temper to produce a corresponding external mien, for mental civility, in particular, has a peculiar ability to do so, though even it requires the assistance of external practice. Mental civility can "of it self teach those ways of Expressing it, which [the child] observes [to be] most acceptable" (§ 67), because it consists chiefly in a concern for others' esteem. It seems to be equated with "a Veneration for [the child's] Parents and Teachers, which consists in Love and Esteem, and a fear to offend them" and, most especially, "*Respect and good Will* to all

111

people" (§ 67). Such sentiments are said here to become habitual by means of esteem and sensual pleasure, which is the source of the concern with esteem: "Be sure to keep up in him the Principles of good Nature and Kindness; make them as habitual as you can, by Credit and Commendation, and the good Things accompanying that State." Similarly, the child is to be made in love with the company of his parents by receiving all his "good things there, and from their hands" (§ 69).

The same views that lead Locke to recommend habituation and the use of esteem as the most effective educational methods also lead him to recognize the importance of example and the influence of company as alternatives to punishment, for they too establish habits and play on the sensitivity to esteem (§§ 67–71). "Children (nay, and Men too) do most by Example. We are all a sort of Camelions, that still take a Tincture from things near us" (§ 67). This view in turn leads to the recommendation for which Locke is probably most famous in the history of education, his preference for a "Privater Education" (§ 70, p. 166) rather than one obtained in schools. One of the advantages he concedes to schools is worth noting as exemplifying both a means and an end of Lockean pedagogy: "the emulation of Schoolfellows, often puts Life and Industry into young Lads" (§ 70, p. 165). However, the innocence and modesty bred at home are "nearer of Kin, and more in the way of those qualities which make an Useful and Able Man"—one who is skilled in "living well, and managing, as a Man should do, his Affairs in the World"—than is "that malapertness, tricking, or violence learnt amongst Schoolboys." In fact, Locke, in rejecting the schoolboy code of manliness, goes so far as to recommend that boys be brought up in the "Retirement and Bashfulness" that girls customarily are raised in (§ 70, p. 166).[116] Just as girls should approximate their brothers' hardiness (§ 9), boys should approximate their sisters' modesty. Locke's moral education reduces sexual differentiation. Instead of being inherently valuable or noble, whatever manliness is necessary to a young man is so "chiefly as a fence to his Vertue when he goes into the World under his own Conduct" (§ 70, p. 167). Locke argues that the manly qualities gained at schools are not, as some fathers think, the way to court fortune and to become thriving men; a father should rather lay "the Foundation of his Son's Fortune in Vertue, and good Breeding" (§ 70, p. 169). For this purpose one does not need cheating, roughness, or schoolboys' "well laid Plots of Robbing an Orchard together" but "the Principles of Justice, Generosity and Sobriety, joyn'd with Observation and Industry."[117] Honesty is the best policy. Lockean education requires the success of Lockean politics or the arrangement of society so that sober, honest industry, not violence, cheating, or insolence, is actually rewarded with fortune and prosperity.

112

Locke sums up this argument thus: " 'Tis Vertue then, direct Vertue, which is the hard and valuable part to be aimed at in Education" (§ 70, p. 170). Virtue is

> the solid and substantial good, which . . . the Labour, and Art of Education should furnish the Mind with, and fasten there, and never cease till the young Man had a true relish of it, and placed his Strength, his Glory, and his Pleasure in it.

This does not mean that virtue is a complete substitute for these other goods of strength, glory, and pleasure; it is understood as the means that leads to them and protects them, just as they must be used to create attachment to it. Locke's argument for keeping the child at home rather than sending him to school concludes, in keeping with what Dunn calls "the egregiously pervasive commercialism of his metaphors,"[118] that it is "the worst sort of good Husbandry, for a Father not to strain himself a little for his Son's Breeding; which let his Condition be what it will, is the best Portion he can leave him" (§ 70, p. 171; see also §§ 15, 90). The commercialism is not, in this instance, only metaphorical, since Locke's argument is not simply that one should sacrifice one's son's fortune to his breeding but that one should lay "the Foundation of [one's] Son's Fortune in Vertue, and good Breeding" rather than in an inheritance.

The influence of example and the importance of employing it rather than punishment as an instrument of government are so great that they require that bad examples be kept from the child (§§ 68 and 76) and that the influence of parental example be facilitated by making the child in love with the company of his parents by joining liberty to that company and making it the exclusive provenance of all good (material) things (§ 69). In the same way, they require that the child be kept in the company of his parents as much as possible instead of being sent to school and being surrendered to "chance or his own Inclination for the choice of his Company" (§ 70, p. 169). Finally, the parent's example must itself be a good one, or all his punishments will be in vain (§ 71). Such an example is of more effect than precepts or punishments, not only because children "better understand what they see, than what they hear" (§ 67), but, most importantly, because rules violated by their authors and the punishments that enforce them are resented as most contrary to liberty. It seems that Locke took more to heart than Hobbes the power of example, which they both recognized, because he, recognizing its connection with the deep human desire for liberty, therefore required that both parents and political rulers be subject to the laws they imposed and enforced if they were not to be resented for "Arbitrary Imperiousness" (§ 71).[119]

Having first restricted the realm of punishment by exempting from it childish play and manners (§§ 63 and 67) and by urging that few rules or "Laws" be imposed on children in the first place (§§ 64–65) and that the method of practice be used instead, and having then gone on to stress the power of example as an alternative to punishment (§§ 68–71), Locke proceeds to restate and extend the spheres exempt from punishment and to provide an even more powerful alternative to it (§§ 72–76). Not only childishness and manners but also learning should be "exempt from the Discipline of the Rod" (§ 72). Instead of the rod, one should rely on motivating: children should be given "a Liking and Inclination to what you propose to them to be learn'd; and that will engage their Industry and Application." This motivation is to be achieved by the use of the previously mentioned rewards and punishments—esteem and disgrace and the accompanying granting or withholding of "all other good Things" (§ 58)—together with several new rules that Locke adds here. The first and greatest of these is that what is wanted of children should not be imposed as a task or required as a duty: "Whatever is so proposed presently becomes irksome: The Mind takes an Aversion to it, though before it were a Thing of Delight or Indifferency" (§ 73; see also § 49).

The reason for the irksomeness of duty becomes explicit now: "Children have as much a Mind to shew that they are free, that their own good Actions come from themselves, that they are absolute and independent, as any of the proudest of you grown Men" (§ 73; see also §§ 35, 41). What makes it necessary or politic to grant liberty is the human desire for liberty.[120] That desire seems to have the same basis in pride as the dangerous desire for mastery (see § 35), yet it can be safely and separately satisfied or accommodated. Perhaps it is even *because* this desire is accommodated that the other can be subjugated. Since Locke emphatically states that this phenomenon applies to grown men as well as children (see §§ 41 and 49), one can appropriately conclude that this argument applies to the wider adult or political context as well, that there, too, it is the human desire for liberty that makes the granting of liberty the most effective way of moving men to do what is wanted of them or to be virtuous or useful. Similarly, the stress on rights rather than duties in Locke's political thought[121] can be viewed in part as a politic response to the fact stated here, that what grown men "do chearfully of themselves" they "presently grow sick of, and can no more endure, as soon as they find it is expected of them, as a Duty" (§ 73).

Locke's discussion here of the proper management of children clarifies the character of the liberty he speaks of, and perhaps not only in the pedagogical context but in the political context as well. For though one should set children to a thing only when they have a disposition to it, "if they are not often enough forward of themselves, a good Disposition should be talk'd into them," which is "no hard matter for a discreet Tutor to do" (§ 74). Indeed, "By these Ways, carefully pursued, a Child may be brought to desire to be taught any Thing, you have a Mind he should learn." Children are actually supposed to be "indifferent to any Thing they can do, so they may be but doing" (§ 76; see also § 129).[122] In warning not to impose as a task what you want done, Locke claims— at first apparently as a hypothetical argument—that if a child is ordered to whip his top he will weary of it (§ 73). But later he actually recommends this policy, saying that the way to incline a child to do what you want is to require him to do what he wants and then permit him to do what you want as a respite or reward (§§ 128–29). The liberty Locke speaks of possesses a malleability that can be systematically exploited and employed as an instrument of government. For Locke explains that the rod is not the only "Instrument of Government" (§§ 47 and 78); allowing liberty rather than imposing duty seems to be one of the "*milder Methods of Government*" (§ 87) Locke prefers, and the "love to be treated as Rational Creatures" can be "made the greatest instrument to turn them by" (§ 81). Only in a modified sense can it be said of creatures so governed that they are free, that their own good actions come from themselves, and that they are absolute and independent (see § 73). This liberty is complementary rather than antithetical to government.

The paradox of liberty as an instrument of government[123] flows from Locke's view that men desire liberty itself more than the particular objects of their desires. This indefiniteness of human desire is related to Locke's minimization of human nature and to his opposition to innatism. The indefiniteness of desire lies at the bottom of his descriptions of the pleasure taken in variety itself as being more powerful than the pleasures taken in various things in particular.[124] If men's primary desire were for the objects themselves, there would be less need for liberty than for those objects or for the specific conditions requisite to attaining them. It is precisely because men are attached primarily to liberty that liberty becomes valuable both as a useful means of government and as a sort of common good or satisfactory common denominator.

At this point it should be noted that, as Locke describes it here, the desire children and grown men have is not necessarily for liberty as such but "*to shew* that they are free, that their own good Actions come from themselves, that they are absolute and independent" (§ 73; my emphasis). The great philosopher of liberty sounds almost condescending toward it when he recommends that matters be so arranged for children that "the enjoyment of their dearly beloved Freedom will be no small Encouragement to them" (§ 76). An older paradox of liberty lies in its combination with the mind's "Mastery over it self" (§ 75). This "habitual Dominion over it self" of the mind is also related to the indefiniteness of desire, which requires liberty yet renders it governable; for this dominion consists in the mind's ability "to take it self off from the hot Pursuit of one Thing, and set it self upon another with Facility and Delight"—to go, that is, from one desire to another.

Locke recommends the appeasement and use of the desire for liberty as a rule (§ 72) to supplement the use of rewards and punishments that develop, and then appeal to, the sensitivity to esteem. Not only can the basic method and the additional rule work together, by employing the separate incentives of esteem and liberty, but the operation of the desire for esteem also necessarily entails the additional action of the spur of "Pleasure in what they have begun by their own desire" (§ 76).[125] For to act from a concern for reputation is, according to Locke, to act freely and from something within (see § 42) even if the particular objects that bring reputation have been carefully selected by others. In this way, the reliance on esteem and the reliance on liberty are complementary parts of one and the same policy.

Locke also gives use of the desire for esteem a new twist here. Esteem is employed particularly in the form of ambition, emulation, and the resultant competition among children: "And if the Things which they observe others to do be ordered so, that they insinuate themselves into them, as the Privilege of an Age or Condition above theirs, then Ambition, and the Desire still to get forward, and higher, and to be like those above them, will set them on work" (§ 76). Similarly, the emulation of the eldest child by the younger ones is used to lead them (§ 74). It is desire "to get forward and higher" that is operative, not desires for specific objects or activities.[126]

Locke has earlier prepared the reader for an exception to his general rejection of corporal punishment (§ 52). This crucial exception is now discussed (§§ 78–79, 84, and 87). It is the use of beating to suppress "*Obstinacy* or *Rebellion*" (§ 78). Contrary to Locke's general preference for the use of esteem and disgrace, this fault must be "master'd with Force and Blows: For this there is no other Remedy." In order to be able to dispense with beating later on, one must use it uncompromisingly to combat this fault, even "eight times successively the same Morning," as did one "prudent and kind Mother" of Locke's acquaintance. To stop "at the seventh Whipping," before prevailing, is only to make more whipping necessary later or to spoil the child forever.[127] Despite his previous contention (§ 48) that the pain of physical punishment establishes only the vicious concern with present pain, Locke asserts here that "The Pain of the Rod" can "bend the Mind, and settle the Parent's Authority." Though he does not explain how this works, one can only infer that it does so through just that concern. There seems to be something irreducible about the effect of physical pain on human pride; perhaps it reminds one of one's dependence, the fact that lies at the bottom of concern for esteem (cf. § 57). It is the ultimate argument or "Instrument of Government," the "last and useful Remedy."

Locke claims that physical pain can induce "a true Sorrow, Shame, and purpose of Obedience" (§ 78). He would have it so ordered[128] "that the shame of the Whipping, and not the Pain, should be the greatest part of the Punishment. Shame of doing amiss, and deserving Chastisement, is the only true Restraint belonging to Vertue." Physical punishment may arouse a moral sentiment of shame at *deserving* chastisement apart from the pain of the chastisement itself through the reminder of dependence and of the importance of the opinion of those whose power you are in (cf. § 40). It is hard to see how else pain alone, even "continued and increased without leaving off till it has throughly prevailed," can convey the notion of desert; and, given that it does, there is no reason offered here to think that it does so only when it *is* deserved. According to the *Essay,* shame "is an uneasiness of the Mind, upon the thought of having done something, which is indecent, or will lessen the valued Esteem, which others have for us."[129] It seems that Locke would found the useful sentiment of shame at having deserved chastisement (like compliance of the will and concern for esteem, §§ 44, 58) on a calculation and then have that calculation be forgotten (cf. "without any Signs of Memory that ever they had been there," § 84). This is of the essence not only of habituation but of the association of ideas. The peculiar relation between the *Essay* and the *Thoughts* is evident in the use here of a principle that Locke warned against there[130] as a great cause of error.

Locke concludes his discussion of beating children with the statement, "I think there are better ways of prevailing with them: And a gentle Perswasion in Reasoning (when the first Point of Submission to your Will is got) will most Times do much better" (§ 80). Given his indications that children are not rational (see §§ 39, 40, 61), and his general reluctance to depend on reason alone, this conclusion may surprise the reader. Indeed, anticipating such surprise, Locke digresses: "It will perhaps be wondered that I mention *Reasoning* with Children: And yet I cannot but think that the true Way of Dealing with them" (§ 81). It soon becomes clear, however, that Locke has not changed his mind and does not, by "Reasoning" with children, mean "Long Discourses, and Philosophical Reasonings," "*Reasonings* from remote Principles," or "long Deductions." He means, first of all, that "you should make them sensible by the Mildness of your Carriage, and the Composure even in your Correction of them, that what you do is reasonable in you, and useful and necessary for them." This notion of reasoning seems to be based less on the rationality of children than on their "love to be treated as Rational Creatures," and it rather flatters that pretension than satisfies their intellects with reasons. Locke says here of this desire that "'Tis a Pride should be cherished in them, and as much as can be, made the greatest instrument to turn them by." One sees again, and more clearly than before, that a useful sentiment can, like the most pernicious one, be characterized as pride. The desire to be thought rational is satisfied here by mildness rather than by reasons, and it is repelled by severity (cf. § 41).

Nevertheless, when Locke states that children understand reasoning "as early as they do Language" (§ 81), he is not referring just to their ability to discern and appreciate mildness and composure in others, for he explains that they may be "convinced" of any "Vertue they should be excited to." But "it must be by such *Reasons* as their Age and Understanding are capable of." These reasons must be "*obvious*, and level to their Thoughts, and such as may (if I may so say) be felt, and touched." These tangible reasons are generally variations of "That it will be a Discredit and Disgrace to them, and displease you," as well as "other more particular" ones. Locke's call for reasoning, or for treating children as rational creatures, is practically identical with his recommendation of the use of esteem and disgrace. The only addition seems to be that one should not only praise and blame for well or ill doing but also point out in advance which actions will lead to one and which to the other: one should promise and threaten. This meaning of reasoning is entirely in accord with the notion that rational creatures are motivated only by rewards and punishments, and that using them to guide children is tantamount to treating children as rational creatures (cf. § 54). Indeed, the use of "motives" here as identical with the "reasons" offered in this sort of "reasoning" is one of the clearest indications of the meaning Locke assigns to rationality: it is a susceptibility to appeals to the motives (reward and punishment) for which one may act. One should not be misled, by such phrases as "the Dignity and Excellency of a rational Creature" (§ 31) or "the Rules and Restraints of Reason" (§ 36), into thinking that reason is, for Locke, an autonomous source of direction. As Lamprecht concludes, Locke in the *Thoughts* "usually aimed to put reason in control, not as itself the moral standard, but as a means to securing the greatest pleasure."[131]

This notion of reasoning is of special interest because Locke indicates here that it is relevant not only to children, for

> The Foundations on which several Duties are built, and the Fountains of Right and Wrong, from which they spring, are not perhaps easily to be let into the Minds of grown Men, not used to abstract their Thoughts from common received Opinions. [§ 81]

Though this statement is qualified by the words "not perhaps easily," it appears from the *Essay* and the *Reasonableness of Christianity* that this qualification should be considered a polite understatement, made as a concession to adult pretensions to rationality (a similar concession seems to be made in some passages of the *Two Treatises,* where it is implied that natural law can easily be known).[132] For in the *Essay* Locke emphasizes the enormous difficulty most men have in abstracting their thoughts from "common received Opinions." If these foundations and fountains are therefore not known to such men, they too must be content with something like the sort of reasoning here provided for children.[133] In the *Two Treatises,* in the crucial instance of the exercise of the right to revolution, the people are credited with just such tangible reasoning: "Are the People to be blamed if they have the sence of rational Creatures, and can think of things no otherwise than as they find and feel them?"[134] It is not clear from this statement in the *Thoughts* whether the "common received Opinions" these grown men are used to are in harmony with these duties, with the result that these men act rightly without knowing truly why they should, or whether the opinions are contrary, with the result that even right action, as well as knowledge, must await the correction of the "common received Opinions."

Some immediate adult reformation is required in any case, for mildness of carriage and composure in administering correction are necessary to give the impression of parental reasonableness. Besides making a virtue of mildness in particular, this necessity entails generally the same sort of self-control on the part of parents that was to be established in children as "the great Principle and Foundation of Vertue and Worth" (§ 33; cf. §§ 38 and 45). For parents must suppress any anger in the course of administering punishment (§ 80; see also §§ 83 and 87). This injunction is related to the general Lockean notion of rationality in that it is future-regarding rather than past- or present-regarding. Punishment not only must appeal to the future-regarding rationality of children but must express that of adults. One should not punish "only to revenge the past Fault, which has raised your Choler" (§ 78), "when you can expect no good from it" (§ 87), but for "a future Compliance" and "prospect of amendment."[135]

Locke returns immediately from "reasoning" (§ 81) to "the plainest, easiest, and most efficacious" method of instruction and formation, the use of examples (§ 82). They "make deeper Impressions" than "any Rules or Instructions." Here Locke is no longer talking about the mere presence of good examples, especially those of the parents themselves, and the absence of bad examples (§§ 68–71), or reliance simply on what children see. Here he means pointing out examples both good and bad, "before their Eyes," to be sure, but accompanied by "some Reflections" as well, that is, by praise or blame of the "good or bad Quality" of the example (see also § 94, p. 194). Thus, though children, as Locke says earlier, "better understand what they see, than what they hear" (§ 67, end), they may understand what they see in terms of what they hear. The visual element adds a great deal, however, to mere "Discourses."

As Locke explains in the *Essay,* the mind grasps ideas from the senses before it grasps them from words, and often more clearly and distinctly as well, so that "the examining and judging of *Ideas* by themselves, their Names being quite laid aside," is "the best and surest way to clear and distinct Knowledge."[136] The special difficulty is, however, that complex ideas, such as the mixed modes of morality here in question, are "for the most part imperfect, confused, and undetermined."[137] Especially because these abstract ideas of mixed modes are "*made by the Understanding*" and "made *very arbitrarily,* made without Patterns, or reference to any real Existence," it is "the ordinary Method, that Children learn the Names of mixed Modes before they have their *Ideas.*" The usual result for men all their lives is that

> without taking the pains necessary to settle in their Minds determined *ideas,* they use their Words for such unsteady and confused Notions as they have, contenting themselves with the same Words other People use . . . this insignificancy in their Words, when they come to Reason concerning either their Tenets or Interest, manifestly fills their Discourse with abundance of empty unintelligible noise and jargon, especially in moral Matters. . . .

The proper remedy for this difficulty, according to the *Essay,* is perfect and exact definition of mixed modes, since in mixed modes, "especially those belonging to Morality," one cannot make use of "the only sure way of making known the significance of the name of any simple *Idea,* [which] is *by presenting to his Senses that Subject which may produce it in his Mind.*" For of such mixed modes "there are not always standing Patterns to be found existing, [so that] the signification of their Names cannot be made known, as those of simple *Ideas,* by any shewing."[138] A partial remedy, however—one more sure, though less extensive in its scope of application, and far more suitable to the capacities of children than that of perfect and exact definition—is presented here in the *Thoughts:* one should point to examples of good and bad with praise and blame. In this way the method of instruction in moral ideas is assimilated as far as possible to that of simple ideas of sense. As such, it is properly added on here to the use of reasons that may be felt and touched.

The method of using examples apparently applies especially to ill qualities, and the reason for that reveals the secret of the power of this method above and beyond that derived from its visual character. Self-love may lead us to ignore or even resent blame placed on bad qualities in ourselves, whereas blame placed on bad qualities in others, even when we possess the same qualities ourselves, encounters no such obstacles and can even move us to reform ourselves. This use of examples is therefore an especially suitable alternative to punishment as an instrument of government, since a father should use it not merely as a general method of instruction but "to reform any Thing he wishes mended in his Son." Locke here makes it clear that this method is suitable not only for children "whilst they are young" or even so long "as they shall be under another's Tuition or Conduct" but even for men, "Nothing sinking so gently, and so deep, into Men's Minds, as *Example*." This fact may serve to strengthen the plausibility of Locke's view of punishment in the *Two Treatises*, that the punished criminal's "Example [can deter] others, from doing the like mischief."[139] It may also help to explain the ferocity of the blame Locke heaps on criminals.[140]

The long part on punishment, including its limitations and alternatives (§§ 63–87), concludes with a discussion devoted largely to the administration of punishment (§§ 83–87). First, as an extension of the notion of reasoning as mildness and composure in one's manner even and especially in punishing, Locke requires that punishment—and here he is speaking of corporal punishment—should not be administered "presently upon the Committing the Fault . . . lest Passion mingle with it" (§ 83). Second, in symmetry with his earlier recommendation that children should "receive all their good things" in their parents' company "and from their hands," not the servants' (§ 69), Locke recommends that "the *Smart* should come more immediately *from another's Hand*, though by the Parent's Order" (§ 83). We have seen that Locke's principle of aversion—that instance of the association of ideas by which corporal punishment "naturally breeds an Aversion to that, which 'tis the Tutor's Business to create a liking to"—leads him to minimize the use of such punishment (§§ 49–50). Although he is not willing to surrender its use entirely, since it is the "last and useful remedy" able to "bend the mind" (§ 78), he is careful, even in its occasional application, to respect the principle of aversion. For when corporal punishment is administered through another's hand, "the Child's Aversion for the Pain it suffers [will] rather be turned on the Person that immediately inflicts it"(§ 83). This policy may remind one of Machiavelli's recommendation that one imitate Cesare Borgia's use of Remirro de Orco to bring "good government" to the Romagna without incurring hatred toward himself.[141] Locke does not seem to have been moved by the thought expressed by G. G. Verdolini, who protests the injustice of Locke's attempt to "turn the resentment for the pain suffered onto the material executor rather than the parent" because

> this would certainly provoke in the child a sense of antipathy and a desire of revenge towards a person who, being simply a material instrument, has no responsibility for the pain caused.

121

The policy may also remind one of Locke's own separation of the executive from the legislative power in *Two Treatises,* for, as Verdolini again remarks, "substituting for the person of the educator that of the executor alters the character of the punishment and gives it a judicial rather than a familial aspect."[142]

Although Locke admits in this part of the *Thoughts* that "Blows are the proper Remedies" for obstinacy (§§ 84, 87),[143] he defines obstinacy (or "Rebellion" or "Stubbornness," as he calls it earlier, § 78) in such a way that blows can never be the first remedy. Disobedience in a child is obstinate only if it is persisted in after "all gentler Ways," all the *milder Methods* of Government, . . . have been *throughly tried* upon him" (§§ 84 and 87). The first remedy should be a show of wonder (see also §§ 110 and 131); the next should be a concerted state of disesteem, accompanied by deprivation of good things (see also §§ 58–59). Blows will, as a result, be needed on "very few Occasions" (§ 84). Locke realizes that this conclusion will provoke the objection that "there are many, who will never apply themselves to their Books, and to what they ought to Learn, unless they are scourged to it" (§ 86). He facetiously explains this objection as having arisen from Greek and Latin being "strange, unnatural, and disagreeable" to children; he then more seriously attributes it to the failure of the grammar schools to employ the "softer Ways of Shame and Commendation" that he elaborates. Although he is unwilling to grant that there are "many" (§ 86) who are not susceptible to the milder methods, he concedes that there are "some so Negligent or Idle . . . . For we must grant, that there will be Children found of all Tempers" (§ 87). But he insists that this latter kind "are not to be the Rule of Education of those, who are better Natur'd." This may be another reason for his preferring private tutors to education in schools; for with the former there is no risk of the worse natures' being the rule for the education of the better. A great gap exists for Locke between the realms of education and civil government; for despite the many parallels between them, stemming from the human nature they both deal with, there are grave differences, owing to the different ways in which they must deal with it. In politics the worse natures must be the rule for the better; civil government is defined by its ability to restrain the worst natures by the harshest methods.[144] Only in this way can it manage to govern the better natures by preserving their liberty.

In education, even in the case of the worse natures, corporal punishment, though it is to be "carried to the utmost Severity," is not to be frequent. If such severe punishment is of no avail when all the milder methods have likewise failed, then frequency will only wear out the influence of the pain (§ 78) or will actually serve to corrupt (§ 48). Therefore, "If it be any Father's Misfortune to have a Son thus perverse and intractable, I know not what more he can do, but pray for him." Locke offers barely more consolation in the face of a complete failure of education than he does in the face of a complete failure of politics, that is, in the face of invincible injustice: "If God has taken away all means of seeking remedy, there is nothing left but patience."[145]

## TUTORIAL DIGRESSION: GOOD BREEDING AND WORLDLY WISDOM (§§ 88–94)

Shortly before the end of the long treatment of parental authority (§§ 40–99, covering its establishment, its instruments, and its relaxation), there is a substantial digression devoted to the tutor, most of it (§§ 93–94) added in the third edition. The first part of this digression (§§ 88–89), which dates from the first edition, is closely related to the subject of authority. Just as the parent is to give the order for, but not be the immediate executor of, the punishment (§ 83), so the tutor is to administer punishment but never "without [the parent's] Consent and Direction" (§ 88). The perfection of this Machiavellian use of the tutor is achieved by "concealing that he has not the Power of the Rod" in order to "keep up his Authority with his Pupil" (§ 88). This concealment may also serve to turn "the Child's Aversion for the Pain it suffers" (§ 83) the more effectively away from the parent. The partial extension of parental authority to the tutor is achieved also by the parent's treating him with "great respect," and arranging for the rest of the household to do so too, for in this matter as in others the force of example counts most. And, just as the example of the parents' respect establishes the tutor's authority more than his own worth and abilities can, so the tutor's example counts more than his precepts: "Ill patterns are sure to be follow'd more than good Rules" (§ 89).[146]

Given the importance of the tutor's example, it is not surprising that Locke insists on the importance of his own qualities (§§ 90–94), though he recognizes that "In all the whole Business of Education, there is nothing like to be less hearkn'd to, or harder to be well observed" than this insistence (§ 90). As a corollary, he points out that since the qualities he recommends are "hardly to be found united in Persons, that are to be had for ordinary Salaries," parents must "Spare no Care nor Cost to get such an one" (§§ 90–94).[147] Locke now repeats that it is better to provide children with virtue and good breeding than to leave them a large inheritance:

> He that at any Rate procures his Child a good Mind, well Principled, temper'd to Vertue and Usefulness, and adorned with Civility and good Breeding, makes a better purchase for him, than if he laid out the Money for an

Addition of more Earth to his former Acres. [§ 90; cf.
§§ 15, 70]

Here it is not clear whether the commercialism is confined to the metaphors of "purchase" and "husbandry" ("'Tis not good Husbandry to
make his Fortune rich, and his Mind poor"), or whether Locke again
advises that one lay the foundation of fortune in virtue and good breeding, with the expectation that the latter qualities will bring prosperity in
their train (cf. § 70). He says here that "A Wise and Good Man can
hardly want either the Opinion or Reality of being Great and Happy.
But he that is Foolish or Vicious, can be neither Great nor Happy, what
Estate soever you leave him" (§ 90). The word "Great" here may mean
"eminent by reason of birth, rank, wealth, power, or position; of high
social or official position."[148] Conversely, Locke shortly after this recommends that youths be made aware of examples of corrupt young men
reduced to ruin and beggary (§ 94, p. 194).

Given the importance of the tutor's example, Locke emphasizes that
he must possess not merely, and not even especially, the learning usually
insisted upon (§§ 92, 93, and 94, esp. pp. 197–98 and 200) but also and
most importantly the other qualities chiefly desired for the pupil. For it
cannot be expected that the pupil "should be better Bred, better Skill'd
in the World, better Principled in the Grounds and Foundations of true
Vertue and Generosity, than his young *Tutor* is" (§ 93). These qualities
of good breeding, knowledge of the world, and virtue, as well as learning,
are precisely the ones that "every Gentleman (that takes any care of his
Education) desires for his Son, besides the Estate he leaves him" (§ 134),
and that provide the framework for Locke's treatment of "the several
parts" of education (§§ 134–95). Of these parts, Locke discusses good
breeding (§ 93) and knowledge of the world (§ 94) at length in the por-
tions of the tutorial digression added in the third edition, but he treats
learning only indirectly and, polemically, as subordinate to the others;
more surprisingly, he treats of virtue hardly at all.

Locke's neglect of virtue as a quality of the tutor is rendered comprehensible by his account of good breeding (§ 93). As he explains,

> Breeding is that, which sets a Gloss upon all his other
> good qualities, and renders them useful to him, in pro-
> curing him the Esteem and Good Will of all that he
> comes near. Without good Breeding his other Accom-
> plishments make him pass but for Proud, Conceited,
> Vain, or Foolish.

Locke does not seem to intend "Accomplishments" here to be understood
in a narrow sense, referring to such skills as dancing, music, and fencing
(cf. §§ 196–200), for he instances courage and "Good Nature" and warns
that even "Vertue and Parts, though they are allowed their due Com-

mendation, yet are not enough to procure a Man a good Reception." The importance of esteem, both as a constituent of happiness and as a principle of virtue, leads to a strong emphasis on good breeding or civility as that which renders virtue pleasing to others and thereby useful to oneself (see also §§ 66–67 and 141–46). Although civility breeds itself, both in the sense that inward civility, or concern for the esteem of others, leads "of it self" to the proper outward expression (§ 67) and in the sense that the example of good breeding breeds good breeding, it does not do so in another sense. It is not good breeding to correct the manners of another;[149] "even those who are Friends, and wish it were mended, scarce ever dare mention it" (§ 93). For this reason, good breeding seems to be the part "most necessary to be form'd by the Hands and Care of a *Governour*"; it "should be the *Governour*'s principal Care."[150]

The part Locke treats at greatest length in his discussion of the tutor's qualities is knowledge of the world (§ 94); indeed, he speaks of it here at far greater length than he does in his thematic treatment of it as a part of the child's education (§ 140). This is only appropriate, since the tutor must have more of this quality than his young pupil should be expected or even desired to have (cf. § 140). This part of education is probably the one most explicitly "historical," that is, designed for a particular time and place.[151] The tutor should know and gradually teach "The Ways, the Humours, the Follies, the Cheats, the Faults of the Age he is fallen into, and particularly of the Country he lives in." This knowledge is historical in that it is of one's own age and country, but it is more than merely historical, for it is conscious of the faults and follies of one's own age and country as faults and follies.

This education in "Skill in Men, and their Manners" (§ 94, p. 192) is intended to teach the youth to judge men "neither with too much Suspicion, nor too much Confidence; but as the young Man is by Nature most inclin'd to either side, rectifie him and bend him the other way" (§ 94, p. 193). Whatever may be the natural bias of most young men, the bias of most education is toward too much ignorance of the world and its dangers, so that Locke's emphasis is, in contrast, decidedly on suspicion (§ 94, pp. 193–95). This suspicion is directed particularly against the "other kind of Tutors" the youth will meet in the world—those who will seek to corrupt him and whom the ordinary education leaves him prey to. Not only must both tutor and pupil know about these "Tutors," but Locke himself seems to have learned something from them and put it to better use. They present vice not only as manliness but, most importantly, as freedom; they claim that "the Freedom belonging to Men, is to take their Swing in a full Enjoyment of what was before forbidden them."[152] As for the youth's following his governors' advice and what Locke terms "the Counsel of his own Reason," these other tutors call that "being govern'd by others"; they say, on the contrary, that in "running counter to all the Rules of Vertue" the youth "goes like a Man of himself, by his own Conduct, and for his own Pleasure." Locke recommends that the youth be forewarned that such men make such statements only "that they may have the government of him themselves" and that he may be "wholly as a Child led by them into those Vices, which best serve their Purposes." Locke emphatically replies to these "other Tutors" in their own terms, that is, in terms of the pursuit of freedom and the avoidance of being governed by others. One can say that he has earlier presented the secret of education as parents' and tutors' making the child "believe, he goes like a Man of himself, by his own Conduct, and for his own Pleasure, when, in truth, he is wholly as a Child led by them" into those virtues that best serve their purposes as well as the child's own (see §§ 72, 73, 76). And he has earlier presented submission to the will of others, which is a preparation for submission to one's own reason, as if it were already that (§§ 32, 34). It seems as if God's education of the first man and woman could have been more effective if it had preempted the appeal of the first corrupting tutor that led to the Fall. Similarly, though the men the youth should be taught most to beware of are those who try to seem what they are not (§ 94, pp. 192–93), he himself should be taught "where he should let them see, and when dissemble the Knowledge of them, and their aims and workings" (§ 94, p. 195). He should thus be able to imitate their dissimulation.

This knowledge of the world is of "much more use," and therefore "much better" for a gentleman, than Greek and Latin or "the abstruse Speculations of Natural Philosophy, and Metaphysicks" (§ 94, pp. 195–96). The only book learning Locke has any good words for at this point is "Greek and Roman Writers," and that precisely because "those antient Authors observed and painted Mankind well, and give the best light into that kind of Knowledge." It may seem odd to us that the best light in this most necessary matter should come from a time without a "sure standard" of morality, a time that had to rest satisfied with a "defective morality" and the "airy commendations" of virtue, that "she is the perfection and excellency of our nature, that she is herself a reward and will recommend our names to future ages."[153] Just as Locke seems to have learned something of how to appeal to human nature on behalf of virtue from the tutors of vice, so it seems that knowledge of human nature is best derived from those lacking a sure standard of morality. It appears, however, from Locke's very explanation of the dispensability of even these useful writers of antiquity that not only knowledge of men but virtue itself, as well as its gloss of civility, can well be found without "the true Principle and Measure of Vertue" (§ 61; see also §§ 136, 139). As he explains:

> He that goes into the Eastern Parts of *Asia,* will find able and acceptable Men without any of these [Greek and Latin, natural philosophy and metaphysics, and knowledge of the ancient authors]: But without Vertue, Knowledge of the World, and Civility, an accomplished, and valuable Man can be found no where. [§ 94, p. 196][154]

Locke does not mention here that these Asiatics are also without Christianity, let alone that, in his understanding, the Siamese and the Chinese, or at least "the Sect of the *Litterati,* or *Learned,* keeping to the old Religion of *China,* and the ruling Party there, are all of them *Atheist.*"[155]

In deploring here the ordinary preference for useless learning over "Prudence and good Breeding," Locke explains that "a Gentleman's Calling . . . is to have the Knowledge of a Man of Business, a Carriage suitable to his Rank, and to be Eminent and Useful in his Country according to his Station" (§ 94, p. 197). His invoking the notion of the gentleman's "Calling" here[156] seems to support the thesis of what is in other ways one of the most sensitive and careful interpretations of Locke, John Dunn's *Political Thought of John Locke.* Dunn's interpretation culminates in the claim that the coherence of Locke's thought, and of his life as well, lies in his Calvinist notion of the calling.[157] The Calvinist notion is that one's line of life or occupation is "a post assigned him by the Lord" and "the vocation of the Lord." For Calvin its point is that a man must not aspire either to desert or to rise above his calling, for "it is unlawful to transgress the bounds assigned him."[158] This doctrine is the quotidian expression of his extreme providentialism. This providentialist character of the doctrine is expounded by Dunn and is attributed by him to Locke.[159] However, Dunn's exposition of the doctrine and its providentialist character is based on Puritan and secondary sources, and he gives no clear evidence for attributing it in this form to Locke. The mere use of the term "Calling," as here in the *Thoughts,* need not indicate the presence of the Calvinist notion or anything more than the sense of "ordinary occupation."[160] This can be seen from the way Locke uses the term in another passage in this same section, where he recommends that the tutor, in giving the pupil knowledge of men, "pull off the Mask, which their several Callings, and Pretences cover them with" (§ 94, p. 192). The notion of one's occupation as a divine calling seems to stem from the interpretation and translation of 1 Corinthians 7:20: "Let every man abide in the same calling wherein he was called."[161] Locke's paraphrase of this decisive scriptural passage, however, avoids the term and, with it, the conflation of the notions of occupation and divine vocation: "Christianity gives not any one any new privilege to change the state, or put off the obligations of civil life, which he was in before." And, as is further indicated in Locke's note to this same passage, the obligations of one's "calling" are civil and not affected by Christianity.[162]

## RELAXATION OF AUTHORITY (§§ 95–98)

After the digression on the tutor, Locke returns to and concludes his account of parental authority with the promised relaxation of that authority (cf. §§ 40–42). This authority is to be relaxed not merely when it comes to an end legally but before then, and not only when the youth has already proved capable of liberty but in order to make him so (§ 95). But liberty serves not only to render capable of it those to whom it is granted but also to remove their resentment of those in authority (§ 96). This is especially true of the consultation, especially in matters of property, that Locke recommends as the first method of relaxing authority. This method not only flatters the desire to be thought rational and to have one's reasons commended (§§ 97–98); it also shows those consulted that those in authority are "not without Care" (§ 96). This mitigates filial envy of paternal property, which otherwise, though it may conduce to obedience,[163] may also lead to the terrible question, *"When will you Die, Father?"* (§ 40).

Locke continues by presenting another method of relaxing authority, one that is complementary to the method of consulting with the pupil about one's own affairs. This method consists in hearing the pupil's reasonings on hypothetical cases involving morality, prudence, and breeding instead of dictating rules and maxims to him (§ 98). It combines one of the chief advantages of the method of consultation—that is, the use of "the Pleasure, and Credit of bearing a Part in the Conversation, and of having his Reasons sometimes approved, and hearken'd to"— with the advantage of the method of pointing out examples (§ 82); namely, it "lets things into the Mind, which stick there, and retain their Evidence with them; whereas words at best are faint Representations, being not so much as the true Shadows of Things, and are much sooner forgotten."

The whole part on authority (§§ 40–99) concludes with a brief summation (§ 99). Here "the great Principle, whereby you will always have hold upon him, to turn his Mind to the Ways of Vertue, and Honour," is presented as a reverence consisting in two parts, love and fear. Fear comes first, established by severity and the consequent awareness of being in the power of another. Love is added by the allowance of liberty and the bestowal of praise or "Caressing," but it does not do away with fear.

For Locke, parental authority serves not merely as a preparation for submission to civil authority, as it does for Hobbes, but as a preparation for civil liberty.

# *THREE*
# The Lockean Virtues

ocke's discussion of the establishment and relaxation of parental authority (*Thoughts*, §§ 40–99) is followed by an account of how that authority should be employed (§§ 103–32). This account contains Locke's fullest and richest analysis of the most important virtues and vices, of their natures and relations, and of the way to nurture the one and cure the other.

## INDIVIDUAL TEMPERS (§§ 100–102)

Between his discussions of authority (§§ 40–99) and its employment (§§ 103–32) Locke writes of the need to observe the individual temper of the pupil, stressing that this is a necessary prerequisite for the proper use of authority (§§ 100–102).[1] He speaks here of the "unalterable Frame of [men's] Constitutions" (§ 101), but he seems to mean by this only that, as he has explained earlier, original tempers "can hardly be totally alter'd, and transform'd into the contrary" (§ 66). Accordingly, though he says here that "These *native Propensities,* these Prevalencies of Constitution, are not to be cured by Rules, or a direct Contest," he does not mean they are not to be cured at all (§ 102). Instead of by rules or a direct contest, it is "with Art they may be much mended, and turned to good purposes." The artful improvement of original tempers is illustrated later, in Locke's discussion of the treatment of timorousness (§ 115) and carelessness (§§ 123–27). But even by art the alteration worked is not total; "the Byass will always hang on that side, that Nature first placed it" (§ 102).

Locke notes here that the use of rules or direct contest is particularly inappropriate in dealing with tempers of "the humbler and meaner sort, which proceed from fear, and lowness of Spirit" (§ 102). Locke means, presumably, that rules or a direct contest will serve only to worsen these tempers, by deepening the underlying fear and further depressing the "Spirit" (cf. §§ 46 and 51). This remark about "the humbler and meaner sort" of tempers may draw the reader's attention to the fact that Locke here presents all of the "tempers" in pairs of opposites: stout/timorous, confident/modest, tractable/obstinate, curious/careless, quick/slow (§ 101),

THE LOCKEAN VIRTUES (Thoughts, §§ 100–132)

fierce/mild, bold/bashful, compassionate/cruel, and open/reserved (§ 102). One may add, as a tenth, the pair gay/melancholy, presented in his first discussion of tempers (§ 66). It may be that Locke opposes in each pair one temper of the humbler and meaner sort, which proceeds from fear and low spirits, and one of the prouder or higher sort, which proceeds from desire or from a deficiency of fear, that is, from high spirits. This possibility is immediately plausible in every case but one, the pair compassionate/cruel.[2] That pair is anomalous in more ways than one. For though Locke here presents cruelty, together with compassion, as a natural temper of the mind, he soon speaks of "unnatural Cruelty." He then also makes this statement:

> The Pleasure [children] take to put any thing in Pain, that is capable of it, I cannot persuade my self to be any other than a foreign and introduced Disposition, an Habit borrowed from Custom and Conversation. . . . Thus, by Fashion and Opinion, that comes to be a Pleasure, which in it self neither is, nor can be any. [§ 116; see also § 37]

These claims—that cruelty is unnatural and that it is one of the "native Propensities"—both date from the first edition of the *Thoughts.* Nearly the same vacillation can be found in Hobbes, for in one passage of *Leviathan* he claims that what men call cruelty is only "little sense of the calamity of others," because "that any man should take pleasure in other mens great harmes, without other end of his own, I do not conceive it possible"; but in another passage he claims that there are some men who take "pleasure in contemplating their own power in the acts of conquest, which they pursue farther than their security requires."[3] Hobbesian rationality tends to deny disinterested malevolence as much as it does disinterested benevolence; yet irrational glory may lead to either. The Hobbesian understanding of cruelty also suggests a way to reconcile the seeming inconsistencies in Locke's statements on the subject in the *Thoughts.* The native propensity to cruelty (§ 102) may be only an insensitivity to the sufferings of others, perhaps from an excess of spirit or a deficiency of fear, unlike the unnatural cruelty taught by others (§ 116), which is actual delight in inflicting pain. The native propensity may leave a child especially open to the bad influence of others but by itself need not lead to taking pleasure in inflicting pain.

## LOVE OF DOMINION (§§ 103–5)

Once parental authority is established and its proper instruments have been recognized and properly employed, it must be applied not only to the carefully observed individual temper of the child but also to the general propensities of human nature. It seems that, for Locke, it is not only the individual temper or "the peculiar *Physiognomy of the Mind*" that is discernible most in "Children, before Art and Cunning hath taught them to hide their Deformities, and conceal their ill Inclinations under a dissembled out-side" (§ 101); it may also have been from artless children that he learned that men are the creatures most "desirous to be Masters of themselves and others" (§ 35). The first inclination to which parental authority must be applied is not an individual temper but the general love of dominion (§§ 103–10). Just as earlier he paired mastery over self and over others as the objects of human pride (§ 35), so here he at least incidentally pairs love of liberty and love of dominion:

> I told you before that Children love *Liberty;* and there-
> fore they should be brought to do the things [that] are
> fit for them, without feeling any restraint laid upon them.
> I now tell you, they love something more; and that is
> *Dominion:* And this is the first Original of most vicious
> Habits, that are ordinary and natural. [§ 103]

Even if their root is the same, love of liberty ought to be accommodated and thereby developed, whereas love of dominion ought to be repressed. It is not clear whether Locke means that children love dominion "more" than liberty or merely that they love it in addition. The love of dominion "shews it self very early" (§ 103)—indeed, "as soon almost as they are born" (§ 104). The earliest evidence of the love of dominion is that children "cry, grow peevish, sullen, and out of humour, for nothing but to have their *Wills*" (§ 104). Children not merely have desires, according to Locke, but "They would have their Desires submitted to by others." Locke's apparent vacillation with respect to the source of man's other inclinations, deriving them sometimes from original sensitivity to sensual pleasure and pain[4] but at other times recognizing the independence of other inclinations, especially pride in its various forms, may again recall Hobbes. Hobbes, too, says that men "naturally love Liberty, and Dominion over others," but he also seems to derive the "perpetuall and restlesse desire of Power after power" from desires for the objects power can obtain and from concern for security.[5] However, in dealing with the crucial *earliest* evidence of love of dominion, the two authors differ. Hobbes presents this early behavior as an expression of mere sensual desire, for he says of men that

> from nature, that is, from their first birth, as they are
> merely sensible creatures, they have this disposition, that
> immediately as much as in them lies they desire and do
> whatsoever is best pleasing to them, and that either
> through fear they fly from, or through hardness repel
> those dangers which approach them . . . . Unless you
> give children all they ask for, they are peevish and cry,

131

aye, and strike their parents sometimes; and all this they have from nature.[6]

Elsewhere Hobbes presents children's crying as an expression of mere dejection or of a recognition of their own weakness and not as a means of getting their wills, let alone as an expression of love of dominion over others:

> . . . *children* weep often; for seeing they think that every thing ought to be given them which they desire, of necessity every repulse must be a check of their expectation, and puts them in mind of their too much weakness to make themselves masters of all they look for.[7]

Locke, however, regards crying as the earliest evidence of a love of dominion, a love that is apparently above and beyond any desire for sensual satisfaction.

This love of dominion shows itself in two desires: desire for the submission of others to one's will (§ 104) and desire for property (§ 105). The reader of the *Two Treatises,* where property is joined with liberty in opposition to absolute and arbitrary power or tyranny, may be surprised to find that, in the *Thoughts,* Locke not only joins desire for property with desire for the submission of others to one's will as an expression of love of dominion; he also says that these are the "two Roots of almost all the Injustice and Contention, that so disturb Humane Life" (§ 105). The desire for property is here described as follows:

> Another thing wherein they shew their love of Dominion, is their desire to have things to be theirs; they would have *Propriety* and Possession, pleasing themselves with the Power which that seems to give, and the Right they thereby have, to dispose of them, as they please. [§ 105]

It may be, however, that what Locke is opposing here is not the desire for property as such but the desire for property as power over others. In the *Two Treatises,* after all, he is concerned not only to defend property from arbitrary government but to deny that property "gives a Man Power over the Life of another."[8] So here, in the *Thoughts,* Locke speaks of the *power* that property "seems" to give; but he speaks without qualification of the right it gives to dispose of things as one pleases.

## SELF-DENIAL (§§ 106–8)

Locke presents three ways to employ parental authority to curb this twofold love of dominion: denial of demands (§§ 106–8), regulation of contests for mastery among children (§ 109), and teaching liberality and justice (§ 110). The first method is already familiar to the reader from

Locke's earlier discussion of the education of the mind, where he presented denial as preparation for self-denial, which is the foundation of virtue (§§ 33–39). Now, in this later discussion, the method of denial is again not of desires as such but more narrowly of desires expressed as demands on others. The point is not simply to suppress "all the Injustice and Contention, that so disturb Humane Life" and that derive from the desire for dominion over others or the demand that they fulfill one's desires; Locke is also saying that the best way to gain the self-control that is necessary for one's own happiness is to learn to refrain from expressing desires as demands on others:

> For giving vent, gives Life and Strength to our Appetites; and he that has the confidence to turn his Wishes into Demands, will be but a little way from thinking he ought to obtain them. [Of this] I am sure, [that] every one can more easily bear a denial from himself, than from any body else. [§ 107]

Locke is thus arguing not only that demanding that others fulfill one's desires leads to injustice and contention but that it is easier to overcome mere desire within oneself, so to speak, than to overcome the *additional* pride or desire for liberty and dominion that is at work once a desire is expressed as a demand on others. This appreciation of the power of pride makes Locke diametrically opposed to later assertions of the healthiness of learning to express one's desires and emotions; on the contrary, "'Tis a great Step towards the mastery of our Desires, to give this stop to them, and shut them up in Silence." The principle of which Locke is particularly sure here, that "every one can more easily bear a denial from himself, than from any body else," may be considered a restatement of his fundamental recognition of the basic human desire for liberty. It may also recall Machiavelli's constitutional principle that "the wounds and every other evil that a man does to himself spontaneously and by choice hurt far less than those which are done to you by others."[9] J. W. Allen suggests that for Machiavelli a version of this principle serves to connect republican liberty and public spirit and thereby to justify republican liberty.[10] This fundamental psychological principle does not render superfluous the largely jural argument of *Two Treatises*, but it does render it plausible and practical. Allen suggests that Machiavelli conceives of popular participation in republican government as "creating a stimulating illusion: a sense that the acts of government are one's own or a hope that they some day will be."[11] Locke is eager in *Two Treatises* to elide the difference between representation and one's own action (he is an advocate of representative government rather than republican government as such or direct popular participation).[12] He writes

133

there of "the Judgments of the Commonwealth . . . which indeed are his own Judgments, they being made by himself, or his Representative."[13]

Locke then proceeds to narrow the denial of desire further to denial of demands for the satisfaction of "Wants of Fancy" as distinguished from "Natural Wants" (§ 107). He grants children "liberty to declare their Wants" (§ 106), meaning only their natural wants. He explains:

> Those are truly Natural Wants, which Reason alone, without some other Help, is not able to fence against, nor keep from disturbing us. The Pains of Sickness and Hurts, Hunger, Thirst and Cold; want of Sleep, and Rest or Relaxation of the Part wearied with Labour, are what all Men feel, and the best dispos'd Minds cannot but be sensible of their uneasiness. . . . [§ 107][14]

Therefore, when a child says "I am hungry" or voices "any other necessity of Nature," one may properly satisfy him, but not when he says "I would have Roast-Meat" (§ 106). If such a want of fancy is declared, it ought to be denied. This austere distinction ought not to be considered puritan, strictly speaking. Calvin specifically denounces it. According to him, God

> intended to provide not only for our necessity, but likewise for our pleasure and delight. . . .
> Let us discard, therefore, that inhuman philosophy . . . allowing no use of the creatures but what is absolutely necessary.[15]

Calvin's almost undiscriminating providentialism rejects the guidance of any philosophic distinction between natural and unnatural or even between necessary and unnecessary. The "inhuman philosophy" he has in mind appears to be Stoicism, for in a similar denunciation, made shortly before, where he speaks of the "iron-hearted philosophy," he explicitly states that he is referring to the ancient Stoics as well as the modern ones.[16] Locke, however, to support the distinction, invokes Horace, whom he has earlier (§ 7) assured us "warm'd not himself with the Reputation of any Sect, and least of all affected Stoical Austerities."[17] It is more likely that Locke derived the distinction between natural and fanciful wants from Epicureanism than from Stoicism.[18]

The basis for the distinction is for Locke a sort of teleological hedonism (or algedonism, since it concerns pain more than pleasure), which renders preservation more fundamental than pleasure or pain. Unlike the wants of fancy,

> The Pains, that come from the Necessities of Nature are Monitors to us, to beware of greater Mischiefs, which they are the Forerunners of: And therefore they must not be wholly neglected, nor strain'd too far. [§ 107][19]

This doctrine is also expounded in the *Essay*, where it is explained that pains serve not "our preservation barely, but the preservation of every part and organ in its perfection."[20]

Locke says it would be "best for Children" for them not to "place any pleasure . . . at all" in matters that nature has made indifferent. But he seems to expect merely that they "learn the Art of stifling their Desires" so that they can "consult, and make use of their Reason, before they give allowance to their Inclinations." We should recall that, according to the *Essay*, the mind's "power to *suspend* the execution and satisfaction of any of its desires [is] the source of all liberty."[21] This liberty includes the mind's "Mastery over it self" or ability "to take it self off from the hot Pursuit of one Thing, and set it self upon another with Facility and Delight" (§ 75).[22]

That Locke does not mean that children should be brought to have no desires of fancy is shown by his statement here that, when children act well, "all things should be contrived, as much as could be, to their Satisfaction, that they might find the ease and pleasure of doing well" (though presumably only as an indirect reward for good conduct, that is, as a natural consequence of parental esteem; see § 107, end, and § 53). He even specifically recommends that their forbearing to demand satisfaction of their wants of fancy should be rewarded "by giving them what they liked." The satisfaction of wants of fancy is thus employed not to eliminate them but to reward, and at the same time instill, the ability to deny those wants and to forbear expressing them as demands on others. Satisfying children's desires serves not only to reward the children for obedience but to "assure them of the love of those, who rigorously exacted this Obedience." Evidence of love or good will is necessary to ensure cheerful obedience to authority (see §§ 38, 53, 115 [pp. 222, 224]).

The importance of giving evidence of love or good will has a partial political parallel. Primitive (patriarchal) political authority rests on recognition of the ruler's tenderness and affection, but once men have examined "more carefully *the Original* and Rights of *Government*," they rely instead on subjecting the government to law, which they do by placing the legislative power in "collective Bodies of Men" and finding out "ways to *restrain the Exorbitances*, and *prevent the Abuses*" of power.[23] Evidence of good will, however, plays a part in two important aspects of Locke's political doctrine: prerogative and the exercise of the right of revolution. These are aspects that are the least legal and most prudential in character. Prerogative, being "*nothing but the Power of doing publick good without a Rule*," that is, "without the prescription of the Law, and sometimes even against it," depends for its operation on the "People observing the whole tendency of their [rulers'] Actions to be the publick good." The exercise of the right of revolution, if not the right itself, depends on the people's sense of the "designs" and "intention" of their rulers, not merely on the rulers' violation of the restraints on them. Locke writes, "It being as impossible for a Governor, if he really means the good of his People, and the preservation of them and their Laws together, not to make them see and feel it; as it is for the Father of a Family, not to let his Children see he loves, and takes care of them."[24] Evidence of good intention is not sufficient, but it can excuse much.

Locke also narrows the policy of denial by exempting from it the realm of recreation or play (§ 108). This exemption is an extension of his earlier exemption of the realm of play from punishment (§ 67); not only are children not to be forbidden to play and not to be punished for playing, but even their requests to play in particular ways should be granted. In this case, "Fancy must be permitted to speak, and be hearkn'd to also." The need for recreation is in itself a natural or necessary want;[25] nevertheless, "there can be no *Recreation* without Delight, which depends not always on Reason, but oftener on Fancy." This concession to delight and fancy in recreation is not merely marginal, for the improvement of children should "be made a *Recreation* to them" and "Care should be taken, that what is of Advantage to them, they should always do with delight." This injunction is the positive side of the prohibition against making what is useful a task or a duty (§ 73). Locke does not repeat here that it is precisely the liberty he recommends that alone "gives the true Relish and Delight" to recreation (§ 76; see also § 74), but he does explain that the prerequisite for applying the kind of "Management" that makes improvement into delightful recreation is first "to raise in [children] the desire of Credit, Esteem, and Reputation." Apparently it is not only by allowing liberty, or by sending or diverting children away from useful activities while they still desire to continue them, or by maintaining a proper balance between "Exercises of the Body and Mind" that children can be brought to "find Delight in the Practice of laudable Things." They must also find delight in the *lauding* of these things; desire for esteem is the prerequisite both for the successful conversion of improvement into recreation and for the allowance of liberty as an effective method of management toward virtue. Locke concludes that "Such a Management [as allows 'a free liberty' in the realm of recreation, which should encompass all that is useful] will make them in love with the Hand that directs them, and the Vertue they are directed to." Liberty can lead to attachment to authority as well as to virtue. This allowance of liberty in recreation, like the method of teaching by practice rather than by precept (see § 66, p. 159), has the additional advantage of revealing the natural temper of the child. This revelation not only serves to guide the proper employment of parental authority by showing what natural biases must be remedied and what propensities may be appealed to, but, according to Locke, it may also "direct wise Parents in the choice, both of the Course of Life, and Imployment they shall design them for." There is no indication, I may note incidentally, that such a choice is a matter of divine calling.

## CIVILITY (§ 109)

The second way in which parental authority should be employed to manage the twofold love of dominion is by the proper regulation of children's contests for mastery over each other (§ 109). Children express their love of dominion not only in fanciful demands upon their powerful parents—demands that Locke recommends should be denied (§§ 106–8)—but, even more, in contests for mastery among themselves, especially over "those that stand near, or beneath them in Age or Degree, as soon as they come to consider others with those distinctions" (§ 104; see also § 117). Locke urges that

> Whoever begins the *Contest,* should be sure to be crossed in it. But not only that, but they should be taught to have all the *Deference, Complaisance* and *Civility* one for another imaginable. This, when they see it procures them respect, Love and Esteem, and that they lose no Superiority by it, they will take more Pleasure in, than in insolent Domineering. . . . [§ 109]

This double policy of punishing the striving for mastery over others and rewarding civility does not mean abandoning concern for having others look up to one, concern for being deferred to, or even concern for superiority. A desire for winning esteem from others replaces the desire for mastery over them—for making them submit their wills to one's own. By teaching and even molding children by getting them to do freely what one wants, one teaches them to act in the same way: to get others to be useful to them freely or from a concern for their esteem and not by mastery (see also § 117). Still, though civility is so pleasing as naturally to procure the rewards of love and esteem (§§ 66 [p. 160], 143 [pp. 247–48]), its practice is not ensured by these natural rewards but seems to depend on the background presence of parents, whose justice protects each child against the insolence of others. So does mutual practice of the law of nature prove insufficient in the state of nature in the absence of an impartial judge to enforce a standing law and to defend the rational and industrious against the quarrelsome and contentious.[26]

Children are not taught civility merely as a more effective means than mastery for getting others to be useful to them; a change must also be worked in what they want from others. They must be taught to desire freely granted esteem rather than fearful submission to their wills. Means and end now merge: if what one wants from others is freely granted esteem rather than slavish submission, the way to get it is not through mastery but through civility. Civility itself, considered internally, is esteem for others; considered externally, it is the expression of such esteem (see §§ 67, 143). This identity of the means to esteem, civility, with its end is at least a paradox if not a vicious circle. For it is not clear that a civility—in the sense of an outward expression of esteem—that is practiced only for the sake of gaining esteem for oneself would provide others with the esteem they seek if it is recognized as such. This difficulty is illustrated by one aspect of a modification that Locke makes in the policy of thwarting desires for mastery and rewarding civility. Although one should thwart those who begin contests for mastery, one should not listen to children's accusations or complaints against each other. This exception is itself qualified by this proviso: if the complaint is sufficiently serious, one should

> reprove the Offender by himself alone, out of sight of him that complained, and make him go and ask Pardon, and make reparation. Which coming thus, as it were from himself, will be the more cheerfully performed, and more kindly received, the Love strengthened between them, and a Custom of Civility grow familiar amongst your Children. [§ 109]

The civil action here, that of asking pardon and making reparation (which is the only action that can end the state of war in the state of nature),[27] is apparently but not truly performed freely or as an expression of inward esteem on the part of the insolent, ill-natured, and injurious toward the complaining and querulous; it is performed because the parent "made him do it." The virtuous circle of mutual esteem rewarding mutual civility (the outward expression of esteem) begins, nonetheless, to revolve on the basis of this initial deception. Civility initiated for an extrinsic purpose, whether in fulfillment of an imposed duty, as here, or in order to obtain the esteem, or simply the cooperation, of others, as in other cases, can become genuine civility by eliciting civility on the part of others, which in turn elicits one's own esteem for them.

Even the initial, deceptive, appearance of freedom with which the offender asks pardon and makes reparation ("*as it were* from himself") is more pleasing to him ("more cheerfully performed") than undisguised fulfillment of an imposed duty would be. This fact can easily be understood if one recalls that the desire for freedom is a desire to *show* that one is free (see § 73). It also extends the notion that "every one can more easily bear a denial from himself, than from any body else" (§ 107) to the denial that merely *seems* to come from himself. For asking pardon and making reparation are a kind of denial—a denial of the desire to show that one's own *good* actions come from oneself (§ 73) or not to have one's "Faults seen in their naked Colours" (§ 132; see also § 143, p. 247); but they are, at the same time, good actions that one desires to show come from oneself. The desire for freedom is so great that one can more easily bear even the denial of the desire for freedom itself when it comes, or seems to come, from oneself.

This policy is also an extension of the defense of hypocrisy in Locke's advocacy of teaching a child to conceal his faults from the world so as to preserve his reputation and thereby his incentive to be virtuous (§ 62). Since here the child who has been offended is, necessarily, all too aware of the offender's fault, the best that can be done is to conceal the fact that the latter's repentance does not come simply from himself. To put it another way: the offender should conceal the fault of being unrepentant or obstinate. As in the general hypocrisy that preserves the incentive to be useful to others, the deception here is not merely self-serving, for it serves to establish the good will, or even love, on the part of the injured that can work as an incentive for the future virtue of the offender. For the appearance of freedom with which the offender repents is not only more pleasing to himself than the undisguised fulfillment of duty would be; it is also more pleasing to the offended party ("more kindly received").

Reflecting on this example and taking a larger prospect, one can say that the identity of means and end involved in showing esteem toward others in order to obtain their show of esteem toward oneself (which in turn may possibly be shown only for an extrinsic purpose) need not imply an empty or unsatisfying circularity. It is true that a show of esteem merely to obtain some material advantage or to avoid some corporal punishment from another, despite one's contempt or hostility for him (see §§ 42, 50), would, if perceived as such, fail to provide the other with the esteem he may seek. But that is not the case when esteem is showed in order to obtain esteem for oneself. For the concern to gain the *esteem* of another, and even the concern to obtain *things* from him but to obtain them from him freely, already includes a kind of esteem for him. For esteem, unlike fear, implies not merely a recognition of the power of others but also a recognition of their desire for freedom, their preference for acting out of esteem rather than from fear. Such a concern therefore allows a reciprocal relation, demanding neither purely disinterested attachment nor deception of the kind that had to be employed in the case of the quarreling children.

Concealing from the offended child that his complaints have brought about the reparation made by the offender not only serves to make that reparation more pleasant for both the offending and the offended child; it also discourages complaining. Indeed, the policy of secretly requiring reparation is in itself an exception, made only in especially serious cases, to the policy of ignoring complaints, which policy in turn modifies the general rule of thwarting those who begin contests for mastery. One should discourage children's complaints because "It weakens and effeminates their Minds to suffer them to *Complain.*" But complaints are discouraged, not to encourage children to stand up and defend themselves against "insolent Domineering," but to teach endurance of "crossing, or pain from others, without being permitted to think it strange or intolerable."[28] Although Locke recommends here a just parental policy of punishing or thwarting insolent domineering and is far from inculcating a slavish disposition (cf. § 50), he does not teach a rigid insistence on one's rights. Too firm an insistence on one's rights, whether expressed in a direct contest for mastery or in complaints to authority, makes civility impossible and some kind of conflict inevitable. As Locke explains in the very next section of the *Thoughts*, "Our first Actions being guided more by Self-love, than Reason or Reflection, 'tis no wonder that in Children they should be very apt to deviate from the just Measures of Right and Wrong" (§ 110; see also § 139). This applies not only to children; in *Two Treatises* Locke explains that "Men being partial to themselves, Passion and Revenge is very apt to carry them too far and with too much heat, in their own Cases."[29]

For this reason, civility will not be ensured simply by men's concern for justice; a further element is required, a complaisance or willingness to endure a measure of being even unjustly crossed by others. Locke explains, further on, that to have civility, given the "Natural *Roughness* which makes a Man uncomplaisant to others, so that he has no deference for their inclinations, tempers, or conditions," it is necessary "to supple the natural stifness and so soften Men's Tempers that they may bend to a compliance and accommodate themselves to those they have to do with" (§ 143, p. 247).[30] Accordingly, complaints are discouraged here, not to encourage self-defense, but to harden children to put up with what they might consider injustice from others. Not only is one apt to mistake the justice of one's own claims, but even defense or complaint against what is actually "insolent Domineering" by another is likely only to express "Anger and Revenge" rather than simply a just desire to maintain one's freedom. Locke does not expect or endeavor to confine self-defense or complaint to a scrupulous observance of justice. To expect to do so is unreasonable, and to endeavor to do so is likely only to license anger and revenge and lead to conflicts and resentments that obstruct civility. It is likely only to produce the propensity Locke decries in his opposition to teaching fencing, that of being "more touchy than needs, on Points of Honour, and slight or no provocations," more "apt to stand upon Punctilios" and "to give Affronts, or fiercely justifie them when given, which is that which usually makes the Quarrel" (§ 199). If the Lockean gentleman is far from having the slavish temper that Hobbes seems to encourage, which, moved by reasonable fear or concerned with self-preservation, excludes honor and consequently submits to tyranny, he is perhaps even farther from the angry and vengeful aristocratic temper that so insists upon honor that it can hardly be distinguished from the tyrannical insolence it is so ready to detect and resist.[31] For though one child "begins the *Contest,*" it is a contest for mastery on the part of both the offender and the offended. Therefore, everyone must experience some "crossing": the insolent initiators must be thwarted by parental authority; the others are thwarted by their insolent peers. Locke's gentleman appears to be one of the people whom he characterizes in *Two Treatises* as being "more disposed to suffer, than right themselves by Resistance."[32] To make his doctrine of individual rights and the right of resistance safe for the world, Locke requires patient people and complaisant gentlemen. Nevertheless, while tolerance is required for civility among equals, vigilance toward authority is required to keep government civil rather than despotic.[33]

## LIBERALITY (§ 110)

The third way in which parental authority should be employed to treat the twofold love of dominion is by teaching liberality or justice (§ 110). This teaching is directed primarily to correcting the second aspect of the love of dominion, its expression in a desire for property (cf. § 105).

Locke's method of teaching liberality to children is to "let them find by Experience, that the most *Liberal* has always most plenty, with Esteem and Commendation to boot." The "Experience" Locke is talking about here is not ordinary experience of the world, for liberality is not necessarily taught by unmediated experience. On the contrary, parents must exert themselves to construct the experience that teaches liberality by rewarding it with "great Commendation and Credit, and constantly taking care, that [the child] loses nothing by his *Liberality.*" This edifying experience, arranged by the parents, is similar to the "settled Experience" that "teaches Children, that the Things they delight in belong to, and are to be enjoyed by those only, who are in a State of Reputation" (§ 58). However, that "settled Experience" is more fundamental; it serves to teach love of reputation itself, whereas this arranged experience uses that love to teach love of liberality. However, in both examples of arranged experience, "the Objects of their Desires are made assisting to Vertue" (§ 58). Both serve to remedy in this world the insufficient attractiveness of "unendowed" virtue, which the ancients failed to remedy with their "airy commendations" and which Christianity reasonably remedied by making virtue "the best bargain" by means of otherworldly rewards and punishments.

Because Locke recommends here that those in charge of a child arrange that his liberality "be always repaid, and with Interest," Rousseau accuses him of rendering the child "in appearance liberal and in fact a miser," of teaching him only a "usurious liberality."[34] Such a child, according to Rousseau, will be liberal only when assured of a return and otherwise will cease to be so. Locke, however, does not seem to intend that his young gentlemen be taught such a narrowly calculating liberality, dependent on favorable circumstances. He intends rather that "good Nature may be setled in them into an Habit," and habits operate without thought or reflection, let alone calculation of interest (see §§ 64, 66, and 110, end). In fact, Rousseau's real opposition to Locke here centers less on self-interest than on habituation, which Rousseau strove to eliminate or at least to minimize and Locke emphatically employed.[35] Since Rousseau's objection is that the force of habit is not only destructive of freedom or independence but is also insufficient to overcome the power of self-interest, it is necessary to note, first, that Locke believes in the great power of habit to overcome even self-interest[36] and, second, that he does not rely here on habituation alone to produce liberality but on pride or emulation as well; the habituation is colored by concern for esteem. As he says:

> Make this a Contest among Children, who shall out-do one another this way: And by this Means, by a constant Practice, Children having made it easie to themselves to part with what they have, good Nature may be setled in them into an Habit, and they may take Pleasure, and pique themselves in being *Kind, Liberal* and *Civil* to others.[37]

The contest for mastery[38] is replaced by a contest in civility, a useful form of competition.[39] Liberality, like kindness and civility itself, is a matter not merely of habit but of pride.

The liberality of the Lockean gentleman is neither calculating and usurious nor a repudiation of the acquisitiveness Locke justifies in the chapter on property in the *Second Treatise*.[40] One should note first of all that liberality does not preclude acquisitiveness but may even be said to presuppose it.[41] One may also note that the liberality taught here to children is limited, at least initially, to parting with what they have, easily and freely, "to their Friends." Finally, the fact that the liberality taught here in effect presupposes acquisitiveness, even if that basis is forgotten as kindness settles into a habit, also warns against concluding that Locke, in praising liberality, repudiates acquisitiveness.

The chief evidence for thinking that Locke here repudiates acquisitiveness is his characterization of the quality that is liberality's contrary, which should be "early and carefully weeded out," namely,

> Covetousness, and the Desire of having in our Possession, and under our Dominion, more than we have need of, being the Root of all Evil.

John Dunn uses this passage to show Locke's opposition to covetousness, which he seems to equate with acquisitiveness or appropriation as such.[42] Claiming that C. B. Macpherson dismisses Locke's condemnation of covetousness far too simply as a vestige of traditional medieval social values, reflecting Locke's place in a transitional society, Dunn maintains that Locke's denunciations of covetousness "were seriously intended, even if they have a hypocritical ring to our ears today."[43] But what Macpherson claimed was rather that Locke distinguishes covetousness from unlimited appropriation, so that his "denunciation of covetousness is a consequence, not a contradiction, of his assumption that unlimited accumulation is the essence of rationality." Macpherson presents this distinction as follows:

> it was rational, i.e., industrious, appropriation that required protection against the covetousness of the quarrelsome and contentious who sought to acquire possessions not by industry but by trespass. It was not the industrious appropriator who was covetous, but the man who would invade his appropriation.[44]

Macpherson seems to understand covetousness not as greediness, that is, the desire to acquire things as such, but as the desire to acquire the possessions of others by trespass rather than by industry. His emphasis on this distinction is in accord with Locke's warning in the *Essay* that we should not confuse covetousness with frugality.[45] Moreover, in the chapter on property in the *Second Treatise*, Locke distinguishes between "the Industrious and Rational" man, whose labor entitles him to "the World," and "the Quarrelsom and Contentious" man, who is characterized by "Covetousness" and who dares to "meddle with what was already improved by another's Labour" because he "desired the benefit of another's Pains, which he had no right to."[46]

If these words of Locke's are insufficient to convince the reader that Locke, in denouncing covetousness, denounces not industrious acquisition but only unjust designs on the honest gains of others, it is possible to refer to a clear statement of his that has not hitherto been noticed in discussions of this point. In Locke's "Paraphrase and Notes on the Epistle of St. Paul to the Ephesians" he comments on Ephesians 4:19, where it is written, in the Authorized Version that serves as Locke's text, that the Gentiles work all uncleanness "with greediness." Locke paraphrases this as uncleanness committed "even beyond the bounds of natural desires"; but he notes that this translation of the Greek term *pleonexia*, though in accord with Pauline usage, is contrary to its common meaning:

143

> . . . "covetousness," in the common acceptation of the
> word, is the letting loose our desires to that which, by
> the law of justice, we have no right to.[47]

This statement indicates that Locke's denunciations of "covetousness" are directed not against those who devote themselves to industrious acquisition or even, like the capitalist, to unlimited industrious acquisition, but only against those who unjustly desire goods belonging to others. Indeed, when covetousness remains simply a desire for the justly acquired possessions of others and does not actually issue in unjust acts of trespass against their property, it is not properly a crime or contrary to the ends of civil society but merely a vice or a sin.[48] Accordingly, here, in the *Thoughts,* covetousness itself is called, not an evil or an injustice, but rather the root of evil or injustice (§ 110; cf. § 105). In this Locke echoes Saint Paul's warning that "the love of money is the root of all evil," made in the context of Paul's preaching contentment with food and clothing or flight from worldly gain.[49] Locke's teaching liberality on the initial basis of concern for worldly gain indicates that liberality is neither incompatible with concern for gain nor based on otherworldly flight from it, though it is opposed to desire for the justly gained property of others.

Locke speaks here, however, of covetousness together with "the Desire of having in our Possession, and under our Dominion, more than we have need of" as being "the Root of all Evil" and to be "weeded out." This desire may seem even less compatible than covetousness with the acquisitiveness Locke justifies in the chapter on property in the *Second Treatise.* But since this desire is directly opposed here to "the contrary Quality of a Readiness to impart to others," which should be "implanted," it may well be understood not as the desire for superfluities as such, but (noting Locke's mention here of "Dominion") along the lines of the desire for property, denounced above, which takes pleasure in the *power* that property seems to give (§ 105). So understood, a desire for superfluities in the face of the needs of others would lead to a lack of liberality—a lack of readiness to give freely of what one has.[50] For though Locke says here that covetousness and the desire for superfluity are "the" root of "all" evil, he says above, more precisely, that the two forms of love of dominion (desire for submission and desire for property as power) are "*two* Roots of *almost* all the Injustice and Contention, that so disturb Humane Life" (§ 105, emphases added).[51] Therefore, when covetousness and the illiberal desire for superfluity are here called "the" root, it seems to be because they are understood here to include, or at least to be suffused by, the desire that others submit to one. As noted above, Locke, in making his quasi-Stoic distinction between natural wants and wants of fancy, does not imply that the gentleman will actually do without all superfluities and lead a life of ascetic severity; he implies only that the gentleman will be able to subdue such desires when his reason tells him it is necessary to do so, whether directly, for the sake of his own happiness, or to avoid offending others.

As we consider the liberality of Locke's gentleman, it is necessary to remember, after all, that he is not expected to give his estate away to the poor but to preserve it and bequeathe it to his son.[52] One can say that the emphasis is neither on acquisition nor on spending but on preservation (§§ 174, 210). Yet ultimately it is only an appreciation of the labor or pain required for acquisition that acts as a restraint on spending and a spur to preservation (§§ 96, 211). However, since the child cannot yet be expected to comprehend the origins of property in labor, another basis (habit and pride) had to be found for the proper attitude toward property in Locke's teaching of liberality.

## JUSTICE (§ 110)

In the third edition of the *Thoughts* Locke adds the teaching of justice to that of liberality as another way to treat the aspect of the love of dominion that is expressed as a desire for property (§ 110). Locke has indicated, to begin with, that his treatment of the love of dominion is in the service of justice, for that love is said to be the root of injustice (§ 105). Calling justice here "this great Social Vertue," he shows that it is as difficult as it is important to teach.

Children are prone to injustice apparently because "the just Measures of Right and Wrong . . . are in the Mind the Result of improved Reason and serious Meditation," which cannot be expected in children. To have justice in the mind requires improved reason and serious meditation first of all because understanding justice presupposes understanding property. One may even say that justice consists in not violating the property of others.

Locke writes in the *Essay* that

> "*Where there is no property, there is no Injustice,*" is a Proposition as certain as any Demonstration in *Euclid:* For the *Idea* of *Property*, being a right to any thing; and the *Idea* to which the name *Injustice* is given, being the Invasion or Violation of that right; it is evident, that these *Ideas*, being thus established, and these Names annexed to them, I can as certainly know this Proposition to be true, as that a Triangle has three Angles equal to two right ones.[53]

As Axtell justly notes, Locke here follows Hobbes's "where there is no *Own*, that is, no Propriety, there is no Injustice."[54] More specifically in the *Essay,* Locke calls injustice "the *Idea* of taking from others, without their Consent, what their honest Industry has possessed them of."[55] Accordingly, Locke writes here in the *Thoughts* that "Children cannot well comprehend what *Injustice* is, till they understand Property, and how particular Persons come by it." But they do not early "have Language and Understanding enough to form distinct Notions of Property." It seems to be for this reason that Locke does not recommend a rational teaching of justice, based on a knowledge "in the Mind" of the "just Measures of Right and Wrong," but urges instead a habituation to an "ingenuous Detestation of this shameful Vice." Such habituation, "the true and genuine Method to obviate this Crime," seems to be achieved not by punishment, let alone by reasoning, but by "a Shew of Wonder and Abhorrency" at any tendency toward injustice on the part of the child. Such a show is one of the most effective methods of shaming (see §§ 85 and 131). The incapacity of children, however, dictates not only a reliance on shaming rather than reasoning as the method of teaching justice; it also requires substituting liberality for justice. For their incapacity lies in their inability to discern not only the ground of justice but also its measures. Since they are without "distinct Notions of Property," "the safest way to secure *Honesty,* is to lay the Foundations of it early in Liberality, and an Easiness to part with to others what they have or like themselves." This recommended substitution explains Locke's initial willingness to omit any discussion of justice as such from the *Thoughts.* Since children know neither the grounds nor the bounds of property and therefore cannot understand justice, they must be made liberal so as to prevent their trespassing those bounds. If they are made liberal, then, despite their ignorance of the bounds of what belongs to others, it seems less likely that they will be tempted to transgress those bounds.

A willingness to give to others does not, however, preclude a willingness to take unjustly from others.[56] It is necessary, therefore, to teach a child not only to be ready to give to others but also *not* to give to others what is not one's own to give. So, though children cannot have "distinct Notions of Property," they ought, nonetheless, to have *some* notion of property:

> And since Children seldom have any thing but by Gift, and that for the most part from their Parents, they may be at first taught not to take or keep any thing, but what is given them by those, whom they take to have a Power over it.

I have suggested so far that it is the danger of the child's *giving* what is not his to give that marks the insufficiency of liberality as the foundation of justice and dictates the necessity of teaching some notion of property. Since Locke, however, writes here only of the danger of the child's *taking*

146

or *keeping* what is not his, it appears that the inadequacy of liberality—Locke's initial foundation of justice—is much greater. A readiness to give to others, it seems, cannot even be relied on to prevent a child from taking *and keeping* what belongs to others; liberality is far from adequate as a foundation for justice.

The notion of property that is relied on here as a foundation for teaching justice to children is a limited one. The first limitation that appears is that children cannot be expected to "understand Property, and how particular Persons come by it" in the sense of understanding *all* the ways that persons "come by it." In the fifth chapter of the *Second Treatise*, "Of Property," Locke argues famously that labor gives a title to property. But that is not the *only* title to property; labor indeed gave a title "in the Beginning," or is the means of the "beginning of Property,"[57] but there are other derivative titles. Indeed, labor itself is a title derived from and subordinate to use. For the very first statement in the chapter is that men "have a right to their Preservation, and consequently to Meat and Drink, and such other things, as Nature affords for their Subsistence." Locke, expanding the basis of property right from bare preservation to a wider sense of "use," proceeds to argue that to enable men to "use" the world "to the best advantage of Life, and convenience" or "for the Support and Comfort of their being," there *must* be a means of establishing property, and this means turns out to be labor. Just as the purpose of property is to "enjoy" it or "to make use of [it] to any advantage of life," so is it accordingly limited to such "use" and is not to be wasted. "Use," however, does not mean simply consumption: "If he gave away a part to anybody else . . . these also he made use of." Not only gift (which includes inheritance), but barter or sale are also counted as "use."[58] Furthermore, though "Labour and Industry began" property, "*Compact* and Agreement, *settled the Property* which Labour and Industry began."[59] One can therefore see that, according to the *Thoughts,* children do have a notion of one of the derivative titles to property—namely, gift—though they have no notion of either the original title, labor, or the conventional one, law. The child's understanding of property as gift cannot even serve as an analogical basis for understanding the original title of property, because that original title, like that of government, is less a matter of (divine) gift than of (human) labor.[60] The child cannot be said to understand *distinctly* what it means for something to belong to him, since, though he knows in a way that something belongs to him because it is given to him by those to whom it belongs, he does not know why it belonged to them in the first place.[61] Locke writes here, accordingly, that children are to regard as their own only what is given them by those "whom they take to have a Power over it." The children's notion of the original title of property, as distinct from the derivative one of gift, is only that of power, which is one of our primary ideas but is not properly either the natural or the conventional title to property; similarly, the children's original notion of authority is not distinct from that of power (§ 40).

Although Locke recommends shame and habit rather than reason and reflection as methods of teaching justice, he does give an instance here of how reason may be appealed to as a sort of last resort:

> And 'tis but for the Father or Tutor to take and keep from them something that they value, and think their own; or order some Body else to do it; and by such Instances make them sensible, what little Advantage they are like to make, by possessing themselves *unjustly* of what is another's, whilst there are in the World stronger and more Men than they.[62]

This method makes one feel the advantage of justice through suffering injustice. It does not presuppose a "distinct" notion of property but merely the subjective "something that they value, and think their own"— a sense of property not distinct from the love of dominion (which is the dangerous inclination here being treated). As such, it might seem to teach not respect for what belongs to others according to "the just Measures of Right and Wrong" but merely respect for what others "value . . . and think their own." But it points away from mere subjectivity to agreement on the bounds of property. This method is practically the same as that employed in the *Second Treatise,* of referring to the state of nature or absence of common authority in order to make men more sensible of the advantages of civil government and more insistent on obtaining them.[63] This method also reminds one of the derivation of justice Locke produced in a fragment of uncertain date entitled "Morality." He there writes:

> If all thing be left in common want rapin and force will unavoidably follow in which state as is evident happynesse cannot be had which cannot consist without plenty and security.
>
> To avoid this estate compact must determin peoples rights.
>
> These compacts are to be kept or broken. If to be broken their making signifies noething if to be kept then Justice is established as a duty and will be the first and generall rule of our happynesse.
>
> But it may be objected it may be sometimes a mans advantage to break his word and then I may doe it as contributing to my happynesse. Resp: All men being equally under one and the same rule if it be permitted to me to break my word for my advantage it is also permitted every one else and then whatever I possesse will be subjected to the force or deceit of all the rest of

148

the men in the world in which state it is impossible for
any man to be happy unless he were both stronger and
wiser then all the rest of man kinde for in such a state
of rapin and force it is impossible any one man should
be master of those things whose possession is necessary
to his well being.[64]

Here, too, Locke appeals to "advantage" and to the fundamental recognition of the existence of many and stronger other men, in order to
show the necessity of justice, that is, of agreeing to respect the rights of
others and of abiding by that agreement.

But this "rougher remedy," as it is called here in the *Thoughts,* is not
"the true and genuine Method" of teaching justice, for the true method
employs shaming and habituation. But neither is it, despite its roughness,
a punishment. It is presented rather as an apparently natural consequence or experience (cf. § 58 and liberality in § 110). This "rougher"
method indeed must be recognized as that of reasoning. For, immediately after presenting it, Locke states his preference for shaming instead,
which "will be a better Guard against *Dishonesty,* than any Considerations
drawn from Interest; Habits working more constantly, and with greater
Facility than Reason: Which, when we have most need of it, is seldom
fairly consulted, and more rarely obey'd." In this way Locke reveals that
he equates reason with serious long-range considerations of interest.
This rough remedy therefore, though not "the true and genuine Method"
of teaching justice, is the rational method; that is, it teaches justice by
teaching the truth. However, even reason understood in this realistic
manner is too weak to be relied on as the foundation of justice.

The end of the paragraph on justice reveals the problem of justice
more clearly than the beginning. The beginning might lead one to suppose that the problem is merely that children do not yet have the developed guidance of reason or a knowledge of the measures of justice,
whereas in fact reason does not in any case work as constantly or easily
as shame or habit, is seldom consulted even when developed, and is
usually not obeyed even when it is consulted. Mere presence in the mind
of knowledge of the just measures of right and wrong is insufficient to
produce just conduct.[65] The beginning, again, might lead one to suppose
that Locke is writing about a problem that pertains only to children, or
even only to young children, whereas in fact he is writing about a problem
that "we" have. Indeed, not merely the tendency to disobey reason when
present, but even the absence of improved reason or serious meditation
is found in most grown men; for, as Locke remarks earlier in the *Thoughts*
(§ 81): "The Foundations on which several Duties are built, and the
Fountains of Right and Wrong, from which they spring, are not perhaps
easily to be let into the Minds of grown Men, not used to abstract their
Thoughts from common received Opinions."[66]

## CRYING (§§ 111–14)

Locke turns next to the subject of crying (§§ 111–14). This subject falls properly within the treatment of the love of dominion, for Locke notes, near the beginning of the whole discussion, that children are expressing their desire for others to submit to them when they "cry, grow peevish, sullen, and out of humour, for nothing but to have their *Wills*" (§ 104).[67] Since such crying expresses "a striving for Mastery," "Insolence, or Obstinacy" (§ 111), "Pride," or "Stomach" (§ 114),[68] it should be strictly forbidden when it occurs and be treated with "severity," even whipping or beating (§§ 112 and 114, beginning). But that is not all that Locke has to say about what crying expresses. Children also use crying to express "Title and Right" or "Claim" (§ 111). It is, in Locke's resonant phrase, "a Declaration of their Right" (§ 112). He even calls it, however ironically, "a sort of Remonstrance against the Oppression and Injustice of those who deny them, what they have a Mind to." This kind of crying and the pride it expresses are another, though suspect, source of the sense of right or justice and injustice.[69] Children cry in this way not simply "when they have not the Power to obtain their Desire" (§ 111) but when their desires are denied by others. For mere physical inability to obtain one's desire does not lead one to cry for it; as Locke notes, children do not cry for the moon (§ 38, end). This sense of right or justice, expressing only the pride that resents the thwarting of one's desires by others, clearly is not in itself a satisfactory sense of justice. But neither is it simply pernicious, nor need Locke's way of describing it be seen as simply ironical; for we have indeed just seen that the rational method of teaching justice derives the sense of justice from the thwarted desire to think things one's own, modified by the recognition that others have the same desire (§ 110).

This sense of justice, derived from resentment at denial of one's desires, is unsatisfactory, however, first of all because the inability to bear the denial of one's own desires is incompatible with one's own pursuit of happiness, one's ability to be useful to oneself as well as to others (§ 45).[70] The severity Locke recommends here might seem to cure this inability only by appealing to it, and as such it would incur the criticism he makes earlier of corporal punishment (§ 48). But Locke emphasizes here the importance of the manner in which the punishment is administered; indeed, he points out that crying often occurs as the *result* of punishment, and he chiefly recommends that it then be subdued by beating the child until crying ceases on command. Locke again does not explain exactly how it is that severe corporal punishment is both able sometimes to appeal to, and thereby strengthen, our propensity to yield to present corporal pleasure or pain and able sometimes to master that propensity and to subdue our insistence on its justice when it is thwarted by others (see §§ 78–79, 84, and 87). He does not explain exactly how it is able to "prevail over [the children's] Wills, teach them to submit their Passions, and make their Minds supple and pliant," or to "do their Minds any good," making them "pliant, penitent and yielding" (§ 112). What he is not saying, however, is that pain is what breaks the children's pride, for he emphasizes here that the punishment must be administered "without Passion, soberly and yet effectually too, laying on the Blows and Smart, not furiously and all at once, but slowly, with Reasoning between" (see also § 87). As he remarks earlier in the *Thoughts*, children "distinguish early betwixt Passion and Reason" (§ 77); they can feel by "the Mildness of your Carriage, and the Composure even in your Correction of them, that what you do is reasonable in you, and useful and necessary for them" (§ 81; see also § 83). This kind of evidently reasonable severity is therefore able not merely to teach children to deny their passions but to "teach them to submit their Passions, and make their Minds supple and pliant, to what their Parents' Reason advises them now, and so prepare them to obey, what their own Reason shall advise hereafter" (§ 112).[71] It appears that for curing obstinacy Locke sees two things as necessary: on the one hand, severity, which alters the calculation of present pleasure and pain and also subdues pride, or the primitive sense of justice, by evoking a sense of dependence in the most vivid way; on the other hand, mildness of manner and intermittent reasoning, which show children that the severity expresses not "passionate Tyranny" (§ 112) but concern for what is "useful and necessary for them" (§ 81).

The primitive sense of justice is by itself unsatisfactory not only because it is incompatible with the ability to deny one's desires, which is requisite for one's own pursuit of happiness, but also because it does not take account of others, or, one might say, it fails to take into account the fact that others have the same sense of justice. It appears that pain makes one most aware of others and of the necessity of taking them into account. In the *Essay* pleasure and especially pain are the ultimate sources of knowledge of one's own existence, knowledge of the existence of other things, and even, in a way, knowledge of the goodness of God.[72] The rational teaching of justice, used as a last resort (§ 110), far from simply suppressing this primitive sense of right and substituting another, uses and generalizes it.[73] By roughly eliciting the first sense of injustice—the sense that resents opposition to one's desires—the rational teaching brings about a recognition that one's own acts of injustice, which the primitive sense of right would otherwise support, elicit similar outrage on the part of others; it also brings about an awareness that, to protect oneself from such acts on the part of others, a generally accepted agreement on the bounds of property and justice is necessary.

Locke distinguishes between the crying that expresses the primitive sense of justice, or frustrated desire, and another sort of crying, one that gives vent to actual pain (§§ 112, beginning, and 113–14). At first this sort is necessary and acceptable, since for infants it is "the first and natural Way to declare their Sufferings or Wants, before they can speak" (§ 113). But, once they can speak, this crying too should be stopped. Locke evidently thinks that, once a child is able to speak of his pain or wants, his crying is no longer merely declarative of wants but becomes, if it is not domineering, merely "bemoaning" himself or "complaining." The bad effect of being permitted to bemoan one's pain is similar to the effect Locke discerned earlier as resulting from being permitted either to express desires of fancy (§ 107) or to complain about being crossed by others (§ 109). The bad effect of "giving vent" is that it "gives Life and Strength to our Appetites" (§ 107) or to our "Anger and Revenge" (§ 109) or, in this case, to our pain. For Locke explains here that children's bemoaning their pain, and, even more, having it bemoaned or pitied by others, "softens their Minds, and makes them yield to the little Harms, that happen to them" (§ 113). Not being pitied by others and even being forbidden to cry for oneself, on the other hand, harden one to become insensitive at least to little harms, "especially of the Body." Pain or suffering are only in the mind, "which alone feels."[74] He even says that "What our Minds yield not to, makes but a slight Impression, and does us but very little Harm: 'Tis the Suffering of our Spirits that gives and continues the Pain." Yet, shortly before this (§ 107), he seems to claim that only bodily pains or wants are natural and that all others are merely wants of fancy, which seems to contradict his claim now that bodily pain is unreal compared to mental suffering. Indeed, he recommends here that one should have an "Insensibility of Mind" for bodily harm but a "Tenderness [that] rises from an ingenuous Shame, and a quick Sence of Reputation." This latter statement suggests that his earlier apparent recognition of only basic bodily wants as necessities of nature (§ 106) and his dismissal of others as wants of fancy (§ 107) are not his last word; for he seems to accept the tenderness of shame as more than a mere want of fancy and to admit that reason can, after all, "fence against" the necessities of nature, if not against the harms they herald (cf. § 107).[75] On the other hand, Locke's dismissal of bodily pain here should be read in the light of his earlier statement that natural bodily pains can be warnings of real harms and, as such, ought to be heeded.

Although Locke cautions against parents' "pitying" or bemoaning their children's pain, he recognizes the duty "to compassionate them," which seems to mean to "help and ease them" (§ 113). The danger may not be merely that the child's complaining or the parent's "pitying" serves to make the pain more lively but that such crying expresses more than a natural desire for help and ease: an irrational and dangerous desire for others to "pity" one, a weakness or "Softness of Mind" that is the opposite of pride (§ 114). The desire to "pity" others, as distinct from helping and easing them—a pity that "softens their Minds" and induces an "Effeminacy of Spirit"—may be akin to the tyrannical desire for dominion (§§ 35, 104, 109).

The two sorts of crying express two tempers, the one "Domineering" (§ 111), stemming from pride (§ 114), the other "Querulous" (§ 111), stemming from "Softness of Mind, a quite contrary Cause" (§ 114). These seem to be the same two tempers that were described shortly before, in the account of how to regulate contests for mastery among children, so as to teach civility: the "insolent Domineering" or "the Insolence and Ill-nature of the Injurious" and the "Anger and Revenge" of the "Querulous" (§ 109). These two tempers also resemble "the *Sylla* and *Charybdis*" (§ 47) that the "great Art" or "true Secret of Education" (§ 46)—and particularly the proper policy of punishment—is meant to avoid: the propensity to indulge present pleasure or pain (§§ 45 and 48) and a "Slavish Temper" or "low Spirits" (§§ 46, 50, 51). In accordance with the diversity of the tempers they express, the two sorts of crying should be suppressed in different ways. To overcome pride and obstinacy, expressed by the first sort, requires a severity that reminds the child of his dependence. Yet even this severity should be administered without passion and be mixed with reasoning to show that the dependence is on a rational or benevolent authority (§ 112). The second sort of crying, however, requires "a gentler Hand," one that leads by means of persuasion, distraction, or ridicule (§ 114).

## COURAGE (§ 115)

There follows a long passage (§ 115, pp. 219–25), added in the third edition, dealing with courage and cowardice; it is inserted at this point because these two tempers are "so nearly related to the forementioned Tempers." Locke does not explicate this near relation (or even make unquestionably clear what previous tempers he refers to), but it would seem at first that courage corresponds to the domineering temper of "Pride, Obstinacy, and Stomach," whereas cowardice corresponds to the querulous temper of "Softness of Mind" (§ 114). Such a correspondence, however, would link the virtue with the temper that has just been dealt with severely and would link the vice with the temper that has just been dealt with gently. The solution to this paradox seems to be provided at once by Locke's introduction of a third quality, "an Excess on the daring side; *Fool-hardiness* and Insensibility of Danger being as little reasonable, as trembling and shrinking at the approach of every little Evil." Courage therefore appears to be the mean between two excesses that correspond to the two tempers corrected in the previous passage.[76]

Locke deals first with excess on the daring side. It seems to be an actual absence of fear. As such, it is dangerous and irrational, for "Fear

153

is a Passion, that, if rightly govern'd, has its use."[77] Its use is to serve "as a Monitor to quicken our Industry, and keep us upon our Guard against the Approaches of Evil."[78] Fear serves this use because it is "an Uneasiness under the Apprehension of that coming upon us which we dislike."[79] Locke also adds to the second edition of the *Essay* at about this same time the useful remark "that the chief if not only spur to humane Industry and Action is uneasiness."[80] It is true that, a little further on in the *Thoughts* (§ 126), Locke writes only of "the two great Springs of Action *Foresight* and *Desire*" and declares that "where there is no Desire, there will be no Industry."[81] Nonetheless, in the *Thoughts,* uneasiness in general, including fear of evil as well as desire for good, is the spur to industry; we can assume this not only from this passage (§ 115) but from the earlier statement that *both* "Good and Evil, *Reward* and *Punishment* . . . are the Spur and Reins, whereby all Mankind are set on work, and guided" (§ 54). It may well be that Locke views fear as more often a rein than a spur (one may say that in this lies the basis of his difference from Hobbes), though he does not exclude its action as a spur. The useful pain or uneasiness that is fear, like the pain or uneasiness that is desire, spurs us to take the pains that are industry or wariness in order to avoid the yet greater future pains that are harms or evils.[82] For Locke, desire is not distinct from fear, as it is for Hobbes. Locke, unlike Hobbes, understands desire, like fear, as an uneasiness or pain.[83] Conversely, for Locke, wherever there is any uneasiness or pain, there is desire, which is "scarce distinguishable" and "inseparable from it."[84]

Fear is not only useful but rational, and foolhardiness is not only dangerous but irrational, for "Good and Evil, *Reward* and *Punishment,* are the only Motives to a rational Creature" (§ 54). The basic cause of foolhardiness is therefore lack of reasoning rather than lack of fear; it is a failure to consider the "Use or Consequence" of running into danger. Fear, the uneasiness at approaching evil, is not only useful and rational but also "so natural to Mankind" that the lack of it must result from being unaware of the approaching evil, being "under the Conduct of Ignorance." The remedy for a foolhardy temper in children is therefore "but a little to awaken their Reason," presumably by pointing out danger and urging them to consider the use or consequence of running into it. However, reason or knowledge cannot by itself overcome heedlessness or ignorance. Reason alone is impotent. To dispose us to hearken to reason requires something else, an "imperious Passion." That passion, Locke says here, is "Self-preservation." As he has already said at the beginning of this passage, where he is explaining the rarity of foolhardiness, "Self-love seldom fails to keep it [fear] watchful and high enough in us." Fear itself, the uneasiness at the approach of evil, is derivative from self-love. As Locke says here, "No Body [is] so much an Enemy to himself, as to come within the Reach of Evil out of free Choice." In the passage on justice, also added to the second edition, Locke indicates that, at least in respect to conduct, self-love is prior to reason and apt to oppose it.[85] Here self-love is equally clearly prior to reason, but it appears more apt to support reason.[86] This difference may be due to self-love's being here primarily self-preservation rather than love of dominion.

Just as courage arises from the self-love (or fear, which derives from it) that lies behind reason, so foolhardiness arises not from simple *ignorance* of danger but from "some more imperious Passion" that lies behind the ignorance or heedlessness. That passion is "Pride, Vain-glory, or Rage, that silences a Child's fear, or makes him not hearken to its Advice." Clearly therefore, apart from simple ignorance of danger, which is easily corrected by information, foolhardiness is not simple lack of fear; it is silenced fear or, rather, fear not listened to. For fear is too natural to be simply absent when one is aware of danger. When Locke writes here that nobody would "court Danger for Danger's sake," he does not so much deny the phenomenon of thrill-seeking as interpret it as pride or rage.[87] The remedy for foolhardiness is therefore to abate the passion that is silencing fear so that the child can consider the consequences of his acts.

Beneath the conflict between reason and ignorance lies the conflict between fear and pride. Beneath the contrast between consideration and heedlessness of consequences lie judgments that certain consequences are worse than others, e.g., that bodily harm or destruction is worse than loss of dominion, of glory, or of vengeance (these being objects of the passions that are competing with fear). The standard of these judgments seems to be "Use." Locke's claim here is that suspension of action and the consideration it permits is more likely to lead to rational choice and action than, for instance, to choosing vengeance over preserving one's life. Locke's remedy for foolhardiness here applies to the realm of fear the *Essay*'s general presentation of rationality and morality as the result of delay or suspension of action and error or vice as the result of haste.[88] Like that presentation, however, it depends on notions of intrinsic good and not merely on a formal notion of good as whatever the result of consideration may be.[89]

Locke turns from the cure of foolhardiness to a longer, more detailed, discussion of the treatment of "Weakness of Spirit . . . the more common Defect." Whereas the previous cure awakens reason or fear, this treatment teaches courage proper, and accordingly it begins with a definition of courage, or "True Fortitude." It is "the quiet Possession of a Man's self, and an undisturb'd doing his Duty, whatever Evil besets, or Danger lies in his way." This definition includes within courage endurance of present evil or pain as well as bearing up against fear of future evil or pain.[90] Locke describes courage here as "Armour," the term he applied to insensibility toward pain in discussing how to treat the second sort of crying.[91] We shall see how essential endurance is to courage for Locke. Courage is not *any* bearing-up against fear or pain; Locke restricts it to the bearing-up that is required for the fulfillment of duty.[92] Courage seems to be not an intrinsic part of the "Character of a truly worthy Man" but only instrumental to the performance of duty. It is "the Guard and Support of the other Virtues." As such it is similar to a "manly air and assurance," which serves a man chiefly "as a fence to his Vertue" (§ 70).[93] As such it may also be one of the "established Habits," which Locke calls the best and surest "Guard" that one can have within one's own mind (§ 10).[94] Although narrowed to the support of virtue, Locke's courage is broad in that it includes "in its full Latitude" not only "Courage in the Field, and a Contempt of Life in the Face of an Enemy," but also courage "in other Places, besides the Fields of Battle," and contempt for "Pain, Disgrace and Poverty" as well as death.[95] Locke does not deny that honors are "justly due to the Valour of those who venture their Lives for their Country" or that death is "the King of Terrors," but he severs courage from an exclusively political or fatal setting. A few pages later, he writes purely metaphorically that his "young Soldier is to be train'd on to the Warfare of Life." We have already seen that foolhardiness, although at first seeming to be simply absence of fear, is rather a lack of reasoning and that serious foolhardiness is silenced fear or fear not listened to. Similarly, we saw that courage, as opposed to foolhardiness, consists in taking the "Advice" of fear. Locke now makes it clear that courage proper—that is, courage as opposed to cowardice—is also not absence of fear.[96] On the contrary, "Where Danger is, Sense of Danger should be; and so much Fear as should keep us awake, and excite our Attention, Industry, and Vigour." Fear is too natural to mankind not to be felt in the presence of danger. Courage is the presence of a fear that excites industry without disturbing either our reasoning or our performing what reason dictates. Courage, as described by Locke, is therefore a sort of fear that combines the advantage of fear as described by Hobbes with the advantage of boldness as described by Bacon: excellence in advice is combined with excellence in execution.[97]

Locke confesses that "Natural Temper" does a great deal toward the production of courage, but he promises that much may be done "even where that is defective," though he does not indicate whether as much can be achieved. It is to this "right Management" of a heart "in it self weak and timorous" that Locke's discussion of courage is chiefly devoted. But, as we have seen before,[98] the natural is not clearly distinct from the artificial, so it is necessary to avoid producing an artificially weak and timorous temper in the first place. Locke states that he has "already taken Notice" of the means of avoiding the two chief forms of this error. The two mistakes are "breaking Children's Spirits by frightful Apprehensions instill'd into them when Young, or bemoaning themselves under every little Suffering." It is entirely clear that Locke took notice of the latter error in his treatment of the second sort of crying (§§ 113–14). But it is not equally clear where he has discussed the former. He has warned against breaking children's spirits by excessive corporal punishment (§§ 46 and 51) but he made no particular mention of frightful apprehensions. If he does refer here to that warning, it would link more closely the two tempers treated here with the "*Sylla* and *Charybdis*" (§ 47) underlying the long discussion of reward and punishment in §§ 43–87. He has also warned against waking children harshly, since that may terrify them (§ 21). It may be, however, that what Locke is referring to is rather his warning against "Notions of *Spirits* and *Goblings*" (§ 138; see also § 191); if so, he forgot, when adding this passage to the second edition, that that warning, though written earlier, comes later on in the work. That warning does refer to "fearful Apprehensions," though it does not refer to breaking children's spirits. The confusion is then further increased; for although Locke says here that, since he has "*already* taken Notice*" of this error, which produces a weak temper, and that, instead, the hardening of a weak temper is now "farther to be consider'd," he proceeds, rather, to discuss "the first Step to get this noble and manly Steadiness," which turns out to be "what I have above mentioned, carefully to keep Children from Frights of all kinds, when they are young." It appears that the importance of avoiding the artificial production of cowardice (especially by supernatural notions, § 138) is so great that Locke is unwilling to leave off and omit it from the treatment of cowardice and the production of courage. To avoid a course that tends to weaken even a sturdy temper seems all the more necessary in hardening an already naturally weak temper. This first step also goes beyond mere refraining from instilling fearful apprehensions into children, for it includes keeping them "out of the way of terrifying Objects." The prevention of artificial cowardice becomes the artificial construction of experience (cf. §§ 58, 110).

The second step presumes the failure, or at least the incomplete success, of the first, for it proceeds "by gentle degrees, to accustom Children to those things, they are too much afraid of." The need for it depends on the failure of the first step not only to keep terrifying objects away from the children but also, as we shall see, to prevent mistaken fears from being "talked into them." Indeed, this step seems at first to be directed only against "mistaken Objects of Terror," in which there is actually "no harm." This step can be taken only partially with infants; it proceeds by distracting them (cf. § 114) or by "mixing pleasant and agreeable appearances" with the frightful object, another application of Locke's discovery of the association of ideas (cf. § 49). Older children, however, can also be *told* that "there is no harm in those frightful Objects." The error itself, as well as the remedy, is explained by the association of ideas and the *tabula rasa* principle that lies beneath it. Although Locke concedes that there is such a thing as an innately timorous temper (see § 101), he maintains that fear of specific objects is not innate; as he states here, "the only thing, we naturally are afraid of, is Pain, or loss of Pleasure." Although he thereby affirms what he calls in the *Essay* "natural tendencies," he denies implicitly here, as he does explicitly there, any innate ideas, let alone innate associations of ideas.[99] Since we are naturally afraid only of pain, we come to fear specific objects only as we associate their ideas with that of pain. Since there are no such innate associations, "when Children are first Born, all Objects of sight, that do not hurt the Eyes, are indifferent to them."[100] Specific fears arise in the two ways by which apprehensions of harm are associated with specific objects: through our own experience of being harmed or pained by them or through being told by others that they will cause us harm or pain. The first way can give rise to mistaken fears when the pain or harm is experienced in a merely accidental connection with the object (see §§ 49, 138), but it seems to be the second way that is of particular concern to Locke here as the cause of "vain Terrors." The cure for such terrors must include not only discourse, to counter whatever talk may have produced them in the first place, but also, and more importantly, habituation, to produce the opposite association.[101] Habituation ought, however, to respect the fear it seeks to supplant by proceeding only by "gentle" or "insensible degrees" to bring the terrifying object "nearer and nearer." Lack of such respect will "increase the Mischief instead of remedying it," presumably because the fear, if fully provoked, will so disturb the child's reason that he will not be able to learn the intended lesson of the experience; but another reason may be that the process of habituation owes its effect to its unconscious or "insensible" character.[102] This second step, of gently accustoming children to mistaken objects of terror, includes, as a crucial element, the method of "mixing pleasant and agreeable appearances," employed with infants; here the child's mastery over his fear is to be rewarded with "Applause." A "Love of Credit" remains "the true Principle, which will constantly work, and incline them to the right" (§ 56).

As I have noted, the second step seems at first to be directed only against *mistaken* objects of terror. But it culminates in such a mastery of the mind over itself and its fears that it becomes "a good preparation to meet more real Dangers."[103] Locke therefore has not digressed from the teaching of courage as the ability to resist danger into a treatment of mere ability to discern the absence of danger. He makes the relatively easy mastery over vain terrors into the way to teach mastery over real terrors. Mastery over mistaken fears accustoms the mind to mastery over fear by showing it that

> Evils are not always so certain, or so great, as our Fears
> represent them; and that the way to avoid them is not
> to run away, or be discompos'd, dejected, and deterr'd
> by Fear, where either our Credit, or Duty requires us to
> go on.

This *salutary* reasoning from vain fears to real fears seems to be a corollary of that reasoning about pleasure, which, as Locke explains in the *Essay*, is the cause of *wrong* judgment; for men are apt to make future pleasure

> give place to any present desire: and conclude with themselves, that when it comes to trial, it may possibly not answer the report, or opinion, that generally passes of it, they having often found, that not only what others have magnified, but even what they themselves have enjoyed with great pleasure and delight at one time, has proved insipid or nauseous at another.[104]

The difference between the two lies in the fact that the salutary reasoning serves the mind's mastery over itself, whereas the wrong one does not; moreover, the former takes account of and seeks to counter the tendency of the timorous temper to exaggerate present dangers, whereas the latter ignores and even serves the tendency to exaggerate present pleasures. The mastery over real or natural fears depends on the prior presence of and mastery over vain, artificial, or supernatural fears. Artificial fears are useful, after all; for experiencing their emptiness can provide the confidence needed for mastery over natural fears.

But the mastery over vain fears of objects that cause no harm or pain is not sufficient to master the natural fear of objects that do cause harm or pain. It is therefore necessary to attack fear in its "Foundation," which, as we have already been told, is "the only thing, we naturally are afraid of," namely, pain. Endurance of present pain is the foundation of courage, which is the bearing up against fear of future pain. It is necessary, therefore, not only to accustom children to mistaken objects of terror but "to accustom them to suffer Pain," employing, again, the power of habituation. Against this recommendation Locke presents the most lengthy anticipated objection that he presents in the *Thoughts*.[105] Like most of the other objections he anticipates, this one is, first of all, an expression of parental fondness.[106] But it will also be objected that this method will not work and even that it will backfire, turning the child against his parents. Finally, it will be objected that this recommendation contradicts Locke's own argument against excessive corporal punishment.[107] Locke finds a certain reassurance in these predicted objections: since his method must be "managed with great Discretion," it is all for the best that it be rejected by those incapable of it.

Locke addresses himself first to the last objection, that of inconsistency. He explains

> I would not have Children much beaten for their Faults, because I would not have them think bodily Pain the greatest Punishment: And I would have them, when they do well, be sometimes put in Pain, for the same Reason, that they might be accustom'd to bear it without looking on it as the greatest Evil.

The premise of this explanation is that whatever is imposed as a reward or a punishment is likely to be accepted as such. This principle of the indefinite content of punishment and reward has already appeared in the arguments against corporal punishment (§ 48) and mercenary rewards (§ 52), in the recommendation that studies not be assigned as tasks (§§ 73–74) but be offered as privileges (§ 76), and in the suggestion of "having their Shooes pulled off" or "some such Punishment" (§ 78).[108] As those passages have shown, the indefiniteness of punishment and reward rests on the natural human love of liberty and resentment of restraint and on concern for the esteem of others, especially those with power over one.

In response to the central objection, that of inefficacy, Locke cites the example of Sparta, which shows "how much Education may reconcile young People to Pain."[109] He is not, however, "so foolish [as] to propose the *Lacedaemonian* Discipline in our Age, or Constitution." Locke does not state what characteristics of the age or constitution—religious, economic, social, or political—rule out this possibility. The extreme part of the objection of inefficacy—that this policy may actually "give the Child an aversion for him that makes him suffer"—seems to pose the most serious difficulty, for it seems to be based on Locke's own principle of aversion, the crucial instance of the association of ideas, associating the idea of pain with the ideas it appears with. For Locke has explained that corporal punishment "naturally breeds an Aversion to that, which 'tis the Tutor's Business to create a liking to," because "offensive Circumstances ordinarily infect innocent things, which they are joined with" (§§ 49, 73–74, 76). Having warned that if their parents' company "be a Prison to [children], 'tis no wonder they should not like it," he has recommended that children be allowed liberty in their parents' company and indeed "receive all their good things there, and from their hands" (§ 69). Conversely and most relevantly, he has urged that corporal punishment be administered by a servant or tutor so that "the Child's Aversion for the Pain it suffers [will] rather be turned on the Person that immediately inflicts it" (§ 83). Especially as Locke does not immediately reply to this portion of the objection, it is incumbent on him to allay it in the course of his exposition of this policy.

As for the first objection, which expresses parental fondness and regards this policy as "unnatural" (whereas the objection of inefficacy regards it as "unreasonable"), Locke responds implicitly to it here, as he has before to similar objections, that his policy is for the child's good; at least he claims that it is conducive to virtue. His exposition of the policy responds more specifically to this objection as well.

The recommended treatment of pain—the great foundation of fear— is in many ways parallel to the treatment of fear itself. It too consists in "the first Step" and "the next thing" (compare p. 224 to p. 221). Also as in that treatment, the first step is avoiding one of the two forms of the error of producing artificial timorousness that Locke has "already taken Notice" of (compare p. 224 to pp. 220–21). The form that is to be avoided here is "to bemoan [children], or permit them to bemoan themselves, on every little Pain they suffer" (compare p. 224 to p. 220). This policy recognizes the power of pride, which makes pains, like desires (see § 107), harder to overcome once they have been expressed or acknowledged by others. As in the error of instilling frightful apprehensions, if it is necessary to avoid a course that tends to weaken even a sturdy temper, it is a fortiori necessary to avoid this if one is trying to harden a temper that is naturally weak. The plausibility of this is not belied here (as it is in the other case) by any paradoxical advantages derived from overcoming artificial weakness. Pitying can cause little pains to seem great (§ 113), but it cannot, after all, produce vain or mistaken pains the way talk can produce vain or mistaken fears, which can then be disproved by experience.

Again as in the treatment of fear proper, the first step in the treatment of pain, which is negative and concerns discourse, is followed by a second step of positive, gradual habituation (compare pp. 224–25 to pp. 221– 23). The habituation is not without discourse, for it consists not simply in accustoming the child to pain but in mixing the pleasure of praise with the idea of pain, or rather with the idea of enduring pain, as it was before with that of fear or of mastering fear (compare p. 225 to p. 223).

Indeed, this policy of accustoming to pain is presented with far more emphasis on praise, pride, reputation, shame, and the good opinion of others than was the policy concerning fear. We have seen that Locke claims that the object of this policy is that pain not be thought the greatest evil; although he does not say what should be thought the greatest,[110] clearly disgrace and shame are to be thought greater evils than pain. Our first impression, that courage is akin to pride, is therefore not entirely misleading. The child accustomed to bearing pain "can take a Pride in giving such Marks of his Manliness." Such endurance is also a kind of "Mastery." As reason depended on fear to overcome pride in a naturally foolhardy temper, so here reason depends on pride to overcome fear in a naturally timorous temper and to produce "the Courage

161

of a rational Creature" (compare p. 225 to p. 219). Yet courage does not entail a complete replacement of concern for bodily pain by concern for esteem. Courage is no more an indifference to pain than it is an absence of fear. Suffering remains; it is not replaced by, it is subordinated to, the concern for esteem. The child comes "to think [that he] himself [is] made Amends [to] for his Suffering, by the Praise [that] is given him for his Courage." The presence of this element of pride does not, how-ever, contradict my previous suggestion, which opposed courage to "Pride, Vain-glory, or Rage" and allied it with fear. For the pride at work here does not seek glory or vengeance or mastery over others but esteem from others for one's mastery over oneself.

Locke's account of the manner in which children should be "de-signedly" put in pain serves to allay the objections that this policy is unkind and that it will produce an aversion toward the parents. In the administration of this policy, praise serves not only as a reward for endurance but also as its context; for the child is assured that the pain is not a punishment or a mark of hostility. As in denying demands for the satisfaction of wants of fancy (§ 107), so here is it a fortiori necessary to assure the children of parental love. For there the denial is a sort of punishment following upon the child's demand, and its opposite satis-faction is employed as a reward; whereas here the infliction of pain does not necessarily follow upon any flinching but, far from being a punish-ment, is imposed "when they do well,"[111] and its opposite is not used as a reward, esteem being the only one. In other words, here the child must be assured, not that his punishment expresses concern for his good, but that his treatment is not punishment at all. This assurance of parental kindness is intended not so much to allay the objections of kind parents as to enable the policy to be successful in two ways: in leading the child not to consider pain the greatest evil and in preventing the pain from producing an aversion toward the parents.

The pain must be exacted when both parent and child are in "good humour" with each other. This requires parental self-control, giving way neither to the harshness of anger nor to the softness of compassion or repenting (cf. §§ 77, 81, 83, 87, 112). Harshness would lead the child to regard the pain as "the Fury of an enraged Enemy" (§ 87) or "passionate Tyranny" (§ 112); softness would "soften" his mind and lead him to regard pain as a very great evil after all (see § 113), contrary to the intention of this policy. The gradualness of the process, besides being appropriate to the "insensible" effect of habituation, also serves the goal of preventing its being considered a punishment or producing an aver-sion. For it must "begin with what is but very little painful" and remain "no more than the Child can bear." In this way this policy respects the power of pain much as the preceding policy respects the power of fear.

Locke concludes this discussion by reminding us that he teaches "the Courage of a rational Creature" (p. 225; cf. p. 219). This courage is not so much a natural temper as a properly educated defective temper. It is not absence of fear or of pride. It is pride tamed by fear or fear enlivened by pride. Courage is a fear that does not disturb the operation of our reasoning or our willingness to listen to it but disposes us to listen to it. Courage is a pride that does not disturb our reasoning about the danger of pain but offers us countervailing pleasures. It requires endurance of pain and is itself required for the fulfillment of duty.

## HUMANITY AND THE LESSONS OF HISTORY (§§ 116–17)

After dealing with the use of parental authority to treat the tempers of foolhardiness and timorousness in order to produce courage, Locke turns to the use of parental authority to curb the temper of cruelty, as revealed in children's treatment of animals, in order to produce a temper or sentiment variously called "good Nature," "Humanity," "Benignity," or "Compassion." As I have noted (p. 130), Locke seems to make contradictory statements about cruelty, saying in one passage that it is a "native propensity" (§ 102) but elsewhere that it is a corruption taught by others (§ 37), and I noted also that he seems to resolve in favor of the latter interpretation. I also suggested that the two statements can be reconciled if Locke viewed the native propensity as mere insensitivity to the suffering of others but regarded actual pleasure in the pain of others as "a foreign and introduced Disposition, an Habit borrowed from Custom and Conversation" (§ 116). This distinction seems to be confirmed here, where Locke describes only delight in tormenting animals as unnatural but speaks of children's simple negligence in caring for their pets as merely a "great Fault." Furthermore, in contrast to the earlier passage (§ 102), Locke does not go so far here as to claim that the opposite temper to cruelty, that of "Benignity and *Compassion,*" is natural *tout court* but only "more natural" (§ 116). He also reveals, however, that "unnatural Cruelty" (§ 116) is rooted in something that is natural, namely, "natural Vanity" or "natural Pride" (§ 117). I conclude that Locke's view is that the insensitivity to the suffering of others, exhibited by some, is a natural propensity but that actual delight in the suffering of others is artificial, though taught by appealing to natural pride.

Locke singles out one way in which unnatural cruelty is taught:

> All the Entertainment and talk of History is of nothing almost but Fighting and Killing: And the Honour and Renown, that is bestowed on Conquerours (who for the most part are but the great Butchers of Mankind) farther mislead growing Youth, who by this means come to think

Slaughter the laudable Business of Mankind, and the most Heroick of Vertues. [§ 116]

Locke's distaste for slaughter and the honor paid to it explains why he separates the virtue of courage from its traditional military context and purpose (§ 115). James Axtell remarks, in his note to this passage, that "Locke's low opinion of history apparently changed by 1697, when he strongly advised its study by her son to the countess of Peterborough," and he adds that "before that time Locke entertained ambivalent feelings about it" and he refers to Locke's manuscript "Of Study" of 1677.[112] I believe that Axtell has misunderstood Locke's opinion of history.

First of all, no change is in fact apparent. Axtell had no need to turn to the letter to the countess of Peterborough, for Locke had already, in the *Thoughts* itself, strongly recommended the study of history. He says here that history "is the great Mistress of Prudence and Civil Knowledge; and ought to be the proper Study of a Gentleman, or Man of Business in the World" (§ 182). It is true that in an earlier passage (§ 94), he demoted learning to a position below virtue, worldly wisdom, and breeding (see also § 147), claiming that most of its usually stressed subjects "belong not to a Gentleman's Calling; which is to have the Knowledge of a Man of Business, a Carriage suitable to his Rank, and to be Eminent and Useful in his Country according to his Station"; he also seemed there to relegate study to "spare Hours." But it is clear that this polemic is against *useless* learning, and it is equally clear that history does not fall into that category but is, on the contrary, a "proper Study" for gentlemen and men of business. Indeed, Locke declares that "A Gentleman's more serious Employment I look on to be Study" (§ 203), and he says that history is one of the "Studies which a Gentleman should not barely touch at, but constantly dwell upon, and never have done with" (§ 186). In the *Thoughts* (§§ 184, 187, and 190–91),[113] Locke particularly recommends Latin history, English history, and biblical history. The letter to the countess of Peterborough, on the other hand, contains not only the strong recommendation of the study of history, quoted by Axtell, but also a warning against "critical expositions" of Roman history that "my Lord neither needs nor ought to be troubled with."[114] In fact, in "Of Study" in 1677, the *Thoughts* in 1693, and the letter of 1697, Locke consistently praises useful history and disapproves of useless history, and it should particularly be noted that in the first two Locke not only denounces *useless* history but something worse: "the greatest part of history [that is] made up of wars and conquest," which leads us "to make butchery and rapine the chief marks and very essence of human greatness."[115]

The utility and danger of history are similar to the utility and danger of knowledge of the world or worldly wisdom generally (see § 94). The utility lies in the fact that both—history and knowledge of the world—

teach "the Ways, the Humors, the Follies, the Cheats, the Faults" of an age or a country, "Skill in Men, and their Manners," "a true Judgement of Men," "the true State of the World," and "Tragical or Ridiculous Examples" of vice (§ 94).[116] In short, they teach us "to think of men as they are," which implies that they teach more about vice than about virtue.[117] The danger common to both is that they present "fashionable and glittering Examples" of vice under the guise of "Credit and Manliness" and being "Brave" (§ 94; see also § 37).

Locke confesses that providing knowledge of the world may teach vice "according as it is done" (§ 94), and the danger or utility of the study of history similarly depends on the way it is studied. In the letter to the countess of Peterborough Locke accordingly requires a "guide" for a young gentleman first reading history and declares that "with the reading of history I think the study of morality should be joined."[118] In "Of Study" he similarly recommends history only to "one who hath well settled in his mind the principles of morality, and knows how to make a judgment on the actions of men."[119] Although he does not make the same point explicit in the *Thoughts,* the learning of virtue there both precedes and is joined with the study of history.[120] What Locke decries is therefore not the study of history per se but only the history in which honor and glory are accorded to killing and to conquerors. Moreover, the danger is posed not simply by the subject of history but by the "style" in which it is treated; for instance, the Roman historians speak of "valour as the chief if not almost the only virtue."[121] A history that spoke of conquerors as butchers rather than heroes would presumably be salutary. It should be clear by now that Locke's objection is not to the study of history per se, for he finds it useful. But it is also dangerous. And both its usefulness and its danger, like the usefulness and the danger of knowledge of the world, result from its being primarily an account of vice.[122]

The *Two Treatises* clearly reveal the same view of history and the same conviction that it should not serve as the rule of conduct. There, even when Locke asserts that there are more "instances out of History" of governments originating from consent than from paternal right, he admits parenthetically that "at best an Argument from what has been, to what should of right be, has no great force."[123] His claim that "the Examples of History" show that governments originate from consent is itself crucially limited to those "that were begun in Peace."[124] For Locke soberly recognizes that "such has been the Disorders Ambition has fill'd the World with, that in the noise of War, which makes so great a part of the History of Mankind, this *Consent* is little taken notice of."[125] He says of conquerors that

Great Robbers punish little ones, to keep them in their Obedience, but the great ones are rewarded with Laurels and Triumphs, because they are too big for the weak hands of Justice in this World, and have the power in their own possession, which should punish Offenders.

Thus Conquerours Swords often cut up Governments by the Roots, and mangle Societies to pieces . . . . The World is too well instructed in, and too forward to allow of this way of dissolving of Governments to need any more to be said of it.[126]

One can also be convinced, by "the History of this, or any other Age," that absolute monarchy fails to correct "the baseness of Humane Nature" and leaves its wielders "insolent and injurious."[127] Yet knowledge of this history is useful to Locke, however bad the examples it offers may be. Far from having a naïve or complacent view of a peaceful and rational past, he is all too aware of the predominant role that force and fraud have played in history.[128]

A knowledge of history is not limited, in its usefulness, to the private lives of gentlemen. It has a specifically political purpose.[129] In the *Thoughts*, for example (§ 182), Locke praises history as the mistress not only of prudence but of "Civil Knowledge," and in the letter to the countess of Peterborough the young gentleman's guide to the study of history is to "teach him to observe the most important things in it relating to a man's private conduct in common life, or to the turns of state in public affairs." In the letter he also particularly recommends that the young gentleman begin his study with Livy, because "the great end of such histories as Livy is to give an account of the actions of men as embodied in society, and so is the true foundation of politics."[130] He calls history "the" true foundation of politics only because in the letter he defines "true politics" as "nothing but the art of governing men right in society and supporting a community amongst its neighbors."[131] In "Some Thoughts Concerning Reading and Study for a Gentleman," however, where he defines politics as "two parts very different the one from the other, the one containing the original of societies and the rise and extent of political power, the other, the art of governing men in society," it is only the latter that "is best to be learned by experience and history," whereas the former is best learned from books such as the *Two Treatises*.[132] In this essay also, he explicitly links the study of history to the character of a gentleman's calling, which is "the service of his country."[133] Since a gentleman is concerned not with government generally but with his own country, Locke adds, when he writes that the art of government is best learned by experience and history, "especially [the history] of a man's own country."[134] In the *Thoughts* itself (§ 187) English history is recommended to the young gentleman, who as such is "concerned diligently to apply himself to that, wherein he may be serviceable to his Country," because it shows the reasons behind laws and thereby "what weight they ought to have."[135]

This survey of Locke's opinion on the use and abuse of history provides a context in which to understand his disparagement of "the Entertainment and talk of History" as one means by which unnatural cruelty is taught. His plea for the prevention of children's cruelty to animals is much more than an expression of quaint English sentimentality.[136] He does not warn against a failure "to be tender to all sensible Creatures" simply because cruelty causes pain or because animals are sensible creatures (and, apart from his use of the term "Creatures," there is no trace here of the argument that animals must be preserved because they are the handiwork of God).[137] Instead, he gives two other reasons against mistreating and for preserving animals. The first is that if parents do not check the habit of cruelty to animals in children, it will, "by Degrees, harden their Minds even towards Men." The second is that one ought not "to *spoil* or destroy any thing, unless it be for the Preservation or Advantage of some other, that is Nobler." The first reason applies especially to inflicting pain; the second applies, rather, to destruction.

The first reason clearly refers to *human* happiness, or at least to the avoidance of human suffering,[138] as its standard; it is ultimately concerned not with animals themselves but with men's attitude toward "those of their own kind." Cruelty toward animals, as deliberate infliction of pain or even as insensitivity to suffering, will lead to cruelty toward men or, at the least, to insensitivity to their sufferings. The English recognize this tendency by excluding butchers from "Juries of Life and Death,"[139] and Locke calls those greatest criminals, honored as military conquerors, "the great Butchers of Mankind." If habit plus praise is able to harden us to our own sufferings (§ 115), it is all the more able to harden us to the sufferings of others, since in the latter case it does not combat our uniquely natural dislike of pain but merely the relatively natural temper of compassion.[140] This is the first reason to motivate parents to prevent childish cruelty to animals. In itself it is unable to motivate children to practice the contrary habit.

The second reason also refers to *human* happiness, or at least to human preservation and convenience, as its standard. For when it states that destruction must serve "the Preservation or Advantage" of some other "Nobler" thing, the nobler things meant are clearly human beings. For in the next sentence Locke writes specifically of "the Preservation of all Mankind." The argument here can also be helpfully compared to the argument in the *Two Treatises* that man in the state of nature has no right to destroy "so much as any Creature in his Possession, but where some nobler use, than its bare Preservation calls for it,"[141] and Locke continues that argument by writing only of obligations toward other

THE LOCKEAN VIRTUES (*Thoughts*, §§ 100–132)

men, whom alone he identifies as the handiwork of God. He also writes incidentally that "the inferior ranks of Creatures" are made for our use, so that we are authorized to destroy them. In his exposition of property in the *Treatises* Locke makes it explicit that the "nobler use" that justifies the destruction of other animals is "the best advantage of Life, and convenience" of men, and he accordingly argues there for a natural-law prohibition against waste—that is, against destroying, spoiling, or even permitting to perish, while it is in one's possession, anything that can be useful to human life or convenience.[142] The argument is not that such destruction of things is a direct offense—that is, to their Creator—but that a thing that one does not use "belongs to others."[143] It is because things can be used by other human beings that one ought not to waste them. It is not God's creation as such that is relevant but rather His intention that His creatures belong to mankind.[144] To recognize that they belong to us, it is not necessary to know that God has given the world to mankind, which we learn from Scripture; on the contrary, "natural Reason . . . tells us, that Men, being once born, have a right to their Preservation, and consequently to Meat and Drink, and such other things, as Nature affords for their Subsistence."[145] That "God has given us all things richly to enjoy" is merely "the Voice of Reason confirmed by Inspiration," and serves to justify property rather than to turn us away from it.[146] Accordingly, this passage in the *Thoughts* does not refer to Scripture or creation but condemns destruction of animals as "*waste*"— that is to say, as waste of things that may serve human life or convenience.

Since both of these reasons refer to *human* ends, one can see why Locke is able to digress here from "our present Business" to make this remark:

> And truly, if the Preservation of all Mankind, as much
> as in him lies, were every one's Persuasion, as indeed it
> is every one's Duty, and the true Principle to regulate
> our Religion, Politicks and Morality by, the World would
> be much quieter, and better natur'd than it is.[147]

The preservation of mankind is thus not simply the principle behind Locke's reasons for opposing cruelty to animals. It is "the true Principle to regulate our Religion, Politicks and Morality by." Preservation is not derived here from a religious argument; on the contrary, it is the principle by which we ought to regulate our religion. The virtue taught here seems to be not simply a more or less natural temper of benignity and compassion, a sentiment of humanity, or a good nature; it is also a certain *persuasion.* But since that persuasion is recommended only in a digression, it may be better not to identify this virtue of humanity with that persuasion of human preservation but rather to say that that persuasion regulates this virtue, as it does all the other virtues that for Locke constitute morality. The virtues of self-denial, civility, liberality, and justice are all taught for the purpose of overcoming "Roots of almost all the Injustice and Contention, that so disturb Humane Life" (§§ 105, 106–10). The virtue of courage, insofar as it is opposed to foolhardiness, is explicitly tied to "Self-preservation," and, insofar as it is opposed to timorousness, it is "the way to avoid" evils, of which death is the most terrifying (§ 115). That the principle of preservation regulates politics for Locke has been remarked by Laslett, who speaks of his "tendency to regard this law of universal preservation as the fundamental natural law."[148]

Locke presents no systematic exposition of how to teach humanity, as he does for teaching courage, for instance. His first reason against tormenting animals—that it leads to cruelty toward men—cannot by itself persuade the children. His second reason, however, can. Locke commends the example of a mother who gave her daughters pets; but, if they neglected the pets, they "forfeited their Possession" or were at least rebuked. Deprivation of these delightful possessions, to which the children may have devoted some diligence, is an artificial analogue of the natural sanction against waste of things useful to human life or convenience and to which some labor may have been devoted. Rebuke is of course another instance of the use of the sanctions of esteem and disgrace, "the most powerful Incentives to the Mind" (§ 56). Besides offering this example, Locke explains only that compassion ought to be settled "by the same gentle Methods, which are to be applied to the other two Faults before mentioned." (These "two faults" appear to be love of dominion [§§ 103–5, treated in §§ 106–10] and crying [§§ 111–14].)[149] The "gentle methods" therefore appear to be habituation, persuasion, employment of esteem and emulation, and contrived rewards and punishments presented as natural consequences; but they also include severity, including beating, which is "gentle" because it is passionless, is mixed with reasoning (§§ 112 and 114), and occurs within a context of parental provision and protection manifesting love.

Locke now enters a caution to the policy of opposing children's mischief and destruction: "the Mischiefs, or Harms, that come by Play, Inadvertency, or Ignorance . . . are not at all, or but very gently, to be taken Notice of." Parents must in fact be willing to tolerate even "considerable Damage." In this they are not guilty of waste but are themselves exercising humanity toward their children by refraining from unnecessary punishment.[150] For punishment must consider not the immediate consequence of the action but only "what Root it springs from, and what Habit it is like to establish." This consideration of the root rather than the consequence is not a departure from Locke's view of punishment as serving only prevention and restraint, not retribution,[151] for the root here is the best evidence of "what Habit it is like to establish." Age will cure playfulness, inadvertency, or ignorance (§§ 63, 72, 80); parental authority must cure cruelty. By failing to consider the root and therefore punishing only the consequences of the child's natural playfulness, the parent would either fail to correct the child or would succeed and thereby spoil the child's temper.[152] By considering the root and therefore ignoring the consequences of natural playfulness, the parent makes clear to the child what is "chiefly Offensive": the fault of the will or mind (§ 80). Rousseau picks up this warning of Locke's and also his claim that mischief is foreign to the child, being introduced by others; putting them together and taking them to the extreme, he concludes against all punishment and regards parental objection to childish damage as expressing mere avarice.[153] Locke, however, distinguishes the artificial delight in mischief or cruelty from the natural love of dominion (compare § 116 to §§ 103–5), permits some very gentle notice to be taken of playful damage (cf. § 80), grants that "*Punishments* must be proposed to Children, if we intend to work upon them" (§ 55), and does not identify as avarice parental objection to childish damage.

Since a concern for human preservation and advantage dictates the virtue of tenderness toward the sufferings of all sensible creatures and aversion to all waste, this virtue is appropriately called "Humanity."[154] In § 117, added in the third edition, Locke turns to a direct application of it to other human beings; he recommends there that children be accustomed to civility toward social inferiors, particularly servants. The usual "Domineering" and "imperious" treatment of servants, "as if they were of another Race, and Species beneath them," fails to consider their "Humane Nature" and to recognize that it is merely "Fortune" that has laid servants low and given the advantage to gentlemen. There is no trace here either of any natural "differentials" between social classes[155] or of social classes being understood as "callings" manifesting a wise and just divine providence.[156] Natural equality is also taught by the *Two Treatises*, where Locke claims that there is "nothing more evident, than that Creatures of the same species and rank promiscuously born to all the same advantages of Nature, and the use of the same faculties, should also be equal one amongst another without Subordination or Subjection" and that servants serve masters only under contract.[157] He also denounces there the theorists of absolute monarchy and the absolute monarchs themselves for treating the people as if they were of an inferior species,[158] the same fault that he here denounces in the treatment of servants. In the case of masters and servants, as in the case of kings and subjects, the superiors should not presume on "their Father's Title" to exercise a power that exists only by consent and must be exercised with respect to their common human nature. For they are all "Brethren," as Locke writes here, and, as he argues in the *First Treatise*, their common Father has not given them title, one over the other.[159]

Locke warns that children's ill treatment of servants will "probably end . . . in Oppression and Cruelty." This dangerous habit is not necessarily taught by "ill Example"; it may stem from "natural Vanity." In any case, it fosters "natural Pride." Locke does not advocate in its stead a treatment that is simply indifferent to inferiority of status.[160] He advocates being "compassionate" precisely in proportion to inferiority of status and wealth. Inferiority of status makes men deserving of compassion and therefore fit objects on whom children can practice the expression of sentiments of humanity, like the helpless "poor Animals, which fall into their Hands" (§ 116). Locke even argues that the humane treatment he advocates will enhance superiority.[161] To elicit love and esteem from one's inferiors is to gain "a more ready and cheerful Service." For to act out of esteem for another, as to act to gain esteem from another, is to act freely, and grown men do cheerfully of themselves what they cannot endure as a duty.[162] Thus the same principle of liberty as the best instrument of government that parents use in governing children they also teach children to use in governing others (see § 109). The common human nature that justifies such humane and civil treatment is men's proud desire "to shew that they are free, that their own good Actions come from themselves, that they are absolute and independent" (§ 73).

Locke's advocacy of showing children that humanity enhances authority only makes obvious what is implicit throughout his discussion of this virtue: that, unlike Rousseau, he does not count on a natural sentiment of compassion to develop it. Neither does he base justice—the virtue of not violating the rights or property of others—on compassion, preferring instead to rely on habit, shame, and rational consideration of self-interest. Nor does he even base liberality—the virtue of being ready to give to others—on compassion, preferring instead habit, emulation, and even the acquisitiveness that liberality transcends (§ 110).

## CURIOSITY AND THE MANAGEMENT OF LABOR AND INDUSTRY (§§ 118–30)

Locke warns in the course of his discussion of curiosity (§§ 118–30) that, "where there is no Desire, there will be no Industry" (§ 126). Since the chief business of children is study, to remove their innate lack of ideas, the most useful desire for spurring their industry is curiosity, which is "but an Appetite after Knowledge" (§ 118). It is a natural desire, and the satisfaction of it is pleasant: "Knowledge is grateful to the Understanding, as Light to the Eyes" (§ 118).[163] What truly justifies the desire for knowledge, however, is not the pleasure provided by its satisfaction but the fact that without it men will be "dull and useless Creatures" (§ 118).[164] So Locke's masterwork, the *Essay*, opens its "Epistle to the

Reader" with an account of Locke's pleasure, as well as his pains, in writing it and a Socratic comparison of the pursuit of truth to hunting, in both of which "the very pursuit makes a great part of the Pleasure."[165] But the serious justification of the desire for knowledge is that "our Business here is not to know all things, but [only] those which concern our Conduct."[166] The most concise statement of Locke's recognition of both the pleasure of knowledge and its more serious justification comes at the beginning of his manuscript "Of Study":

> The end of study is knowledge, and the end of knowl-
> edge practice or communication. 'Tis true delight is com-
> monly joined with all improvements of knowledge; but
> when we study only for that end, it is to be considered
> rather as diversion than business, and so is to be reck-
> oned amongst our recreations.[167]

As Locke says here in the *Thoughts,* curiosity is a "great *Instrument*" (§ 118; my emphasis).

The value of curiosity, as well as Locke's appreciation of children, is beautifully illustrated by his extended comparison of children to "Travellers newly arrived in a strange Country, of which they know nothing" (§ 120). Their characteristic questions are "*What is it?*", by which Socratic question they do not ask the nature of a thing but "mean nothing but the Name," and "*What is it for?*" Curiosity is directed to utility. Children are inferior to adults insofar as they are "wholly Ignorant," but they are superior insofar as they are curious, that is, concerned with remedying their ignorance and lacking any adult "Conceit" or "all our Prudence and Knowledge." Their curiosity is therefore not only deserving of satisfaction; it is also more able to "set a considering Man's Thoughts on work" than can "the Discourses of Men, who talk in a road [in a rut, as we might say today], according to the Notions they have borrowed, and the Prejudices of their Education." One can even say that the *Essay*— itself a project of adult education—aims to make us more like children, not only by making us more curious but by freeing us from the prejudices of our education, which so often masquerade as innate ideas.

Curiosity, the tendency to ask about "any new thing [that] comes in their way" (§ 120), also leads to a child's "reasoning about things that come in his way" (§ 122). Reason, Locke declares here,

> as the highest and most important Faculty of our Minds,
> deserves the greatest Care and Attention in cultivating
> it; The right improvement, and exercise of our Reason,
> being the highest Perfection, that a Man can attain to in
> this Life. [§ 122]

One must note, first, that "the use and end of right Reasoning, [is] to have right Notions, and a right Judgment of things; to distinguish betwixt Truth and Falsehood, Right and Wrong; *and to act accordingly*" (§ 189; my emphasis). One must remember, second, that reason, man's "only Star and compass" to steer by,[168] takes its bearings not from perfection but from happiness. Locke writes, of "the happiness that all Men so steadily pursue, consisting in pleasure," that "Power and Riches, nay Vertue it self, are valued only as Conducing to our Happiness" (§ 143). Indeed, Locke understands an innate "desire of happiness and an aversion to misery" not only to be determinable by empirical observation[169] but to be a natural and necessary characteristic of any intellectual or intelligent being,[170] even God,[171] or to be an "unavoidable concomitant of consciousness."[172] Thus, perfection of reason for its own sake is not the goal; rather, "the highest perfection of intellectual nature lies in a careful and constant pursuit of true and solid happiness."[173]

The nature and power of curiosity are clarified by Locke's account of the ways to encourage it (§§ 118–21). The first and basic way is to answer intelligibly all of a child's questions and never to neglect, disapprove, ridicule, or overanswer them (§ 118). At first it appears that this method is effective simply because knowledge itself pleases children and operates as an incentive or reward. For it is in explaining this point that Locke says "Knowledge is grateful to the Understanding." But answering questions does not operate simply by providing children with the delight of knowing something. Locke continues, "Children are pleased and delighted with [knowledge] exceedingly, especially if they see, that their *Enquiries* are regarded, and that their Desire of Knowing is encouraged and commended." In other words, answering children's questions rewards them with respect as well as knowledge. Locke makes the pleasure of knowledge dependent on pleasure in esteem when he recommends hearing the child rather than merely lecturing him; for "he will then begin to value Knowledge when he sees, that it inables him to Discourse; and he finds the Pleasure, and Credit of bearing a Part in the Conversation, and of having his Reasons sometimes approved, and hearken'd to" (§ 98; see also §§ 97, 156).

Locke thus shows that, in encouraging curiosity by answering questions, the pleasure of esteem is practically inseparable from that of knowledge, and he also shows that it is not simply the truth of knowledge that pleases. For in explaining why children would prefer learning over "silly Sports," if only their inquiries were satisfied, he says that they would find more pleasure in learning than in such play because "there would be still Newness and Variety, which is what they are delighted with." Learning delights not simply by providing knowledge but by its novelty and variety, the desire for which Locke links to love of liberty.[174] In "silly

Sports" one returns "over and over to the same Play and Play-things," but in learning one continually learns new and different things (§ 118).

Given that the first and basic way of encouraging curiosity—answering children's questions—relies inseparably on the pleasure of esteem and the pleasure of knowledge, it should be no surprise that the second way is to give additional commendation (§ 119). Locke explains: "since we are all, even from our Cradles, vain and proud Creatures, let their Vanity be flattered with Things, that will do them good; and let their Pride set them on work on something which may turn to their Advantage." Although he warns against flattering the desire for *things* in order to encourage learning (§ 52), he does not scruple to flatter vanity or pride for a good end.[175] Human pride is powerful; it is also useful, given its close connection to the desires to be free and rational or to be recognized as such (§§ 73, 76, 81). In particular, Locke recommends here that the eldest sibling be encouraged to learn by teaching the younger ones. Locke has earlier suggested that the eldest can be used to lead the younger ones by exploiting the latter's "Ambition, and the Desire still to get forward, and higher, and to be like those above them" (§§ 74, 76).[176] Now he adds that such emulation is also a great spur to the eldest himself. Locke may not rely on this generous pleasure—of displaying one's superiority by sharing it—when he treats teaching liberality with things (§ 110), because he does not want to encourage pride in having things to give[177] and because liberality with things means losing them, whereas communicating one's knowledge leads one to know it better oneself.

The third way to encourage curiosity is a corollary of the first: it is never to give deceitful or evasive answers to children's questions (§ 120). To do so, if perceived (which it "easily" is), both discourages their curiosity and teaches children "the worst of Vices."[178] If they ask something "they should not know," they should be plainly told that "it is a thing that belongs not to them to know" (§ 121).[179]

The fourth and last way to encourage curiosity is deliberately to bring "strange and new things in their way" (§ 121). For as we have seen, novelty and variety are what delight children about learning.

As he did in discussing foolhardiness and courage, Locke now discusses the fault of excess. The fault of excess belonging to curiosity is "pertness" (§ 122). Pert talk seems to be encouraged by parents as an agreeable amusement. It is also a result of school education (§ 70, p. 170). Locke frowns on this; he recommends instead that a child be encouraged not only to ask questions but to reason: "When his Reasons are any way tolerable, let him find the Credit and Commendation of it; And when they are quite out of the way, let him, without being laugh'd at for his Mistake, be gently put into the right" (§ 122; see also §§ 97–98). Good reasoning, encouraged in this way, will be more pleasant for reasonable parents than pert prattle.

Locke is far more concerned, however (as he also was in discussing timorousness and courage), with the fault of deficiency. The fault of deficiency belonging to curiosity is "carelessness" or "Sauntring" (§§ 123–29). Even more than in his discussion of timorousness, Locke is concerned to distinguish between the natural form of the fault, resulting from the child's innate temper, and its acquired form, resulting from bad education (§§ 123 and 125). The artificial form—the fault consisting in "acquir'd aversion to Learning" (§ 125)—is also "natural"; that is, it is a natural result of learning's being "forced upon [the child] as a Task" (§ 123; see also §§ 49, 73, 74, 76). This fault in the child is the sad result of the parents' failing to pay adequate respect to his deep, proud desire for liberty or to take Locke's advice not to impose learning as a task (advice given when he exempted learning from the sphere of punishment [§§ 72–76]). This artificially produced fault can be distinguished from the natural "*Sauntring* Temper" because the child who has it will be "vigorous and eager," "stirring and active," in his own free play but "slow and sluggish" when it comes to studying; on the other hand, if the lack of curiosity is natural, the child will be "*listless* and *indifferent* in all his Actions" (§ 123). This analysis of the natural fault—carelessness, the temper "contrary" to curiosity (§ 123)—shows that curiosity is not a separate desire, naturally aimed at knowledge, but simply one direction that a general temper of busy activity or industry may take. To distinguish the artificial from the natural forms requires not only careful observation but spying; the child must be watched without even "a Suspicion, that any body has an Eye upon him" (§ 125).[180] Successful concealment of this kind does not offend "Conscience," like the easily perceived falsehood excluded in the third way of encouraging curiosity (§ 120). It is necessary because otherwise the child may fear to reveal his busy pursuit of his own designs, preferring to appear entirely idle.

If a child's "carelessness" is only an "acquir'd aversion to Learning" (§ 125), the cure is easy. The "first step"—the "softer application," the "most desirable way"—is reasoning (§ 124). Locke's general recommendation to reason with children makes it clear that "such *Reasons* as their Age and Understanding are capable of" must be employed; that is, the reasons must be obvious and tangible ones, appealing to their interests as they understand them (§ 81). Accordingly, reasoning with the child who has an acquired aversion to learning appeals precisely to his love of play by pointing out to him that he would have more time for it if only he would apply himself to his studies. If this reasoning fails to overcome the aversion he has developed toward his studies because they have been required of him as a task, the second step should be employed: the use of shame, ridicule, and concerted disapproval.

If these steps fail, then, instead of making a reasoned appeal to the child's love of his favorite play, the parent must eliminate that love by

175

surfeit. In recommending, in § 73, that learning not be imposed as a task, Locke, to prove that imposition causes aversion, made what then appeared to be a hypothetical suggestion: that if a child is ordered to "whip his Top" regularly "as a Duty," he will soon weary of it. Now he seriously and systematically recommends this very policy (§§ 124, 128, and 129).[181]

This policy of surfeit uses the love of liberty and the dislike of duty, both of which gave rise to the child's aversion to study, to replace that aversion with an aversion to play and a desire for study. It would have been better in the first place to have made learning into play (§§ 74, 108, 148–54), but, once the mistake is made, it is too late; "the Cure is [now] to be applied at the other end," and "the contrary Course" is to be taken of making the child's favorite play into a task (§ 128). The "Task of Play" must not, however, be imposed "as a Punishment for Playing," for then, like other punishments, it might serve to endear the crime to the child and also raise an aversion to the inflicter and his purpose.[182] It must be imposed, rather, "as if it were the Business required of him" (§ 128). One must, for example, plead the expense of a tutor (§ 124) or "some Pretence or other" (§ 129). In short, Locke says that parents must use this method to "deceive" their children into studying (§ 128) (and this despite his warning against giving "Deceitful" answers [§ 120]).[183] For thus does learning become a recreation after all: as a relief from the task of playing (§ 129). Play is not to be imposed as a punishment; study, however, is to be offered as a reward for the task of play, and it will be accepted as such. This method assumes children's fundamental indifference to particular activities: they "find little Difference so they may be doing: The Esteem they have for one thing above another, they borrow from others" (§ 129; see also § 76). Locke thinks that we have no innate ideas of particular objects or actions, only undirected desires for pleasure and avoidance of pain, directed by experience to particular things and taking shape in desires, also undirected to particular objects, for liberty, variety, and esteem. Children desire to be "busie, as they imagine, in things of their own choice, and which they receive as Favours from their Parents, or others for whom they have respect, and with whom they would be in credit" (§ 129). Because, as this statement reveals, there is a close connection between the desire for liberty and the desire for esteem, the things that children imagine to be of "their own choice" can in fact be of "their Governour's Choice" (§ 129).

If parental espionage discovers that the fault is a natural idleness rather than an acquired one, the cure is much harder. Since love of liberty and dislike of duty are not the cause of the problem, they cannot be used to provide an easy solution. The temper of natural idleness lacks "the two great Springs of Action, *Foresight* and *Desire*" (§ 126). It is necessary, therefore, to "plant and increase" them. Locke explains, however, only how to "increase" an already existing desire, not how to plant or increase foresight. Presumably the increased desire overcomes "unconcernedness for the future" and stimulates foresight.[184] The parent must first discover what the child's desire is—whether it is positive, for praise, play,[185] or even fine clothes (contrast § 37), or negative, for the avoidance of pain or disgrace.[186] He must then work to increase it, presumably by encouraging its expression, by satisfying it, by using it as a reward, and even by invitation and temptation, the very methods excluded earlier in teaching self-denial (cf. §§ 36–39, 52, 57, 107). For in this case even "an excess of Appetite" is to be welcomed, for it is to be used to motivate the child's industry. "For where there is no Desire," Locke concludes, "there will be no Industry." Similarly, in the chapter on property in the *Second Treatise*, Locke writes that the "desire of having more than Man needed" led to the invention of money, which in turn motivated men to greater degrees of industry.[187]

If this method of exciting industry by increasing appetite fails, then one must resort to "constant bodily Labour," preferably of a kind involving "some little hardship and shame" (§ 127). This labor has the positive value of habituating to activity and the negative value of driving the child to "desire to return to his Book." In this it resembles using the "Task of Play" to combat the acquired aversion to study. But here one cannot offer study as a reward for the task and expect it to be freely embraced; one cannot rely on dislike of duty as one could when that was itself the cause of the problem (and this is why shame and hardship are employed here, as well as imposition). Instead, one must impose study as an additional task and, as a reward, gradually reduce the required labor as the child gradually becomes more "Industrious at his Book." In the first method of curing natural idleness—by increasing appetite (§ 126)—Locke excludes "Sloth" from the list of desires that may be satisfied as a reward for study ("for that will never set him on work"), but here he seems to find a way of doing so after all. It is not clear, however, whether Locke means here that bodily labor is intrinsically more repulsive than study, either in general or specifically for the naturally idle, or whether the difference centers more on using shame rather than reward. Other passages indicate that he does not consider the pains of bodily labor to be necessarily more repulsive than those of study.[188] His view is rather that the pains of bodily and mental exercise should each be a pleasant recreation from the other: to do so is "none of the least Secrets of Education" (§ 197; see also § 108).[189]

Finally, in what may be considered an appendix to his discussion of curiosity and the industry that it excites, Locke discusses "Play-things" (§ 130). He suggests three related policies regarding playthings: they should not be in the child's own "Custody," they should not be bought, and they should be made by the children themselves. According to the first, "the Child should have in his Power but one at once, and should not be suffered to have another, but when he restor'd that." One may infer that this policy limits the satisfaction and so discourages the children's desire to "have *Propriety* and Possession, pleasing themselves with the Power which that seems to give, and the Right they thereby have, to dispose of them, as they please" (§ 105) or the "Desire of having in our Possession, and under our Dominion, more than we have need of" (§ 110). Children should be able to use and enjoy their playthings but not to have needless power over them. Locke explicitly claims for this policy the merit that it discourages spoiling or wasting, cardinal violations of the principle of preservation (§ 116). In discussing the way to teach children about justice, he says that children should understand property only as a gift from "those, whom they take to have a Power over it" (§ 110); there is thus no attempt to teach them the distinct notions of property, set forth in the *Second Treatise*, as ultimately derived from labor and settled by consent. Lodging their toys in the power of their tutors, who dole them out with restraint, teaches some notion of the limits of "plenty" and the costs of waste.[190] In this way it also teaches "Good Husbandry."

The second policy, that playthings should not be bought, forecloses

> that great variety they are often over-charg'd with, which
> serves only to teach the Mind to wander after change,
> and superfluity; to be unquiet, and perpetually stretch-
> ing it self after something more still, though it knows
> not what: and never to be satisfied with what it hath.

This love of variety, Locke protests, is an obstacle to achieving "Moderate Desires" or becoming "a contented happy Man." But we must not forget that this love of variety or desire for more does not have to be taught, since it is natural (§ 74);[191] nor should we forget that Locke understands it as the cause of the pleasure of learning and that he eagerly employs it as a motive (cf. §§ 118, 128). Similarly, although he writes here that failure to follow this policy with respect to playthings teaches children pride and vanity as well as covetousness, "almost before they can speak," we cannot help recalling that he elsewhere acknowledges that "we are all, even from our Cradles, vain and proud Creatures" and that he proposes to flatter that vanity and use that pride to advantage (§ 119).

Although only some desires or wants, "the Necessities of Nature," are natural—in the sense that reason alone is not able to keep them from disturbing us because they are monitors of greater mischiefs—whereas others are "Wants of Fancy" (§ 107), that does not mean that the distinction between the two kinds lies in this: that the natural wants occur by themselves, without having to be taught, while the wants of fancy are always taught. For fancy or imagination is a natural faculty, and the desires for esteem, dominion, liberty, change, variety, and unnecessary possessions are likewise natural in this sense. In other words, nature does not limit men to desires for the necessities of nature—men are not naturally moderate.[192] It is necessary, therefore, for them to be "taught Moderation in their Desires," both for the sake of their own happiness and for the sake of others.

Moderation of desires is taught not only by the awareness of scarcity instilled by the first policy's penalty for waste and by the avoidance of getting "accustomed to abundance," instilled by the second, but, above all, by the recognition that labor is necessary for the satisfaction of desire. This lesson is taught by the third policy, which requires children to make their own playthings as far as practicable. The only exception Locke is willing to make here is for playthings, like tops, that are themselves "to be used with labour." Children should be taught self-reliance, understood along the lines of what is currently called the "work ethic" as opposed to the "welfare ethic." They should be accustomed "to seek for what they want in themselves, and in their own indeavours" and should not expect "to be furnish'd from other hands, without imploying their own." For the latter attitude characterizes "the Quarrelsom and Contentious," who, as Locke says in the *Second Treatise,* unlike "the Industrious and Rational," "desired the benefit of another's Pains, which he had no right to."[193] The awareness that labor must precede satisfaction tames the desire for variety and the desire for "something more," both of which can be used as motives but which, left untamed, undermine our happiness and make us dangerous to others. This awareness teaches not only moderation of desire but also "Application, Industry, Thought, Contrivance, and Good Husbandry." This guiding insight clearly links several key Lockean virtues: self-denial, avoidance of waste, and industry.

Locke's *Thoughts* has been criticized for treating labor merely as a recreation and not recognizing either its formative value or its being the principal economic resource.[194] Francesco de Bartolomeis, however, notes that "what he says about the utility that children derive from making their own toys gives the impression of a sufficiently exact singling-out of the character of educative labor, which is understood in a modern way." This scholar even suggests that

> Certainly, without recourse to any artifice, we are able to establish a correlation between the experimental concept of knowledge, which implies construction, and the demand that children themselves construct their toys. That is, to put children in front of toys already beautiful and made is like putting them in front of something extraneous. Such toys are extraneous in the same way that innate ideas—logical entities constituted prior to the use of the natural faculties—are extraneous.

Even Bartolomeis, however, concludes that this "happy intuition" of the utility of children's making their toys "remains almost without consequences in the work of Locke," that "at bottom he did not succeed in developing the reasons outlined in regard to the construction of toys." He also, like others, charges that Locke views labor only as a recreation, opposed to education, and so fails to recognize "the effective value that it has in social reality." I would not dismiss Locke's remarks about "the restricted sphere of play or pleasant labor" even if they seemed otherwise to be "almost without consequences" in his work.[195] For Locke emphasizes that these "little things" because they "form Children's Minds," are "not a small thing in [their] Consequences."[196] It is hard for me to believe that the author of the chapter on property in the *Second Treatise* did not recognize the effective value of labor in social reality.[197] I can understand the opposite interpretation only as proceeding from dogmatic assumptions about the limitations imposed on Locke's thought by his class connection or historical situation. As for the formative or educative value of labor, not only is it fully recognized in this important passage, but the recommendation of manual labor in §§ 201–9 is misunderstood if it is regarded as applying solely to labor used as recreation. For before listing its utility as a recreation from study, a recreation that contributes to our health, Locke first lists the skill and dexterity it gives in "useful Arts" (§ 202). Although he says that the ability "to govern and teach" one's gardener and the "great many Things both of delight and use" that one gains from both gardening and carpentry are not "the chief end of his Labour," he does not say that that end is simply recreation in itself. It is rather "Diversion from his other more serious Thoughts and Employments, by *useful* and healthy manual Exercise" (§ 204; my emphasis). The usefulness of labor is not unrelated to its chief aim.[198] However, what best reveals Locke's consistent recognition of the educative and formative value of labor is his recommendation, immediately following this one, of something besides manual labor but also "relating to Trade," namely, "*Merchant's Accompts*" (§ 210). Keeping accounts teaches in a more sophisticated way the same lesson, that labor must precede the satisfaction of desire, as is taught by having to make one's own toys. This is illustrated by Locke's story of the noble Venetian who required his extravagant son to count his money before he could spend it, until he learned good husbandry by reflecting soberly: "If it be so much Pains to me barely to count the Money, I would spend, What Labour and Pains did it cost my Ancestors, not only to count, but get it?" (§ 211). Locke not only recognizes that labor is the source of wealth but claims that labor can teach that recognition and the virtues that follow from it.

Locke strongly denounces lying, not only as being "so ill a Quality" itself but as "the Mother of so many ill ones that spawn from it, and take shelter under it" (§ 131). Earlier in the *Thoughts* he paired it with obstinacy as a fault requiring the most severe punishment (§§ 84 and 99), perhaps because lying challenges parental authority by sheltering faults from it. Precisely because this vice is "so much in fashion amongst all sorts of People," it is necessary to counter social encouragement of it by employing a social stigma, branding it as "wholly inconsistent with the Name and Character of a Gentleman," belonging, instead, to "the abhorred Rascality." That is to say, Locke himself is not under the illusion he says should be fostered among children: that lying is *not* in fashion among *all* sorts of people. This illusion and this abhorrence should be instilled in children as soon as they observe this fault in others; one should not wait first for them to engage in it themselves. If they do, their lying should be met first with wonder (cf. §§ 84, 85, 110), then with rebuke and concerted disapproval, and finally, if necessary, with blows.

Locke also deals here with making excuses, "a Fault usually bordering upon, and leading to untruth" (§ 132; see also § 139). Locke does not attribute this fault to social fashion but seems to regard it as natural, since he views it as common to all "the Sons of *Adam*."[199] For it expresses their fear "to have their Faults seen in their naked Colours,"[200] which is perhaps a perverse corollary of their proud desire "to shew that they are free, that their own good Actions come from themselves" (§ 73).[201] Perhaps because this fault expresses a concern for one's reputation or even a desire to think well of oneself, Locke recommends that it "be cured rather with Shame than Roughness." To encourage ingenuousness, it is therefore necessary not only to pardon any fault that is directly confessed, and even to pardon it so completely as never to mention it again, but to reward the confession with commendation. Indeed, Locke goes so far as to urge that, if the excuse cannot be disproved, one should "let it pass for True, and be sure not to shew any Suspicion of it." For it is necessary to preserve the child's reputation, which is "a great and your best hold upon him."

This policy of overlooking "some slips in Truth" is an extension of the policy of not blaming children in public and of teaching them to conceal their faults from the world and thus preserve their reputations and their incentives to be virtuous (§ 62; see also § 109). There is a fine line between overlooking a child's excuses (and the faults they cover) in order to preserve his reputation as an incentive for him to preserve it, on the one hand, and flattering him that he is getting away with lying, on the other. But making excuses can well be overlooked when it expresses a desire to preserve one's reputation rather than a desire simply to avoid punishment. And Locke's policy of offering "perfect Impunity" for confession makes it possible for children to avoid punishment without their making any excuses. However, making excuses cannot be overlooked and must be punished severely when it ceases to express concern for reputation and comes to express obstinacy by being persisted in when challenged. Just as Locke's mention of the sons of Adam may remind us of original sin, so his policy of exchanging pardon for confession may remind us of priestly practice. Locke, however, is not recommending the use of confession to encourage a sense of sin or guilt; instead he encourages parents to use it to "keep up [the child's] Reputation with you as high as is possible."

Locke's recommendation that parents pretend not to suspect their children's excuses in certain circumstances and to overlook "some slips in Truth" suggests more than that the child's excuse-making can express a useful concern for his reputation; it also shows that a kind of deceit, or at least dissimulation, is allowable on the part of the parents. Despite his strong denunciation of lying here and his earlier warning against teaching falsehood or dissimulation to children by example (§ 120; see also §§ 37, 84, 99, 100, 139–40), this is not the only example of his recommending useful dissimulation. Children should be brought to believe things that are not strictly true, such as that "those that are commended, and in Esteem for doing well, will necessarily be beloved and cherished by every Body, and have all other good Things as a Consequence of it" (§ 58), or that "the most *Liberal* has always most plenty, with Esteem and Commendation to boot" (§ 110). That the tutor does not have the power of the rod should be concealed (§ 88). The child himself should be taught when to dissemble his knowledge of men (§ 94, p. 195). One should not let the child perceive that one observes him in his play (§§ 102 and 125). One should not let the complainer perceive that one reproves the offender and should even make the latter ask pardon of the former as if moved to do so of himself, dissembling that he has been made to do so (§ 109). When a child has been turned away from study, one must "under some Pretence or other" (§ 129) impose play "as if it were the Business required of him," though of course it is not (§ 128). In this way one should "deceive" children into studying, just as one may "cozen" or "cheat" them into reading (§§ 128, 149, and 155). Parents must also sometimes feign a "Shew of Wonder" (§§ 85, 110, 131).

The moral virtues toward which Locke directs the application of parental authority include self-denial, civility, liberality, justice, courage, hardiness, humanity, industry, the avoidance of waste, and truthfulness. These virtues are not simply natural but must be taught by habituation and by reward and punishment, especially praise and blame; by example, reasoning, and allowance of liberty but denial of mastery; and by maintaining a balance between gentleness and severity accompanied by evidence of love; and by other, sometimes elaborate, artifices. They are taught, however, by appealing to or manipulating the child's natural sensibilities—to pleasure and pain, to self-preservation and fear, to love of dominion, love of liberty, love of novelty and variety, to ambition and emulation—and by carefully observing the child's individual nature and accommodating the teaching to it. The virtues themselves are founded on two fundamental insights: that almost everything that is of value comes from human labor and that there are more and stronger men in the world than oneself.

These virtues are not taught in a directly political context, but they directly address the problems of Locke's politics. Locke does not associate these virtues, even justice and courage, with patriotism, nor does he directly teach love of country, as Plato does in the *Republic* or Rousseau in the *Government of Poland*. He apparently expects love of country, to which he appeals in the Epistle Dedicatory of the *Thoughts*, to grow out of the private attachments one develops for the people around one. But the virtues he teaches are based on the same insights as his politics and serve the same goals, the preservation of oneself and others and avoidance of the injustice and contention that so disturb human life. The *Two Treatises* present "the Natural Vanity and Ambition of Men"—the passion or imagination that substitutes for reason, and the fancy or covetousness that desires the benefits of others' labor—as the chief psychological roots of political threats to preservation of life, liberty, and property.[202] These are precisely the tendencies that the Lockean moral virtues are intended to counter.

In the *Two Treatises,* reason, which is the law of nature, teaches two fundamental duties, self-preservation and, when that "comes not in competition," the preservation of the rest of mankind.[203] Self-preservation is based solidly on the "first and strongest desire God Planted in Men, and wrought into the very Principles of their Nature being that of Self-preservation"; but the natural duty to preserve others, at least apart from one's children, does not seem to have any similar basis in human nature.[204] The moral education in the *Thoughts* provides Locke's complex account of how to build concern for the life, liberty, and property of others on a solid basis in human nature. In the *Treatises*, the right to liberty is derived as a "Fence" or security to preservation, but they begin by invoking a more generous, less calculating, contempt for slavery, and end by justifying resistance that risks life for liberty.[205] The moral education in the *Thoughts* provides Locke's subtle account of the nature of the human attachment to liberty and how to nurture and direct it.

183

# *FOUR*

# The Completion
# of Education

### The Parts of Education (§§ 133–34)

Having completed his thoughts concerning the general *method* of educating a young gentleman, Locke turns to consider "the several parts of his Education" (§ 133). He first warns that, although the general method should influence "the whole course of his Education," it does not contain "all those Particulars, which his growing Years, or peculiar Temper may require." The method is inherently limited by the requirement that it be adapted to the child's years and temper. It must be adapted to his temper because it teaches by habits rather than by rules or precepts and motivates by exciting desires rather than by imposing duties and threatening with punishments (see §§ 64, 66, 74, 126). It must be adapted to his years because it establishes authority by initial severity and relaxes it by later familiarity, and it seeks to exploit the child's desire to be thought rational and to affect to be a man (see §§ 40–41, 43, 71, 80, 81, 95).

Before moving into his discussion of the parts of education—which he defines as "*Virtue, Wisdom, Breeding,* and *Learning*" (§ 134), the same qualities that are needed in the tutor (§§ 93–94)—Locke warns that

> I will not trouble my self, whether these Names do not some of them sometimes stand for the same thing, or really include one another. It serves my Turn here to follow the popular Use of these Words; which, I presume, is clear enough to make me be understood; and I hope there will be no Difficulty to comprehend my Meaning.

This warning is echoed in his definition of "Wisdom," which begins "*Wisdom* I take, in the popular acceptation" (§ 140).

Axtell concludes, on the basis of this warning, that the *Thoughts* is "not a proper philosophical discourse."[1] For in the *Essay* Locke distinguishes between the "*civil*" use of words, such "as may serve for the upholding common Conversation and Commerce, about the ordinary Affairs and Conveniencies of civil Life, in the Societies of Men, one amongst another,"

184

and the "*philosophical* use of words," which is "to convey the precise Notions of Things, and to express, in general Propositions, certain and undoubted Truths, which the Mind may rest upon, and be satisfied with, in its search after true Knowledge."[2] Locke then remarks (as Axtell notes) that "Common use *regulates the meaning of Words* pretty well for common Conversation; but . . . is not sufficient to adjust them to philosophical Discourses."[3] For "Exactness is absolutely necessary in Enquiries after philosophical Knowledge, and in Controversies about Truth," but "Vulgar Notions suit vulgar Discourses."[4]

It might be argued that in following the popular use of words in the *Thoughts* Locke adopts only the third remedy set forth in the *Essay* for the imperfections and abuses of words, namely, to "follow common Use."[5] But it is his fourth remedy—to declare the meaning in which one uses words, "because Men in the Improvement of their Knowledge, come to have *Ideas* different from the vulgar and ordinary received ones"—that is especially necessary in discussions of morality, because the common use of moral terms leaves "great uncertainty and obscurity in their signification" owing to their complexity, and it leaves them "very various and doubtful" owing to their having no "*Standards* in Nature."[6] Because of the lack of natural standards for moral terms, not only is it especially *necessary* to define moral terms rather than merely to rely on their popular acceptation; it is also especially *possible* for them to be "perfectly and exactly *defined.*" For they are merely "Combinations of several *Ideas*, that the Mind of Man has arbitrarily put together, without reference to any Archetypes."[7] Locke therefore concludes, in the *Essay*, that one may "lay great blame on those who make not their discourses about *moral* things very clear and distinct." If men fail "in all their moral discourses, to define their Words when there is Occasion . . . it must be great want of Ingenuity (to say no worse of it) to refuse to do it."[8]

Locke's unwillingness to trouble himself about the key moral terms in the *Thoughts,* his willingness, instead, to follow their popular use because it serves his turn, and the conclusion Axtell draws from these facts indicate the popular or civil character of the *Thoughts.*[9] Locke himself writes at the end of the *Thoughts* that he "would not have it thought that I look on it as a just Treatise on this Subject" (§ 216). But by this he seems to mean chiefly that, because it fails to set forth "proper Remedies" for "the various Tempers, different Inclinations, and particular Defaults, that are to be found in Children," it is "far from being a compleat Treatise on this Subject, or such, as that every one may find, what will just fit his Child in it"; in short, he repeats the first warning (§ 133) mentioned above, not the second (§ 134).[10]

Richard Cox goes further than Axtell on the basis of the passage in § 134. He indicates that it is only because Locke follows popular use that he speaks of virtue as consisting in "having a 'true notion of God' and a 'love and reverence of this Supreme Being,' speaking the truth, and being 'good-natured to others.' "[11] That is far from clear; but it is clear that Locke's following popular use means that he fails to define virtue or to distinguish it from the other qualities he mentions here. In particular it excuses him from precisely discussing the classical question of the relation between virtue and wisdom, whether they are really "the same thing, or really include one another." In employing the popular distinction of virtue from wisdom, he does not say whether he accepts it. However tenable or untenable that distinction may be in other respects, it is consonant with his teaching virtue by habit rather than by precept, reason, or reflection (§§ 10, 64–66, 110, 185). We shall see that in his account the distinction between virtue and breeding is also very questionable and that following popular use acquits him from explaining it. Although in ranking the four qualities of a gentleman Locke clearly puts virtue first, wisdom and breeding next, and learning last and least, the clarity of that ranking is somewhat obscured by his refusal to vouch for the distinctions between the qualities.[12]

## VIRTUE (§§ 135–39)

Of the four parts of education, Locke places virtue as "the first and most necessary" for "a Man or a Gentleman" (§ 135). From this last phrase John Yolton rightly infers that, although much of the *Thoughts* is written specifically for gentlemen, "in the matter of rationality and virtue, Locke is writing for all men."[13] Locke indeed states that "all Men . . . steadily pursue" happiness (§ 143), that virtue is for a man "absolutely requisite to make him valued and beloved by others, acceptable or tolerable to himself" (§ 135),[14] and that without such esteem and self-esteem a man "will be happy neither in this, nor the other World."[15] Yet, though Locke claims that virtue is necessary for happiness, he does not claim that it is sufficient.

He recommends that as "the Foundation" of virtue[16] one ought to imprint "very early" on the minds of children (for it is not there innately)[17]

> a true Notion of *God,* as of the independent Supreme
> Being, Author and Maker of all Things, from whom we
> receive all our Good, who loves us, and gives us all Things.
> [§ 136]

One should also instill "a Love and Reverence of this Supreme Being" and accustom children to "some plain and short Form of Prayer" (§§ 136, 137, 139). Locke's emphasis, however, is negative. This simple notion of God is "enough to begin with." One should not be "unseasonably forward to make [the child] understand the incomprehensible Nature of that infinite Being" (§ 136). It quickly becomes apparent, however, that this simple notion is not only enough, "to begin with," for little children but that for most men there is *no* season for understanding the incomprehensible; for Locke remarks here, "And I think it would be better if Men generally rested in such an Idea of *God,* without being too Curious in their Notions about a Being, which all must acknowledge incomprehensible."[18] Curiosity is not necessarily a virtue; it is one only when it is directed to useful and comprehensible knowledge. Curiosity about the incomprehensible or a failure to recognize the limits of human understanding[19] lead in this case to "Superstition or Atheism" and eventually to persecution or lawlessness.[20]

This simple notion of God, recommended for little children and for men generally, is even more purely reasonable than Locke's Christianity. It contains, first of all, nothing specifically Christian or referring to positive revelation.[21] But it also contains nothing of the fear and punishment characteristic of Locke's other accounts of a natural religious foundation of morality.[22] Only the good that God does to men is mentioned.[23] Although "Love and Reverence" of God should be instilled, nothing is said here of true reverence's containing two parts, "*Love* and *Fear,*" as filial piety does (§ 99).[24] Divine government seems to have learned something of the limitations of punishment and fear from the art of government taught in the *Thoughts.*

The largest portion (§ 138) of the discussion of virtue is devoted to preserving children from "Notions of *Spirits* and *Goblings,* or any fearful Apprehensions in the dark." Such notions "sink deep" because of the accompanying dread, and they produce "strange Visions" and make children almost incurable "dastards." These notions so prepossess men's "Fancies" that they overpower the advice of reason that there is "no cause to fear invisible Beings more in the Dark, than in the Light." (It should be noticed that Locke fails to address two objections: first, that there is more cause to fear visible beings in the dark, where they become invisible, and, second, that there is cause to fear invisible beings everywhere if one is taught to believe in them at all.) Locke denies that fear of the dark is natural: "If Children were let alone, they would be no more afraid in the Dark, than in broad Sun-shine: They would in their turns as much welcome the one for Sleep, as the other to Play in."[25] To counter any artificially instilled fear of the dark, one should teach "That God, who made all Things good for them, made the Night that they might sleep the better and the quieter; and that they being under his Protection, there is nothing in the dark to hurt them." Thus the very notion of God is deprived of everything threatening, and it is employed to counter frightening notions of other beings.

In Locke's teaching of courage (§ 115), he spoke of the danger that frightful apprehensions may be "talked into" children, breaking their spirits (perhaps through some "Motion of the Animal Spirits" or other physiological cause [§ 115, p. 221]) and producing cowardice; however, he also said that overcoming artificial, mistaken fears prepares children to acquire courage in facing more real dangers. Locke here reveals the hidden cause of the teaching of such notions and implicitly indicates another danger present in them. It is the "usual Method" of servants to "awe Children, and keep them in subjection, by telling them of *Rawhead* and *Bloody Bones*" and other terrifying "Names" or "invisible Beings" (§ 138).[26] Locke is frequently concerned to counter "the Folly and Perverseness of Servants, who are hardly to be hinder'd from crossing herein the Design of the Father and Mother" (§ 59) and from trying to "lessen their Authority" (§ 68). He repeatedly emphasizes that the parents' ability to employ concerted disapproval must not be undermined by the servants' flattery (§§ 57, 59, 68, 84, 131). Servants also undermine parental authority by giving "Forgiveness" without "Reformation" (§ 59). Not only must their independent bestowal of praise or forgiveness be controlled; they must be watched in their dispensation of food or wine as well.[27] Locke is as concerned to preserve parental authority undivided within the family and undisturbed by servants' efforts to keep children in subjection by fear of invisible beings as he is to preserve civil authority undivided within civil society and undisturbed by priestly efforts to keep people in subjection by fear of invisible beings.[28]

After imprinting a true notion of God and a custom of prayer, the next thing in teaching virtue is to require truthfulness and to encourage "good nature" or love of others (§ 139). For teaching truthfulness, Locke emphasizes the policy of discouraging excuse-making by sooner forgiving twenty confessed faults than a single excused one (cf. § 132). And, although he has just called a true notion of God "the Foundation" of virtue (§ 136),[29] here he says that good nature is "the true Foundation of an honest Man," apparently because "All Injustice generally [springs] from too great Love of our selves, and too little of others."[30] Locke does not say that injustice springs from loving ourselves *more than* others, and accordingly he does not insist that we love others more than or even as much as ourselves.[31] He has already argued that good nature or love of others will be rewarded by the love they return as well as by other advantages for oneself (§§ 109, 110, 116, 117).

Locke concludes by saying that this is "enough for laying the first Foundations of Vertue in a Child." These "first Foundations" include "the Foundation" as well as "the true Foundation." Locke does not include directly teaching either justice or courage in laying the first foundations of virtue because "Children cannot well comprehend what *Injustice* is, till they understand Property" (§ 110) and "so few Men attain to" true fortitude "that we are not to expect it from Children" (§ 115, p. 220). He does, however, counter the foundation of injustice by teaching love of others, and he counters the foundation of cowardice by ridding children of frightful apprehensions.

Locke's discussion of virtue is necessarily incomplete, not only because it is confined to first foundations but also because it is "in general," whereas "the Business of Education" is to remedy the biases of the particular natural tempers of most of "*Adam*'s Children."[32] As he explains,

> to enter into Particulars of this, would be beyond the
> Design of this short Treatise of Education. I intend not
> a Discourse of all the Vertues and Vices, and how each
> Vertue is to be attained, and every particular Vice by its
> peculiar Remedies cured.

This disavowal justifies Cox's statement that Locke's discussion of the virtues in the *Thoughts* "as distinguished, for example, from the elaborate analysis of the *nature* of the virtues in Aristotle's *Ethics*—is eminently practical and popular."[33] Invidious comparisons aside, it is only fair to note that Locke adds to this disavowal the following claim: "Though I have mentioned some of the most ordinary Faults, and the ways to be used in correcting them." He is referring here to his discussion of the ways that parental authority should be used to correct the tempers of children (§§ 103–32). It is true that in that discussion he speaks less of virtues and vices and more of "Faults,"[34] along with biases, tempers, humors, constitutions, inclinations, dispositions, habits, customs, qualities, and even passions, sentiments, and appetites, some good and useful, others ill.[35] However, I devoted much of my account of the *Thoughts* to that discussion precisely because I hoped to show that it does indeed contain an analysis of the natures and relations of the most important virtues and vices as well as advice on how to attain the former and cure the latter.

The Lockean virtues are self-denial, civility, liberality, justice, courage, humanity, curiosity (or, more properly, industry), and truthfulness. In addition, hardiness or endurance of pain is a foundation of courage (§ 115), and good husbandry or avoidance of waste is closely tied to humanity (§ 116). Just as it is not clear whether virtue, wisdom, breeding, and learning do not "sometimes stand for the same thing, or really include one another" (§ 134), so is it with the particular virtues. Civility, liberality, and humanity, for instance, all seem to be referred to as "good nature" (§§ 67, 110, 116). They are all aspects of good nature or love of others, civility being the expression in one's manner of one's good will toward others or of a disposition not to offend them, liberality a readiness to give to others, and humanity an aversion to causing pain to those in one's power.[36] As for other relations between the virtues, liberality especially is the foundation of justice (§ 110; cf. § 139). Courage is the guard and support of the other virtues (§ 115, p. 220). Self-denial, however, holds first place. Not only is it the first remedy that parents must use to free their children from the universal love of dominion (§§ 106–8); it is also, in the whole education of the mind, "the great Principle and Foundation of all Vertue and Worth" (§ 33).[37]

Aside from these virtues, there are other qualities, related to them, including religion as "the Foundation" or one of "the first Foundations" of virtue (§§ 136, 139). Then there is the love of credit or reputation, which is perhaps even more fundamental than the habit or power of self-denial. Although not itself called a virtue, it is still "the true Principle, which will constantly work, and incline them to the right" (§ 56), and it contributes more than anything else to the habit of self-denial (§ 200).[38] So fundamental to the power of self-denial is concern for esteem that in one crucial summary (§ 185) Locke conflates the two, speaking of "the love of Reputation instead of satisfying his Appetite, being made habitual in him."

Given that unreflective self-love is prior to reason or reflection and that habits work more constantly and with greater facility than reason (§ 110), Locke relies less on rules or knowledge than on habits, especially the habit of self-denial, first based on and perpetually strengthened by self-love, especially the love of reputation. For "The Foundations on which several Duties are built, and the Fountains of Right and Wrong, from which they spring, are not perhaps easily to be let into the Minds of grown Men, not used to abstract their Thoughts from common received Opinions" (§ 81). On the contrary,

> if a true estimate were made of the Morality, and Religions of the World, we should find, that the far greater part of Mankind received even those Opinions and Ceremonies they would die for, rather from the Fashions of their Countries, and the constant Practice of those about them, than from any conviction of their Reasons. [§ 146]

Still, Locke's low estimate of the power of reason and his reliance on habit and on concern for esteem do not lead him to do entirely without rules, principles, and knowledge in moral education. He includes a true notion of God among the foundations of virtue. It is true that he opposes children's "promiscuous reading" of Scripture or reading "all the Parts of the *Bible* indifferently as the Word of God, without any other distinction," for he regards such practices as perhaps the worst way of "principling their Religion" (§ 158). He favors, instead, excerpting "easy and plain moral Rules" from Scripture for a child to read and memorize and later to be "inculcated as the standing and sacred Rules of his Life and Action" (§ 159). More generally, Locke explains that once one has taught a constant habit of self-denial and has artfully instilled a love of praise, one has planted "the proper Stock, whereon afterwards to graft the true Principles of Morality and Religion" (§ 200; see also § 61).[39] Something of the content of those principles can be inferred from what Locke says about excerpting rules from Scripture. He does not explain by what standard it is that moral rules should be "fitly chosen" from Scripture, but he does give one example: *What you would have others do unto you, do you the same unto them.*" In the *Essay* he calls this rule "that most unshaken Rule of Morality, and Foundation of all social Virtue," and the *Second Treatise* almost begins with a quotation of Hooker's argument for that rule. That this rule is only an example and not itself the standard of selection or a first principle appears from the passage in the *Essay*, where Locke explains that it is not self-evident but depends on some antecedent truth.[40]

Scripture is not the only reading Locke recommends in the *Thoughts* for becoming "informed in the Principles and Precepts of Vertue" (§ 185). He also recommends Cicero's *Offices* (§ 185) and Pufendorf's works. Immediately thereafter, he does suggest the basis of at least some virtues when he recommends instruction in "the natural Rights of Men, and the Original and Foundations of Society, and the Duties resulting from thence" (§ 186). But above all, as we have seen in the teaching of humanity, Locke proclaims "the Preservation of all Mankind, as much as in him lies" as not only "every one's Duty" but "the true Principle to regulate our Religion, Politicks and Morality by" (§ 116). If not exactly "a Discourse of all the Vertues and Vices," the *Thoughts* is, nonetheless, the most elaborate source we have for Locke's analysis of moral qualities.

## Wisdom (§ 140)

By "wisdom" Locke does not refer to any theoretical, contemplative, or otherworldly knowledge but to the meaning the word has "in the popular acceptation, for a Man's managing his Business ably, and with foresight in this World." In his discussion of knowledge of men as a quality of the tutor (§ 94), Locke did not so completely follow popular use, for he described it only as "containing one great part of Wisdom" (p. 195). Locke discusses this worldly wisdom far more briefly here than in the tutorial digression, for although "the *Tutor* should know the World well" (§ 94), worldly wisdom is "above the reach of Children" (§ 140; see also § 214). For it is the product not only of "a good natural Temper" and "application of Mind" but also of "Experience" or "an Acquaintance with Men, their Tempers, and Designs" (§ 140).[41] It "is not the product of some Superficial Thoughts, or much Reading; but the effect of Experience and Observation in a Man, who has lived in the World with his Eyes open, and conversed with Men of all sorts" (§ 94, p. 195). Accordingly, Locke is concerned here only with "the fittest preparation of a Child for *Wisdom*" (§ 140).

That preparation consists above all in preventing children from becoming "Cunning; which, being the Ape of *Wisdom,* is the most distant from it that can be."[42] Locke maintains that cunning is not merely a dishonest perversion of worldly wisdom but actually its opposite, because cunning lacks the "Understanding" proper to wisdom, as the ape lacks that proper to a man. Cunning is a failure to manage one's business ably and with foresight because it fails to recognize that "a *cunning* Trick helps but once, but hinders ever after." One can successfully conceal a cunning trick, but one cannot conceal one's being cunning.[43] When one is seen to be cunning, one encounters distrust and opposition on the part of others and, ultimately, defeat at their hands. But "the open, fair, *wise* Man has every Body to make way for him, and goes directly to his Business," and that is why it is wise to be open and fair. Locke says nothing here about teaching a young man when to "dissemble" his knowledge of men (cf. § 94, p. 195). Perhaps that can come only later, after this preparation.

Besides teaching the child to avoid cunning and falsehood (see also §§ 120, 131–32) the preparation for wisdom includes accustoming a child "to have true Notions of things, and not to be satisfied till he has them." This quality appears to be what Locke refers to as "Truth" as distinct from "Sincerity" in his restatement at the end of this section: a concern to have the truth oneself, as distinct from being truthful to others. In this context, this quality implies not general curiosity but being accustomed to make "a true Judgement of Men," knowing "the true State of the World," and being disposed "to think no Man better or worse, wiser or foolisher, than really he is" (§ 94, p. 193). This preparation also includes raising a child's mind to "great and worthy Thoughts," but Locke does not elaborate what these thoughts might be. In the restatement, however, he writes, instead, of accustoming children "to a submission to Reason; and as much as may be, to reflection on their own Actions." He is clearly referring here to the habit of self-denial, which plays so important a role as "the great Principle and Foundation of all Virtue and Worth" (§ 33).[44]

Locke has earlier remarked that worldly wisdom is "the only Fence against the World" (§ 94, p. 195).[45] It protects one's virtue against the vice of others, just as courage guards virtue against one's own fears (§ 115, p. 220). As such it is subordinate to virtue but second only to it, since it is necessary for its preservation. Finally, because it enables one to manage one's business with foresight, worldly wisdom also contributes directly to happiness.[46]

The next part of education, good breeding, differs from virtue and wisdom in being suitable peculiarly for a gentleman rather than for man as such (compare § 141 to §§ 135 and 140). It is a counterpart of wisdom, which is "a Man's managing his Business ably" (§ 140), for it is "the managing our selves well" in one "part of our Behaviour," namely, in our conversation with others (§§ 144 and 145, p. 250).

Locke explains what good management of oneself in conversation consists in in far greater detail than he explains what good management of one's business consists in. Good management of oneself in conversation with others consists in the exercise of one quality, civility (cf. §§ 66–67, 93, 109, 117). Civility is "a disposition of the Mind not to offend others" (§ 143, p. 246) or "a care not to shew any slighting, or contempt, of any one in Conversation" (§ 145, p. 250).[47] More positively stated, it is a "general Good will and Regard for all People,"[48] but the emphasis is on the negative avoidance of offense or of "making any one uneasie in Conversation" (§ 143, p. 247). As such, civility is not entirely distinct from virtue, especially the virtues of good nature.[49] Indeed, Locke calls it here "this first, and most taking of all the Social Virtues" (§ 143, p. 247), just as he called justice "this great Social Vertue" (§ 110).[50] Civility is one of the terms Locke uses to describe the second virtue taught by the application of authority (§ 109).

Besides this "internal Civility of the Mind," there is also its external expression, "that decency and gracefulness of Looks, Voice, Words, Motions, Gestures, and of all the whole outward Demeanour, which takes in Company, and makes those with whom we may converse, easie and well pleased" (§ 143, p. 246).[51] Inward civility is the same in all men everywhere, but its outward expression, which Locke compares to a language, is "very much governed by the Fashion and Custom of every Country" (ibid.).[52] Accordingly, he speaks of "an English Gentleman's Behaviour" (§ 94, p. 201). Because, like language, it depends on the custom of the country, good breeding must be "learn'd chiefly from Observation, and the Carriage of those, who are allow'd to be exactly *well-bred*,"[53] just as languages should be taught primarily by conversation rather than by rules (compare §§ 162, 165–68). As Locke has earlier explained, "that, which will most influence their Carriage, will be the Company they converse with, and the fashion of those about them" (§ 67). Perhaps because it is so dependent on the influence of others, it "has the Name of *Good Breeding*, as if peculiarly the effect of Education" (§ 145, p. 250). Locke earlier (§ 67) exempted breeding or manners from the spheres of rules and punishment because the example of the company one keeps is of more effect than "all the Rules in the World, all the Correction imaginable," and here he also claims that internal civility leads of itself to outward civility (compare §§ 143 [pp. 246–47] and 145 [p. 250] to § 67). A disposition not to offend others leads one to observe and adopt "the most acceptable, and agreeable way of expressing that Disposition."[54] Locke therefore urges parents to teach their children "to love and respect other People," which is inward civility, and not "perplex" them about the rules and modes of outward civility or manners (§ 145; cf. § 67). To teach manners, and especially to make them able to "converse with Strangers, and Persons of Quality" or "Persons above us" (§ 142), one should provide them simply with good Company, not with rules.

But one should not infer that Locke regards outward civility as entirely relative to time and place or that he simply defers to the examples of those socially above him (cf. § 131). On the contrary, in discussing faults of incivility he pointedly castigates his social superiors. For example, he complains that "Railery" is often introduced "amongst People of the better rank" (§ 143, p. 248), and he deplores the fact that "forwardness to talk, frequent *Interruptions* in arguing, and loud *wrangling,* are too often observable amongst grown People, even of Rank amongst us" (§ 145, p. 252). He even illustrates this last remark with a story about "two Ladies of Quality" who once argued "as fiercely as two Game-Cocks in the Pit." As for the relativity of the ways of expressing esteem, Locke refers us not simply to the fashion and custom of the country but to qualities "most directly opposite" to civility, some of which are specific modes of behavior (§§ 143, 145). Among these are censoriousness or finding fault with another, including raillery and contradiction. Censoriousness is in "direct opposition to *Civility*" not because of some parochial fashion but because of a fundamental human propensity; for "Men, whatever they are or are not guilty of, would not have their faults displaid, and set in open view and broad day light before their own or other People's Eyes" (§ 143, p. 247; see also §§ 82, 132). Similarly, interruption is intrinsically uncivil, and to illustrate its civil opposite Locke offers this example from another country:

> The *Indians,* whom we call Barbarous, observe much more Decency and Civility in their Discourses and Conversation, giving one another a fair silent Hearing, till they have quite done; and then answering them calmly, and without Noise or Passion. And if it be not so in this civilized Part of the World, we must impute it to a Neglect in Education, which has not yet reform'd this ancient Piece of Barbarity amongst us. [§ 145, p. 252]

Thus, though such outward matters as "putting off their Hats and making Legs modishly" (§ 145; see also § 67) may vary with fashion and custom from country to country, it appears that censoriousness or interruption cannot consist anywhere with civility or expression of esteem. We may also recall Locke's earlier statement that "He that goes into the Eastern Parts of *Asia,* will find able and acceptable Men without any of these [classical learning, speculative natural philosophy, and metaphysics]: But without Vertue, Knowledge of the World, and Civility, an accomplished, and valuable Man can be found no where" (§ 94, p. 196). Independent of mere modes and ceremonies, there is also a universal civility that forms an element of genuine civilization.[55]

Just as civility is not clearly distinct from virtue, neither is it simply inferior to it. Despite the conspicuous priority of virtue (§§ 70 [p. 170], 135, 177, 200), Locke has already explained that, at least for a gentleman, "Breeding is that, which sets a Gloss upon all his other good qualities, and renders them useful to him, in procuring him the Esteem and Good Will of all that he comes near" (§ 93). Among the good qualities rendered useful by civility, he explicitly included "Vertue," which is, by itself, "not enough to procure a Man a good Reception, and make him Welcome where ever he comes" (ibid.). Accordingly, he concluded that breeding should be "the *Governour's* principal Care" and that the tutor himself ought "in the first place to be well Bred." Breeding, then, is what enables virtue to gain esteem, and the importance of this dependence is underlined by the explanation in the very statement of the priority of virtue, that to possess it is "first and most necessary" for a man or a gentleman, "as absolutely requisite to make him valued and beloved by others" as well as "acceptable or tolerable to himself" (§ 135).[56] If the very priority of virtue rests on its being needed to gain esteem, and if esteem cannot be gained without civility, then virtue's need for civility is crucial. To gain esteem and thereby happiness, virtue is necessary but not sufficient. Locke explains the dependence of virtue on civility in a portion of a passage added to § 143 in the fifth edition:

> The happiness that all Men so steadily pursue, consisting in pleasure, it is easie to see why the *Civil,* are more acceptable than the useful. The Ability, Sincerity, and good Intention, of a Man of weight and worth, or a real friend seldom atones for the uneasiness that is produced by his grave and solid Representations. Power and Riches, nay Vertue it self, are valued only as Conducing to our Happiness. And therefore he recommends himself ill to another as aiming at his Happiness, who in the services he does him, makes him uneasie in the manner of doing them. [§ 143, p. 249]

Virtue is valued only as conducing to our happiness, which consists in pleasure; civility is more pleasant than virtue. Civility therefore enjoys a kind of priority over virtue in that, by making others easy and happy, it gains a hearing for virtue. Locke accordingly concludes here that "*Civility* therefore is what in the first place should with great care be made habitual to Children and Young people."

Like courage and curiosity, civility lies between two extremes, one of excess and one of deficiency. The excess, "too great a concern, how to behave our selves towards others" (§ 143, p. 246), expresses itself in "*sheepish Bashfulness*" (§ 141) or being so "confounded in . . . Thoughts, Words, and Looks" as "not to be able to do any thing, or at least not do with that freedom and gracefulness, which pleases, and makes [one] acceptable" (§ 142). This excess of concern with others is also a deficiency; it is not thinking "so well of our selves, as to perform those Actions which are incumbent on, and expected of us, without discomposure, or disorder" (§ 142). The other extreme is "too *little care* of pleasing, or *shewing respect* to those we have to do with" (§ 143) or, presumably, "to think so well of our selves, as to stand upon our own Value; and assume to our selves a Preference before others" (§ 142).

To avoid both of these extremes, Locke proposes "this one Rule, *Not to think meanly of our selves, and not to think meanly of others*" (§ 141). This rule expresses the connection between self-esteem and esteem for others in civility, which gains the esteem of others for oneself. Locke assures us that "The first Part of this Rule, must not be understood in opposition to Humility, but to Assurance" (§ 142). Despite this remark, it is hard to see how the rule "*Not to think meanly of our selves*" can be a rule against assurance, let alone an injunction to humility. On the contrary, it soon appears to be an injunction to think well of ourselves (ibid.). Earlier, Locke has indeed recommended "assurance" as a fence to one's virtue (§ 70, p. 167). Now, though he urges that, to encourage inward civility, one should teach children "Humility, and to be good-natur'd" (§ 145, p. 250), he alters this almost immediately into teaching them merely "to love and respect other People," with no mention of humility.

Of the various faults of incivility that Locke deals with here,[57] contradiction seems to be of special concern to him, for he deals with it twice, first as a "sort of Censoriousness," the third of four qualities "most directly opposite" to civility (§ 143), and second as forming, together with interruption, a "sort of Unmannerliness" that should be "early restrain'd" (§ 145).[58] Contradicting another person is a sort of censoriousness and is therefore uncivil, because "All opposition to what another Man has said" is "apt to be suspected of *Censoriousness*" and is "seldom received without some sort of humiliation" (§ 143, p. 249).[59] Whether or not civility is compatible with humility on one's own part, it cannot be compatible with humiliation of another, with running counter to his desire for what Locke earlier called "the Pleasure, and Credit . . . of having his Reasons sometimes approved, and hearken'd to" (§ 98; see also §§ 97 and 122).

196

Locke concludes, therefore, that we should not "intrude our selves for Teachers; and take upon us, either to set another right in his Story, or shew the Mistakes of his Judgment" (§ 145, p. 251). To say that teaching—at least unsolicited teaching—is inconsistent with civility might seem an odd remark in a discourse of education. But we may also recall Locke's saying that, since civility itself forbids one to correct others' incivilities, the correction must be made only by tutors, "who have Authority over them" (§ 93). Parental and tutorial authority is a necessary exception to the model of social relations it is trying to teach. Yet even that exception is modeled as far as possible on the pattern of civility. Even tutors should not intrude themselves on the children they teach: "Get them but to ask their Tutor to teach them . . . instead of his Calling upon them to learn" (§ 74).

Locke grants, however, that civility, though it excludes contradiction, "does not require that we should always admit all the reasonings or relations that the company is entertain'd with, no, nor silently to let pass all that is vented in our hearing" (§ 143, p. 248). Civility does not actually require "opposing the opinions, and rectifying the mistakes of others," as "truth and charity sometimes" do, but it does not oppose that either, "if it be done with due caution and care of circumstances." For Locke condemns neither

> Difference of Opinions in Conversation, nor Opposition in Men's Discourses: This would be to take away the greatest Advantage of Society, and the Improvements [that] are to be made by ingenious Company; where the light is to be got from the opposite Arguings of Men of Parts, shewing the different Sides of things, and their various Aspects, and Probabilities, would be quite lost, if every one were obliged to assent to, and say after the first Speaker. [§ 145]

This celebration of difference of opinion befits the author of *A Letter on Toleration*. Whereas that work teaches a narrow conception of security as the end of coercive civil society, this passage suggests a broader understanding of the advantages of society understood as "civil" in another sense.[60] Locke's insistence here on "due caution and care of circumstances," which he himself always observed in dissenting from the opinions of others, means above all that one should dissent with "the gentlest manner, and softest words," showing all "marks of respect and good will" (§ 143, p. 249), or "with some civil Preface of Deference and Respect to the Opinions of others" (§ 145, p. 252). Young people, especially, should express their opinions only when asked and then "by way of Enquiry, not Instruction." The reason for this caution is not simply that it is more important to procure credit and esteem than to "get the better of it in the Argument,"⁶¹ for civility will gain "the more favourable Attention, and give what they say the greater Advantage." As Locke writes in the *Letter on Toleration,* by "the true and only method of propagating the truth, I mean when the weight of rational arguments is accompanied by humanity and benevolence."⁶²

## LEARNING (§§ 147–95)

Learning is the last and the least part of education, though it receives by far the longest treatment (§ 147). Not only is it subordinate to virtue and wisdom, as wisdom and breeding are subordinate to virtue; it is actually an evil without them. Learning is "a great help" to virtue and wisdom, but without them it produces only "the more foolish, or worse Men."⁶³ Locke is aware that this demotion of learning "may seem strange in the mouth of a bookish Man" like himself.⁶⁴ But he is "not here considering of the Education of a profess'd Scholar, but of a Gentleman" (§ 195, p. 307).⁶⁵ But an even more fundamental consideration is his subordination of theory to practice. Virtue and wisdom belong to any man; good breeding is especially appropriate to a gentleman; but learning is both required by gentlemanship and to a certain extent restricted by it. For a gentleman requires "the Knowledge of a Man of Business" (§ 94, p. 197), and Locke even declares that "A Gentleman's more serious Employment I look on to be Study" (§ 203); yet "there is nothing less becoming a Gentleman" than having the learning of a "Pedant" (§ 175). Frequently in this discussion of learning, the pupil's status as a gentleman is invoked to require or to restrict his learning in a particular respect.

A thorough examination of the curriculum and of the pedagogical methods to be employed in the intellectual part of education, which occupies so much of the *Thoughts,* would require another study. I shall present here only a cursory survey. The methods exemplify the principles expounded earlier, and I have indeed made anticipatory references to them in presenting that exposition. The fundamental psychological premise here, as there, is the natural love of liberty, which expresses itself especially in a delight in play, a sensitivity to esteem, and an aversion to duty (compare § 148 to §§ 73–76). Accordingly, Locke writes here that

> I have always had a Fancy, that *Learning* might be made
> a Play and Recreation to Children; and that they might
> be brought to desire to be taught, if it were propos'd to
> them as a thing of Honour, Credit, Delight and Recre-
> ation, or as a Reward for doing something else; and if
> they were never chid or corrected for the neglect of it.
> [§ 148]

Learning as play and the use of esteem are the cardinal marks of this pedagogy. The two are combined most delightfully in Locke's recommendation that one teach the alphabet by means of playing with lettered dice, which the child should think "a Game belonging to those above him" (§ 151).[66] Locke relies on exciting desires, not on evoking fear; for fear, precisely the passion that "makes the strongest impression on their yet tender and weak Spirits," is at odds with the easiness of mind conducive to learning (§ 167, pp. 274–76). In excluding punishment and fear from learning, however, Locke does not fail to recognize that authority is originally established through awe (ibid.; cf. §§ 40, 42, 44). This gentle pedagogy also relies on the natural love of novelty and variety (§ 167, pp. 273–74).

Locke writes here of "the pleasure of knowing things" as a motive for learning (§ 178). But the tutor cannot count on finding this in the child; he must "raise in him a love and esteem of Knowledge" (§ 195, p. 307). To do this, the teacher should

> make the Child comprehend (as much as may be) the Usefulness of what he teaches him, and let him see, by what he has learnt, that he can do something, which he could not do before; something, which gives him some Power and real Advantage above others, who are ignorant of it. [§ 167, p. 275][67]

Learning is valued for its utility, for procuring esteem, for power, and for comparison with others (cf. §§ 76, 98, 119, 148).

Locke begins with teaching children to read (§§ 148–55). The first reading should be *Aesop's Fables* (§ 156), "the only Book almost that I know fit for Children" (§ 189, p. 298).[68] Some stories and moral rules may also be excerpted from the Bible, to serve as reading matter, but the book as a whole is unsuitable; early reading of it has led "some Men" never to have "clear and distinct Thoughts" of religion their whole lives (§§ 157–59). After reading comes writing (§ 160) and, after that, drawing, which is "very useful to a Gentleman in several occasions; but especially if he travel," since it enables him to describe buildings, machines, and costumes, though not necessarily faces (§ 161).[69] Locke also hesitantly suggests shorthand, for "Dispatch" and for "Concealment" (§ 161).[70] After English, Locke advises teaching children to speak and read French, which, as a living language (presumably to be used in traveling and in conversing with travelers), must be pronounced well and so should come before any dead languages (§ 162; see also § 168, pp. 278–79). It should be learned by "constant Conversation, and not by Grammatical Rules" (§ 162; cf. § 165). Reliance on practice, habit, and example rather than rules marks the learning of languages just as it does the learning of virtue and breeding.[71]

THE COMPLETION OF EDUCATION (*Thoughts*, §§ 133–216)

Locke recommends Latin (§§ 163–77) as "absolutely necessary to a Gentleman," though not "requisite to Trade and Commerce and the Business of the World" or for those destined solely for such a life (§ 164). It is the language not only of the Roman historians, orators, and poets whom Locke recommends (§ 184) but also of such modern works of learning as those of Pufendorf and Grotius (§ 186) and "the incomparable Mr. *Newton*" (§ 194), to say nothing of Locke's own first published work, his *Epistola de Tolerantia*. Latin should, like French, be learned by conversation and by reading, at first from interlinear texts (§§ 163, 165–67); it should not be learned by doing grammar exercises (§ 168), or by composing themes or verses (§§ 170–74, for poetry of any sort will only "waste his Time and Estate"), nor should it be learned by memorization (§ 176). Finally, the learning of the language should be combined with as much "real" or useful knowledge as possible (§§ 166, 169, 178).

Useful or "real" knowledge is of "Things, that fall under the Senses" (§ 166; see also § 187) and should begin with what "lies most obvious to the Senses, such as is the Knowledge of *Minerals, Plants,* and *Animals;* and particularly Timber and Fruit-Trees, their parts and ways of propagation" (§ 169). Such matters will "not be useless to the Man," presumably because they will assist him in managing his estate (cf. § 204). Of the sciences, geography should come first (§ 178) and then arithmetic, which, aside from being of "so general use in all parts of Life and Business, that scarce any thing is to be done without it," permits further progress in geography and astronomy (§§ 179–80). Close to these subjects is geometry, though only so much as is "necessary or useful" to "a Man of Business" (§ 181). Arithmetic also permits the study of chronology (§§ 182–83).

Except for the direct utility to business that some of these subjects possess, all this seems to culminate in history (§ 184), "which is the great Mistress of Prudence and Civil Knowledge; and ought to be the proper Study of a Gentleman, or Man of Business in the World," and which depends on the knowledge of geography and chronology (§ 182) and uses the ability to read Latin (§ 184; cf. § 177). Sandwiched between Locke's recommendations of Roman and English history are two crucial subjects. The first is the study of ethics from the Bible, Cicero, and Pufendorf, though its basis has been taught "all along from the beginning," though "more by Practice than Rules" and by "the love of Reputation instead of satisfying [the pupil's] Appetite, being made habitual in him" (§§ 185–86). The second is the "general Part of Civil-law" from Grotius and from Pufendorf, who "perhaps is the better of the two," and it teaches "the natural Rights of Men, and the Original and Foundations of Society, and the Duties resulting from thence" (§ 186). It "concerns not the chicane of private Cases, but the Affairs and Intercourse of civilized Nations in general, grounded upon Principles of Reason." This study, like that of history (cf. § 182), is not merely for the youth, since a gentleman should "constantly dwell upon, and never have done with it." (Locke includes his own *Two Treatises* in this part of politics.)

Because the pupil is "an *English* Gentleman" and should be "concerned diligently to apply himself to that, wherein he may be serviceable to his Country"[72] in any station, "from a Justice of the Peace, to a Minister of State," he must know not only this general part of civil law, based on "Principles of Reason," but also "*Our Law*" (§ 187). The "reason" and the "true ground" of English laws are understood not purely from principles of reason but from the study of "our *English* Constitution and Government" and "our History." Understanding these constitutional and historical grounds of laws teaches "what weight they ought to have," at least after one has already studied general civil law.

Locke excludes formal rhetoric and logic (§ 188) as well as disputing, which substitutes victory for truth, produces an obstinate refusal to "yield to.plain Reason" that is "inconsistent with civil Conversation," and leads to "a captious and fallacious use of doubtful Words, which is the most useless and most offensive way of talking, and such as least suites a Gentleman or a lover of Truth of any thing in the World" (§ 189, pp. 296–97).[73] He strongly insists, however, on the skills of speaking and writing English well (§§ 188–89). Gentlemen are men "the greatest part of whose Business in this World, is to be done with their Tongues, and with their Pens"; they should therefore have the ability to "let their Thoughts into other Men's minds, the more easily and with the greater impression" (§ 168, p. 278).[74] This can be called "Rhetorick" (§ 168, p. 280). Just as "There can scarce be a greater Defect in a Gentleman, than not to express himself well either in Writing or Speaking" (§ 189, pp. 297–98), so there is "nothing more becoming a Gentleman, nor more useful in all the Occurrences of Life, than to be able, on any Occasion, to speak well, and to the purpose" (§ 171). Writing well is also both becoming and useful to a gentleman; writing letters, for instance (which "has so much to do in all the occurrences of Humane Life, that no Gentleman can avoid shewing himself in this kind of Writing"), not only "always lays him open to a severer Examination of his Breeding, Sense, and Abilities, than oral Discourses," but there are "Consequences, that in his Affairs, his well or ill managing of it often draws after it" (§ 189, p. 299). Speaking and writing well should be taught by examples, practice, and habit rather than by rules or, when by rules, only by those furnished with "fit examples," so that they are "Patterns" rather than rules (§ 189, pp. 298–99). All this effort "to polish and perfect his Style" should be in English rather than Latin or Greek, since its purpose is use. This concern with one's own language is itself an imitation of the ancients (§ 189, pp. 300–301, and § 168, pp. 279–80).[75]

Locke turns from the paradigmatically conventional realms of style and language[76] to *"Natural Philosophy"* (§§ 190–94).[77] This should not be taught "as a speculative Science" (§ 190) or strictly "as a Science" at all (§§ 190, 193), for we have no certain and systematic knowledge of "the Principles, Properties, and Operations of Things, as they are in themselves" (ibid.).[78] A gentleman should nevertheless learn about "some of the Systems of the *Natural Philosophy* in Fashion," not to gain "satisfactory Knowledge of the Works of Nature" but to "fit himself for Conversation" in "this learned Age" (§ 193). Locke does note, however, that, of "the several Sects," the "Modern *Corpuscularians* talk, in most Things, more intelligibly than the *Peripateticks.*" Besides this knowledge of speculative systems for the purpose of, as we might say, cocktail chat, the study of nature also contains very many things that, although not "brought into a Science," are nevertheless

> convenient and necessary to be known to a Gentleman: And a great many other, that will abundantly reward the Pains of the Curious with Delight and Advantage. But these, I think, are rather to be found amongst such Writers, as have imploy'd themselves in making rational Experiments and Observations, than in starting barely speculative Systems. Such Writings therefore, as many of Mr. *Boyle*'s are, with others, that have writ of *Husbandry, Planting, Gardening*, and the like, may be fit for a Gentleman.[79]

Thus gentlemen return from their brief ascent up the heights of speculation back down to the useful things "most obvious to the Senses" (cf. § 169). Speculative natural philosophy, however lacking in certainty, is necessary for conversation. Experimental natural philosophy, on the other hand, is useful to life, even though it does not yet form a system. Locke does hold out some hope that it will do so—a hope, inspired by the achievements of his friend, "the incomparable Mr. *Newton*," that mathematics may be "applied to some Parts of Nature" (or "this stupendious Machine") but "upon Principles that Matter of Fact justifie" (§ 194). He recommends the *Principia*, which will "give no small light and pleasure,"[80] though he does not expect that Newton's readers will "understand his Demonstrations" but will only "carefully mind his Conclusions." (How early did the modern scientific popular enlightenment become the acceptance of one authority in place of another!)

Locke earlier explained that "the true way, our Knowledge should begin" is by laying the foundation, not in "Metaphysicks," but in "Things, that fall under the Senses" (§ 166; see also §§ 169, 181). Here, however, he insists that the study of spirits, "usually referr'd to *Metaphysicks*," must come before the study of bodies or matter (§§ 190–92).[81] This priority is defended not on the grounds that spirits are "the most Excellent and Powerful Part of the Creation" (§ 190),[82] but

> because Matter being a thing, that all our Senses are constantly conversant with, it is so apt to possess the Mind, and exclude all other Beings, but Matter, that prejudice, grounded on such Principles, often leaves no room for the admittance of Spirits, or the allowing any such things as *immaterial Beings in rerum natura:* when yet it is evident, that by mere Matter and Motion, none of the great Phoenomena of Nature can be resolved, to instance but in that common one of Gravity, which I think impossible to be explained by any natural Operation of Matter, or any other Law of Motion, but the positive Will of a Superior Being, so ordering it. [§ 192]

Axtell comments: "Locke was aware of his inconsistency; nevertheless, he had to suspend the operation of the very 'Principles of Knowledge' to make room for this bow to religion."[83] Locke, however, does not explicitly limit science here for the sake of religion; he introduces religion or metaphysics to support science. A parallel inconsistency is present within this passage, for Locke treats the study of spirits both as a part of natural philosophy, which is the knowledge of things "as they are in themselves" (§ 190), and as distinct from it (§§ 192, 193).

This study of spirits, like that of bodies, should not be taught "as a Science that can be methodized into a System" (§ 190).[84] Although we are led "both by Reason and Revelation" toward "a truer and fuller comprehension of the intellectual World," the study of it here seems to be only from Scripture, or rather from an abridged "good History of the Bible" or even, to begin with, from "a short and plain Epitome" of *that* (§§ 190–91; cf. §§ 158–59). For "the clearest and largest Discoveries we have of other *Spirits,* besides God, and our own Souls, is imparted to us from Heaven, by Revelation" (§ 190). And Locke does not discuss here our rational knowledge of God and of our own souls as spirits.[85] Not only does Scripture teach us of the spirits presupposed by natural philosophy, but natural philosophy helps to explain Scripture, for one can explain God's causing the Flood in terms of (Newtonian) natural philosophy (§ 192).

Locke concludes his treatment of learning by justifying his omission of Greek (it is unnecessary to a gentleman, however needed by a "profess'd Scholar") and by adding some observations on learning languages, culled from La Bruyère, and a statement of the importance of "Method" (§ 195).

## ACCOMPLISHMENTS (§§ 196–99)

Besides the learning he gains from "Study and Books," a gentleman needs "*Accomplishments.*" These are gained from "exercise" and "Masters" (§ 196). The first accomplishment is dancing, which teaches gracefulness, manliness, and confidence. Locke has admitted that "I know not how" it does this (§ 67). This confession of ignorance marks his single recognition of the moral role played by any element of aesthetic education. Music, however, he regards as a waste of time, being almost as pernicious as writing poetry (§ 197; cf. § 174). Locke recognizes that "since Fencing and Riding the great Horse, are so generally looked upon as necessary Qualifications in the breeding of a Gentleman, it will be hard wholly to deny any one of that rank these Marks of Distinction" (§ 199). Along with this bow to fashion, Locke warns that these accomplishments have "very little to do with civil Life" and "were yet formerly unknown to the most Warlike Nations." He is willing to allow "Riding the great Horse" up to a point, since it is "of use to a Gentleman both in Peace and War," and, moreover, it is about as healthful an exercise as is available in a great town (§ 198). But one should not devote too much time to it, since, as Locke writes here, sounding one of the keynotes of the *Thoughts*, one should remember

> in all the parts of Education, that most time and application is to be bestowed on that, which is like to be of greatest consequence, and frequentest use, in the ordinary course and occurrences of that Life, the young Man is designed for.

Locke is far more reluctant to allow fencing (§ 199). Skill in it encourages one to be provocative and easily provoked to quarrels. An inability to fence is far less dangerous, for it makes one "careful to keep out of Bullies' and Gamesters' Company, and . . . not be half so apt to stand upon Punctilios, nor to give Affronts, or fiercely justifie them when given." Such care is not incompatible with Lockean courage (see § 115). In any case, for fighting, fencing is less useful than wrestling, which Locke accordingly prefers.

## TRADE (§§ 201–11)

After a brief summary, emphasizing virtue and wisdom, and especially self-denial, as well as the methods of practice and praise (§ 200), Locke turns to what he fears will be considered inconsistent with gentlemanship: "*a Manual Trade*" (§ 201). Learning a manual trade not only teaches skill in a useful art but contributes to our health, especially as a recreation from study, which does not (§ 202). Locke suggests ironwork, perfuming, engraving, working with precious stones or optical glasses, among others; but, above all, he recommends woodwork and gardening, or *"Husbandry in general,"* as most useful and healthful for a "Country-Gentleman" (§§ 202, 204, 209). His greatest emphasis is thus on agriculture, and he gives examples of "great Men" among the Jews and the ancients who combined it with "the Arts of War or Government" (§ 205). But he rejects painting as a waste of time and a sedentary recreation, just as he excludes writing poetry from learning (§ 174) and excludes music from accomplishments (§ 197). These exclusions reveal Locke's judgments of the unimportance of these aesthetic activities for the formation of gentlemen and of the probable results of an untalented indulgence in them; that is, they do not betray a total lack of aesthetic appreciation on his part. Two remarks of his suggest this; in one he says that "reading the excellent *Greek* and *Roman* Poets is of more use [for the pupil] than making bad Verses of his own" (§ 174; but note the context), in the other, that "ill Painting is one of the worst things in the World" (§ 203). It remains true, however, that Locke is more concerned with the dangers that result from *having* a talent for poetry or painting than from lacking one.

The manual trades are more useful than such fashionable diversions as cards, dice, and drinking, which are dangerous to one's estate or one's health (§§ 207–8; cf. §§ 19 and 174). For recreation should not only provide "Delight and Ease" but "produce, what will afterwards be profitable" (§ 207). The best policy to adopt regarding cards and dice, as well as fencing (cf. § 199), is ignorance, which removes one from temptation (§ 208; but what then of the alphabetical dice of §§ 150–55?). Locke's eagerness to teach gentlemen *"a Manual Trade; nay two or three"* (§ 201), or even *"dexterity and skill in hundreds of Things"* (§ 208), is a far cry from the Platonic insistence on "one man, one art."

Locke insists even more strongly on "one thing relating to Trade," *"Merchant's Accompts"* (§§ 210–11). This is "a Science not likely to help a Gentleman to get an Estate, yet possibly there is not any thing of more use and efficacy, to make him preserve the Estate he has." Unlike the more fundamental treatment in the *Second Treatise,* which is concerned above all with the origin or acquisition of property, the *Thoughts* emphasizes the preservation of inherited property rather than its acquisition or, for that matter, its spending.[86] Not only should the young man be taught accounting, but he should be required to keep accounts of his allowance (§ 211). This requirement is not designed to enable his father "to criticize on his Expences"; for a young man must "be fully Master of" his allowance (§ 211) if he is to "form distinct Notions of Property, and to know what is [his] by a peculiar Right exclusive of others" (§ 110). For, according to the *Two Treatises,* property "is for the benefit and sole Advantage of the Proprietor," and a man has *"Liberty* to dispose, and order, as he lists, his Person, Actions, Possessions, and his whole Property, within the Allowance of those Laws under which he is."[87] Children do not have a *right* to manage their property before the age of reason,[88] but it may be educational for them to do so; keeping accounts is required for giving a young man the habit of managing his own money. Locke tells a story of a noble Venetian who required his extravagant son to count his allowance until he learned good husbandry by reflecting soberly: "If it be so much Pains to me barely to count the Money, I would spend, what Labour and Pains did it cost my Ancestors, not only to count, but get it?" The emphasis in the *Thoughts* is on preservation rather than acquisition or spending; but what will ultimately act to restrain spending and foster preservation of property is the fundamental insight that labor or pain necessarily precedes acquisition. It is through this insight that the heir of property can have something like the same appreciation of it that its first acquirer had.[89]

## Travel (§§ 212–15)

Locke turns last of all to what is usually considered the "last part" of education, namely, "*Travel,* which is commonly thought to finish the Work, and compleat the Gentleman" (§ 212). Locke, however, argues that travel should either come much earlier or be postponed until after the youth has already become a gentleman. The usual time parents select is the period between their son's sixteenth and twenty-first years—"the worst part of a Man's Life," at least for this purpose (§ 215). At this age youths "think themselves too much Men to be governed by others, and yet have not Prudence and Experience enough to govern themselves" (§ 212). In this "boyling boistrous part of Life" a youth actually "comes to relish, and pride himself in manly Vices, and thinks it a shame to be any longer under the Controul and Conduct of another" (cf. §§ 71, 94 [pp. 193–94]). It is therefore useless to send a tutor abroad with him, for he will only consider him "the Enemy to his Freedom." Far from being the time for foreign travel, this is "the Season of all his Life, that most requires the Eye and Authority of his Parents, and Friends to govern it." The love of liberty and desire to think oneself a man can be accommodated and even usefully employed in the carefully constructed environment of home (§§ 73–76, 124, 128–29, 148), but they can hardly be contended with abroad at the time when they are strongest.

The two main advantages to be gained from foreign travel are learning languages and an "Improvement in Wisdom and Prudence" (§ 212). The first can be picked up best between the ages of seven and fourteen or sixteen, at which time children will still submit to a tutor sent to accompany them. The second is gained "by seeing Men, and conversing with People of Tempers, Customs, and Ways of living, different from one another, and especially from those of his Parish and Neighbourhood."

After he is twenty-one, a young man is more likely to make "useful Observations" on his own (§ 213), to have information about his own country to exchange with foreigners (§ 212), and to be admitted into conversation with "Men of Worth and Parts" (§ 214). He must also be "inquisitive" (§ 214), in this respect resembling children, who are like "Travellers newly arrived in a strange Country, of which they know nothing" (§ 120). He should learn not only of the specific "Customs, Manners, Laws, and Government of the Country he is in" but also something of—though he cannot be expected to become perfect in—"the Knowledge of Men" (§ 214; cf. §§ 94, 140). The knowledge of men consists above all in becoming "cautious and wary," becoming accustomed to look "beyond the outside" of men (to their "inside" or "Designs" [§ 94, p. 193]), and gaining the proper relation between one's own outside and inside: the young man should, "under the inoffensive Guard of a civil and obliging Carriage, keep himself free and safe in his Conversation with Strangers, and all sorts of People, without forfeiting their good Opinion" (§ 214).

The reason for the usual error about the best time for travel is not merely a lack of insight into the advantages of travel and the ages appropriate to them but parental desire for their son to "be back again by One and twenty, to marry, and propagate" (§ 215). Although God "bid mankind increase and multiply," and nature "willeth the increase of Mankind,"[90] these are not the true reasons for parental hurry in this matter. The true reasons are rather the father's anxiety to get the dowry and the mother's "for a new Sett of Babies to play with." Locke, however, is in no such hurry; he is anxious for the young man to get more of a head start than usual on his children. If he is to give them an education like the one Locke is designing for him, he will need considerable wisdom.

### Conclusion (§ 216)

Locke concludes the *Thoughts* by saying that he "would not have it thought that I look on it as a just Treatise" on education (§ 216). It contains only "some general Views, in reference to the main End, and aims in Education" for "a Gentleman's Son." It does not deal with all "the various Tempers, different Inclinations, and particular Defaults, that are to be found in Children." Nor does it deal with conditions other than those of a gentleman.

Locke does, however, permit himself to voice the hope that his *Thoughts*

> may give some small light to those, whose Concern for
> their dear little Ones makes them so irregularly bold,
> that they dare venture to consult their own Reason, in

the Education of their Children, rather than wholly to rely upon Old Custom.

If such bold parents do consult their own reason, letting it be guided by Locke's *Thoughts*, they will have joined him in his project of taking men who are by nature free but naturally love freedom and even dominion over others, and making them into gentlemen who are able not only to govern themselves but to help in governing their country.

# CONCLUSION

Ⅰn our time, individualist principles of freedom, equality, and consent seem to be tearing the family apart, theoretically and practically, by justifying and producing divorce, abandonment, and runaways. Locke used the principles of natural freedom and equality, as well as subjection by consent, to criticize the authoritarian patriarchal family. He stressed that husbands' powers fall short of dominion, and he limited them to what wives might consent to. He argued the natural legality of divorce, once the children produced by the union had been raised, and he even suggested the natural legality of so unconventional a familial form as polyandry. He argued that parental "power" is, rather, a matter of children's rights—that it exists only for the children's good and must be directed toward their eventual freedom, equality, and friendship with their parents. He not only emancipated adult children from any obligation of obedience but advised that parents use authority and coercion sparingly with younger children, instead offering as much liberty and imposing as few duties as possible. Despite his critique of the authoritarian patriarchal family, Locke's individualism was far from being aimed at the destruction of the family. Locke was eager to preserve a liberal version of the family as the home of pleasant study and educative play, a home founded on liberty, civility, and love rather than patriarchal tyranny. He placed women's rights and children's rights within the family, not in opposition to it. This was not because he took his individualist principles only halfway but because he saw that the greatest desideratum for the preservation of individual liberty is the limitation of government to the protection of individual rights. If government should not try to form character, except by the example of its protecting rights, then that function must be fulfilled privately, by agencies that do not have the ultimate destructive power of government. If government by consent is to be meaningful, the formation of that consent or dissent must be entrusted to other agencies. For Locke, the family was the natural and safest agency for these crucial purposes. Natural affection could keep parents concerned for the good of their children while leaving them open to enlightened calculation. The family's small size could permit the attention to individuality required by an education for liberty.

Locke's educational proposals might seem irrelevant to our situation insofar as they rest on education within the home rather than the school. Locke himself confesses that "both sides [domestic and school education] have their Inconveniences," and he ends by thinking that "there might be ways found out to avoid the Inconveniences on the one side and the other" (§ 70). For Locke, "schools" meant boarding schools, which meant separating children from their families when they were very young. In our time, of course, the concentration of population and the improvement of transportation make division of labor between family and school commonplace, but the usual allocation of moral and religious education to the family or its chosen church, and of learning and some aspects of social education to the school, is not far from where Locke's arguments point. It is with Locke's proposals for moral education that I have been chiefly concerned.

Contemporary dissatisfaction with Lockean liberalism rests in part on the dominant interpretations of Locke's moral vision. These attribute to him a mean-spirited, selfish materialism, a naïve reliance on rationalism or natural virtue, or an outmoded and anxious Calvinism. Locke, however, constructs modern moral virtues, including civility, liberality, justice, and humanity, on the basis of his egoistic and hedonistic psychology. He both taught a generous concern for others and recognized the power of self-love, pride, and passion. To understand his view of human life as an entirely degraded one, bereft of any dignity, is to do an injustice not only to Locke but to liberalism and ourselves. To exaggerate his rationalism or his otherworldliness is to miss the mundane and hard-headed practicality that makes him useful. Finding nothing decent or inspiring in the interpretations of Locke that are offered to them, students of our political culture have gone off seeking "non-Lockean" elements in our heritage. They should discover, instead, the "non-Lockean" elements in Locke.

Even if we recognize Lockean decency and realism, we may be apt to regard the moral virtues toward which he directed education as merely bourgeois or middle-class morality, hard and narrow, low and colorless. He may offend our moral taste by seeming to slight imagination, passion, and sexuality in favor of reason, self-expression in favor of self-denial, beauty in favor of utility. Our egalitarian but affluent society seems to yearn for some of the aristocratic ethos Locke had to criticize to make us possible. His emphasis on the harsh virtues of self-denial, courage, hardiness, and industry may offend our easy-going self-gratification, but these virtues may still be necessary to the individual liberty and comfort that we join with him in valuing. Locke saw that we have to be willing to deny our desires, face our fears, endure our pains, and take pains in labor in order to preserve our equal liberty and avoid being either tyrants or slaves. Lack of that self-mastery makes us prone to prey on the rights of others and willing to surrender our own. For Locke, passion and imagination make us subject to the authority of others, exploited by their ambition and covetousness.[1] Rationality enables and entitles us to be free, whether from political tyranny, as in the *Two Treatises,* or from intellectual superstition and authority, as in the *Essay.*

# *NOTES*

### Introduction

1. See Peter Laslett, Introduction to Locke's *Two Treatises of Government* (New York, 1965), pp. 16–18; James L. Axtell, Introduction to *The Educational Writings of John Locke* (Cambridge, Eng., 1968), pp. 15, 98. All of my references to the *Treatises* and to the *Thoughts Concerning Education* will be to these editions.

2. Diogenes Laertius 8. 16.

3. *Republic* 423e–424a.

4. Ibid., 520b.

5. Ibid., 520a–d; *Crito* 50c, 51c–d.

6. Ernest Barker, Introduction to *The Politics of Aristotle* (London, 1958), pp. lviii and li.

7. *Leviathan*, ed. C. B. Macpherson (Harmondsworth, Eng., 1968), chap. 30, p. 384, and "Review and Conclusion," p. 728.

8. The quotation is from Locke's early (1667) "Essay Concerning Toleration" in H. R. Fox Bourne, *The Life of John Locke* (New York, 1876), vol. 1, p. 181.

9. *Leviathan*, "Review and Conclusion," p. 728.

10. *Patriarcha and Other Political Works of Sir Robert Filmer*, ed. Peter Laslett (Oxford, 1949), p. 63; emphasis added. All page references to Filmer's works will be to this edition.

11. *Two Treatises*, II, § 173.

12. Locke, "Some Thoughts Concerning Reading and Study for a Gentleman," in Axtell, ed., *Educational Writings of John Locke*, p. 400.

13. See *Some Thoughts Concerning Education* (in Axtell, ed., *Educational Writings of John Locke*), § 186: ". . . the natural Rights of Men, and the Original and Foundations of Society, and the Duties resulting from thence."

14. Ibid., §§ 182 and 186–87.

15. Laslett, in *Two Treatises*, p. 35.

16. Ibid., pp. 37–55, and Maurice Cranston, *John Locke: A Biography* (London, 1957).

17. John Harrison and Peter Laslett, *The Library of John Locke*, 2d ed. (Oxford, 1971), pp. 21–22; Laslett, in *Two Treatises*, pp. 100–101.

18. *Library of John Locke*, p. 24.

19. See Michael Oakeshott, Introduction to Thomas Hobbes, *Leviathan* (Oxford, 1957), pp. xliii–xliv, lvii.

20. See Herbert Marcuse, "Repressive Tolerance," in Robert Paul Wolff, Barrington Moore, Jr., and Herbert Marcuse, *A Critique of Pure Tolerance* (Boston, 1969), pp. 90 and 106; see also John Rawls, *A Theory of Justice* (Cambridge, Mass., 1971), pp. 31–32, 192, 259–63, 327, 436–37, 497–98, 515, 544, 569, and 584.

21. See *Two Treatises,* II, chaps. 14 and 19, esp. §§ 168 and 224–30.
22. Ibid., §§ 170, 174.
23. See *Some Thoughts Concerning Education,* §§ 73, 76, 124, 128–29.
24. Ibid., § 73.
25. Ibid., § 81.

CHAPTER ONE

1. Quentin Skinner allows that Locke was one of the founders of liberalism, but he objects to calling him a liberal ("Meaning and Understanding in the History of Ideas," *History and Theory* 8 [1969]: 19, 24). Skinner's first reason for this view is that Locke's earliest works, the so-called *Two Tracts on Government,* are "markedly authoritarian" and that to call him a liberal is thus to speak as if "Locke at thirty is evidently not yet 'Locke'—a degree of patriarchalism to which even Filmer did not aspire." Locke, however, published the *Two Treatises* and the *Letters Concerning Toleration* and acknowledged them in his will, and he did not publish the *Two Tracts.* He took care that we would remember him for his liberalism, not for his authoritarianism. The *Two Tracts* are valuable, however, for showing that the liberal goal of maximizing liberty is distinguishable from the specific line that liberals draw to limit government (see John Locke, *Two Tracts on Government,* ed. Philip Abrams [Cambridge, Mass., 1967], pp. 120–23). Skinner's second reason is that to suppose Locke "intended to contribute to a school of political philosophy which . . . it was his great achievement to make possible" is to commit prolepsis. Locke, however, makes it clear in his Preface to the *Two Treatises* that he intends his hypothesis of natural freedom to be accepted.

2. *Two Treatises,* I, § 67; II, §§ 4, 87.

3. Ibid., I, § 92; II, §§ 3, 57, 87, 88.

4. See John Locke, *Epistola de Tolerantia: A Letter on Toleration,* ed. Raymond Klibansky and J. W. Gough (Oxford, 1968), pp. 66–69, 122–23.

5. *Two Treatises,* II, chap. 16, "Of Conquest"; see also II, § 1, on force as the alternative to Locke's and Filmer's hypotheses.

6. James Daly, in *Sir Robert Filmer and English Political Thought* (Toronto, 1979), suggests that Filmer was never very influential and was treated as being so by the Whigs only to tar their opponents with absurdity and un-English extremism.

7. See *Two Treatises,* II, § 4.

8. Compare II, § 4, to I, § 67.

9. *Patriarcha,* p. 53. On Filmer, see Laslett's Introduction to *Patriarcha;* Daly, *Filmer and Political Thought;* Gordon J. Schochet, *Patriarchalism in Political Thought: The Authoritarian Family and Political Speculation and Attitudes, Especially in Seventeenth-Century England* (Oxford, 1975), pp. 115–58; John Dunn, *The Political Thought of John Locke: An Historical Account of the Argument of the "Two Treatises of Government"* (Cambridge, Eng., 1969), pp. 58–76; W. H. Greenleaf, *Order, Empiricism, and Politics: Two Traditions of English Political Thought, 1500–1700* (Oxford, 1954), pp. 80–94; Charles R. Geisst, "The Aristotelian Motif in Filmer's *Patriarcha,*" *Political Studies* 21 (1973): 490–99; R. W. K. Hinton, "Husbands, Fathers and Conquerors: I. Filmer and the Logic of Patriarchalism," *Political Studies* 15 (1967): 291–300; J. W. Allen, "Sir Robert Filmer," in *The Social and Political Ideas of Some English Thinkers of the Augustan Age,* ed. F. J. C. Hearnshaw (London, 1928), pp. 27–45. Generally, I view "providentialism" as a more precise and historical way of describing Filmer's central thought than "order," the "ge-

netic doctrine," or even "sovereignty"; I am therefore closer to Dunn's view than to Greenleaf's, Schochet's, or Daly's.

10. *Patriarcha*, p. 78. (The examination of Suarez's argument is on pp. 74–78.)

11. Ibid., p. 57. Compare Locke's complaint, in reference to this first quotation, that citing Bellarmine does not make "any sort of proof at all" (*Two Treatises*, I, § 12).

12. See Robert Bellarmine, *Extracts from the Supreme Pontiff*, trans. George Albert Moore (Chevy Chase, Md., 1951), p. 6.

13. On this problem see Dunn, *Political Thought of John Locke*, pp. 58–59 and 63, and Laslett's Introduction to Filmer's *Patriarcha*, pp. 11 and 15; see also Schochet, *Patriarchalism*, p. 150.

14. *Patriarcha*, pp. 76, 63.

15. See Laslett's Introduction, ibid., pp. 21–33, and Dunn, *Political Thought of John Locke*, pp. 72–76.

16. *Patriarcha*, p. 194.

17. *Two Treatises*, I, §§ 6, 11, 60–66. For Locke on Filmer's use of ancient authors, see I, § 154.

18. *Laws* 690a–d.

19. *Republic*, 449c–466d.

20. *Statesman*, 258e–259c.

21. *Patriarcha*, p. 80.

22. Ibid., pp. 57–61, 187–89, 231, 241, 283–84, 288–89, and passim. The process of patriarchal division is indeed supposed to have gone so far that it became necessary later to have a counteracting process of patriarchal unification in order to form the larger monarchies of modernity (ibid., pp. 61–62).

23. Ibid., pp. 60–61. The seventeenth-century printed versions, such as the one Locke used, lacked the chapter headings available in Laslett's edition, which is based on a manuscript; see Laslett's note, ibid., p. 44.

24. Unless the reference to Jacob's purchase of Esau's birthright and his obtaining Isaac's blessing is regarded by Filmer as an instance of usurpation; if so, part of the force of Locke's mockery of this passage is obviated. Locke presents the passage as if Filmer intended it as an illustration or even a proof of primogeniture (*Two Treatises*, I, §§ 113–18, 137).

25. George H. Sabine comments that "the feebleness of this 'are to be reputed' was lost on none of Filmer's critics" (*A History of Political Theory* [New York, 1937], p. 513). But this is to ignore Filmer's providentialist doctrine of usurpation.

26. *Patriarcha*, pp. 61–62; see also Filmer's later *Anarchy of a Limited or Mixed Monarchy*, in *Patriarcha*, p. 288.

27. *Patriarcha*, p. 62.

28. See Bernard Mandeville, *The Fable of the Bees* (Harmondsworth, Eng., 1970), p. 371 and also 54–55, 167, 222. It may also be added that whereas Mandeville's private vices serve the public benefits of wealth and power, Filmer's express divine punishment. For Mandeville, divine punishment is indeed performed by means of private virtues (see *The Fable*, pp. 70–75).

29. *Patriarcha*, p. 62.

30. On this, see Dunn, *Political Thought of John Locke*, p. 72, n. 2.

31. *Patriarcha*, p. 232.

32. Filmer lived from 1588 to 1653; *Patriarcha* was written sometime between 1635 and 1642, before the Civil War. See Laslett's Introduction to *Patriarcha*, pp. 1, 3, and 9.

33. Ibid., pp. 5–8.

34. Ibid., pp. 231–35. Filmer's tracts were published between 1648 and 1652. *Patriarcha* was published only posthumously, in 1680, during the Exclusion crisis, when it became of concern to Locke; but it served as the basis for the tracts, which include extracts from it.

35. *Two Treatises,* Preface; I, §§ 71–72, 79–80, 121; and—as appears from these passages and is noted by Laslett in his note to the last of them—a part of the missing section of the *First Treatise.*

36. Dunn, *Political Thought of John Locke,* p. 63, n. 3.

37. *Patriarcha,* p. 232; consider also this statement, which appears on p. 233: "in grants and gifts that have their original from God or nature, as the power of the Father hath, no inferior power of man can limit, nor make any law of prescription against them: upon this ground is built that common maxim, that *Nullum tempus occurrit regi,* no time bars a King."

38. See ibid., pp. 94–95.

39. Dunn, *Political Thought of John Locke,* p. 65, n. 3.

40. See *Patriarcha,* pp. 234–35. Grotius, in *The Law of War and Peace,* trans. Francis W. Kelsey (Oxford, 1925), bk. 1, chap. 4, § xv, makes the same distinction, but in the next four sections (xvi–xix) he permits not only passive obedience but, in some cases, actual resistance.

41. *Patriarcha,* p. 235.

42. *Two Treatises,* I, §§ 3, 104–5, 124, 126; *Patriarcha,* p. 65.

43. *Patriarcha,* p. 234. On Filmer's curious partial Hobbism see Dunn, *Political Thought of John Locke,* p. 70, n. 3, and p. 71, nn. 1–4; see also Sabine, *History of Political Theory,* p. 513.

44. *Patriarcha,* pp. 66–67, 247–48, 294–95, 300; *Two Treatises,* II, §§ 21, 168, 240, 241.

45. *Patriarcha,* p. 234: "in obeying a usurper, we may obey primarily the true superior, so long as our obedience aims at the preservation of those in subjection, and not at the destruction of the true governor."

46. See Dunn, *Political Thought of John Locke,* p. 71, n. 2.

47. *Patriarcha,* p. 234.

48. In a note to *Two Treatises,* I, § 79, Laslett reproaches Locke for perpetually reproaching Filmer "with statements made under such necessity." But Filmer already justified obedience to usurpers in *Patriarcha,* pp. 61–62; indeed, his doctrine there was more simply accommodating to them than his later *Directions,* with their exceptions and indelible divine right. A practitioner of passive obedience he may have been, but a trimmer of theory it seems he was not.

49. *Patriarcha,* pp. 54–55 (emphases mine); see also pp. 99–100 and 321–22 (the last passage is from Bodin).

50. Filmer employs the classic biblical passages "Be subject unto the higher powers" (Romans 13:1) and "Submit yourselves unto every ordinance of man" (1 Peter 2:13) (*Patriarcha,* pp. 67, 100–101, 189–91, 291). Contrast Allen's statement ("Filmer," p. 29) that Filmer "did not argue from the Epistle to the Romans."

51. Luke 20:25; Matthew 22:21; Mark 12:17.

52. See Dunn, *Political Thought of John Locke,* p. 60, and W. H. Greenleaf, "Filmer's Patriarchal History," *Historical Journal* 9 (1966): 159.

53. *Patriarcha,* pp. 241–42.

54. Ibid., p. 65.

55. Ibid., p. 56; cf. p. 225.

56. Ibid., pp. 72, 77, 268–69, 287.

57. Ibid., pp. 81–82, 223–26, 285–88. These criticisms are most sympa-
thetically presented by Allen in "Filmer," pp. 33–38.

58. See Dunn, *Political Thought of John Locke*, pp. 60, 67.

59. Filmer, *Patriarcha*, pp. 262, 266, 274; 82; 233.

60. Nor did he "obviously" assume it, as Laslett asserts (Introduction to
Filmer, *Patriarcha*, pp. 15 and 21) and as Greenleaf claims is "almost certain"
("Filmer's Patriarchal History," p. 163).

61. *Two Treatises*, I, chaps. 9, 10, and 11, on the inheritance of Adam's
sovereignty.

62. *Patriarcha*, p. 62; see also pp. 60–61, 232–33, 288–89.

63. See, e.g., Howard Warrender, *The Political Philosophy of Hobbes* (Oxford,
1957), pp. 237–49, and Sterling Power Lamprecht, *The Moral and Political Philosophy of John Locke* (New York, 1962), pp. 146–48.

64. *Two Treatises*, I, § 121.

65. Filmer, *Patriarcha*, pp. 80, 187–88, 241.

66. *Two Treatises*, I, chap. 9.

67. Filmer, *Patriarcha*, p. 278; cf. pp. 84–85 and 189.

68. Ibid., p. 53.

69. Ibid., pp. 53, 55, 89–90, 206, 224, 244.

70. *Two Treatises*, I, §§ 3, 4; see also II, § 112, where Locke says that men
"never dream'd of Monarchy being *Jure Divino*, which we never heard of among
Mankind, till it was revealed to us by the Divinity of this last Age."

71. Contrast the statements (ibid., II, §§ 94, 111) about "the negligent, and
unforeseeing Innocence of the first Ages," which failed to "examine more carefully *the Original* and Rights of *Government.*" Elsewhere Locke argued that
novelty is not an argument either for or against a thought ("Letter to the Bishop
of Worcester," *The Works of John Locke*, 8 vols. [London, 1823], vol. 4, pp. 135–
39).

72. *Two Treatises*, I, § 6. Here, using the Greek version of 1 Peter 2:13,
Locke finds a scriptural foundation for government by consent.

73. *Two Treatises*, I, § 4.

74. *Patriarcha*, p. 53; Laslett's edition, based on the manuscript—which
Locke of course did not have—reads "Within the last hundred years . . . ," which
makes the novelty more precise. Moreover, in the manuscript version, the first
chapter is entitled "The Natural Freedom of Mankind, a New, Plausible and
Dangerous Opinion."

75. *Two Treatises*, Preface. The comical phrase "Drum Ecclesiastick," al-
luding to the pulpit that divines bang on, may come from Samuel Butler's anti-
Puritan *Hudibras* (see *OED*, sv. Drum), one of the few works of English literature
Locke owned; see John Harrison and Peter Laslett, *The Library of John Locke*, 2d
ed. (Oxford, 1957), p. 29.

76. Filmer, *Patriarcha*, pp. 53–57. Locke, *Two Treatises*, I, §§ 2–6, 67; II,
§§ 4, 87, 95, 119, 123, 190–91.

77. *Two Treatises*, II, § 4.

78. *Two Treatises*, I, § 4 (the nonitalicized phrase is Locke's sarcastic addition); cf. I, § 67, and Filmer, *Patriarcha*, p. 54.

79. *Patriarcha*, pp. 53–57, 256.

80. Ibid., pp. 53–54.

81. R. Doleman (pseud. Robert Parsons), *A Conference about the Next Succession to the Crowne of Ingland* (1594), pp. 1–3, 14, 25, 103 (misnumbered as 203)
(hereditary right); 21–23, 35 (monarchy); 9–12, 44 (forms of government); 13,
21–23, 29, 35, 72, 82 (laws and conditions); 1–3, 14, 25, 128–96 (succession);

37–81 (deposition); 196–218 (pretenders). This pseudonymous work by the Jesuit Robert Parsons cautiously refrains from explicitly and conclusively arguing for the Spanish claim to the English throne and avoids open signs of Roman Catholicism. Nevertheless, its author, one of "the *bêtes noires* of Anglican divines," is "the most frequent subject of attack by supporters of James, and his work is evidently regarded as the most salient exposition of the treasonable character of the Papal aims" (J. N. Figgis, *The Divine Right of Kings* [New York, 1965], pp. 101–4; see also J. W. Allen, *A History of Political Thought in the Sixteenth Century* [London, 1960], pp. 208, 260–62). According to a printed notice appended to the copy of *A Conference* in Houghton Library, Elizabeth I decreed that possession of the book was high treason, and the printer is said to have been hanged, drawn, and quartered.

82. Doleman (Parsons), *A Conference*, pp. 33, 53, 81; cf. pp. 199–200.

83. Ibid., pp. 3–4; cf. p. 7.

84. Ibid., p. 8; cf. p. 4.

85. Ibid., pp. 7, 202, 204–6.

86. Although Parsons means an end taught by nature and recognized by the ancients, he emphasizes its religious side, relevant to the current problem of succession and opposed to Machiavelli's opposition between political virtue and religion (ibid., pp. 41, 203–18; but cf. pp. 154–55).

87. George Buchanan, *De Jure Regni apud Scotos* (London, 1689), pp. 5, 10–13, 16, 20, 22–23, 34–36, 39–41, 44–45, 59, 64, 66. Buchanan's work was published in 1578 but was probably written in the 1560s to defend the deposition of Mary Stuart from the throne of Scotland. He appears, however, not to have been a Calvinist fanatic but a humanist poet who lived in France, associating with Catholics. See Allen, *Political Thought in the Sixteenth Century*, pp. 336–42; J. N. Figgis, *Political Thought from Gerson to Grotius* (New York, 1960), pp. 167–73; R. W. and A. J. Carlyle, *A History of Medieval Political Theory in the West* (New York, 1936), vol. 6, pp. 332–34, 387, 399–401; Quentin Skinner, *The Foundations of Modern Political Thought*, vol. 2, *The Age of Reformation* (Cambridge, Eng., 1978), pp. 339–45.

88. J. W. Gough, *The Social Contract* (Oxford, 1957), p. 63, n. 4; Allen, *Political Thought in the Sixteenth Century*, p. 340; but cf. Otto von Gierke, *Natural Law and the Theory of Society* (Cambridge, Eng, 1934), vol. 2, p. 243, n. 63.

89. Buchanan, *De Jure Regni*, pp. 6–7, 16.

90. Gough, *Social Contract*, p. 63, n. 4; Buchanan, *De Jure Regni*, pp. 7–9.

91. Calvin, *Institutes of the Christian Religion*, trans. John Allen, 7th ed. (Philadelphia, n.d.), bk. 4, chap. 20, § 25; see also Allen, *Political Thought in the Sixteenth Century*, pp. 52–60.

92. Calvin, *Institutes*, bk. 4, chap. 20, § 32; cf. Filmer, *Patriarcha*, pp. 54–55, 99–100, 321–22.

93. Calvin, *Institutes*, bk. 4, chap. 20, § 31.

94. Filmer, *Patriarcha*, p. 62. He does not, however, recognize any mixed government; see pp. 93, 198–99, 279–313.

95. See Michael Walzer, *The Revolution of the Saints* (New York, 1969), pp. 23, 58–59; Allen, *Political Thought in the Sixteenth Century*, pp. 58, 68, 103–20; Skinner, *Foundations of Modern Political Thought*, vol. 2, pp. 191–94, 214, 219–20, 230–34, 314–16.

96. Calvin, *Institutes*, bk. 2, chap. 2, §§ 13, 22; cf. bk. 4, chap. 20, § 16.

97. Ibid., bk. 2, chap. 1, § 8, and chap. 3, § 2; see also chap. 1, § 9.

98. Ibid., bk. 2, chap. 2, §§ 12, 3; see also bk. 1, chap. 15, § 6; bk. 2, chap. 1, § 2, and chap. 2, §§ 2, 22.

99. Ibid., bk. 2, chap. 2, §§ 15–16.

100. Ibid., bk. 1, chap. 5, § 7.

101. Walzer, *Revolution of the Saints*, p. 35; Leo Strauss, *Spinoza's Critique of Religion* (New York, 1965), p. 196.

102. Calvin, *Institutes*, bk. 1, chap. 5, §§ 4, 6–7, 11; chap. 14, § 20; chap. 16, §§ 1–8; chap. 17, § 5.

103. See Walzer, *Revolution of the Saints*, pp. 32–33, 60.

104. Calvin, *Institutes*, bk. 4, chap. 20, § 4.

105. Filmer, *Patriarcha*, p. 289.

106. Compare Calvin, *Institutes*, bk. 4, chap. 20, §§ 7–8, to Filmer, *Patriarcha*, pp. 206, 229, 284, 288–89.

107. Calvin, *Institutes*, bk. 4, chap. 20, §§ 8, 12, 25.

108. Ibid., §§ 25, 30.

109. Ibid., bk. 1, chap. 18, § 4; Filmer, *Patriarcha*, p. 62.

110. Calvin, *Institutes*, bk. 4, chap. 20, § 31.

111. Ibid., § 9; cf. ibid., § 3, and "Dedication to Francis I," vol. 1, p. 22.

112. Filmer, *Patriarcha*, p. 56; cf. p. 54 n. See also Robert Bellarmine, *De Laicis*, trans. Kathleen Murphy (New York, 1928), chap. 6, p. 27. When Filmer quotes this statement he refers to it as coming from chapter 4; but when he notes it to support his claim that Bellarmine "looks asquint," he cites chapter 6. James I attacked the same passage; see *The Political Works of James I*, ed. C. H. McIlwain (Cambridge, Mass., 1918), p. 153.

113. Bellarmine, *De Laicis*, chaps. 1 and 2 passim.

114. Filmer, *Patriarcha*, p. 57; Bellarmine, *Supreme Pontiff*, bk. 5, chap. 1, § 5, and, generally, bk. 5, chaps. 2–8. Cf. Skinner, *Foundations of Modern Political Thought*, vol. 2, pp. 175–80.

115. Bellarmine, *Supreme Pontiff*, bk. 5, chap. 7, §§ 11–12; Bellarmine, *Power of the Pope in Temporal Affairs against William Barclay* (Chevy Chase, Md., 1949), chaps. 20, 21, 22, and 26, pp. 126–28, 137–39, 154. Cf. Allen, *Political Thought in the Sixteenth Century*, p. 359; Carlyle and Carlyle, *Medieval Political Theory*, vol. 6, p. 404.

116. Bellarmine, *Power of the Pope*, chap. 21, p. 134; cf. chaps. 3 and 5, pp. 37, 48. The original statement does not make this basis explicit; see *Supreme Pontiff*, bk. 5, chap. 7, §§ 11–12, 15.

117. Filmer, *Patriarcha*, pp. 56–57.

118. Bellarmine, *De Laicis*, chap. 6.

119. Ibid., chap. 5. According to Bellarmine, "the correct meaning of St. Paul when he says, 'he that resisteth the power, resisteth the ordinance of God' " is that government is by natural law, and, since "natural law is Divine law, therefore, government was instituted by Divine law" (chap. 6). He derives the scriptural warrant for civil power from natural law.

120. Ibid., chap. 5, pp. 22–23, chap. 7, pp. 31–32; cf. Doleman (Parsons), *A Conference*, p. 4, and Leo Strauss, *Natural Right and History* (Chicago, 1953), pp. 184, 215–16.

121. Filmer, *Patriarcha*, pp. 289–90; Bellarmine, *De Laicis*, chap. 2, p. 11.

122. Filmer, *Patriarcha*, pp. 53–54.

123. Locke, *Two Treatises*, I, §§ 4, 67.

124. John Hayward, *An Answer to the First Part of a Certaine Conference Concerning Succession, Published not long since under the name of R. Dolman* (London, 1603). Hayward describes his work, in the dedication to James I, as a "defence, both of the present authorite of Princes, and of succession according to proximitie of bloud: wherein is maintained, that the people have no lawfull power,

to remove the one or repell [repeal] the other." See Allen, *Political Thought in the Sixteenth Century,* pp. 256–62; Schochet, *Patriarchalism,* pp. 47–50.

125. Hayward, *An Answer,* p. $A_4$ verso.

126. Ibid., pp. $B_4$–$C_2$ verso. The argument from consent does not contradict Hayward's objection to Parsons's use of historical examples, that "there is no action either so impious or absurd, which may not be paralleled by examples" and that "examples suffice not to make any proffe" (pp. $F_2$, $P_1$ verso; cf. p. $O_4$ verso). For the secondary law of nature is "the received custome, successively of al, and alwaies of most nations in the world"; though it is immutable "in *abstracto,*" it is not so "in *subjecto*"; it can be transgressed though not changed (pp. $B_1$, $B_2$ verso). See Daly, *Filmer and Political Thought,* p. 65, n. 26.

127. Hayward, *An Answer,* pp. $C_2$ verso–$D_2$.

128. Ibid., p. $C_1$; cf. Doleman (Parsons), *A Conference,* pp. 15–18.

129. Doleman (Parsons), *A Conference,* pp. 21–24.

130. Cf. Buchanan, *De Jure Regni,* pp. 10–12, 19–20, 38; Bellarmine, *De Laicis,* chap. 6, p. 27; *Supreme Pontiff,* bk. 1, chaps. 1–4, esp. chap. 2, § 16. Filmer brings out this difficulty in Bellarmine (*Patriarcha,* pp. 57, 84). Bellarmine avoids the rigidity of a natural-law doctrine that would render all forms of government but one unlawful, by deriving forms of government not directly from natural law but from "the law of nations"—"a sort of conclusion drawn from the natural law by human reason" (*De Laicis,* chap. 6, p. 27); but cf. Thomas Aquinas, *Summa Theologica,* I–II, qu. 95, a. 4.

131. Calvin, *Institutes,* bk. 4, chap. 20, §§ 7–8; cf. Walzer, *Revolution of the Saints,* p. 39.

132. Filmer, *Patriarcha,* pp. 62, 206, 229, 284, 289; cf. Daly, *Filmer and Political Thought,* pp. 45–47, 112, n. 32; Dunn, *Political Thought,* p. 65.

133. Filmer, *Patriarcha,* p. 54. Filmer seems to have read Hayward, for he quotes him later in *Patriarcha* as "a learned historian of our age" (pp. 94–95).

134. For such reasons Allen concludes not only that Hayward was not an exponent of the theory of the divine right of kings but that there is no full expression of that theory in England before Filmer (see Allen, *Political Thought in the Sixteenth Century,* pp. 258, 260, 270).

135. Doleman (Parsons), *A Conference,* p. 72. Parsons seems to mean, however, only that forms of government are not determined by God but are left to each commonwealth to choose; all kings are from God only by his "universal providence," and sometimes they rule by his permission rather than his ordinance, so that he still leaves men authority to dispose of government for the public benefit (pp. 9, 123).

136. Hayward, *An Answer,* p. $K_4$ verso.

137. Hayward does, however, at one point reckon that it is wise of God to send persecutors, since men prove more pious under them (p. $T_4$ verso).

138. Ibid., pp. $N_4$ verso, $P_2$; Doleman (Parsons), *A Conference,* pp. 12, 39.

139. Hayward, *An Answer,* pp. $B_2$, $E_3$. In his Preface to his "Observations upon Aristotle's Politiques," Filmer writes that at the time of the Judges there was "some small show of government," yet truly "there was no form of government"; in *Patriarcha,* he notes that "even then, the Israelites were under the kingly government of the Fathers of particular families" (*Patriarcha,* pp. 189, 84). Filmer agrees that Nimrod was the "first founder of monarchy" only in the sense that he was the first to usurp the rights of other patriarchal kings (p. 59). Hooker, writing shortly before Hayward, calls the time before the Flood "those times wherein there were no civil societies" (which in Locke become the times of "the state of nature"); yet Hooker claims with Hayward that "the Law of

Nature doth now require of necessity some kind of regiment." Compare Hooker, *Laws of Ecclesiastical Polity,* bk. 1, chap. 10, § 3, to Locke, *Two Treatises,* II, § 91 n.

140. Hayward, *An Answer,* p. E$_3$; Filmer, *Patriarcha,* p. 63 (but cf. *An Answer,* p. L$_3$).

141. Hayward, *An Answer,* pp. D$_4$–E$_1$, E$_3$, K$_3$ verso; the English monarchy specifically rests on William the Conqueror's title "by dinte of sworde" (p. R$_2$ verso). Filmer's recognition of usurpers' heirs rests on providence, not prescription (*Patriarcha,* pp. 232–33; see Daly, *Filmer and Political Thought,* pp. 119–22).

142. Hayward, *An Answer,* pp. B$_4$–F$_1$ verso.

143. Filmer, *Patriarcha,* pp. 81–82.

144. Allen, *Political Thought in the Sixteenth Century,* p. 258. Right before introducing Hayward, Filmer writes that the people's right to punish princes "follows (as the authors of it conceive) as a necessary consequence" of natural freedom (*Patriarcha,* p. 54); the parenthesis holds open the possibility of a position that accepts natural freedom without sedition.

145. Filmer, *Patriarcha,* pp. 81–82; cf. pp. 225–26, 243–44, 255–56, 273–74, 285–88.

146. Ibid., p. 256; Hayward, *An Answer,* p. D$_3$.

147. Filmer, *Patriarcha,* p. 54. William Barclay was the author of *De Regno et Regali Potestate adversus Buchananum, Brutum, Boucherium et reliquos Monarchomachos* (1600). Although Filmer credits it to John Barclay, Laslett in his note to this passage identifies the author as William Barclay, as does Figgis implicitly (*Divine Right,* p. 131); Locke, in quoting this passage, omits the perplexing first name (*Two Treatises,* I, §§ 4, 67). John Barclay was William Barclay's son, and he continued his father's work as a vindicator of the right of kings. William wrote *De Potestate Papae* to refute Bellarmine's assertion (in *De Summo Pontifice*) of the papal right to authorize the deposition of kings, and John, after his father's death in 1608, wrote *Pietas Sive Publicae pro Regibus* (1612) to refute Bellarmine's reply (published as *De Potestate Summi Pontificis in Rebus Temporalibus* in 1610). Since Filmer refers to Barclay as one of those who "have learnedly refuted both Buchanan and Parsons," the great patriarchalist probably mistakenly referred to the father by the son's name, for in *De Regno et Regali Potestate* William Barclay refutes the *De Jure Regni* of his fellow Gallicized Scot, Buchanan, and also the monarchomachic works of "Brutus," the pseudonym of the author of the *Vindiciae contra Tyrannos,* and Jean Boucher, the Catholic author of *De Justa Abdicatione Henrici tertii,* which defends tyrannicide as well as revolution. (See note 165, below, for evidence that Filmer used or misused *De Regno* in *Patriarcha.*) On William Barclay, see Allen, *Political Thought in the Sixteenth Century,* pp. 385–93, and Carlyle and Carlyle, *Medieval Political Theory,* vol. 6, pp. 445–50.

148. *Two Treatises,* II, § 232.

149. Allen, *Political Thought in the Sixteenth Century,* pp. 387, 389.

150. William Barclay, *The Kingdom and the Regal Power,* trans. G. A. Moore (Chevy Chase, Md., 1954), bk. 1, pp. 22, 24, 26; bk. 2, p. 100.

151. Ibid., bk. 2, p. 106; cf. Bellarmine, *De Laicis,* chap. 7, pp. 31–32; Bellarmine, *Supreme Pontiff,* bk. 1, chap. 2, § 15; Filmer, *Patriarcha,* pp. 80, 84.

152. Barclay, *Kingdom,* bk. 2, p. 111; Hayward, *An Answer,* pp. B$_2$, E$_3$; cf. Filmer, *Patriarcha,* p. 59.

153. Barclay, *Kingdom,* bk. 1, pp. 37–39.

154. Ibid., bk. 2, pp. 100–105, 109–29.

155. Ibid., bk. 3, chaps. 2–3, pp. 143–49.

NOTES TO PAGES 32–34

156. Ibid., bk. 3, chap. 2, pp. 145–46. The Roman *lex regia,* whereby the people conferred their sovereignty and power on the emperor, is an instance; Barclay's native Scotland is another (see ibid., bk. 2, pp. 123, 128).

157. Ibid., bk. 3, chap. 2, pp. 144–45; chap. 3, pp. 149–59; chap. 4, pp. 160–61, 167; bk. 6, chap. 16, p. 541. Barclay even allows that the people may establish no law of succession and keep kingship elective (bk. 2, p. 114; bk. 3, chap. 3, p. 159).

158. Ibid., bk. 3, chap. 10, pp. 214, 223–24; chap. 12, p. 235; contrast Filmer, *Patriarcha,* pp. 100–101, 189–90.

159. Barclay, *Kingdom,* bk. 3, chap. 16, p. 268; cf. chap. 10, pp. 223–24; bk. 4, chap. 10, pp. 335–37; chap. 21, pp. 386–87; bk. 5, chap. 14, p. 465.

160. Ibid., bk. 3, chap. 4, pp. 165–66.

161. *Two Treatises,* II, §§ 232–39.

162. Barclay, *Kingdom,* bk. 3, chap. 3, pp. 156–58; contrast Hayward, *An Answer,* p. A₁ verso.

163. Barclay, *Kingdom,* bk. 3, chap. 16, pp. 273–74.

164. Ibid., bk. 1, pp. 38–39; bk. 3, chap. 8, p. 205; chap. 12, p. 237; bk. 4, chap. 10, pp. 335–37.

165. Ibid., bk. 1, pp. 37–38; bk. 2, pp. 105–7, 109, 118. Barclay adduces as evidence of this natural propensity the great number of kings in the earliest times. This passage appears to have been the source for a similar passage in Filmer's *Patriarcha,* pp. 59–60. Filmer repeats seven of Barclay's eight examples in the same order and in much the same words, only substituting ancient kings of "our county of Kent" (Filmer's own county) for Barclay's ancient German examples. He also omits Barclay's identification of Melchizedek as Shem (see *Kingdom,* bk. 2, p. 82), probably because Shem, as "Adam's heir," should be more than a mere king of Salem. Locke vigorously points out that Shem was still alive at times when Filmer attributes patriarchal power to all sorts of other rulers (*Two Treatises,* I, §§ 146–47). Filmer uses Barclay's examples in his history of the "footsteps" of paternal government, which they are not particularly suited to. The origin of this passage helps to explain why its examples "are all impertinent and directly contrary to what he brings them to prove" (*Two Treatises,* I, § 149).

166. Filmer, *Patriarcha,* p. 82; see also pp. 81, 225–26, 243–44, 255–56, 273–74, 285–88.

167. Locke noted in 1679 Filmer's challenge (see Filmer, *Patriarcha,* p. 226), in connection with the problems of majority rule, representation, tacit consent, etc., that "amongst all them that plead the necessity of the consent of the people, none of them hath ever touched upon these so necessary doctrines; it is a task it seems too difficult, otherwise surely it would not have been neglected, considering how necessary it is *to resolve the conscience,* touching the manner of the peoples passing their consent; and what is sufficient, and what not, to make, or derive a right, or title from the people" (Locke Ms. f. 28, p. 119, discussed by Laslett in his Introduction to Locke's *Two Treatises,* p. 72).

168. Filmer, *Patriarcha,* pp. 239–50 (Filmer's "Observations on . . . Leviathan" is included in Laslett's edition of *Patriarcha*).

169. Quotations from *De Cive* are from Thomas Hobbes, *Man and Citizen,* ed. Bernard Gert (New York, 1972). Quotations from *Leviathan* are from Thomas Hobbes, *Leviathan,* ed. C. B. Macpherson (Harmondsworth, Eng., 1968). Quotations and translations from other works of Hobbes are from *The English Works of Thomas Hobbes,* ed. William Molesworth, 11 vols. (London, 1839–40), and *Opera Latina,* ed. William Molesworth, 5 vols. (London, 1845). References are to Hobbes's part, chapter, and section numbers, except for *Leviathan,* the chapters of which

are not divided into sections, where page numbers from the Macpherson edition are also provided. For Hobbes on the family, see Richard Allen Chapman, "*Leviathan* Writ Small: Thomas Hobbes on the Family," *American Political Science Review* 69 (1975): 76–90; Schochet, *Patriarchalism,* pp. 225–43; Leo Strauss, *The Political Philosophy of Hobbes: Its Basis and Its Genesis* (Chicago, 1963), pp. 60–70, 102–4; Richard Peters, *Hobbes* (Baltimore, 1967), pp. 185, 197–98; John Laird, *Hobbes* (London, 1934), pp. 197, 209–11, 216; Warrender, *Political Philosophy of Hobbes,* pp. 123–24, 236, 238–39, 247, n. 1; Keith Thomas, "The Social Origins of Hobbes's Political Thought," in *Hobbes Studies,* ed. K. C. Brown (Oxford, 1965), pp. 188–89; R. W. K. Hinton, "Husbands, Fathers, and Conquerors: II. Patriarchalism in Hobbes and Locke," *Political Studies* 16 (1968): 55–67; Nathan Tarcov, *Locke's Thoughts Concerning Education, the Family, and Politics* (Ph.D. diss., Harvard University, 1975), pp. 138–280.

170. *Leviathan,* chap. 17, p. 228, and chaps. 18, 20; in *De Cive,* natural as distinguished from institutive or political (chap. 5, § 12; chap. 8, § 1); in *De Corpore Politico,* patrimonial as distinguished from commonwealth (pt. 1, chap. 6, § 11) or from institutive (pt. 2, chap. 3, § 1).

171. *Leviathan,* chap. 17, p. 228, chap. 18, pp. 228–29, chap. 20, pp. 251–52; *De Cive,* chap. 5, § 12, chap. 8, § 1; *De Corpore Politico,* pt. 1, chap. 6, § 11; pt. 2, chap. 1, § 3, chap. 3, § 2.

172. *De Corpore Politico,* pt. 2, chap. 1, § 1; cf. pt. 2, chap. 4, § 10; *De Cive,* chap. 1, § 10; *Leviathan,* chap. 20, pp. 252–53.

173. *Leviathan,* chap. 17, p. 228; *De Cive,* chap. 5, § 12, chap. 8, § 1; *De Corpore Politico,* pt. 2, chap. 1, § 1.

174. Compare *Leviathan,* chap. 17, p. 227; *De Cive,* chap. 5, § 4; and *De Corpore Politico,* pt. 1, chap. 6, §§ 4, 6.

175. *De Corpore Politico,* pt. 2, chaps. 3, 4; *De Cive,* chaps. 8, 9; *Leviathan,* chap. 20, pp. 253–56. In the first two presentations, Hobbes presents paternal dominion only after despotic dominion, perhaps because its nature is made clearest that way.

176. *De Corpore Politico,* pt. 2, chap. 4, §§ 1–3; *De Cive,* chap. 9, §§ 2–3; *Leviathan,* chap. 20, p. 254.

177. *De Corpore Politico,* pt. 2, chap. 4, § 1.

178. *De Corpore Politico,* pt. 1, chap. 4, § 2, to which pt. 2, chap. 4, § 1, specifically refers; cf. *De Cive,* chap. 3, § 14; *Leviathan,* chap. 15, pp. 211–12.

179. *De Corpore Politico,* pt. 1, chap. 2, § 10, chap. 6, § 1, pt. 2, chap. 1, §§ 5–6, chap. 8, § 8; *De Cive,* chap. 2, § 11, chap. 5, § 4; *Leviathan,* chap. 14, p. 196, chap. 15, p. 202, chap. 17, p. 225.

180. Cf. *De Corpore Politico,* pt. 1, chap. 1, § 10; *De Cive,* chap. 1, §§ 7–10; *Leviathan,* chap. 14, pp. 189–90; cf. Locke, *Two Treatises,* II, §§ 26–28.

181. *De Corpore Politico,* pt. 2, chap. 4, § 2; *De Cive,* chap. 9, § 1; *Leviathan,* chap. 20, p. 253.

182. *De Corpore Politico,* pt. 1, chap. 3, § 6; this exception is not made explicitly in *De Cive* or *Leviathan,* perhaps because it is practically impossible to determine whether a benefactor acts only for benefit without any element of glory; indeed, it would seem practically impossible for anyone who is able to confer a benefit not to take pleasure in his power to do so.

183. *De Corpore Politico,* pt. 1, chap. 2, § 1, chap. 3, § 6, chap. 4, § 15; *De Cive,* chap. 2, §§ 1–2, chap. 3, § 8; *Leviathan,* chap. 15, pp. 209, 214, 216.

184. *De Corpore Politico,* pt. 1, chap. 3, § 10; *De Cive,* chap. 3, § 11; *Leviathan,* chap. 15, p. 210.

185. *Human Nature,* chap. 9, §§ 15, 17; this might seem to be part of Hobbes's paraphrase of "the opinion of Plato," but a contrast with *Symposium* 208e makes it clear that it is Hobbes's own comment.

186. *Human Nature,* chap. 8, § 5, chap. 9, §§ 15–17; *De Corpore Politico,* pt. 2, chap. 9, § 3. Hobbes omits this duty of the sovereign in *De Cive,* chap. 13, and *Leviathan,* chap. 30 (even though, as I show above, he there presents natural human sexuality as even less directed to generation). Presumably he omits it as a part of his omission of the sovereign's duty to provide for the eternal good of subjects; for multiplying population, as distinct from providing for prosperity, peace, and defense, has a scriptural rather than a natural basis (compare *De Corpore Politico,* pt. 2, chap. 9, § 3, "having created but one man, and one woman," to pt. 2, chap. 3, § 2, "all at once created male and female"; cf. *Two Treatises,* I, §§ 33, 41; II, § 42). Willis B. Glover claims that concern for the eternal salvation of subjects is imposed by Hobbes on sovereigns by natural law "in all three of his political treatises," but the passages he cites do not bear this out (see Glover, "God and Thomas Hobbes," *Hobbes Studies,* ed. K. C. Brown [Oxford, 1965], pp. 151–52, n. 16).

187. *Leviathan,* chap. 6, pp. 123–24, chap. 10, p. 151; cf. *De Homine,* chap. 11, § 5, chap. 12, § 8 ("*solet*").

188. *Leviathan,* Introduction, p. 81.

189. Compare *Patriarcha,* p. 233, to *Leviathan,* chap. 31, p. 397, and *De Cive,* chap. 15, § 5.

190. *Human Nature,* chap. 7, § 5; *De Corpore Politico,* pt. 1, chap. 1, § 6; *De Cive,* Epistle Dedicatory (*summum naturae malum* in the Latin version), chap. 1, § 7; *Leviathan,* chap. 6, pp. 129–30, chap. 11, pp. 160–61; *De Homine,* chap. 11, §§ 6, 15; cf. Oakeshott, *Leviathan,* Introduction, pp. xxxi, n. 1, xxxiv; Strauss, *Political Philosophy of Hobbes,* pp. 15–17, 124–25, 132–33; Strauss, *Natural Right,* pp. 180–81.

191. Compare *Politics* 1278b25–30 to *Nicomachean Ethics* 1158b21–22, 1161b19, 1162a4–7, 1165a21–24, and to *Politics* 1262a25–29.

192. See Schochet, *Patriarchalism,* pp. 229–31; H. C. Mansfield, Jr., "Hobbes and the Science of Indirect Government," *American Political Science Review* 65 (1971): 103.

193. *De Corpore Politico,* pt. 2, chap. 4, §§ 3–7; cf. *De Cive,* chap. 9, §§ 3–4 and 6; *Leviathan,* chap. 20, pp. 253–54.

194. *Leviathan,* chap. 20, p. 253.

195. *Leviathan,* chap. 11, p. 163, chap. 13, p. 183, chap. 15, p. 211; *De Cive,* chap. 1, § 3, chap. 3, § 13; *De Corpore Politico,* pt. 1, chap. 1, § 2, chap. 4, § 1, chap. 6, § 1; cf. Thucydides, *History* 3. 83, translated by Hobbes in *English Works,* ed. Molesworth, 8:351.

196. *Leviathan,* chap. 20, p. 253.

197. *Human Nature,* chap. 9, § 1, chap. 9, § 17; *De Corpore Politico,* pt. 1, chap. 3, § 6.

198. Cf. Schochet, *Patriarchalism,* pp. 230–31, 235, 241–42.

199. *Leviathan,* chap. 15, p. 209; *De Cive,* chap. 3, § 8; *De Corpore Politico,* pt. 1, chap. 3, §§ 6–7; in all three presentations gratitude is the one natural law Hobbes goes to the trouble to explicitly contrast with justice.

200. *De Cive,* chap. 9, § 3.

201. *Leviathan,* chap. 11, p. 163.

202. See Strauss, *Political Philosophy of Hobbes,* pp. 123–25.

203. *De Corpore Politico,* pt. 2, chap. 4, § 3 referring back to pt. 1, chap. 1, § 13; *De Cive,* chap. 1, §§ 13–14; chap. 5, § 3.

204. *De Corpore Politico,* pt. 2, chap. 4, § 3; cf. pt. 1, chap. 1, § 13; *De Cive,* chap. 9, § 3; *Leviathan,* chap. 20, pp. 253–54.

205. See *De Corpore Politico,* pt. 2, chap. 3, § 3; *Leviathan,* chap. 20, p. 254 ("supposed to promise").

206. *Leviathan,* chap. 26, p. 317; *De Cive,* Author's Preface.

207. *Leviathan,* chap. 20, pp. 253, 255; cf. Warrender, *Political Philosophy of Hobbes,* pp. 123–24, 256; Laird, *Hobbes,* p. 210; F. C. Hood, *The Divine Politics of Thomas Hobbes* (Oxford, 1964), pp. 173–74; Schochet, *Patriarchalism,* pp. 231–33; Filmer, *Patriarcha,* p. 245.

208. *Leviathan,* chap. 15, pp. 204–5.

209. See Locke's criticism, *Two Treatises,* II, §§ 13, 90–94, 137.

210. For obligation by consent, see *De Cive,* chap. 8, § 3, "all obligation derives from contract"; even the dominion of God is supposed to be by covenant (*Leviathan,* chap. 35, pp. 442, 444–45).

211. Schochet, *Patriarchalism,* pp. 226, 236–43.

212. Filmer, *Patriarcha,* pp. 239, 241.

213. *Leviathan,* chap. 17, p. 228; chap. 19, p. 250; chap. 20, p. 255; *De Cive,* chap. 9, § 10, chap. 9, §§ 14–19; *De Corpore Politico,* pt. 2, chap. 4, §§ 10–17.

214. *De Corpore Politico,* pt. 2, chap. 3, § 2; *De Cive,* chap. 8, § 1; *De Homine,* chap. 1, § 1; cf. Filmer, *Patriarcha,* p. 241. For Isaac de La Peyrère's later, partly scriptural, argument for multiple creation, see Strauss, *Spinoza's Critique,* pp. 64–85.

215. For the state of nature as a war of every man against every man, see *De Corpore Politico,* pt. 2, chap. 8, § 8; *De Cive,* chap. 1, § 12, chap. 5, § 2, chap. 10, § 1; *Leviathan,* chap. 13, pp. 185, 188, chap. 14, pp. 189–90, 196, chap. 15, p. 204, chap. 19, p. 249, chap. 21, p. 266, chap. 28, p. 354, chap. 30, p. 376.

216. *Leviathan,* chap. 20, p. 257. On "small Families" in the state of nature, see ibid., chap. 13, p. 187, chap. 17, p. 224.

217. See ibid., chap. 13, pp. 185–86.

218. See Warrender, *Political Philosophy of Hobbes,* p. 124; Chapman, "*Leviathan* Writ Small," pp. 78–79.

219. See *De Corpore Politico,* pt. 1, chap. 4, § 10, chap. 6, § 1; *De Cive,* chap. 3, § 27, chap. 5, § 1; *Leviathan,* chap. 15, p. 215, chap. 17, pp. 223–24.

220. *Leviathan,* chap. 16, pp. 219–20; Schochet, *Patriarchalism,* p. 238.

221. See *De Cive,* chap. 14, § 9; Filmer, *Patriarcha,* pp. 62, 72, 188, 233, 283, 289. For the tremendous importance of the Fifth Commandment for patriarchal thinking generally, see Laslett, Introduction to Filmer, *Patriarcha,* pp. 26–27; Schochet, *Patriarchalism,* pp. 6, 14–16, 38–39, 73–74, 78–81, 89–92, 94.

222. *Leviathan,* chap. 21, p. 266.

223. *De Corpore Politico,* pt. 1, chap. 6, § 3; *De Cive,* chap. 5, § 3; *Leviathan,* chap. 17, p. 224. In each of these passages Hobbes's argument moves from the insufficiency of small groups for security to the need of large groups for a common power to rule them.

224. Compare Schochet, *Patriarchalism,* p. 242, to Mansfield, "Indirect Government," p. 103, n. 23.

225. *De Corpore Politico,* pt. 2, chap. 9, § 3; *De Cive,* chap. 14, §§ 9–10, chap. 17, § 10, chap. 6, § 16.

226. In the accompanying reinterpretation of the Eighth Commandment, against theft (*De Cive,* chap. 6, § 16, chap. 14, §§ 9–10, chap. 17, § 10), Hobbes gives the example of a Spartan law which, by sanctioning *successful* theft by youths, thereby rendered it not theft; he does not mention the Spartans' sanction of

what Christians might call adultery (see Plutarch, *Lycurgus* 15. 6–7 and 17. 3–4).

227. *De Cive*, chap. 14, § 9. Filmer quotes only "Honor thy Father," omitting "and thy Mother," as Locke frequently points out (see *Two Treatises*, I, §§ 6, 11, 60–66).

228. This difference may be related to a shift in concern away from refuting the claim of Roman Catholic clergy to judge "of the lawfulnesse of Marriages" (*Leviathan*, chap. 47, p. 707) by virtue of their sacramental character. Cf. esp. *De Cive*, chap. 6, § 16 n., and chap. 18, § 14.

229. *Leviathan*, chap. 43, p. 614.

230. *Leviathan*, chap. 30, p. 376. Equal justice, equal taxes, public charity, and prevention of idleness seem to belong to legislation; counselors, commanders, and international relations seem not to fit into the division (see pp. 385–87, 391–94). Neither the division nor the emphasis on instruction is present in the earlier *De Corpore Politico* (pt. 2, chap. 9) and *De Cive* (chap. 13).

231. *Leviathan*, chap. 30, p. 378, in preparation for chap. 42, pp. 545–47.

232. Ibid., chap. 30, pp. 377–82.

233. See ibid., chap. 22, p. 285, where the father or master "obligeth his Children, and Servants, as farre as the Law permitteth, though not further, because none of them are bound to obedience in those actions, which the Law hath forbidden to be done."

234. See *De Cive*, chap. 9, § 8.

235. *Leviathan*, chap. 27, p. 352 (emphasis added).

236. *De Cive*, chap. 9, § 8.

237. *Leviathan*, chap. 30, p. 382.

238. Ibid.

239. Schochet presents this statement as if it were adduced by Hobbes to justify the "authority over their offspring that fathers have in society." Instead of beginning it with Hobbes's words, "To which end they are to be taught," Schochet adds, in brackets, "It must be remembered" (*Patriarchalism*, pp. 238–39); contrast Chapman, "*Leviathan* Writ Small," p. 82.

240. Chapman, "*Leviathan* Writ Small," pp. 85–86.

241. *Leviathan*, chap. 30, pp. 382–83.

242. *De Corpore Politico*, pt. 2, chap. 1, § 10; cf. chap. 5, § 2, chap. 8, § 8; *De Cive*, chap. 6, § 9, chap. 14, § 6; *Leviathan*, chap. 18, p. 234, chap. 24, pp. 295–96.

243. *Leviathan*, chap. 13, p. 185.

244. Ibid., chap. 21, p. 271.

245. Ibid., chap. 11, p. 161; chap. 13, pp. 184–85; chap. 10, p. 156; chap. 12, p. 175.

246. *De Corpore Politico*, pt. 2, chap. 4, § 13; *De Cive*, chap. 9, § 15; *Leviathan*, chap. 19, p. 250.

247. *Leviathan*, chap. 11, p. 166; *De Homine*, chap. 13, § 4.

248. *De Cive*, chap. 1, § 2, n. 1; *Human Nature*, chap. 9, § 14; *De Cive*, Author's Preface.

249. *De Homine*, chap. 13, § 3.

250. *Human Nature*, chap. 10, § 8; chap. 5, § 14.

251. For an interpretation of reliance on example rather than precept as the original guiding thought of Hobbes, see Strauss, *Political Philosophy of Hobbes*, pp. 79–102.

252. *De Homine*, chap. 13, § 7.

253. *Leviathan*, chap. 8, pp. 138–39; cf. the Introduction, p. 83.

254. Ibid., "Review and Conclusion," p. 728; see also chap. 30, pp. 383–85; *De Cive*, chap. 13, § 9; *De Corpore Politico*, pt. 2, chap. 9, § 8.

255. Hood, *Divine Politics*, p. 217.

256. *Leviathan*, chap. 31, p. 408; "Review and Conclusion," p. 728.

257. *Leviathan*, chap. 18, p. 233; see also chap. 42, pp. 567–68; *De Cive*, chap. 6, § 11.

258. See *De Corpore Politico*, pt. 2, chap. 8, § 3 (ambition); *De Cive*, chap. 12, § 1 ("the *doctrines* and the *passions*"); chap. 12, § 10 (ambition); cf. *De Corpore Politico*, pt. 2, chap. 8, §§ 4–10; *De Cive*, chap. 12, §§ 1–8; *Leviathan*, chap. 29, pp. 365–68.

259. *Leviathan*, chap. 30, p. 379.

260. Ibid., "Review and Conclusion," p. 729.

261. *De Cive*, chap. 13, § 12; cf. *De Corpore Politico*, pt. 2, chap. 9, § 7.

262. *De Cive*, chap. 6, § 11; *Leviathan*, chap. 18, p. 233, chap. 30, p. 382.

263. *Leviathan*, chap. 21, p. 264.

264. See Thomas, "Social Origins," p. 228.

265. The sovereign's judgment over doctrines seems to apply only, or at least chiefly, to books and men "speaking to Multitudes of people" (*Leviathan*, chap. 18, p. 233).

266. See *De Corpore Politico*, pt. 2, chap. 9, §§ 1, 4; *De Cive*, chap. 13, § 15; *Leviathan*, chap. 30, p, 388; and Laird, *Hobbes*, p. 215: "He did not suppose that *all* education was necessarily the State's business."

267. *Human Nature*, chap. 10, § 8.

268. *Leviathan*, chap. 43, p. 614.

269. *De Corpore Politico*, pt. 2, chap. 9, § 8 (emphasis added); the emphasized claim is omitted in *De Cive*, chap. 13, § 9, and in *Leviathan*, chap. 30, p. 384.

270. The subject matters of the "true doctrine" referred to in the passage just quoted are those of his own work; see *Human Nature*, chap. 1, § 1. For Hobbes's confidence, see, e.g., the Dedication to the *Elements*.

271. *Leviathan*, chap. 30, p. 384.

272. *Six Lessons to the Savilian Professors*, Lesson VI, in Hobbes, *English Works*, 7:345.

273. *Leviathan*, chap. 6, p. 124; cf. chap. 8, p. 139, on the desire to know, and *Decameron Physiologicum*, chap. 1, in *English Works*, 7:71–72. See also Thomas, "Social Origins," pp. 220–21, and Dorothea Krook, *Three Traditions of Moral Thought* (Cambridge, Eng., 1959), pp. 117–18, 129.

274. Chapman, "*Leviathan* Writ Small," pp. 87–88.

275. *De Corpore Politico*, pt. 2, chap. 5, § 3. Such arguments may be found not only in Filmer but also in such authors as Dante and Bellarmine; see *De Monarchia*, bk. 1, chaps. 5–9, and *Supreme Pontiff*, bk. 1, chaps. 2 and 4 (the latter work is argued against by both Hobbes, *Leviathan*, chap. 42, pp. 576–609, and Filmer, *Patriarcha*, pp. 56–57 and 84, where such arguments are quoted).

276. *De Corpore Politico*, pt. 1, chap. 1, § 12, and chap. 6, § 2; pt. 2, chap. 4, §§ 3–4; pt. 1, chap. 6, § 5; pt. 2, chap. 3, § 2.

277. *De Cive*, chap. 10, § 3. Compare his answer to Bellarmine, "that Examples prove nothing" (*Leviathan*, chap. 42, p. 608). Thomas nevertheless presents one of these arguments—that God instituted paternal government—as if it were simply Hobbes's own (Thomas, "Social Origins," p. 188 and n. 36).

278. Compare *De Cive*, chap. 5, chapter title, and chap. 5, § 2, to chap. 10, § 3. In *De Corpore Politico* (pt. 2, chap. 5, § 3) Hobbes does not say by whom paternal government is "instituted."

279. *Leviathan*, chap. 19, p. 241.

280. See Strauss, *Political Philosophy of Hobbes*, p. 152; cf. Hobbes, *De Cive*, Author's Preface.

281. *Leviathan*, chap. 22, p. 284; chap. 26, pp. 316, 328; *De Cive*, chap. 3, §§ 31–32; *Leviathan*, chap. 15, p. 216.

282. See Strauss, *Political Philosophy of Hobbes*, p. 104.

283. See *Leviathan*, chap. 26, p. 320, and "Review and Conclusion," pp. 718–19.

284. Indeed, the only place Hobbes's name appears in the *Two Treatises* is in the title of Filmer's criticism of Hobbes, cited by Locke in the Preface and in I, § 14.

285. See Filmer's *Observations Concerning the Originall of Government*, including the Preface and the first part, "Observations on Mr. Hobbes's *Leviathan: or His Artificial Man—a Commonwealth*," in *Patriarcha*, pp. 239–50.

286. Laslett, in his Introduction to Filmer, *Patriarcha*, p. 39; see also pp. 39–42 and Laslett's Introduction to Locke, *Two Treatises*, pp. 80–92, 45–48, 103–5.

287. Filmer, *Patriarcha*, p. 239.

288. *Leviathan*, chap. 13, p. 187.

289. Filmer, *Patriarcha*, p. 241.

290. Ibid. Cf. *Leviathan*, chap. 14, pp. 189–90.

291. *Patriarcha*, pp. 241–42. The accusation of familial cannibalism was flung back at Filmer by Locke in *Two Treatises*, I, §§ 57 and 59.

292. *Leviathan*, chap. 14, p. 190.

293. E.g., *De Corpore Politico*, pt. 2, chap. 4, § 3: "the mother, in whose power it is to save or destroy it, hath right thereto by that power."

294. *De Cive*, Author's Preface, end.

295. Ibid., chap. 1, § 10 n.

296. *Patriarcha*, p. 242.

297. Schochet, *Patriarchalism*, pp. 236–37, referring to *De Cive*, chap. 9, § 2; see also *De Cive*, chap. 1, § 3: "if we look on men *full grown* . . . there is no reason why any man, trusting to his own strength, should conceive himself made by nature above others" (emphasis added).

298. Filmer, *Patriarcha*, p. 239.

299. *De Cive*, chap. 9, §§ 2–3; chap. 5, § 3, and chap. 6, § 3; chap. 2, § 18, and chap. 1, §§ 9–10.

300. Filmer, *Patriarcha*, pp. 245, 242.

301. Ibid., p. 245, quoting from *Leviathan*, chap. 26, p. 333. Filmer cites "page 249," but in the first edition of *Leviathan*, the pagination of which appears in brackets in the Macpherson edition, this is the beginning of chapter 40, where a related passage does appear but without the phrase that Filmer quotes.

302. See *Leviathan*, chap. 14, p. 191; *De Cive*, chap. 8, § 3.

303. See *De Cive*, Author's Preface, where children are said to be "exempted from all duty."

304. It should be noted that Filmer characteristically misquotes Hobbes here as saying that the government over children originally resides in the mother "because she *brings forth* & first nourisheth them" (emphasis added); what Hobbes actually says is "*aluntur et educantur*" ("nourished & brought up") (*De Cive*, chap. 9, § 7; cf. chap. 9, § 4). Hobbes, unlike Filmer, does not argue from generation.

305. *De Cive*, chap. 9, § 3, and chap. 9, § 6; the first example (Amazonian warfare), unlike the second (Amazonian contracts for children), is not retained in *Leviathan*, chap. 20.

306. *De Cive*, chap. 9, § 4. The statement in this passage that "the mother in the state of nature, where all men have a right to all things, may recover her

son again, namely, by the same right that anybody else might do it" must mean by theft or robbery; compare chap. 1, § 10.

307. Filmer, *Patriarcha*, p. 245. Compare Filmer's apparent acceptance (*Patriarcha*, p. 283) of Hunton's reference to Genesis 3:16 ("where God ordained Adam to rule over his wife") as "the original grant of government" to his statement (p. 289) that "Eve was subject to Adam before he sinned" and to his use of Genesis 1:28 (e.g., on pp. 63–64 and pp. 187–88). Cf. Locke, *Two Treatises*, I, §§ 16, 44, and 55.

308. Filmer, *Patriarcha*, p. 245, referring to *De Cive*, chap. 9, § 3; cf. *Leviathan*, chap. 20, p. 254.

309. *Patriarcha*, p. 74.

310. Ibid., pp. 72–73.

311. Filmer, "Directions for Obedience to Government in Dangerous or Doubtful Times," in *Patriarcha*, pp. 232–33.

312. Ibid.

313. All references in parentheses in the rest of this chapter are to *Two Treatises*.

314. Locke does not mention donation or property in the first statement, and in the second he divides fatherhood into a claim from begetting and a claim from the Fifth Commandment.

315. See the title of chapter 6.

316. Locke's denial that historical example is a rule flows from his refusal to perceive the workings of particular providence in history.

317. See Harvey C. Mansfield, Jr., on the "grandfather problem" in *Statesmanship and Party Government: A Study of Burke and Bolingbroke* (Chicago, 1965), p. 57.

318. This is the "grandfather problem" again.

319. Locke's opposition to dual sovereignty here, as well as his remarkably repeated denunciation of the danger of a single heir to Adam in the world, who challenges all present rulers (see, e.g., I, §§ 104–5), suggests rejection of the most powerful claimant of divided sovereignty in his time, even though the *Two Treatises* explicitly distinguish civil government only from paternal, conjugal, and despotic government, not from ecclesiastical government.

320. See the Preface and I, § 121. On "Fate," see also I, § 2.

321. Cf. II, § 124, and Hobbes, *Leviathan*, chap. 26, p. 322, and Machiavelli, *The Prince*, chap. 15.

322. Cf. I, §§ 73–77.

323. Note also I, §§ 133–34, 144–45, and 168–69.

324. Laslett, in his note to this passage, claims that what he calls "the chronological argument" becomes the main theme at I, §§ 168–69, but that it is unfinished, for he conjectures that "it presumably occupied the early part of the missing portion." Indeed, he asserts that it "breaks off abruptly in the middle of a phrase" and that it "made nonsense" to treat it as a sentence. He even alters the sentence himself without any textual support, making it into nonsense by changing "1750 Years" to "1150 Years," the total of the two nearest numbers (500 plus 650). Laslett appears not to have followed the argument of I, §§ 129–69, the last quarter of the *First Treatise*, which, as I explained above, is a close examination of Filmer's "History out of Scripture" for evidence of the conveyance of Adam's sovereignty (see Locke's explicit statement to this effect in § 128). Laslett claims that the passage consists of "comments on Filmer's sentences . . . wandering far from its [the chapter's] title 'Who Heir?' " He then surmises that what we have here is "a stringing together of surviving fragments of the lost portion of Locke's original manuscript" (note to §§ 159–60). But one should

recall the summary, at § 150, of the argument beginning at § 129, which concludes that during the "2290 Years" from Adam until the exile in Egypt there was *no* "Absolute Monarchical Power descending from *Adam,* and exercised by Right of *Fatherhood.*" Similarly, the last sentence (for so it is) summarizes the argument that began in § 151 by concluding that, during the 1,750 years the Jews were the chosen people (200 years in Egypt, plus 400 years till the monarchy, plus 500 years of monarchy, plus 650 years to their dispersion by the Romans; see §§ 163, 165, and 168–69), they were ruled by hereditary monarchs less than a third of the time (500/1,750; 500 is *more* than a third of Laslett's 1,150); moreover, even these monarchs did not achieve the throne by primogeniture "from *David, Saul, Abraham,* or which upon our *A*'s [Filmer's] Principles is the only true [Fountain]; From *Adam.*" For other peculiarities of Laslett's understanding of Locke's references to scriptural chronology, see his notes to I, §§ 136 and 150; he seems to think that Locke lived in the seventh century and that the exile in Egypt took place in 706 B.C.

325. Figgis, *Divine Right,* p. 152; Allen, "Filmer," p. 43, and *Political Thought in the Sixteenth Century,* p. 270.

326. Figgis, *Divine Right,* pp. 154–55.

327. Ibid., p. 152.

328. Ibid., pp. 154–55, 157. Cf. Sabine, *History,* p. 513.

329. See also I, § 153.

330. *Two Tracts,* pp. 171–72.

331. *Works,* vol. 8, p. 367; see also *A Letter on Toleration,* pp. 116–17. On Locke's use of Scripture in *Two Treatises,* see Strauss, *Natural Right,* pp. 214–19; Richard H. Cox, *Locke on War and Peace* (Oxford, 1960), pp. 47–57; and M. Seliger, *The Liberal Politics of John Locke* (New York, 1969), pp. 56–62.

332. See Filmer, *Patriarcha,* pp. 54–55, 67, 99–101, 189–91, 291, 321–22.

333. Filmer, *Patriarcha,* p. 191.

334. See II, §§ 138–40, 142.

335. Filmer, *Patriarcha,* p. 54.

336. See also, e.g., I, § 101.

337. See *An Essay Concerning Human Understanding,* ed. Peter Nidditch (Oxford, 1975), bk. 4, chaps. 18–19.

338. Cf. ibid., chap. 19, § 10: "For where a Proposition is known to be true, Revelation is needless: And it is hard to conceive how there can be a Revelation to any one of what he knows already."

339. On the relation of reason and revelation in Locke, see, e.g., Lamprecht, *Moral and Political Philosophy of Locke,* pp. 2–3; Strauss, *Natural Right,* pp. 202–20; E. E. Worcester, *The Religious Opinions of John Locke* (Geneva, N.Y., 1889), pp. 25–35; and S. G. Hefelbower, *The Relation of John Locke to English Deism* (Chicago, 1918), pp. 71–73, 101–6, 115–16.

340. Cf. II, § 25.

341. *Essay,* bk. 4, chap. 19, § 4.

342. Seliger (*Liberal Politics,* p. 59) understands this to mean that "where scriptural language is obscure, we are entitled to doubt whether the words reported 'must be understood literally to have been spoken.' " However, it is their superfluity, not their obscurity, that seems to justify the doubt in this passage. It may be possible, however, to understand this parenthesis of Locke's to question merely whether God literally "speaks" when positive revelation takes place. Yet Locke himself refers to this as "this Grant spoken to *Adam*" (*Two Treatises,* I, § 31).

343. Compare *Two Treatises*, I, § 39, to I, § 92, and II, §§ 6, 25, 26, and 30.

344. See also I, § 67.

345. See also I, § 118.

346. He implies that, on the contrary, she "may endeavor to avoid it."

347. See Hobbes, *De Corpore Politico*, pt. 1, chap. 2, § 1, and *De Cive*, chap. 2, § 1.

348. See also Locke's early *Essays on the Law of Nature*, ed. Wolfgang von Leyden (Oxford, 1954), pp. 164–77, and *Essay*, bk. 1, chap. 2, §§ 4, 24, 9–13, and chap. 3, § 20.

349. See also *Essays on the Law of Nature*, pp. 160–63, 176–79.

350. See also ibid., pp. 171–73, and *Essay*, bk. 1, chap. 2, §§ 9, 12.

351. See also *Some Thoughts Concerning Education*, § 146.

352. *Two Treatises*, I, § 47 (cf. II, § 82), and I, § 88.

353. See also ibid., II, §§ 197–98, and cf. Filmer, *Patriarcha*, p. 289.

354. See Machiavelli, *The Prince*, chap. 15, and his *Discourses*, bk. 2, chap. 2, and bk. 3, chap. 1.

355. Seliger, *Liberal Politics*, pp. 63–64. See also Strauss, *Natural Right*, pp. 214–15.

356. See, esp., II, § 176. On Locke on providence, see Hefelbower, *English Deism*, pp. 91–92; Worcester, *Religious Opinions*, p. 34; and H. McLachlan, *The Religious Opinions of Milton, Locke, and Newton* (Manchester, Eng., 1941), pp. 97–98.

357. Locke explicitly states that God is bound by natural law, at least in the case of grants or promises (I, § 6; II, § 195), and in his *The Reasonableness of Christianity* (Chicago, 1965), § 180, God appears to be bound by the law of nature, by his and human nature, or by the nature of things.

358. Locke incidentally admits (I, § 61) that "the Law of the Old Testament" gives the parents of false prophets "Power in this Case of Life and Death." But in the *Letter on Toleration* he explains that the law of the Old Testament is "not obligatory to us Christians," because " 'Hear, O Israel,' sufficiently restrains the obligation of the law of Moses only to that people" (*A Letter on Toleration*, p. 117). That call introduces the Ten Commandments in Deuteronomy 5:1 and the command to love the one God in Deuteronomy 6:4.

359. See also II, §§ 52, 67–68.

360. Cf. II, § 149: "this Fundamental, Sacred, and unalterable Law of *Self-Preservation*."

361. See also I, § 86.

362. Cf. II, § 25.

363. Locke claims a duty to preserve children once they are begotten but not a duty to beget, contra Wolfgang von Leyden, "John Locke and Natural Law," *Philosophy* 31 (1956): 27. See *Essays on the Law of Nature*, pp. 196–97.

364. *Essay*, bk. 2, chap. 21, § 52. See also ibid., § 51, and A. P. Brogan, "John Locke and Utilitarianism," *Ethics* 69 (1959): 88, and Raymond Polin, *La Politique morale de John Locke* (Paris, 1960), p. 29.

365. John W. Yolton, *John Locke and Education* (New York, 1971), pp. 27–28. Cf. Strauss, *Natural Right*, pp. 226–27. On natural parental fondness, see also Locke's *Some Thoughts Concerning Education*, §§ 99, 107. As the context of Yolton's quotation shows, natural parental love is not naturally enlightened.

366. Locke frequently expands mere "Preservation" or "Subsistence" into "convenience" and "Comfort"; see, e.g., II, §§ 25–26.

367. See Schochet, *Patriarchalism*, p. 254, n. 48.

368. Cf. *Some Thoughts Concerning Education*, § 215, where Locke speaks of a maternal desire "for a new Sett of Babies to play with."

369. This almost echoes the Eighth Psalm.

370. II, §§ 10, 11, 26, 55, 58, 60, 61, 63, 163–64, 170, 172, 181, 230; but cf. II, § 34.

371. See *Oxford English Dictionary*, s.v. Irrational.

372. See his references to "all inferior or irrational Creatures"; "the Irrational Inhabitants of the dry Land"; "the Irrational Animals of the World"; "the Terrestrial irrational Animals"; "the Terrestrial irrational Creatures" (I, §§ 23–27). The burden of the argument here is precisely that the dominion conveyed by God according to Genesis 1:28 is not "of one Man over another, but only the Dominion of the whole Species of Mankind, over the inferior Species of Creatures" (§ 28).

373. Cf. Jean-Jacques Rousseau, *The First and Second Discourses*, ed. Roger D. Masters (New York, 1964), pp. 113–15.

374. See *Essay*, bk. 1, chap. 3, §§ 3, 13. Laslett, in his note to *Two Treatises*, I, § 86, remarks that the language of the two principles is "very close." On the relation of preservation and the pursuit of happiness, cf. Strauss, *Natural Right*, pp. 226–28.

375. Compare I, § 86, to I, § 88.

376. Compare I, § 56, to I, § 88.

377. Locke of course denies that to act contrary to nature is man's privilege, or permitted by God, in the sense that it is rational.

378. Cf. I, § 97, "as a part of themselves," and note that a parent has "a Right to be maintain'd by his Children where he needs it, and to enjoy also the comforts of Life from them, when the necessary Provision due to them, and their Children will afford it" (§ 90). Similarly, the subordination to self-preservation of the more general concern for the preservation of other men (II, § 6) suggests that the latter may be derived from self-preservation. The *Thoughts Concerning Education* may be regarded as an account of how this is best done.

379. See also I, § 98: "the Power of the Husband being founded on Contract."

380. Schochet, *Patriarchalism*, pp. 249–50.

381. Compare I, § 48, to I, § 47. Note also I, § 123: "what in Nature is the difference betwixt a Wife and a Concubine?" See also II, § 65.

382. Laslett, in his note to I, § 130, says that Locke "accepted the political character of the family under such circumstances," but that is the opposite of Locke's point.

383. Civil societies may nonetheless be originally constituted by "several Families . . . uniting into Society," though still by individual consent (II, § 110).

384. See Geraint Parry, "Individuality, Politics, and the Critique of Paternalism in John Locke," *Political Studies* 12 (1964): 163–77.

385. See I, §§ 88–89.

386. Cf. II, §§ 3, 45, 88, 123, 124, 127, 131, 134, 137–40, 199, 222, 239, and *A Letter on Toleration*, pp. 66–67, 90–91, 124–27.

387. See *Essay*, bk. 2, chap. 28, §§ 10–12; *Some Thoughts Concerning Education*, Epistle Dedicatory, §§ 1, 32.

388. *A Letter on Toleration*, pp. 88–89, 138–39.

389. See also I, §§ 90, 93.

390. See also II, § 68.

391. Schochet, *Patriarchalism*, p. 250. However, it is hardly *will* that the child lacks but rather understanding, judgment, or reason; see II, §§ 58–59, and *Some Thoughts Concerning Education*, §§ 35–36.

392. Parry, "Individuality," p. 173.

393. See also II, §§ 55, 56, 58, 60.

394. See also II, § 202, where a king "is supposed from the advantages of Education, imployment and Counsellors to be more knowing in the measures of right or wrong."

395. See also II, § 54.

396. Note Parry's use of the terms "supposed" and "presumed" immediately after the passage I have quoted above.

397. *The Reasonableness of Christianity*, § 252. Cf. Hobbes's requirement that the laws of nature be contracted into his negative form of the Golden Rule so as to be "intelligible, even to the meanest capacity" (*Leviathan*, chap. 15, p. 214).

398. *A Letter on Toleration*, pp. 132–35.

399. Cf. *Some Thoughts Concerning Education*, § 67.

400. Contrast I, § 63.

401. Cf. Hobbes, *De Cive*, Author's Preface, where children "are exempted from all duty," and Locke, *Essays on the Law of Nature*, pp. 203, 270.

402. Cf. *Essay*, bk. 1, chap. 3, § 23, where filial veneration is said to derive not from nature but from education.

403. See also Locke's "An Essay Concerning Toleration," in Fox Bourne, *Life*, vol. 1, p. 178.

404. See also II, §§ 105–12.

405. Laslett's note to II, § 74. See also Seliger, "Liberal Politics," pp. 209 ff.

406. Schochet, *Patriarchalism*, p. 257.

407. See, e.g., ibid., pp. 255–59.

## CHAPTER TWO

1. Friedrich Nietzsche, *Beyond Good and Evil*, trans. Walter Kaufmann (New York, 1966), § 186, p. 97.

2. Dunn, *Political Thought of John Locke*, pp. 191–92.

3. Ibid., p. 192, n. 1, quoting Locke's "Ethica," Ms. c. 28, p. 113.

4. Locke, "Some Thoughts Concerning Reading and Study for a Gentleman," in Axtell, *Educational Writings of John Locke*, p. 400.

5. *Two Treatises*, I, § 42.

6. The *Thoughts* is an example of what Rosalie Colie calls "the publication of the private"; see her "John Locke and the Publication of the Private," *Philological Quarterly* 45 (1966): 41–44.

7. All references in parentheses in this and the following chapters are to *Some Thoughts Concerning Education* by section and, for the longer sections, by page numbers, which refer to Axtell, ed., *The Educational Writings of John Locke*.

8. Locke wrote jocularly to Clarke, "You know I am a meddling man in all your affairs"; this remark appears at the end of the first installment of what Clarke endorsed as his "instructions about the education of my son." See Benjamin Rand, ed., *The Correspondence of John Locke and Edward Clarke* (Cambridge, Mass., 1927), p. 115.

9. See §§ 19, 47, 55, 63, 64, 67, 74, 86, 87, 94 (pp. 196 and 200), 110, 138, 145 (p. 251), 156, 158, 165, 167 (p. 274), 168 (p. 267), 171, 175, 189 (p. 300), 212.

10. *Two Treatises*, I, §§ 56, 88; II, §§ 6, 135, 129, 171.

11. Ibid., I, Preface, §§ 2–3.

12. For the other examples of children on whom some aspect of Locke's method worked, see §§ 27, 78 (two examples), 115 (p. 224), 116, 148, and 166. The one in § 115 was added in the third edition.

13. See Axtell, *Educational Writings of John Locke,* p. 109.

14. The qualification, "this" world, seems to be ignored in the rest of the sentence: "He that has these Two, has little more to wish for," and it is dropped in the rest of the section. This may be only because a sound mind is also the chief prerequisite for happiness in the other world; consider §§ 61 and 135.

15. See the *Essay Concerning Human Understanding* (ed. Peter Nidditch [Oxford, 1975]; hereafter referred to as *Essay*), bk. 1, chap. 4, §§ 22–24, and bk. 4, chap. 20, § 8. Cf. Francesco de Bartolomeis, *John Locke: Il Pensiero Filosofico e Pedagogico* (Florence, 1967), pp. 23, 98.

16. See also Locke, *Of the Conduct of the Understanding,* § 2 (in *Works,* vol. 3), and *Essay,* bk. 2, chap. 9, § 15, chap. 10, § 8, chap. 11, § 2, and bk. 4, chap. 20, § 5.

17. When the importance of education is restated (§ 32) with reference back to this passage, the exception of the tenth part is dropped. This procedure may remind one of the passages in the chapter on property in the *Second Treatise,* where labor progresses from constituting nine-tenths of useful things, to ninety-nine hundredths, to nine hundred ninety-nine thousandths, until, finally, nature contributes "only the almost worthless Materials" (*Two Treatises,* II, §§ 40 and 43). There, as here, the contribution of human effort is increased, while that of nature (though it is human nature in the case of education) is minimized.

18. See, e.g., §§ 64–66, 67, 110, end, and 185.

19. *Essay,* bk. 1, chap. 1, § 2; bk. 2, chap. 8, § 4, and chap. 10, § 5; but see also bk. 2, chap. 8, § 12. Contrast Hobbes, *Leviathan,* chaps. 1, 2, and 6.

20. This view is reminiscent of Machiavelli's praise of relying on one's own *virtù* rather than on inheritance or, more generally, *fortuna.* This apparent and possibly surprising belittling of money, especially in the two later passages, might be said to show that Locke's "individualism," or respect for self-reliance, takes precedence over his "capitalism," or respect for economic acquisition.

21. As Axtell notes, the term "crazy" meant physically frail, not mentally so (*Educational Writings of John Locke,* p. 114, n. 2).

22. "Business," according to the *Oxford English Dictionary,* meant diligent activity in any calling, not, as later, specifically in commerce.

23. Cf. Lamprecht, *Moral and Political Philosophy of Locke,* p. 117, n. 29; but cf. also Parry, "Individuality," p. 167.

24. Cf. Locke's *The Reasonableness of Christianity,* § 245, where the ancient philosophers' chief moral "arguments were from the excellency of virtue, and the highest they generally went was the exalting of human nature, whose perfection lay in virtue . . . that she [virtue] is the perfection and excellency of our nature."

25. Yolton, *Locke and Education,* p. 34; his other reference is to § 52.

26. Lamprecht, *Moral and Political Philosophy of Locke,* p. 117, n. 29.

27. Similarly, in *Essay,* bk. 4, chap. 17, §§ 2–3, Locke distinguishes between reason as making a proof and reason as perceiving it when made by another. It appears that this is an even lower form or looser sense of reason. As Ginevra Guglielmina Verdolini remarks, Locke's rational progression "threatens sometimes to resolve itself into a moral strictness of puritan flavor that risks coercing the spontaneous development of the spirit by subordinating it to the obliged acceptance of an end extraneous to the child's spirit" (*Giovanni Locke: Il Pensiero Pedagogico* [Rovigo, 1954], p. 93; my translation).

28. It is also of some use now, for the children will not be "half so uneasy to themselves or others" (§ 38).

29. According to Locke's probable source, Bacon (*Apophthegmes New and Old*, § 190) or Montaigne (*Essays,* bk. 1, chap. 23), and the original source, Diogenes Laertius, *Lives of the Philosophers* 3. 38, the sage in question was Plato; see Axtell's note to this passage.

30. That men desire that others should not be their master may be called the first principle of the *Two Treatises* (see I, § 1).

31. See *Two Treatises,* II, § 17.

32. See §§ 48, 107 (p. 210), and 200.

33. Cf. § 66 (p. 160). In § 75 the special form of it is also called the mind's "Dominion over it self."

34. As Verdolini remarks (*Giovanni Locke,* pp. 92–93), "the foundation of education is liberty, understood not as liberty pure and simple but rather as reasonableness in its use; that is, liberty is mastery of oneself"; see also her remark (ibid., pp. 95–96) that "for Locke *liberty* is thus a spontaneous aspiration of every being, but this still must not expand in an irrational form; on the contrary, it must develop under the guidance of reason" (my translation).

35. Compare Harold J. Laski, *The Rise of European Liberalism* (London and New York, 1962), p. 61, to Dunn, *Political Thought of John Locke,* pp. 245–46.

36. Hobbes, *De Cive,* Author's Preface; see also *Leviathan,* chap. 27, beginning.

37. See the Epistle Dedicatory (p. 112), and §§ 3, 15, 94 (p. 197), 133, 195, 216, and passim.

38. Cf. Aristotle, *Nicomachean Ethics* 1095b4–8.

39. The examples given of the vice of lying—lying for one's parent's or one's own profit or for that of the master to whom one is apprenticed—provide a distinctly bourgeois or commercial context, unusual in the *Thoughts;* but disapproval of the vice is not necessarily aristocratic or antibourgeois. Cf., e.g., Max Weber on honesty as the best policy and the spirit of capitalism in *The Protestant Ethic and the Spirit of Capitalism* (New York, 1958), pp. 57, 282–83.

40. Cf. *Essay,* bk. 2, chap. 28, §§ 7, 14.

41. Yolton, *Locke and Education,* p. 34.

42. Lamprecht, *Moral and Political Philosophy of Locke,* p. 118.

43. See the Epistle Dedicatory (p. 112), and §§ 66 (p. 159, parenthesis), 94 (p. 200), 116, 146, 164, 176, 189 (p. 299), 207, and the very end of the *Thoughts.*

44. See, especially, *Two Treatises,* II, chap. 6.

45. See Parry, "Individuality," p. 173.

46. *Two Treatises,* II, § 59; cf. "one and Twenty, or any other Age" (ibid., § 75).

47. "*Natural rights*" are mentioned (§ 186) as a subject of the book-learning that takes place after actual moral formation. The books mentioned include works of Cicero, Grotius, and Pufendorf, who would, to be sure, speak of natural law; but Locke himself does not. The silence here is even more consistent than that observed in the *Essay* (see *Essay,* bk. 1, chap. 3, §§ 2, 6, 13; bk. 2, chap. 28, § 11). In the *Treatises,* too, it was "besides my present purpose, to enter here into the particulars of the Law of Nature" (II, § 12).

48. In the *Two Treatises* themselves there is a greater difficulty insofar as knowledge of natural law is supposed to be the prerequisite for sharing in natural freedom and equality, while Locke himself not only presents no rational demonstration or even enumeration of its propositions but even gives some positive basis for doubting whether any men in a state of nature or most men ever come

rationally to know the law of nature (II, § 124). If most men do not come to know the natural law by their own reason, it is not clear that they have a title to enjoy full liberty, unsubjected to the will of others.

49. Jean-Jacques Rousseau, *Emile; or, On Education,* trans. Allan Bloom (New York, 1979), pp. 68, 85–86.

50. See ibid., p. 80. De Bartolomeis (*John Locke,* pp. 102–3) goes too far in assimilating Locke's procedure in this matter to Rousseau's, apparently on the basis of Locke's recommendation (in § 100) that parental authority "operate as a natural Principle." Locke, however, does not mean by this that authority should be disguised as the operation of natural (extrinsic, physical) forces; he means, rather, that acceptance of authority should seem to the child to be part of *his* nature, so that "it will always be Sacred to him, and it will be as hard for him to resist it, as the Principles of his Nature" (§ 100).

51. In this connection, see Bruno Bettelheim, "Moral Education," in *Moral Education,* ed. Nancy F. Sizer and Theodore R. Sizer (Cambridge, Mass., 1970), pp. 90, 94, 98, 99–102. Locke even traces the child's sense of dependence and its accompanying fear back to the earliest experience of nursing (§ 115, p. 222).

52. *Essay,* bk. 2, chap. 21, § 73 (where three of the ideas listed are modes of power); see also ibid., chap. 7, § 8, and chap. 21 passim.

53. Cf. the replacement of obedience by honor in *Two Treatises,* II, § 66.

54. Cf. §§ 3 and 32.

55. But he does not slight it either: "Fear is a Passion, that, if rightly govern'd, has its use" (§ 115).

56. Yolton, *Locke and Education,* p. 35.

57. Cf. *Essay,* bk. 2, chap. 10, §§ 4–5.

58. See Machiavelli, *Discourses,* bk. 3, chaps. 1, 3, and 49.

59. See *Two Treatises,* II, §§ 19, 21, 127, 212, 226, and 230.

60. It is hard to believe that Locke added "present" otherwise than to allow for this possibility, though it could be claimed that he meant merely that it is especially hard to resist present pleasure or pain.

61. De Bartolomeis (*John Locke,* p. 100) remarks that "Locke, although to express his thought he makes use of the traditional opposition of reason and sentiment, does not entirely share the Platonic-mediaeval conception" (my translation).

62. In § 33 the ability to resist desire served "Vertue and Worth"; in § 38 it served "Vertue and Excellency."

63. Cf. *Two Treatises,* II, § 42.

64. See Peter Gay, *John Locke on Education* (New York, 1964), Introduction, pp. 9–11. For Locke's own teaching of humanity, see *Thoughts,* §§ 116–17.

65. "For extravagant young Fellows, that have Liveliness and Spirit, come sometimes to be set right, and so make Able and Great Men" (§ 46). Greatness is more than Locke promises from his own method of education alone; see, e.g., the Epistle Dedicatory, where he speaks of producing "vertuous, useful, and able men."

66. The notion of "spirit" in the psychology of the *Thoughts* is most difficult. The term varies from a medical or physiological usage (§§ 25 and 115, p. 221) to a religious one (§§ 137 and 190–92).

67. Locke also speaks in § 126 of "the two great Springs of Action *Foresight* and *Desire*"; cf. *Essay,* bk. 2, chap. 20, § 6: "the chief if not only spur to humane Industry and Action is uneasiness."

68. The low-spirited man is "an useless thing to himself and others" (§ 51).

69. See Locke, *The Reasonableness of Christianity,* §§ 9–11, 175, 245.

70. See the manuscript "Of Study" (Ms. Locke, c. 28, p. 86; published in Axtell, *Educational Writings of John Locke,* p. 406): "delight is commonly joined with all improvements of Knowledge" (though not that, but practice is "the end of Knowledge"). Cf. also the manuscript "Thus I Think" (Ms. Locke, c. 28, p. 143; published in Lord King, *The Life and Letters of John Locke* [New York, 1972], pp. 306–7).

71. See "Thus I Think" (King, *Life and Letters,* pp. 306–7): "Reputation, for that I find everybody is pleased with, and the want of it is a constant torment." (Locke also lists reputation as one of "the most lasting pleasures of this life.") See also *Essay,* bk. 2, chap. 28, § 12.

72. Cf. *Essay,* bk. 2, chap. 20, §§ 2, 7–10, and 15, and Hobbes, *Leviathan,* chap. 6, p. 122, and chap. 11, p. 162.

73. This has already been suggested by "Love of Vertue and Reputation" (§ 42).

74. The principle of association of ideas is the subject of *Essay,* bk. 2, chap. 33. See also Axtell, *Educational Writings of John Locke,* pp. 122, n. 4, and 150, n. 1.

75. For in this way "Children come to hate things which were at first acceptable to them," and thus grown men can become "disgusted with any innocent Recreation" (§ 49).

76. The situation is different, however, when it comes to rewards (see §§ 52–53) or to praise and blame.

77. Locke distinguishes covetousness from acquisitiveness (the desire that spurs industry) by defining it as a desire for things belonging to others or, more generally, as a desire not ruled by reason (see *Two Treatises,* II, § 34).

78. See, e.g., Lamprecht, *Moral and Political Philosophy of Locke,* pp. 89–102, and Strauss, *Natural Right,* pp. 249–53.

79. See I. A. Snook, who remarks, in "John Locke's Theory of Moral Education" (*Educational Theory* 20 [1970]: 367), that if the child knows "which action of his has led to the loss of esteem . . . then the loss of esteem and the accompanying deprivation is punishment for that action and contravenes Locke's main principle."

80. Parents are said to make use of the pernicious sensual rewards and punishments to make children "industrious" (§ 52).

81. Cf. *Essay,* bk. 2, chap. 28, §§ 5–6.

82. See *Two Treatises,* II, §§ 8 and 12, and Lamprecht, *Moral and Political Philosophy of Locke,* pp. 161–63. Like other versions of utilitarian psychology, this one seems to permit an entirely formal interpretation, one that would neutrally allow all phenomena (it would allow revenge, for example, by understanding revenge as done for the sake of a pleasure that results from it), though its thrust or bias is toward accepting only some rewards, pleasures, or utilities as truly rational (e.g., the pleasure of esteem but not that of revenge). Thus it seems to take a neutral standard of rationality, but it arrives at moral conclusions. This view makes divine punishment a particular problem; see, e.g., the note from Locke's journal in 1681, published in King, *Life and Letters,* pp. 123–24.

83. See also references to natural law as reason, e.g., the one in *Two Treatises,* II, § 6.

84. See §§ 35, 45, 48, and 50 ("his natural Inclination").

85. In Rousseau's *Emile* this recognition is understood to be the source of both the desire for domination and of *amour-propre,* or internal domination by others. Rousseau, therefore, would rather conceal that dependence (see *Emile,* pp. 65–68). For Locke, awareness of the dependence is the source of the very

237

passion that is to control the desire for mastery, love of esteem. Here one can see what it is in the *Thoughts* that would particularly repel Rousseau or even influence him by posing in a self-conscious form the alternative to his rejection of *amour-propre*. This explains Rousseau's negative judgment on Locke's pedagogy at the beginning of *Emile* (p. 33). Rousseau seems to have studied Locke's *Thoughts* with some care (see *Emile*, pp. 55, 89, 103, 117, 126, 128, 197, 202, 255, 357, and also Pierre Villey, *L'Influence de Montaigne sur les idées pédagogiques de Locke et de Rousseau* [Paris, 1911]).

86. Cf. the contrast that John Dunn points to (*Political Thought*, pp. 195–96) between "the artificial and insulated process of child-rearing" and "this world" in Locke's similar procedure for teaching liberality in § 100.

87. Snook, "Locke's Theory."

88. For praise and commendation or rebukes or reproofs, see §§ 57, 62, 131; see also "a cold and neglectful Countenance," looking "sowre," "the Severity of their Brows," or "a Look or a Nod" (§§ 57, 59, 60, 77).

89. Lamprecht, *Moral and Political Philosophy of Locke*, p. 116.

90. See Plato, *Apology* 23c, 30b, and 31c.

91. Cf. § 44, where compliance, induced by severity before the child acquires memory, comes to seem natural.

92. Freedom is treated in a similar way in *Two Treatises*, II, § 17, and property in II, §§ 37–38 and 47–50.

93. *The Reasonableness of Christianity*, § 245.

94. Ibid. Cf. Dunn's use of this passage in his *Political Thought of John Locke*, pp. 195–96, 217–18.

95. See the scheme for reform of the Poor Laws that Locke prepared when he was a member of the Board of Trade in 1697 (Fox Bourne, *Life*, vol. 2, p. 378), and his letter of May 21, 1701, to his friend Philip van Limborch, in which he discusses Limborch's son's commercial training (ibid., p. 491). Although in the passage from the reform scheme he comes close to assuming that the poor are vicious (he probably means only the idle poor) and in the letter to Limborch he assumes that the virtuous prosper, he never assumes that the prosperous are virtuous, contrary to the implications of Macpherson's analysis in his *The Political Theory of Possessive Individualism* (Oxford, 1962), pp. 222–47; see also his "The Social Bearing of Locke's Political Theory," in *Locke and Berkeley*, ed. C. A. Martin and D. M. Armstrong (London, n.d.), pp. 215–16, 220.

96. Cf. the use of the term "neglect" in that context in § 58.

97. Cf. *Essay*, bk. 2, chap. 28, §§ 4–17, esp. § 5.

98. Snook, "Locke's Theory," p. 365; see also Yolton, *Locke and Education*, p. 36, on the distinction between reasons for and motives of action. For further discussion, see Yolton, "Locke on the Law of Nature," *Philosophical Review* 68 1958): 477–98; von Leyden, "John Locke and Natural Law," pp. 23–35; Raghuveer Singh, "John Locke and the Theory of Natural Law," *Political Studies* 9 (1961): 105–18; and George H. Moulds, "The 'Right' and the 'Good' in Locke's Writings," *Locke Newsletter* 3 (1972): 17–25.

99. For Locke's distinction between prudence and morality, see below, my note 132 to chapter 3.

100. Cf. *Essay*, bk. 1, chap. 3, § 6; bk. 2, chap. 28, § 8 (note additions in the second edition), and chap. 21, § 70; bk. 4, chap. 12, § 11; and *The Reasonableness of Christianity*, §§ 183–84, 212, 243, 245.

101. Cf. the Pascalian argument in the *Essay*, bk. 2, chap. 21, § 70, from the "bare possibility" of another life, though Locke claims there that he has merely "foreborn to mention anything of the certainty, or probability of a future

State." See also the entries in Locke's Journal for July 29, 1676, and February 8, 1677 (Locke Ms., f. 1, pp. 367–70, and f. 2, pp. 49–51, published in Richard Aaron and Jocelyn Gibb, *An Early Draft of Locke's "Essay," Together with Excerpts from His Journals* [Oxford, 1936], pp. 81–82, 87–88).

102. Cf. *Essay*, bk. 4, chap. 3, § 29, chap. 17, § 23, chap. 18, § 7, and *The Reasonableness of Christianity*, § 245.

103. This shift begins in § 58, where attaching other *"agreeable or disagreeable Things"* to parental esteem and disapproval is used to arouse a general concern for reputation. Locke may say only *"as it were* by a common Consent" (§ 61, emphasis added) because of his long-standing criticism of common consent or *consensus gentium* as a standard, running from the early so-called *Essays on the Law of Nature*, written about 1660 (see pp. 160–79), to the *Essay*, the masterwork of his maturity (see bk. 1, chap. 2, §§ 3–4, 24; chap. 3, §§ 6–14, 20–23).

104. See Locke's letter to William Molyneux of March 30, 1696, in *Works*, vol. 3, p. 377.

105. See *The Reasonableness of Christianity*, § 243.

106. Cf. Hobbes's position, discussed above, p. 46.

107. Cf. de Bartolomeis, *John Locke*, pp. 97–98.

108. See *Essay*, bk. 1, chap. 4, §§ 22, 24, and bk. 4, chap. 20, § 8.

109. Yolton, *Locke and Education*, p. 4; see also pp. 9–10.

110. Ibid., p. 40.

111. See Yolton's *John Locke and the Way of Ideas* (Oxford, 1956), esp. pp. 26–48.

112. De Bartolomeis, *John Locke*, p. 23.

113. Cf., e.g., *Second Treatise*, chap. 2, where, though all men are the "Workmanship" of God and are therefore not authorized to destroy one another (§ 6), they may "destroy things noxious to them," including their fellows (§ 8), who may then "be destroyed as a *Lyon* or a *Tyger*" (§ 11).

114. Cf. *Essay*, bk. 1, chap. 3, §§ 3, 13, and chap. 4, § 12.

115. Cf. *Thoughts*, §§ 20, 48, and *The Reasonableness of Christianity*, §§ 2 and 4.

116. Compare the recommendation, perhaps equally grating to the traditionally aristocratic among the gentry, that their children be raised in some respects like the children of farmers and yeomen (§ 4).

117. According to Axtell (*Educational Writings of John Locke*, p. 169, n. 1), the reference to the orchard is a "gibe" at Francis Osborne's *Advice to a Son* (1656), where such exploits are praised. Osborne recommends the exploits as a preparation for military life, not for seeking one's fortune—the goal in terms of which Locke responds.

118. Dunn, *Political Thought of John Locke*, p. 255.

119. See *Two Treatises*, II, §§ 90–94, 136–37, 138, 142, 143, 151, 162, 199–200, 222, and 214. Cf. Machiavelli, *Discourses*, bk. 1, chap. 45.

120. This desire is explicitly restated in terms of liberty shortly: "they want their Liberty" (§ 74) and " . . . that natural Freedom they extreamly affect. And 'tis that Liberty alone which gives the true Relish and Delight to their ordinary Play-Games" (§ 76). The term *"good* Actions" (§ 73; emphasis added) is not exclusive, as the context shows ("a Thing of Delight or Indifferency"), and we shall see shortly that the desire to show that one's actions come from oneself can apply to anything.

121. This stress is denied by Laslett (Introduction to the *Two Treatises*, p. 134), who finds what he calls "the doctrine of natural political virtue" to be the central doctrine of *Two Treatises* (pp. 122–26, 130). But if political virtue

were natural, Locke would never have had to write *Some Thoughts Concerning Education* or, for that matter, his *Two Treatises of Government.* Men's "first and strongest desire" is "Self-preservation," they are "partial to themselves," and, as a result, "the greater part [are] no strict Observers of Equity and Justice" (*Two Treatises,* I, § 88; II, §§ 123, 125). In discussing justice in the *Thoughts,* he begins with these words: "Our first Actions being guided more by Self-love, than Reason or Reflection," and he sees "All Injustice generally springing from too great Love of our selves" (§§ 110 and 139). Locke himself never mentions "natural political virtue"; indeed, "virtue" is mentioned only marginally in *Two Treatises;* it is mentioned, for instance, as distinct from the basis of political obligation (II, § 54) and as characterizing a primitive situation, in which proper political institutions are absent (II, §§ 94, 110–11).

122. This is not contrary to Locke's emphasis on the individual tempers and constitutions of children (§§ 66, 87, 100–101, 123, 174, 202, 216). Children's tempers are inclinations to particular passions, not attachments of their passions to particular objects. Passions (like abilities) may be innate, unlike the ideas of things, to which the passions are attached by experience (see *Essay,* bk. 2, chap. 20, § 14).

123. On Locke's combination of liberty and authority in the *Thoughts,* see Verdolini, *Giovanni Locke,* pp. 87, 92–95, and de Bartolomeis, *John Locke,* pp. 98–100.

124. For the pleasure in variety, see §§ 74, 118, 128, 130 (where its danger is discussed), and 167 (pp. 273–74); on the indefiniteness of human desire, compare Hobbes, *Leviathan,* chap. 11, beginning, and Machiavelli, *Discourses,* bk. 1, chap. 37, and bk. 2, Proemium.

125. Locke connects the concern for esteem with the desire for liberty, which is also a desire to be thought and be treated as a rational creature, one motivated by reward and punishment. But it is misleading to assimilate Locke to Kant in regarding "the sentiment of honor" as "indisputably the sign of moral conscience," as Pasquale Rosa does (*Il Pensiero Filosofico e Pedagogico de Giovanni Locke* [Naples, 1965], p. 20).

126. One is reminded of Hobbes's comparison of the life of man to a "*race* we must suppose to have no other *goal,* nor other *garland,* but being foremost" and in which "Continually to out-go the next before, is *felicity*" (*Human Nature,* chap. 9, § 21).

127. Cf. Machiavelli's distinction between cruelty well used and badly used at the end of chapter 8 of the *Prince;* see also chapter 17.

128. The words "if it can be" seem to concede some doubt as to its possibility.

129. The word "indecent" (*Essay,* bk. 2, chap. 20, § 17) seems to be a term of the law of reputation (ibid., chap. 28, § 11).

130. Ibid., chap. 33.

131. Lamprecht, *Moral and Political Philosophy of Locke,* p. 117.

132. See *Essay,* bk. 1, chap. 3, §§ 21–27, and bk. 4, chap. 20; *The Reasonableness of Christianity,* § 241; *Two Treatises,* I, § 86, and II, §§ 11, 12, and 124.

133. In *The Reasonableness of Christianity* they are provided with the Christian revelation instead (§ 252; see also §§ 238, 241, 243, 245).

134. *Two Treatises,* II, § 230; see also II, § 94: "But whatever Flatterers may talk to amuze Peoples Understandings, it hinders not Men, from feeling."

135. For Locke's theory of punishment, see Lamprecht, *Moral and Political Philosophy of Locke,* pp. 161–63.

136. *Essay,* bk. 4, chap. 6, § 1; see also chap. 5, §§ 3–5, and "Of Study" (published in Axtell, *Educational Writings of John Locke,* p. 419), where he says,

"when a man thinks, reasons, and discourses within himself, I see not what need he has of them [words]. I'm sure 'tis better to lay them aside and have an immediate converse with the Ideas of the things."

137. *Essay,* bk. 4, chap. 5, § 4.

138. Ibid., bk. 3, chap. 5, §§ 2–3, 15; chap. 10, § 4; chap. 11, §§ 14–15.

139. *Two Treatises,* II, § 8; see also II, §§ 11–12. That is, punishment may serve not only to "terrifie others" (II, § 12) but also, through the shameful example of the punished criminal, to turn them against the fault they otherwise incline to.

140. See Laslett's comments on Locke's "ferociousness," "savagery," and "hostile, even spiteful terms" (notes on *Two Treatises,* title page and II, § 172). Laslett, however, speaks as if these remarks apply only to despots or even particularly to James II; but some refer to any murderer or perhaps even any violator of the law of nature (II, §§ 8, 10, 11, 16, 181).

141. *The Prince,* chap. 7.

142. Verdolini, *Giovanni Locke,* p. 33. Incidentally, since Locke is willing to delegate the execution of punishment to a "discreet Servant" (§ 83) as well as to the tutor, there is no reason for Rosa to claim that Locke recommends that punishments be "inflicted by persons not inferior in social rank to the pupil" (*Pensiero Filosofico,* p. 20).

143. See also §§ 78–79 and 99; one therefore should not attribute to Locke the view that "Beating a child has no educational function of any sort" (Gay, *Locke on Education,* p. 11), an impression also given by accounts that ignore Locke's emphatic exception (e.g., Yolton, *Locke and Education,* p. 35).

144. *Two Treatises,* II, §§ 3, 11–12, 87–89, 123–30, and 136; note especially the quotation from Hooker at 135 n. and cf. *A Third Letter for Toleration* in *Works,* vol. 6, pp. 504–5.

145. *Two Treatises,* II, § 176.

146. Cf. again Hobbes, *De Homine,* chap. 13, § 7: "the dispositions of youths are not less but much more disposed to bad morals by example than to good ones by precept."

147. If Locke ever advanced the economic interests of his own class, it is here; he was a long-time tutor (see Axtell, *Educational Writings of John Locke,* pp. 36–47).

148. *OED,* s.v. Great, mng. 12; the first example given of the sense "eminent in point of mental or moral attainments" (mng. 15b) is from 1709, though it may have been used by Locke in § 46. Note his uses of the term in §§ 206 and 207.

149. See § 143 on censoriousness in opposition to civility.

150. See §§ 94 (pp. 197 and 200), and 143, end.

151. Cf., e.g., Yolton, *Locke and Education,* pp. 17–18, 87–90.

152. Cf. the distinction in *Two Treatises* between liberty and license (II, § 6; see also II, §§ 22, 57, 59–60, 63, 123).

153. *The Reasonableness of Christianity,* §§ 242–43 and 245.

154. Cf. *Two Treatises,* I, § 141: "the *Chineses,* a very great and civil People," do not "believe the Bible." This passage in the *Thoughts* calls into question Yolton's notion that the laws of nature, which "constitute for Locke the most important standards of conduct," are simply "seventeenth-century renditions of Christian morality" (Yolton, *Locke and Education,* p. 87; cf. Dunn, *Political Thought of John Locke,* pp. 98–100, 190–95).

155. *Essay,* bk. 1, chap. 4, § 8; for Locke's interest in China, see his reading notes on the subject, Ms. c. 27, pp. 179–212.

156. See also the Epistle Dedicatory and §§ 187 and 201, and (though they do not refer to the gentleman's calling specifically) §§ 94 (p. 192), 174, and 207. See, further, the *Conduct of the Understanding,* §§ 7–8 and 23; "Some Thoughts Concerning Reading and Study for a Gentleman," in Axtell, *Educational Writings of John Locke,* p. 398, and "Of Study," ibid., pp. 409, 411; "Recreation," Ms. c. 10, pp. 66–67, published in King, *Life and Letters,* p. 332; and the letter to the Reverend Richard King, dated August 25, 1703, in Locke's *Works,* vol. 10, p. 309.

157. See Dunn, *Political Thought of John Locke,* pp. 196, 218–20, 231–32, 245–54, and 262–65.

158. Calvin, *Institutes,* bk. 3, chap. 10, § 6. See also Walzer, *Revolution of the Saints,* p. 43. J. W. Gough attributes to Locke this notion that one "may not try to better himself" (*John Locke's Political Philosophy* [Oxford, 1950], p. 19). He misunderstands Locke's statement, in *Two Treatises,* II, § 6, that everyone is bound "not to quit his Station," which is in fact a prohibition against suicide.

159. Dunn, *Political Thought of John Locke,* pp. 219–20, 222–23.

160. See *OED,* s.v. Calling, mng. 11.

161. Weber, *Protestant Ethic,* pp. 79, 84, 207–10; *OED,* s.v. Calling, mngs. 9–10.

162. *A Paraphrase and Notes on the Epistles of St. Paul,* in *Works,* vol. 8, p. 116 and note f; cf. paraphrases of verses 17 and 24 and note h.

163. *Two Treatises,* II, §§ 72–73.

## CHAPTER THREE

1. Cf. §§ 66, 87, 123, and 216.

2. For the association of confidence and boldness, as opposed to modesty and bashfulness, with "Spirit," see § 70 (p. 166); for curiosity as desire and carelessness as the lack of it, see §§ 118–27; for timorousness as weakness of spirit, see § 115. Obstinacy, however, may be more a matter of "will" than of "spirit" (see §§ 78–79 and 87).

3. Hobbes, *Leviathan,* chap. 6, p. 126; chap. 13, pp. 184–85.

4. This appears in his eagerness to employ material rewards, albeit indirectly, to establish concern for esteem (§§ 58, 67, and 69), his willingness to employ corporal punishment as the ultimate remedy (§§ 78 and 87), and his view that the only natural wants are physical (§ 107).

5. See *Leviathan,* chap. 17, p. 223, and chap. 11, p. 161. In chap. 13, pp. 184–85, the two views appear as two different kinds of men, though even here it may be that the irrational love of conquest derives from rational origins that it loses sight of. On this point, contrast Strauss, *Political Philosophy of Hobbes,* esp. pp. 10–11, with C. B. Macpherson, *The Political Theory of Possessive Individualism: Hobbes to Locke* (Oxford, 1962), pp. 42 ff.

6. Hobbes, *De Cive,* Author's Preface. Rousseau appears to understand this passage to mean that men are naturally wicked, which is precisely the opposite of the point Hobbes explicitly makes (see the "Second Discourse," *Du Contrat Social,* Garnier ed. [Paris, 1962], pp. 57–58, and *Emile,* p. 67). Hobbes does say, however, or at least his spokesman "B." does in *Decameron Physiologicum,* that "men from their very birth, and naturally, scramble for every thing they covet, and would have all the world, if they could, to fear and obey them" (*English Works,* vol. 7, p. 73). The second desire, however, may be merely instrumental to the first. On this passage, see the discussions by Strauss and Macpherson cited in the preceding note.

7. Hobbes, *Human Nature,* chap. 9, § 14; see also *De Homine,* chap. 12, § 7, and *Leviathan,* chap. 6, p. 125.

8. *Two Treaties*, I, §§ 41, 42, 43, 73, 92–93, 97; II, §§ 72–73. See also Herbert H. Rowen, "A Second Thought on Locke's *First Treatise*," *Journal of the History of Ideas* 17 (1956): 130–32.

9. Machiavelli, *Discourses*, bk. 1, chap. 34 (my translation).

10. Allen, *Political Thought in the Sixteenth Century*, p. 461.

11. Ibid. See also Harvey C. Mansfield, Jr.'s, presentation of Machiavelli's new regime as "indirect government," in "Machiavelli's New Regime," *Italian Quarterly* 13 (1970): 63–95.

12. Locke's only use of the term "republic" in the *Two Treatises*, as far as I am aware, is to call a prince whose person is sacred by the law "the head of the Republick" (II, § 205); as for his use of "commonwealth," compare I, §§ 132–34, to II, § 132. However, Gough, for instance, goes too far in concluding that "The power of the people, in his system, is exercised at the foundation of the state, but after that it remains dormant unless a revolution becomes necessary" (Gough, *Locke's Political Philosophy*, p. 115). Locke frequently refers to "the people" also having a "power of chusing" at least a part of the legislature at regular intervals in the form of government he supposes (II, §§ 140, 142, 154, 157, 158, and 213).

13. *Two Treatises*, II, § 88; see also § 138 ("their own consent" and "my consent"), § 139 ("their own consent"), and § 140 ("his own Consent, *i.e.* the Consent of the Majority, giving it either by themselves, or their Representatives chosen by them").

14. Cf. *Essay*, bk. 2, chap. 21, § 45.

15. Calvin, *Institutes*, bk. 3, chap. 10, §§ 2–3. Contrast also *Two Treatises*, II, § 46 ("Gold, Silver, and Diamonds, are things, that Fancy or Agreement hath put the Value on, more than real Use, and the necessary Support of Life") and II, § 184.

16. Calvin, *Institutes*, bk. 3, chap. 8, §§ 9–10. Stoicism seems to be the chief target of the polemic against philosophy running through this portion of the *Institutes;* cf. chap. 6, § 3, chap. 7, §§ 1–2, chap. 8, §§ 9–11, and chap. 10, §§ 1–3.

17. Horace also supplies the motto of the *Thoughts* and is praised as one of the "most difficult and sublime of the *Latin* Authors," along with Tully and Virgil (§ 184). In "Some Thoughts Concerning Reading and Study for a Gentleman" (Axtell, *Educational Writings of John Locke*, p. 403), Locke lists Horace as one of the authors who teach the knowledge of men. Coste, in his "Character of Mr. Locke," also reports Locke's praise of Horace (Locke, *Works*, vol. 10, pp. 170–71). Horace was one of the best-represented authors in Locke's library (see Harrison and Laslett, *Library of John Locke*, pp. 157–58).

18. Cf. Diogenes Laertius 10. 127–28, 149 (on Epicurus), and Cicero, *Tusculan Disputations* 5. 93. Locke was familiar with such doctrines not only from Diogenes Laertius and Cicero (see Harrison and Laslett, *Library*, pp. 108–9, 125; he quotes from the *Tusculans* in *Essay*, bk. 2, chap. 28, § 11) but also from his knowledge of Gassendi and his acquaintance with Bernier; see Gabriel Bonno, "Les Relations intellectuelles de Locke avec la France," *University of California Publications in Modern Philology* 33 (1955): 37–264, and Cranston, *Locke: A Biography*, pp. 102–3, 169–70. For Locke's Stoicism, see Axtell's notes to *Thoughts*, §§ 113 and 115 (pp. 218–20), and Polin, *Politique morale*.

19. See also § 115 (p. 219): "Fear was given us as a Monitor to quicken our Industry, and keep us upon our Guard against the Approaches of Evil."

20. *Essay*, bk. 2, chap. 7, § 4; but cf. bk. 2, chap. 21, § 34.

21. Ibid., bk. 2, chap. 21, § 47.

22. Cf. Locke's *Conduct of the Understanding*, § 45: "The mind should be always free and ready to turn itself to the variety of objects that occur, and allow them as much consideration as shall for that time be thought fit."

23. See *Two Treatises*, II, §§ 75, 105, 107, and 94, 111.

24. Ibid., §§ 160, 164, 165, 166; 225, 230; 209.

25. Cf. §§ 107 ("want of . . . Rest or Relaxation of the Part wearied with Labour") and 63.

26. Cf. *Two Treatises*, I, § 81; II, §§ 13, 21, 34, 38, 45, 123–27, 136, and *A Letter on Toleration*, pp. 124–25.

27. Cf. *Two Treatises*, II, § 20. Since children have not consented to enter civil society, they can be considered in the state of nature, especially among themselves; and since they do not know the law of nature, they also tend to be in a condition approaching the state of war, lacking only the element of deadly force (compare II, §§ 57, 59, and 63 to II, §§ 16–20, and 123–24.

28. In Plato's *Republic* 464c–465a, on the other hand, assault is decriminalized so that men will be required or encouraged to defend themselves; see also Plato's *Laws* 879e–880 and Rousseau's *Emile*, p. 250 n.

29. II, § 125; see also II, §§ 13, 123–24.

30. This is a milder version of the fifth law of nature in *Leviathan*, chap. 15 (p. 209), that of "Mutuall accommodation, or Complexance," "a man that by asperity of Nature will strive to retain those things which to himselfe are superfluous, and to others necessary; and for the stubbornness of his Passions, cannot be corrected, is to be left, or cast out of Society, as combersome thereunto." See also Hobbes, *De Cive*, chap. 3, § 9.

31. Locke is less willing to accept the connection between the desire for freedom and anger and revenge than Aristotle, for instance (see *Politics* 1328a). The desire for freedom has a correspondingly higher status for Locke, and anger and revenge a lower one.

32. II, § 230; see also II, § 168, end, and §§ 208, 223–25.

33. See Nathan Tarcov, "Locke's *Second Treatise* and 'The Best Fence against Rebellion,'" *Review of Politics* 43 (1981): 198–217.

34. *Emile*, p. 103.

35. Contrast *Emile*, pp. 62–63, 160, with *Thoughts*, §§ 10, 17, 18, 42, 64, 66, 67, 130, end, 145, 147, end, 185, 200.

36. Consider not only the sections of the *Thoughts* referred to in the preceding note but, above all, Locke's view that most men receive "even those Opinions and Ceremonies they would die for . . . from the Fashions of their Countries, and the constant Practice of those about them" (§ 146).

37. To "pique" oneself clearly means here to "pride oneself," though the word occurs here twelve years earlier than the first such usage listed in the *OED*.

38. Cf. § 109; see also §§ 35, 38, 78, 80.

39. Cf. §§ 74, 76, 119, 129, 148.

40. See Axtell's note to § 105 (p. 207, n. 3).

41. Cf. Machiavelli's *Prince*, chap. 16.

42. Dunn, *Political Thought of John Locke*, p. 246, n. 1, and p. 248. Peter Laslett, opposing Macpherson and Strauss, uses similar language from the *Second Treatise* to dissociate Locke from the "spirit of capitalism" (Introduction to his edition of *Two Treatises*, p. 119), and in this he is followed by Dunn (p. 246, nn. 1–2) and by Alan Ryan ("Locke and the Dictatorship of the Bourgeoisie," *Political Studies* 13 [1965]: 224). Martin Seliger expresses similar reservations (*Liberal Politics*, pp. 142–43, 155), but he still believes it is justifiable to associate Locke with the spirit of capitalism "in the sense established by Max Weber and adopted

by R. H. Tawney—i.e., as expressive of views which alleviate scruples about acquisitiveness and stimulate industry, thrift and the accumulation of wealth" (p. 142, n. 6).

43. Dunn, *Political Thought*, pp. 212, 215, 228; cf. Seliger, *Liberal Politics*, p. 143.

44. Macpherson, *Possessive Individualism*, p. 237; this statement is quoted by Dunn, *Political Thought*, p. 214, n. 3, to illustrate that Macpherson claims that Locke reduces rationality to appropriation, but he makes no note of it in his comments on Locke's denunciations of covetousness.

45. *Essay*, bk. 3, chap. 10, § 33.

46. *Two Treatises*, II, § 34. The covetous seems to misunderstand the character of God's bounty; He did not spare men pains or present them with things already improved. Human industry and labor are necessary for plenty and even for subsistence; without them there would be nothing to quarrel over. Without security from meddling there would be no industry to produce anything to meddle with. See II, §§ 42 and 93.

47. See also Locke's note on Ephesians 5:3.

48. Cf. *A Letter on Toleration*, pp. 114–15, and Locke's early (1667) "Essay on Toleration," in Fox Bourne, *Life*, vol. 1, p. 182; see also *Essay*, bk. 2, chap. 28, §§ 7–10. Macpherson's contrast between Locke and Hobbes on covetousness is misleading. According to him, "Locke was not prepared to go as far as Hobbes," for the latter regarded "Covetousnesse of great Riches" as "Honourable" (Macpherson, *Possessive Individualism*, p. 237, quoting *Leviathan*, chap. 10. p. 156). Macpherson then argues that, though "for both thinkers unlimited accumulation was morally justified," Hobbes "made no distinction between covetousness and unlimited accumulation." However, though Hobbes, in the passage noted, states that great covetousness is "Honourable," that is, a "signe of Power"—along with, for that matter, any "great, but unjust" act (whereas "covetousness . . . of little gains" is dishonorable)—he did not regard it as "morally justified." Though he said that "covetousness" is "a name used alwayes in signification of blame," he recognized that men apply it to "Desire of Riches" generally—that is to say, *in others*—"because men contending for them, are displeased with one anothers attaining them." Hobbes, however, suggests, in opposition to this subjective usage, an objective one: "the desire in it selfe, be to be blamed, or allowed, according to the means by which those Riches are sought" (*Leviathan*, chap. 6, p. 123). Hobbes accepts the Second Table of the Decalogue (as interpreted by him and ultimately by the sovereign), including, in particular, the Tenth Commandment, *Thou shalt not covet,* as being natural law, known to human reason apart from Scripture (see *De Cive*, chap. 16, § 10, and *Leviathan*, chap. 42, p. 546). It is true, however, that he regards covetousness as forbidden *only* by natural law and *not* by civil law and as being, therefore, a sin but not a crime (*De Cive*, chap. 14, § 14, and *Leviathan*, chap. 27, p. 336). But that should not be taken to suggest that he regards it as "morally justified" any more than does Locke, who takes the same position. Indeed, for Hobbes, though the sovereign cannot forbid covetousness by law, any more than he can for Locke, it is part of his duty to teach the people that "not onely the unjust facts, but the designes and intentions to do them" are injustice, which is "the intention of the tenth Commandement" (*Leviathan*, chap. 30, p. 383). For covetousness as an unjust intention not only shows contempt for the legislator (chap. 27, p. 336); it is also an obvious source of crimes (p. 342). Hobbes's condemnation of covetousness involves, however, a reinterpretation, for he explains that "To be delighted in the Imagination onely, of being possessed of another mans goods, servants, or wife, without any

intention to take them from him by force, or fraud, is no breach of the Law, that sayth, *Thou shalt not covet*" (p. 336). This is a position Locke generally accepts in the *Thoughts*, i.e., that fault lies not in having desires but in being unable to deny them (§ 38). For Hobbes, even covetousness in his strict sense is one of the "infirmities, so annexed to the nature, both of man, and all other living creatures, as that their effects cannot be hindred, but by extraordinary use of Reason, or a constant severity in punishing them" (*Leviathan*, chap. 27, p. 342).

49. 1 Timothy 6:5–11 and 15–17; cf. *Two Treatises*, I, § 40, and II, § 31.

50. As such it would again resemble Hobbes's fifth law of nature in *Leviathan*, chap. 15, p. 209.

51. The qualification "almost" may indicate Locke's view that contention and even injustice disturb human life even in the absence of love of dominion, given merely the concern for necessities, self-preservation, and liberty in the state of nature, with its penury and lack of a known law. Cf. *Two Treatises*, II, §§ 32, 124.

52. See, e.g., §§ 96 and 134. As for Locke's interpretation of Luke 18:22–25 ("sell all that thou hast, and distribute unto the poor"), see *The Reasonableness of Christianity*, § 203. Cf. Hobbes, *Leviathan*, chap. 25, p. 306, and chap. 43, p. 622.

53. *Essay*, bk. 4, chap. 3, § 18.

54. Axtell, *Educational Writings of John Locke*, p. 215, n. 1; Hobbes, *Leviathan*, chap. 15, p. 202.

55. *Essay*, bk. 4, chap. 4, § 9. Cf. *Two Treatises*, I, § 42.

56. Cf. Machiavelli's *Prince*, chap. 16.

57. *Two Treatises*, II, §§ 30, 45, 51.

58. Ibid., §§ 25, 26, 27 ff.; §§ 31, 36; § 46; §§ 72, 116.

59. Ibid., § 45; cf. §§ 38 and 50, end. See also the notion of justice as "such a treatment of the Person or Goods of another, as is according to Law" in *Essay*, bk. 3, chap. 11, § 9.

60. *Two Treatises*, II, §§ 32, 34, 35. Also, compare §§ 13 and 101 to §§ 87, 89, 95–99, and 104.

61. This is the ground for Rousseau's insistence on teaching property on the basis of the child's labor and not on the basis of gift: "for him to be able to have this idea [property], he must have something that belongs to him. To mention to him his clothing, his furniture, his toys, is to say nothing to him, since, although he disposes of these things, he knows neither why nor how he came by them. To say to him that he has them because they were given to him is hardly to do better, for, in order to give, one must have. Here is, therefore, a property anterior to his, and it is the principle of property one wants to explain to him; not to mention that a gift is a convention and that the child cannot yet know what convention is. . . . The thing to do therefore is to go back to the origin of property, for it is there that the first idea of it ought to be born" (*Emile*, p. 98).

62. On the policy of ordering somebody else to do the taking, cf. § 83; on reasoning as making men "sensible" of advantage, cf. § 81.

63. *Two Treatises*, II, §§ 123–27, 131, and chap. 11 generally.

64. Ms. c. 28, pp. 139–40, published in Thomas Sargentich, "Locke and Ethical Theory: Two MS Pieces," *Locke Newsletter* no. 5 (Summer 1974): 27–28. Sargentich not unjustly calls this "a Hobbesian argument" (p. 24).

65. Cf. *Essay*, bk. 2, chap. 21, §§ 31–70, esp. 35 and 61–67.

66. Cf. ibid., bk. 3, chap. 11, § 9: "*Justice* is a Word in Every man's Mouth, but most commonly with a very undetermined loose signification."

67. See also § 106, beginning, § 35, beginning, and § 38, end.

68. Cf. *OED*, s.v. Stomach, mng. 8b (pride) and c (anger).

69. Cf. Rousseau, *Emile,* pp. 65–66.

70. See also §§ 33, 38, 48, 52.

71. On obedience to others' reason as preparation for obedience to one's own reason, see §§ 36 and 61.

72. *Essay,* bk. 4, chap. 9, § 3, and chap. 10, § 2; bk. 4, chap. 2, § 14, and chap. 11, §§ 3, 6–8; and bk. 2, chap. 7, §§ 3–6.

73. The rational teaching of justice did not begin with an improved sense of justice—with a recognition of the just measures of property—but with a sense of what "they value, and think their own" (§ 110).

74. Cf. *Essay,* bk. 2, chap. 20, § 2; chap. 21, § 41.

75. For the acceptance of shame, see chapter 2, note 71, above.

76. Cf. *Nicomachean Ethics* 1107a34–b4 and 1115b24–1116a9.

77. This pithy sentence may recall, but falls far short of, Hobbes's "The Passion to be reckoned upon, is Fear" (*Leviathan,* chap. 14, p. 200).

78. In this respect fear resembles certain bodily pains themselves: "The Pains, that come from the Necessities of Nature are Monitors to us, to beware of greater Mischiefs, which they are the Forerunners of" (§ 107).

79. Cf. *Essay,* bk. 2, chap. 20, § 10.

80. Ibid., § 6; see also ibid., chap. 21, §§ 29–37, also added in the second edition. The second edition of the *Essay* was published in 1694, the third edition of the *Thoughts* in 1695. Locke specifically includes the uneasiness of fear as a source of action in *Essay,* bk. 2, chap. 21, § 40 (also from the second edition).

81. The first phrase is added in the third edition, but the second phrase is already in the first edition as well as in the letter to Clarke of March 9, 1691, on which this passage is based (see Axtell, *Educational Writings of John Locke,* p. 391). This thought seems therefore to originate in connection with the *Thoughts* rather than with the *Essay.* See also § 46.

82. Cf. Strauss, *Natural Right and History,* p. 250: "Hobbes identified the rational life with the life dominated by the fear of fear, by the fear which relieves us from fear. Moved by the same spirit, Locke identifies the rational life with the life dominated by the pain which relieves pain [labor]." I am suggesting that Lockean rationality includes Hobbesian rationality.

83. Compare *Essay,* bk. 2, chap. 20, § 6, and chap. 21, §§ 31–33 and 64, to *Leviathan,* chap. 6, pp. 129–30.

84. *Essay,* bk. 2, chap. 21, §§ 30–31 and 71.

85. "Our first Actions being guided more by Self-love, than Reason or Reflection, 'tis no wonder that in Children they should be very apt to deviate from the just Measures of Right and Wrong" (§ 110).

86. In the passage on justice, however, self-love also turns out to be not entirely opposed to reason, which is identified with "Considerations drawn from Interest" (§ 110).

87. This interpretation is of a piece with Locke's disapproval of schoolboy pranks and fights (§ 70) and perhaps also with his philistine attitude toward poetry, music, and painting (§§ 174, 197, 203).

88. See, esp., *Essay,* bk. 2, chap. 21, §§ 46–52, 56, 67, and 71.

89. See ibid., § 53, "the true intrinsick good or ill, that is in things," and § 56, "the eternal Law and Nature of things."

90. Cf. *Nicomachean Ethics* 1117a32–b5 and Cicero, *Tusculan Disputations* 2. 32–33 and 43. Locke quotes the latter (2. 46) in *Essay,* bk. 2, chap. 28, § 11.

91. "This Brawniness and Insensibility of Mind is the best Armour we can have, against the common Evils and Accidents of Life" (§ 113); cf. Cicero, *Tusculan Disputations* 2. 33, "tectus Volcanis armis, id est, fortitudine."

92. Cf. *Nicomachean Ethics* 1115b17–24 and Cicero, *De Officiis* 1. 62–63.

93. Cf. Locke's statement that knowledge of the world is a fence against it (§ 94, p. 195).

94. Contrast Plato's views on the best internal "guard," *Republic* 549b and 560b.

95. Contrast *Nicomachean Ethics* 1115a24–b6. Cicero (*De Officiis* 1. 83–84) allows for a broader arena for courage, but it is still a political one.

96. Contrast *Nicomachean Ethics* 1115a6–b1; but note b11–13.

97. Cf. Hobbes, *English Works,* vol. 8, p. vii, where "fear . . . for the most part adviseth well, though it execute not so, " and Bacon, "Of Boldnesse" (*Essays,* no. 12), where boldness "is ill in Counsell, good in Execution."

98. See §§ 35, 42, 59, 64, 66, 100, 101–2, 110.

99. See *Essay*, bk. 1, chap. 3, § 3: "Nature, I confess, has put into Man a desire of Happiness, and an aversion to Misery. . . . I deny not, that there are natural tendencies imprinted on the Minds of Men; and that, from the very first instances of Sense and Perception, there are some things, that are grateful, and others unwelcome to them; some things that they incline to, and others that they fly: But this makes nothing for innate Characters on the Mind."

Locke speaks of "natural" connections of ideas and "natural antipathies" in the *Essay* (bk. 2, chap. 33, §§ 5–8), but he means only that the causes of their being acquired through experience are natural or even physiological rather than fortuitous, not that they are innate or prior to experience.

100. Pain and pleasure, Locke says here, "are not annexed to any shape, colour, or size of visible Objects." Locke here specifically excludes racial prejudice from being innate: "they are no more afraid of a Blackmore . . . than of their Nurse." Locke's example of fire proves so much that it undermines his position; for to show that the fear of fire is acquired only through experience, he remarks that "the pleasant brightness, and lustre of flame, and fire, so delights Children," and this remark concedes an innate association of a specific object with pleasure and therefore with desire. Why not then concede an innate association of the visible aspects of specific objects with pain and therefore fear?

101. On habits as of greater importance than discourse, see §§ 10, 64, 66, 67, 110.

102. Cf. §§ 44, 64, 66, 84, and 100. In its dependence on proceeding by degrees, mental habituation resembles bodily habituation; cf. § 7, "in this, as in all other *Alterations* from our ordinary way of Living, the Changes must be made by gentle and insensible Degrees; and so we may bring our Bodies to any thing, without Pain, and without Danger"; see also § 9. The emphasis on alteration indicates that gradualism is especially necessary when a previous habituation is to be reversed, as is the case in the present discussion.

103. On the mind's mastery over itself as a goal of moral education, see §§ 45, 48, 66, 75, 107, 200.

104. *Essay*, bk. 2, chap. 21, § 65.

105. For other anticipated objections, see §§ 4, 7, 9, 54, 78, and 107, and perhaps 81.

106. Cf. "the Mothers possibly may think this a little to hard" (§ 4); "How fond Mothers are like to receive this Doctrine, is not hard to foresee" (§ 7); and "This may perhaps be thought a little too severe by the natural Indulgence of tender Parents" (§ 107). See also §§ 9, 13 and 34.

107. For Locke on excessive corporal punishment, see §§ 43–51, 60, 72, 78–80, 84–86.

108. The principle appears again in the treatment of laziness, especially in § 129, where Locke says that "The Esteem they have for one thing above another, they borrow from others: So that what those about them make to be a Reward to them, will really be so."

109. Locke took notes on the pedagogical section of Plutarch's *Lycurgus* in October, 1678; see Ms., f. 3, pp. 305–7.

110. Locke calls death "the King of Terrors" (§ 110, p. 221). Similarly, at the start of the *Second Treatise* (§ 3) his definition of political power includes "*a Right* of making Laws with Penalties of Death, and consequently all less Penalties"; disgrace is thus a lesser penalty than death. But cf. *Essay*, bk. 2, chap. 28, § 12.

111. On the other hand, it must be remembered that this policy is to be applied to those whose natural temper is "weak," and proportionately to that weakness: "the softer you find your Child is, the more you are to seek Occasions, at fit times, thus to harden him." Locke even writes that, once this process of gradual habituation to pain is begun, "whenever he is observ'd to flinch from what one has reason to think he would come off well in, if he had but Courage to undertake; That he should be assisted in at first, and by Degrees shamed to"—a sequence that is dangerously likely to be perceived as punishment.

112. Axtell, *Educational Writings of John Locke*, p. 227, n. 1, referring to Locke's letter that appears on pp. 393–96. "Of Study" is included on pp. 405–22.

113. There is thus as much evidence for saying that Locke "entertained ambivalent feelings" about study or learning generally as there is about history in particular. But it is more accurate to say he disparages useless learning and praises useful learning.

114. Axtell, *Educational Writings of John Locke*, p. 394.

115. Ibid., p. 410. Both the disparaging of history in § 116 and the praises of it in §§ 182, 184, 186, 187, and 190–91 date from the first edition of the *Thoughts*. The distinction may be clearest in "Of Study" where Locke praises and blames in the same sentence: "I do not deny but history is very useful and very instructive of human life; but if it be studied only for the reputation of being an historian, it is a very empty thing" (Axtell, *Educational Writings of John Locke*, p. 409; see also p. 422).

116. In "Some Thoughts Concerning Reading and Study for a Gentleman," written in 1703 (in Axtell, *Educational Writings of John Locke*, pp. 397–404), Locke says (p. 403) that the "knowledge of men" is "to be had chiefly from experience, and next to that from the judicious reading of history," and in "Of Study" he says that history shows "a picture of the world and the nature of mankind" (ibid., p. 422).

117. "Of Study," p. 422. He continues, "there also one may learn great and useful instructions of prudence, and be warned against the cheats and rogueries of the world." Cf. Bacon, *The Advancement of Learning*, bk. 7, chap. 2: "we are beholden to Machiavel, and writers of that kind, who openly and unmasked declare what men do in fact, and not what they ought to do; for it is impossible to join the wisdom of the serpent and the innocence of the dove, without a previous knowledge of the nature of evil; as without this virtue lies exposed and unguarded."

118. "Letter to the Countess of Peterborough," in Axtell, *Educational Writings of John Locke*, pp. 394 and 395.

119. Ibid., p. 422; note that the reading of history recommended in "Some Thoughts Concerning Reading and Study for a Gentleman" (p. 403) is "judicious."

120. Locke discusses virtue in §§ 185–86 in the midst of his discussion of history. He does explicitly require a guide for learning knowledge of the world, so that it will lead to virtue rather than vice (see § 94).

121. "Of Study," *Educational Writings of John Locke,* p. 410. This point reveals most clearly the link between Locke's criticism of history and his desire to sever courage from the military context.

122. De Bartolomeis, however, suggests that Locke recommends a history of "the civil progress of man, his works of peace, his discoveries, his sense of liberty and of virtue" (*John Locke,* pp. 122–23).

123. *Two Treatises,* II, § 103. This appeal to historical instances is part of Locke's reply to an objection rather than part of his own argument; note the distinction between reason and history in II, § 104, and see also I, § 57: "But if the Example of what hath been done, be the Rule of what ought to be, History would have furnish'd our A—— [Filmer] with instances of this *Absolute Fatherly Power* in its heighth and perfection, and he might have shew'd us in *Peru,* People that begot Children on purpose to Fatten and Eat them."

124. Ibid., II, § 104; see also § 112: "as far as we have any light from History . . . all peaceful beginnings of *Government* have been *laid in the Consent of the People.* I say *peaceful,* because I shall have occasion in another place to speak of Conquest."

125. Ibid., § 175.

126. Ibid., §§ 176, 211.

127. Ibid., § 92. On the insolent and injurious, see also *Thoughts,* § 109.

128. On fraud, see *Two Treatises,* I, § 58: "when Fashion hath once Established, what Folly or craft began, Custom makes it Sacred. . . . He that will impartially survey the Nations of the World, will find so much of their Governments, Religions, and Manners brought in and continued amongst them by these means, that he will have but little Reverence for the Practices which are in use and credit amongst Men." Cf. *The Reasonableness of Christianity,* § 238: "what dread or craft once began, devotion soon made sacred, and religion immutable." See also the role of learning and religion in justifying the crimes of absolute monarchy, *Two Treatises,* II, § 92, and I, § 1.

129. See "Some Thoughts Concerning Reading and Study for a Gentleman," in Axtell, *Educational Writings of John Locke,* p. 403: "To fit a gentleman for the conduct of himself, whether as a private man or as interested in the government of his country, nothing can be more necessary than the knowledge of men; which [is] to be had chiefly from experience, and next to that from a judicious reading of history."

130. Ibid., p. 394. Locke emphasizes political changes and their causes as the focus of history, "the turns of state and the causes upon which they depended"; cf. ibid., p. 400: "the several turns of state and how they have been produced."

131. Ibid., pp. 395–96.

132. Ibid., p. 400; cf. the similar distinctions made between morality and prudence, which is best taught by history, and between "the ground and nature of civil society," including property, which "I have nowhere found more clearly explained, than in a book intitled, Two Treatises of Government," and "the interest of any country," attained by "all the arts of peace and war" (Locke, letter to the Reverend Mr. Richard King, August 25, 1703, in *Works,* vol. 10, pp. 306–9). See also the argument in his journal of June 26, 1681, that, unlike mathematics

and morality, "physique, politie and prudence are not capable of demonstration but a man is principally helpd in them by the history of matter of fact" (*An Early Draft of Locke's Essay*, ed. Aaron and Gibb, pp. 116–17).

133. "Thoughts Concerning Reading and Study," p. 398.

134. Ibid., p. 400.

135. Although in "Some Thoughts Concerning Reading and Study for a Gentleman" and the letter to the Reverend Mr. Richard King Locke recommends works on "the ancient constitution of the government of England," he does not seem to be much interested in it or to regard it as politically decisive. On Locke's lack of interest in this literature, see J. G. A. Pocock, *The Ancient Constitution and the Feudal Law* (Cambridge, Eng., 1957), pp. 235–38.

136. Note that he remarks that "our Practice takes Notice" of his argument by excluding butchers from juries of life and death. Rousseau probably picks up this point from the *Thoughts*, but he seems to think that the much-vaunted humanity and "good nature" of the English are belied by their love of hunting (*Emile*, p. 153).

137. That argument is suggested by *Two Treatises*, II, § 31; see Dunn, *Political Thought of John Locke*, pp. 87–95, especially this statement on p. 95: "if God had created all of it for some good purpose, clearly none of it should be destroyed without good purpose. Hence that other central axiom of Lockean politics, the duty to maximize preservation and its curious consequence, the iniquity of waste."

138. Cf. *Essay*, bk. 2, chap. 21, §§ 36, 40, 41–42, and 71.

139. Presumably because butchers will be insensitive to the suffering of the convicted criminal (not that of the injured victim). Locke himself encourages us to regard the execution of a criminal as the destruction of a wild beast in *Two Treatises*, II, §§ 8, 10, 11, 16, 172, 181, and 182.

140. Compare the "more natural Temper" Locke speaks of in § 116 to the "Compassionate or Cruel" native propensities mentioned in § 102.

141. *Two Treatises*, II, § 6.

142. Ibid., § 26. See also I, §§ 86, 92, 97; II, §§ 25 and 31; Dunn, *Political Thought of John Locke*, p. 166, n. 4; and *Two Treatises*, II, §§ 31, 37, 46.

143. *Two Treatises*, II, § 31; see also Dunn, *Political Thought of John Locke*, p. 108, n. 4.

144. *Two Treatises*, II, §§ 31, 34; see also I, §§ 41, 86.

145. Ibid., II, § 25; cf. I, chap. 4 and §§ 86, 88.

146. Ibid., II, § 31; cf. I, § 40, and 1 Timothy 6:17.

147. Richard Cox begins his "Justice as the Basis of Political Order in Locke" by quoting this sentence of Locke's as "a highly condensed version of his understanding of justice" (in the volume *Nomos VI: Justice*, ed. Carl J. Friedrich and John W. Chapman [New York, 1963], pp. 243–61).

148. Laslett's note to *Two Treatises*, II, § 16, in which he also quotes this sentence from the *Thoughts*. Preservation is not only a natural law (II, §§ 7, 16, 134, 135, 149, 159) but a natural right (II, §§ 11, 25, 220), a natural power (II, §§ 128, 129, 171), a natural desire or principle of action (I, §§ 86, 88), or, more vaguely, the will of nature or of God and nature (II, §§ 168, 182; the law of nature is said to be a declaration of the will of God in II, § 135). It is not only universal in the sense of pertaining to the preservation of all mankind (II, §§ 6, 7, 11, 16, 128, 129, 135, 171, 182), but particular in the sense of pertaining to a particular society (II, §§ 129, 134, 149, 159, 171, 220) or as self-preservation (I, §§ 56, 86, 88; II, §§ 6, 11, 25, 128, 129, 135, 149, 168, 171). Gough's claim (*Locke's Political Philosophy*, p. 19, n. 1; see also Raghuveer Singh, "John Locke

and the Theory of Natural Law," *Political Studies* 9 [1961]: 116) that "apparently individualist" passages on preservation "occur mainly near the beginning of the *Second Treatise*" is therefore not correct.

149. The passage on foolhardiness and timorousness (§ 115) dates from the third edition, later than this passage on the "two Faults."

150. Note Locke's remark that purposely to make children "uneasie . . . would relish too much of Inhumanity, and ill Nature; and be apt to infect them with it" (§ 107). The principle of preservation dictates that punishment in itself be regarded as an evil: "the *end of Government* being the *preservation of all*, as much as may be, even the guilty are to be spared, where it can prove no prejudice to the innocent" (*Two Treatises*, II, § 159).

151. See *Two Treatises*, II, §§ 8 and 11.

152. Cf. § 63; and see §§ 60, 65, and 78 for the first possibility and §§ 43, 46, 51, and 66 (p. 159) for the second.

153. *Emile*, pp. 92–93.

154. See also § 66, where Locke uses the phrase "an Humane, Friendly, civil Temper," and § 107, on inhumanity. Contrast the references to brutality in §§ 93 and 143.

155. See Macpherson, *Possessive Individualism*, pp. 221 ff.

156. See Dunn, *Political Thought of John Locke*, pp. 219–23.

157. *Two Treatises*, II, § 4; cf. I, § 67, and II, § 6; II, § 85.

158. Ibid., I, § 156; II, §§ 93 and 163.

159. Ibid., I, § 93; I, §§ 67, 81, 95; II, § 1.

160. See § 142, where Locke speaks of "that respect and distance, which is due to every one's Rank and Quality," and § 143, where he says that civility expresses "a respect and value" for all people "according to their Rank and Condition."

161. This is an elaboration of an argument made in the first edition in § 109.

162. See §§ 73, 74, 76, 97, 99, 109, 129, 148, 167.

163. On the pleasure of light, see § 115 ("the pleasant brightness, and lustre of flame, and fire, so delights Children") and *Essay*, bk. 2, chap. 9, § 7.

164. Cf. the arguments against useless learning in §§ 94 and 147. For a combination of both points, as well as an indication of the role of curiosity on a much higher level, cf. § 193, where Locke says that in natural philosophy, besides very many things "that are convenient and necessary to be known to a Gentleman," there are "a great many other, that will abundantly reward the Pains of the Curious with Delight and Advantage."

165. Cf., e.g., Plato, *Republic* 432b.

166. *Essay*, bk. 1, chap. 1, § 6; cf. bk. 4, chap. 12, §§ 11–12.

167. "Of Study," in Axtell, *Educational Writings of John Locke*, p. 406.

168. *Two Treatises*, I, § 58.

169. *Essay*, bk. 1, chap. 3, § 3.

170. Ibid., bk. 2, chap. 21, § 52; see also § 62, where Locke says, "I lay it for a certain ground, that every intelligent Being really seeks Happiness, which consists in the enjoyment of Pleasure, without any considerable mixture of uneasiness."

171. Ibid., chap. 21, §§ 49–50.

172. Ibid., chap. 27, § 26: "a concern for Happiness, the unavoidable concomitant of consciousness, that which is conscious of Pleasure and Pain, desiring, that that *self*, that is conscious, should be happy." Cf. "Of Ethics in General," § 7: "an understanding free agent naturally follows that which causes pleasure

to it and flies that which causes pain; i.e. naturally seeks happiness and shuns misery" (in King, *Life and Letters of John Locke*, p. 310).

173. *Essay*, bk. 2, chap. 21, § 51.

174. See § 74: "the Change and Variety is that which naturally delights them. The only Odds is, in that which we call Play, they act at liberty"; § 76: " 'tis that Liberty alone which gives the true Relish and Delight to their ordinary Play-Games"; § 128: "We formerly observed, that Variety and Freedom was that that delighted Children, and recommended their Plays to them"; and § 167 (pp. 273–74).

175. The reference to pride in § 52 seems to refer only to vanity about one's appearance, given the examples there and the recommendation, in §§ 55–62, of rewards of esteem. Section 105 recommends weeding out the love of dominion, not pride in general, which includes love of liberty (§ 103).

176. See §§ 129 and 148. Cf. § 70 (p. 165): "the emulation of Schoolfellows, often puts Life and Industry into young Lads."

177. The discussion of curiosity begins, in § 118, by referring back to § 108, where Locke emphasized the different policies appropriate for responding to the desires for a "thing they would *have*" or a "thing they would *know*."

178. On the vice of lying or falsehood, see § 131 and also §§ 37, 84, 99, 100, 139, and 140. The mention of "Dissimulation" here, however, reminds us that the child should be taught when to "dissemble" his knowledge of men (see § 94 [p. 195]).

179. Rousseau instead cleverly suggests that the question that Locke himself says children ask, "What is it for?" (§ 120), should be asked them about their questions when they ask what they should not know (*Emile*, p. 179).

180. Cf. § 102: "observe your Son's *Temper;* and that, when he is under least restraint, in his Play, and as he thinks out of your sight." Concealment is necessary presumably because even children have some "Art and Cunning" to "hide their Deformities, and conceal their ill Inclinations under a dissembled out-side" (§ 101; see also § 50).

181. The policy of surfeit may be suggested by "Turn the Tables" in § 76, and it is briefly touched on in § 108.

182. The point, after all, is that this method is "a better Cure" than the usual remedy for a preference for play over study, namely, "forbidding, (which usually increases the Desire)"; see also §§ 50, 83, 85, and 115 (pp. 223, 224).

183. But see also § 149, on how a child may be "cozen'd" into reading as play, and § 155, where Locke says, "cheat him into [learning to read] if you can, but make it not a Business for him."

184. Cf. *Essay*, bk. 2, chap. 21, §§ 35–39 and 58–65. Accordingly, since desire seems to lead to foresight, Locke writes there (ibid., chap. 20, § 6) simply that "the chief, if not only spur to human industry and action is uneasiness."

185. A desire for play would make it hard to distinguish this child from the one with the acquired aversion to learning.

186. Locke's counting aversions as desires here is consonant with his assimilation of the two as uneasiness in the *Essay*, bk. 2, chap. 20, § 6, and chap. 21, §§ 30–33, 66, 73.

187. See *Two Treatises*, II, §§ 37, 48, 49; the prince who encourages honest industry is "wise and godlike" (II, § 42). Laslett alters "Man," in the phrase "desire of having more than Man needed," to "Men," following the first edition rather than the later ones, which Locke corrected, and he also makes other alterations, without textual authority, in a way that diminishes the connection between this desire and the invention of money. Cf. Tocqueville, *Democracy in America*, vol.

1, pt. 2, chap. 9: "The most enlightened, patriotic, and humane men in Canada make extraordinary efforts to render people dissatisfied with the simple happiness that still contents them. They extol the advantages of wealth . . . and are at greater pains to goad human passions" (trans. George Lawrence [New York, 1969], pp. 284–85).

188. See § 74, where learning "might be made as much a Recreation to their Play, as their Play is to their Learning. The Pains are equal on both sides: Nor is it that which troubles them, for they love to be busie," and in play they "employ their Pains, (whereof you may observe them never sparing) freely." See also § 115 (pp. 224–25), where Locke says that "to bear very painful, and rough Usage . . . without flinching or complaining . . . this we see Children do every Day in play one with another," and § 206, where he says that "he that thinks *Diversion* may not lie in hard and painful Labour, forgets the early rising, hard riding, heat, cold and hunger of Huntsmen, which is yet known to be the constant Recreation of Men of the greatest Condition."

189. Rousseau repeats Locke's formula, only making it "the great secret" (*Emile,* p. 202; contrast *Thoughts,* § 56). See also Locke's "Essay Concerning Recreation" (1677; reprinted in King, *Life and Letters of John Locke,* pp. 330–33).

190. Cf. the chapter on property in the *Second Treatise,* where "the Plenty God had given" to man (§ 28) was only a "plenty of natural Provisions" (§ 31), so that man's condition was one of "penury" until his labor transformed it (§ 32).

191. See § 167 (pp. 273–74), "The Natural Temper of Children disposes their Minds to wander. Novelty alone takes them. . . . They . . . have almost their whole Delight in Change and Variety. It is a Contradiction to the Natural State of Childhood for them to fix their fleeting Thoughts." Locke is describing what today is called the "short attention span" of children. See also §§ 105 and 110 on the natural desire for unnecessary possessions.

192. Cf. § 45, where the ability to resist present pleasure or pain is said to be a temper "so contrary to unguided Nature."

193. *Two Treatises,* II, § 34. Cf. *Essay,* bk. 4, chap. 4, § 9.

194. Verdolini, *Giovanni Locke,* pp. 97 and 184, n. 1.

195. De Bartolomeis, *John Locke,* pp. 128–31 (my translations).

196. Cf. Plato, *Republic* 424e–425a and 558b and *Laws* 643b–c and 797a–b; see also Rousseau, *Emile,* p. 107 and *Considérations sur le Gouvernement de Pologne,* in *Du Contrat Social* (Garnier ed., Paris, 1962), p. 343.

197. See, e.g., the statements in *Two Treatises,* II, § 42, that "*labour makes the far greatest part of the value* of things, we enjoy in this World" and that "the increase of lands and the right imploying of them is the great art of government."

198. See § 207, "the learning or putting their hands to any thing, that was useful"; and § 208, "to acquire *dexterity and skill in hundreds of Things.*"

199. Cf. §§ 20 and 139. Adam's first excuse was that he feared to have his nakedness seen (Gen. 3:10). For his second excuse and those made by Eve and Cain, see Gen. 3:12–13 and 4:9. But cf. Locke on "untimely Prohibitions" (§ 85).

200. Cf. § 90, where parents are admonished "to cover that, which is the most Shameful Nakedness, *viz.* their [children's] natural wrong Inclinations and Ignorance"; that is, to cover these faults not with excuses but with "Vertue and Usefulness . . . Civility and good Breeding."

201. Cf. § 143 (p. 247): "Men, whatever they are or are not guilty of, would not have their faults displaid, and set in open view and broad day light before their own or other People's Eyes."

202. *Two Treatises,* I, §§ 10, 58; II, §§ 34, 107, 111, 199, 230.

203. Ibid., II, § 6; cf. II, §§ 7, 8, 11, 16, 25, 128–29, 135, 149, 171.

204. Ibid., I, § 88; cf. I, §§ 56, 97 and II, §§ 56, 58, 60, 63, 67, 170.
205. Ibid., II, §§ 17, 18, 23, 149; cf. I, § 1, and II, chap. 19.

## CHAPTER FOUR

1. Axtell, *Educational Writings of John Locke,* p. 241, n. 1.
2. *Essay,* bk. 3, chap. 9, § 3.
3. Ibid., § 8.
4. Ibid., chap. 11, § 10; cf. § 25.
5. Ibid., § 11.
6. Ibid., § 12; chap. 9, §§ 6–9; chap. 10, § 33; chap. 11, §§ 9 and 18; bk. 4, chap. 3, § 19.
7. Ibid., bk. 3, chap. 11, § 15; see also bk. 2, chap. 22, and bk. 3, chap. 5.
8. Ibid., bk. 3, chap. 11, §§ 15, 17.
9. A suggestion similar to Axtell's about the *Thoughts* has been made about the *Two Treatises* by Strauss (*Natural Right and History,* pp. 220–21), based on similar passages in the *Treatises* (I, § 109, and II, § 52) and the same distinction from the *Essay.* Strauss's suggestion has been rejected by Laslett, who says, in his Introduction to the *Two Treatises* (p. 99, n. 45), that Locke insists in the *Treatises* that the language of politics be "philosophic," though he "may have contradicted his own rules in practice." Locke, however, maintains in the *Treatises* (I, § 109) that "certainly Propriety of Speech is necessary in a Discourse of this Nature," though in the *Essay* (bk. 3, chap. 9, § 8) he explains that "*common Use, that is, . . .* Propriety . . . *regulates the meaning of Words* pretty well for common Conversation; but . . . is not sufficient to adjust them to philosophical Discourses." Laslett, however, denies that the *Treatises* are "political philosophy," and he classifies them instead with "Machiavelli and the writers of political advice . . . a convention of discussing politics and its theory outside the area of philosophy" (pp. 97–101). Dunn (*Political Thought of John Locke,* p. 198, n. 1) follows Laslett in rejecting Strauss's suggestion and adds, "There is no reason to suppose that Locke would have considered *any* of his works as samples of 'vulgar discourses,' such as those of 'merchants and lovers, cooks and tailors' " (quoting *Essay,* bk. 3, chap. 11, § 10; my emphasis).
10. By its not being a "just" treatise on education Locke also means that it is designed only for a young gentleman, not for a prince or a nobleman, to say nothing of young men of lower conditions (§ 216); see also, especially, the Epistle Dedicatory and §§ 4, 6, 15, 70 (pp. 169–71), 92–94, 131, 133–35, 141, 161, 164–68, 171–72, 175, 182–83, 186–89, 193, 195 (p. 307), 196, 198–99, 201–4, and 208–15.
11. Cox, "Justice as the Basis of Political Order in Locke," pp. 252–53, quoting from §§ 136 and 139 but citing only § 139.
12. For the ranking, see §§ 135, 141, and 147, and cf. §§ 70 (pp. 165 and 170), 93, 94 (pp. 195–200), 177, and 200. That virtue ranks first and learning last is far clearer than the relative positions of wisdom and breeding.
13. Yolton, *Locke and Education,* p. 31; see also p. 87.
14. See also §§ 41 and 45, and, on liberality, particularly § 110.
15. Cf. *Essay,* bk. 2, chap. 28, § 12, and Locke's "Thus I Think," in King, *Life and Letters of John Locke,* pp. 306–7.
16. To say that a true notion of God is the foundation of virtue is not the same as to say that it is what virtue consists of, as in Cox's account.
17. Cf. *Essay,* bk. 1, chap. 4, §§ 8–17, and bk. 4, chap. 10, § 1.
18. Cf. ibid., bk. 2, chap. 17, § 1, and chap. 23, §§ 33–36; bk. 4, chap. 10, § 19.

19. Ibid., bk. 1, chap. 1, § 7.

20. Cf. Locke, *A Letter on Toleration,* pp. 132–33. Although Locke equates superstition here (§ 136) with men's "making *God* like themselves," such anthropomorphism is to some extent inevitable because our notion of God enlarges ideas "taken from the Operations of our own Minds" (*Essay,* bk. 2, chap. 23, §§ 33–36).

21. Axtell refers to "the moral teachings of Holy Scripture" in his note to § 136 without mentioning this fact. It is true that in Locke's restatement in § 139 he writes of "a true Notion of a God, such as the Creed wisely teaches." But presumably he refers only to the first phrase of the Apostle's Creed, which proclaims belief in God the Father as creator of everything (a belief included within Locke's own statement here of the notion of God), and not to the creedal notions of Jesus, the Holy Ghost, or the Church. On creeds, see also §§ 157 and 159 and Locke's *A Third Letter for Toleration,* in *Works,* vol. 6, pp. 152–54, 408–11.

22. Cf. *Essay,* bk. 1, chap. 3, § 6 (where Locke says, of "the true ground of Morality," that it "can only be the Will and Law of a God, who sees Men in the dark, has in his Hand Rewards and Punishments, and Power enough to call to account the Proudest Offender"). See also bk. 3, chaps. 12–13, bk. 2, chap. 21, § 70, chap. 28, § 8, and *The Reasonableness of Christianity,* § 243 (where the law of nature cannot be known "without a clear knowledge and acknowledgement of the law-maker, and the great rewards and punishments for those that would or would not obey him"), and "Of Ethics in General," §§ 4 and 10, in King, *Life and Letters of John Locke,* pp. 308–9, 312–13.

23. The possibility of punishment may be suggested by the limitation that God "hears and sees every Thing, and does all manner of Good *to those that love and obey him*" (emphasis added). In any case, Locke adds, "You will find that being told of such a *God,* other Thoughts will be apt to rise up fast enough in [the child's] Mind about him"; perhaps divine punishment is one of those unspecified other thoughts.

24. See also § 67: "a Veneration for his Parents and Teachers, which consists in Love and Esteem, and a fear to offend them."

25. Although sleep may not have the charm of liberty that graces play (§§ 74, 76, and 128), it is a natural want (§ 107) in which children should be indulged "their full Satisfaction" or at least "a large Allowance" (§ 21). This "great Cordial of Nature" (§ 22) is so naturally attractive that in one of the most touching passages in the *Thoughts* Locke warns that "being forced from their *Sleep,* how gently soever you do it, is Pain enough to them" (§ 21). Wakefulness is not a pleasure for the philosopher, for whom life is an almost "constant succession of *uneasinesses*" (*Essay,* bk. 2, chap. 21, § 45). Indeed, being hastily awakened is itself a source of frightful apprehensions (§ 21).

26. In § 191, servants teach children such notions "to fright them into a compliance with their Orders," thereby ultimately "subjecting their Minds" to "Weakness" and "Superstition" or, in reaction, to "the other but worse extream" (presumably materialism or even atheism), the same dangers as result to most men from "too Curious" inquiries into the nature of God (cf. § 136).

27. See §§ 19 and 69. On the bad examples set by servants, see §§ 70 (p. 171), 76, and 89; on the importance of subordinating even the tutor's authority to the parent's, see §§ 83 and 88. Servants should be treated with humanity and not with "Domineering Words" or an "imperious Carriage," but this behavior in itself serves to maintain "Superiority" and to strengthen "Authority" (§ 117).

28. See Locke, *A Letter on Toleration*, pp. 66–77, 84–87, 94–97, 130–33, 146–49; *The Reasonableness of Christianity*, §§ 238 and 241; and *Two Treatises*, Preface, and I, § 64, II, §§ 22, 87, 89, 92, 112, 134, 149, and 210. Locke's discussion of subjection through belief in invisible beings and names in the *Thoughts* may also recall Hobbes's reference to priestly dominion as the "Kingdom of Darkness" in the last part of *Leviathan*. Rousseau, in *Emile* (pp. 133–38), rejects Locke's explanation of fear of the dark; he claims instead that, like superstition, it has a natural cause; his discussion climaxes in a mysterious story about a Bible and a church. Compare Thomas Jefferson's remark in his "profession of political faith," that "I am for encouraging the progress of science in all its branches; and not for raising a hue and cry against the sacred name of philosophy; for awing the human mind by stories of raw-head & bloody bones to a distrust of its own vision, & to repose implicitly on that of others" (letter to Elbridge Gerry, January 26, 1799, in *The Portable Thomas Jefferson*, ed. Merrill D. Peterson [New York, 1975], pp. 477–78).

29. Cf. § 139 on a true notion of God and a custom of prayer as "the Foundations of Vertue." Contrast § 33 on self-denial as "the great Principle and Foundation of all Vertue and Worth." In other passages, the "Foundations on which several Duties are built" and the "Grounds and Foundations of true Vertue and Generosity" are left unspecified (§§ 81 and 93).

30. Cf. § 110: "the safest way to secure *Honesty*, is to lay the Foundations of it early in Liberality" (which is also called "good Nature" in this passage).

31. Cf. *Two Treatises*, II, § 6. Locke's quotation from Hooker in § 5 is, as Laslett remarks in his note to the passage, "not quite exactly quoted," with the result that Locke prevents anyone from understanding Hooker to require us to love others as much as ourselves. See Hooker, *Laws of Ecclesiastical Polity*, bk. 1, chap. 8, § 7.

32. Cf. §§ 133 and 216. For "the Sons of Adam" see § 132; Locke can hardly be referring here to original sin, for he exempts a "few" from unhappy natural biases (cf. § 1, where a "few" are endowed with happy constitutions).

33. Cox, "Justice as the Basis of Political Order in Locke," p. 252.

34. Cf. *OED*, s.v. Fault, mng. 3a, "Expressing a milder censure than *vice*."

35. He does, however, call self-denial a virtue in § 107; justice a virtue and injustice a vice in § 110; courage a virtue in § 115 (p. 220); and lying a vice (though not in his thematic treatment of it) in § 120. See also § 108.

36. See §§ 67, 143, 110, and 116–17. See also Locke, "Morality" Ms. c. 28, pp. 139–40, in Sargentich, "Two MS Pieces," p. 28, where Locke says that "Civility Charity Liberality" are virtues "which relate to society and soe border on Justice."

37. See also § 38, where self-denial is "the Principle of all Vertue and Excellency," and § 45, where it is "the true Principle of Vertue and Industry"; see also § 200.

38. See also §§ 42 ("the Love of Vertue and Reputation"), 53, 57–58, 76, 81, 94 (p. 198, where "love of Reputation," along with the first three parts of education and industry, is placed above learning), 98, 108–10, 113, 115 (pp. 223 and 225), 118–19, 131–32, 145 (p. 252), 148, and 155.

39. In the same passage Locke calls love of praise "a Principle." We should note that he uses the ambiguous term "principle" sometimes to mean merely a "fundamental quality which constitutes the source of action" (*OED*, mng. 4), sometimes a "fundamental truth or proposition" (*OED*, mng. 5), and sometimes in such a way that one cannot be sure which he means. The outstanding example of his play with the ambiguity of this term is in chapter 3 of the *Essay*, "No Innate

Practical Principles," where he confesses that there *are* innate practical principles but that they are "Inclinations of the Appetite to good, not Impressions of truth on the Understanding," that they are "natural tendencies" not principles of knowledge (bk. 1, chap. 3, § 3). See also ibid., § 13, where he says that "Principles of Actions indeed there are lodged in Men's Appetites." There is a similar ambiguity in *Two Treatises* as to which kind of principles natural law consists in; see I, §§ 86, 88; II, §§ 6, 124. See also note 148 to chap. 3.

40. *Essay*, bk. 1, chap. 3, § 4. The same point emerges from *Two Treatises*, II, § 5, since Locke indicates there that the rule is derived from the natural equality of men.

41. In this respect, as in its definition, Locke's "wisdom" corresponds to Hobbes's "prudence" rather than his "sapience" ("wee usually have one name of Wisedome for them both") and to Aristotle's *phronēsis* rather than his *sophia;* cf. *Leviathan*, chap. 5, p. 117, and *Nicomachean Ethics* 1142a11–16.

42. On cunning, see also § 101, and cf. Bacon's distinction between cunning and wisdom in his essay "Of Cunning."

43. Cf. Bacon's essay "Of Simulation and Dissimulation." In his account of the "other kind of Tutors" in § 94 (pp. 193–95), Locke is not so confident that cunning is easily discovered.

44. Compare, especially, § 107: "They should therefore be accustomed betimes to consult, and make use of their Reason, before they give allowance to their Inclinations."

45. See also § 70 (p. 167), where knowledge of the world gives a young man "a manly air and assurance," valued "chiefly as a fence to his Vertue when he goes into the World under his own Conduct."

46. Compare § 1 on the mind's ability to direct "wisely" as the first prerequisite for happiness.

47. Compare the manuscript "Morality" (Ms. c. 28, pp. 139–40, in Sargentich, "Two MS Pieces," p. 28), where Locke says that "Civility is noething but outward expressing of goodwill and esteem or at least of noe contempt or hatred."

48. Compare § 67: *"Respect and good Will to all People."*

49. Compare §§ 67, 110, 116, 139.

50. Locke includes civility as one of the virtues "which relate to society and soe border on Justice" in the manuscript "Morality." The reference to justice as a social virtue dates from the third edition of the *Thoughts*, whereas that to civility dates from the fifth.

51. Compare § 67 on "Civility in the Carriage" and "in the Mind" ("inward Civility"). For a beautifully detailed account of gracefulness, see § 66, p. 160.

52. See also § 145 (p. 250): "It is as peculiar and different, in several Countries of the World, as their Languages."

53. See also § 93 (p. 190), "Nothing can give it but good Company, and Observation joyn'd together," and § 94 (p. 201), "This is a Knowledge he must have about him, worn into him by Use, and Conversation, and a long forming himself by what he has observed to be practised and allowed in the best Company."

54. See also § 67: "that respect will of it self teach those ways of Expressing it, which he observes most acceptable."

55. Compare § 66 (p. 160): "those little Expressions of Civility and Respect, which *Nature* or Custom has established in Conversation" (my emphasis).

56. See also § 41, where Locke says that children should come to recognize that parental restraints are "to make them capable to deserve the Favour of their Parents, and the Esteem of every Body else."

57. On the first fault of incivility, "Natural *Roughness*," compare § 9 and also § 66 (p. 161).

58. The passage in § 143 dates from the fifth edition, the one in § 145 from the third.

59. Cf. Hobbes, *Leviathan*, chap. 10, p. 153: "To agree with in opinion, is to Honour: as being a signe of approving his judgement, and wisdome. To dissent, is Dishonour; and an upbraiding of errour; and (if the dissent be in many things) of folly."

60. Compare *A Letter on Toleration*, p. 123: "laws are not concerned with the truth of opinions, but the security and safety of the commonwealth and of each man's goods."

61. See also § 143 (p. 249): "that whilst we gain the argument we may not lose the esteem of those that hear us."

62. *A Letter on Toleration*, p. 85.

63. See also § 177, where Locke says that learning without virtue will "make the worse, or more dangerous Man."

64. His recommendation of deliberately inflicting pain in order to harden children, though rarely to punish them, may also be said to be "strange" (§ 115, p. 223).

65. See also §§ 195 (p. 309), 168 (p. 279), and 189 (p. 297: "a Gentleman or a lover of Truth").

66. This method seems to have been used by Locke's pupil, the third earl of Shaftesbury, in educating the fourth earl; see "Mr Locks Play Things," by Horst E. Meyer, in *Locke Newsletter* no. 4 (Summer, 1973): 38–40.

67. Cf. Hobbes, *Human Nature*, chap. 8, § 4: "And because the power of one man resisteth and hindereth the effects of the power of another, *power* simply is no more, but the *excess* of the power of one above that of another."

68. See also §§ 167 (p. 271) and 177. For a brief account of Locke's own project of supervising an edition of Aesop and the role it played in his opposition to the renewal of the Licensing Act in 1695, see Axtell, *Educational Writings of John Locke*, p. 271, n. 2; see also "Locke's Aesop's Fables," by Robert H. Horwitz and Judith B. Finn, in *Locke Newsletter* no. 6 (Summer, 1975): 71–89.

69. For samples of Locke's own drawings of buildings and machines, see *Locke's Travels in France 1675–79*, ed. John Lough (Cambridge, Eng., 1953), pp. 5, 11, 129, 158, 197, 205, 212, 240, 263, 269, 285.

70. For Locke's use of shorthand for both purposes, see von Leyden's introduction to Locke's shorthand writings in Locke, *Essays on the Law of Nature*, pp. 246–51.

71. Compare §§ 10, 64–71, 93, 110, 145, and 185.

72. In the Epistle Dedicatory, Locke says, "I think it every Man's indispensable Duty, to do all the Service he can to his Country."

73. Locke traces the fault of contradiction to "the Custom of Disputing, and the Reputation of Parts and Learning usually given to it" (§ 145, p. 251).

74. Compare § 189 (p. 300): "To Write and Speak correctly gives a Grace, and gains a favourable Attention to what one has to say."

75. For Locke's view of the proper attitude toward the ancients, see his *Of the Conduct of the Understanding*, § 24, in *Works*, vol. 3, pp. 246–47.

76. Languages are "very much governed by the Fashion and Custom of every Country" (§ 143, p. 246) and "were made not by Rules or Art, but by Accident, and the common Use of the People" (§ 168, p. 276).

77. See Axtell's chapter "Locke and Scientific Education," in *Educational Writings of John Locke*, pp. 69–87, and also his "Locke, Newton, and the Two

Cultures," and Yolton's "The Science of Nature," both in Yolton, ed., *John Locke: Problems and Perspectives* (Cambridge, Eng., 1969), pp. 183–93 and 234–61. See also, of course, Locke's own *Elements of Natural Philosophy* in *Works*, vol. 3, pp. 303–30.

78. Compare *Essay*, bk. 4, chap. 3, §§ 26, 29, chap. 6, §§ 11–13, and chap. 12, §§ 10–12.

79. Compare ibid., bk. 4, chap. 12, §§ 11–12. Axtell, *Educational Writings of John Locke*, pp. 80–81, quotes this passage from the *Thoughts* but omits the last sentence and then comments: "Just *why* they were necessary, and of *what* advantage they were, Locke never said explicitly" (his emphases). However, the last sentence makes the necessity and advantage tolerably clear to one who has noted that Locke's gentleman should not contemn his "dirty Acres" (§ 174) and should learn gardening (§§ 204–6).

80. Compare § 216, where Locke says that his *Thoughts* "may give some small light."

81. The contrary passages all date from the first edition of the *Thoughts*.

82. Axtell, *Educational Writings of John Locke*, p. 79, assumes that this phrase refers to "the Creator, God," but Locke could hardly refer to God as a part of his own creation.

83. Ibid., p. 78.

84. Compare *Essay*, bk. 4, chap. 3, § 27.

85. Locke was not so certain of the immateriality of our souls in the most controversial section of the *Essay* (bk. 4, chap. 3, § 6; see also bk. 2, chap. 23, § 5).

86. See §§ 15, 40, 42, 96, 97, 110, 134, and 174; cf. *Two Treatises*, II, §§ 25–51; Aristotle, *Nicomachean Ethics* 1119b22–1122a17; Machiavelli, *The Prince*, chap. 16.

87. *Two Treatises*, I, § 92, and II, § 57; see also II, §§ 59, 138, and 140.

88. Ibid., II §§ 173–74.

89. Compare § 96; compare also Plato's *Republic* 330b–c and Aristotle's *Nicomachean Ethics* 1120b11–14.

90. Compare *Two Treatises*, I, §§ 41 and 59.

## Conclusion

1. *Two Treatises*, I, § 58.

# BIBLIOGRAPHY

Aaron, Richard, and Gibb, Jocelyn. *An Early Draft of Locke's Essay, together with Excerpts from His Journals.* Oxford, 1936.

Allen, J. W. *A History of Political Thought in the Sixteenth Century.* London, 1960.

———. "Sir Robert Filmer." In *The Social and Political Ideas of Some English Thinkers of the Augustan Age,* edited by F. J. C. Hearnshaw. London, 1928.

Aristotle. *The Politics of Aristotle.* Edited by Sir Ernest Barker. London, 1958.

Axtell, James. "Locke, Newton, and the Two Cultures." In *John Locke: Problems and Perspectives,* edited by John W. Yolton. Cambridge, Eng., 1969.

Barclay, William. *The Kingdom and the Regal Power.* Translated by George Albert Moore. Chevy Chase, Md., 1954.

Bartolomeis, Francesco de. *John Locke: Il Pensiero Filosofico e Pedagogico.* Florence, 1967.

Bellarmine, Robert. *Extracts on politics and government from the Supreme Pontiff from third general controversy.* Translated by George Albert Moore. Chevy Chase, Md., 1951.

———. *De Laicis.* Translated by Kathleen Murphy. New York, 1928.

———. *Power of the Pope in Temporal Affairs against William Barclay.* Translated by George Albert Moore. Chevy Chase, Md., 1949.

Bettelheim, Bruno. "Moral Education." In *Moral Education: Five Lectures,* edited by Nancy F. Sizer and Theodore R. Sizer. Cambridge, Mass., 1970.

Bonno, Gabriel. "Les Relations intellectuelles de Locke avec la France." *University of California Publications in Modern Philology* 33 no. 2 (1955): 37–264.

Brogan, A. P. "John Locke and Utilitarianism." *Ethics* 69 no. 2 (January 1959): 79–93.

Buchanan, George. *De Jure Regni apud Scotos.* London, 1689.

Calvin, John. *Institutes of the Christian Religion.* Translated by John Allen. 7th ed. Philadelphia, n.d.

Carlyle, R. W., and Carlyle, A. J. *A History of Medieval Political Theory in the West.* New York, n.d.

Chapman, Richard Allen. "*Leviathan* Writ Small: Thomas Hobbes on the Family." *American Political Science Review* 69 (1975): 76–90.

Colie, Rosalie. "John Locke and the Publication of the Private." *Philological Quarterly* 45 (1966): 24–45.

Cox, Richard. "Justice as the Basis of Political Order in Locke." In *Nomos VI,* edited by Carl J. Friedrich and John W. Chapman. New York, 1963.

———. *Locke on War and Peace.* Oxford, 1960.

Cranston, Maurice. *John Locke: A Biography.* London, 1957.

Daly, James. *Sir Robert Filmer and English Political Thought.* Toronto, 1979.

Doleman, R. [Robert Parsons]. *A Conference about the Next Succession to the Crowne of Ingland.* 1594.

Dunn, John. *The Political Thought of John Locke: An Historical Account of the Argument of the "Two Treatises of Government."* Cambridge, Eng., 1969.

Figgis, J. N. *The Divine Right of Kings.* New York, 1965.

———. *Political Thought from Gerson to Grotius: 1414–1625.* New York, 1960.

Filmer, Sir Robert. *Patriarcha and Other Political Works.* Edited by Peter Laslett. Oxford, 1949.

Fox Bourne, H. R. *The Life of John Locke.* New York, 1876.

Gay, Peter. *John Locke on Education.* New York, 1964.

Geisst, Charles R. "The Aristotelian Motif in Filmer's *Patriarcha.*" *Political Studies* 21 (1973): 490–99.

Glover, Willis B. "God and Thomas Hobbes." In *Hobbes Studies,* edited by K. C. Brown. Oxford, 1965.

Gough, J. W. *John Locke's Political Philosophy: Eight Studies.* Oxford, 1950.

———. *The Social Contract: A Critical Study of Its Development.* Oxford, 1957.

Greenleaf, W. H. "Filmer's Patriarchal History." *Historical Journal* 9 no. 2 (1966): 158–71.

———. *Order, Empiricism, and Politics: Two Traditions of English Political Thought, 1500–1700.* Oxford, 1954.

Grotius, Hugo. *The Law of War and Peace.* Translated by Francis W. Kelsey. Oxford, 1925.

Harrison, John, and Laslett, Peter. *The Library of John Locke.* 2d ed. Oxford, 1971.

Hayward, John. *An Answer to the First Part of a Certaine Conference Concerning Succession, Published Not Long Since under the Name of R. Dolman.* London, 1603.

Hefelbower, S. G. *The Relation of John Locke to English Deism.* Chicago, 1918.

Hinton, R. W. K. "Husbands, Fathers, and Conquerors: I. Filmer and the Logic of Patriarchalism." *Political Studies* 15 (1967): 291–300.

———. "Husbands, Fathers, and Conquerors: II. Patriarchalism in Hobbes and Locke." *Political Studies* 16 (1968): 55–67.

Hobbes, Thomas. *The English Works of Thomas Hobbes of Malmesbury.* Edited by William Molesworth. 11 vols. London, 1839–45.

———. *Leviathan.* Edited by C. B. Macpherson. Harmondsworth, Eng., 1968.

———. *Man and Citizen.* Edited by Bernard Gert. New York, 1972.

———. *Opera Latina.* Edited by William Molesworth. 5 vols. London, 1845.

Hood, F. C. *The Divine Politics of Thomas Hobbes: An Interpretation of "Leviathan."* Oxford, 1964.

Horwitz, Robert H., and Finn, Judith B. "Locke's Aesop's Fables." *The Locke Newsletter* 6 (Summer, 1975): 71–89.

James I of England. *The Political Works.* Edited by C. H. McIlwain. Cambridge, Mass., 1918.

Jefferson, Thomas. *The Portable Thomas Jefferson.* Edited by Merrill D. Peterson. New York, 1975.

King, Peter. *The LIfe and Letters of John Locke.* New York, 1972.

Krook, Dorothea. *Three Traditions of Moral Thought.* Cambridge, Eng., 1959.

Laird, John. *Hobbes.* London, 1934.

Lamprecht, Sterling Power. *The Moral and Political Philosophy of John Locke.* New York, 1962.

Laski, Harold J. *The Rise of European Liberalism: An Essay in Interpretation.* London, 1962.

Locke, John. *The Correspondence of John Locke and Edward Clarke.* Edited by Benjamin Rand. Cambridge, Mass., 1927.

———. *The Educational Writings of John Locke.* Edited by James L. Axtell. Cambridge, Eng., 1968.

———. *Epistola de Tolerantia/A Letter on Toleration.* Edited by Raymond Klibansky and J. W. Gough. Oxford, 1968.

———. *An Essay Concerning Human Understanding.* Edited by Peter Nidditch. Oxford, 1975.

———. *Essays on the Law of Nature.* Edited by Wolfgang von Leyden. Oxford 1954.

———. *The Reasonableness of Christianity.* Edited by George W. Ewing. Chicago, 1965.

———. *Locke's Travels in France: 1675–1679.* Edited by John Lough. Cambridge, Eng., 1953.

———. *Two Tracts on Government.* Edited by Philip Abrams. Cambridge, Eng., 1967.

———. *Two Treatises of Government.* Edited by Peter Laslett. New York, 1965.

———. *The Works of John Locke.* 10 vols. London, 1823.

McLachlan, H. *The Religious Opinions of Milton, Locke, and Newton.* Manchester, Eng., 1941.

Macpherson, C. B. *The Political Theory of Possessive Individualism: Hobbes to Locke.* Oxford, 1962.

———. "The Social Bearing of Locke's Political Theory." In *Locke and Berkeley,* edited by C. B. Martin and D. M. Armstrong. London, n.d.

Mandeville, Bernard. *The Fable of the Bees.* Edited by Phillip Harth. Harmondsworth, Eng., 1970.

Mansfield, H. C., Jr. "Hobbes and the Science of Indirect Government." *American Political Science Review* 65 (March 1971): 97–110.

———. "Machiavelli's New Regime." *Italian Quarterly* 13 no. 52 (1970): 63–95.

———. *Statesmanship and Party Government: A Study of Burke and Bolingbroke.* Chicago, 1965.

Marcuse, Herbert. "Repressive Tolerance." In *A Critique of Pure Tolerance,* edited by Robert Paul Wolff and Barrington Moore, Jr. Boston, 1969.

Meyer, Horst E. "Mr Locks Play Things." *Locke Newsletter* 4 (Summer, 1973): 38–40.

Moulds, George H. "The 'Right' and the 'Good' in Locke's Writings." *Locke Newsletter* no. 3 (1972): 17–25.

Nietzsche, Friedrich. *Beyond Good and Evil.* Translated by Walter Kaufmann. New York, 1966.

Oakeshott, Michael, ed. Introduction to Hobbes's *Leviathan,* edited by Michael Oakeshott. Oxford, 1957.

Parry, Geraint. "Individuality, Politics, and the Critique of Paternalism in John Locke." *Political Studies* 12 no. 2 (1964): 163–77.

Parsons, Robert. *See* Doleman, R.

Peters, Richard. *Hobbes.* Baltimore, 1967.

Pocock, J. G. A. *The Ancient Constitution and the Feudal Law: A Study of English Historical Thought in the Seventeenth Century.* Cambridge, Eng., 1957.

Polin, Raymond. *La Politique morale de John Locke.* Paris, 1960.

Rawls, John. *A Theory of Justice.* Cambridge, Mass., 1971.

Rosa, Pasquale. *Il Pensiero Filosofico e Pedagogico de Giovanni Locke.* Naples, 1965.

Rousseau, J.-J. *Du Contrat social.* Garnier ed. Paris, 1962.

———. *Emile, or On Education.* Translated by Allan Bloom. New York, 1979.

———. *The First and Second Discourses*. Edited by Roger D. Masters. New York, 1964.

Rowen, Herbert H. "A Second Thought on Locke's First Treatise." *Journal of the History of Ideas* 17 (1956): 130–32.

Ryan, Alan. "Locke and the Dictatorship of the Bourgeoisie." *Political Studies* 13 (1965): 219–30.

Sabine, George H. *A History of Political Theory*. New York, 1937.

Sargentich, Thomas. "Locke and Ethical Theory: Two MS Pieces." *Locke Newsletter* no. 5 (Summer, 1974): 24–31.

Schochet, Gordon J. *Patriarchalism in Political Thought: The Authoritarian Family and Political Speculation and Attitudes, Especially in Seventeenth Century England*. Oxford, 1975.

Seliger, Martin. *The Liberal Politics of John Locke*. New York, 1969.

Singh, Raghuveer. "John Locke and the Theory of Natural Law." *Political Studies* 9 (1961): 105–18.

Skinner, Quentin. *The Foundations of Modern Political Thought*. Vol. 2: *The Age of Reformation*. Cambridge, Eng., 1978.

———. "Meaning and Understanding in the History of Ideas." *History and Theory* 8 (1969): 3–53.

Snook, I. A. "John Locke's Theory of Moral Education." *Educational Theory* 20 (1970): 364–67.

Strauss, Leo. *Natural Right and History*. Chicago, 1953.

———. *The Political Philosophy of Hobbes: Its Basis and Its Genesis*. Chicago, 1963.

———. *Spinoza's Critique of Religion*. New York, 1965.

Tarcov, Nathan. "Locke's Thoughts Concerning Education, the Family, and Politics." Ph.D. Dissertation. Harvard University, 1975.

———. "Locke's *Second Treatise* and 'The Best Fence Against Rebellion.' " *Review of Politics* 43 (1981): 198–217.

Thomas, Keith. "The Social Origins of Hobbes's Political Thought." In *Hobbes Studies*, edited by K. C. Brown. Oxford, 1965.

Tocqueville, Alexis de. *Democracy in America*. Translated by George Lawrence. New York, 1969.

Verdolini, Ginevra Guglielmina. *Giovanni Locke: Il Pensiero Pedagogico*. Rovigo, 1954.

Villey, Pierre. *L'Influence de Montaigne sur les idées pédagogiques de Locke et de Rousseau*. Paris, 1911.

Von Gierke, Otto. *Natural Law and the Theory of Society: 1500–1800*. Cambridge, Eng., 1934.

Von Leyden, Wolfgang. "John Locke and Natural Law." *Philosophy* 31 (1956): 23–35.

Walzer, Michael. *The Revolution of the Saints: A Study in the Origins of Radical Politics*. New York, 1969.

Warrender, Howard. *The Political Philosophy of Hobbes*. Oxford, 1957.

Weber, Max. *The Protestant Ethic and the Spirit of Capitalism*. Translated by Talcott Parsons. New York, 1958.

Worcester, E. E. *The Religious Opinions of John Locke*. Geneva, N.Y., 1889.

Yolton, John W. *John Locke and Education*. New York, 1971.

———. "Locke on the Law of Nature." *Philosophical Review* 68 (1958): 477–98.

———. *John Locke and the Way of Ideas*. Oxford, 1956.

———. "The Science of Nature." In *John Locke: Problems and Perspectives*, edited by John W. Yolton. Cambridge, Eng., 1969.

# INDEX

Adam: and the desire for liberty, 21; and divine right, 20; and Filmer's patriarchalism, 11, 13, 14, 19, 58; and original sovereignty, 31, 58–60, 64

adults: education of, 172; and reason, 105, 118

Allen, J. W.: on Barclay, 31; on Buchanan, 24; on Filmer, 61; on Hayward, 30; on Machiavelli, 133

ambition: of children, 174; and desire for esteem, 116; in Lockean pedagogy, 183

Aquinas, Thomas, 52

Aristotle, 2, 11, 12, 15, 24, 37, 52, 56, 97, 189; *Nicomachean Ethics*, 97, 189; *Politics*, 11, 12

authority: and advantages of government, 148; civil, 128, 188; and consent, 71; and force, 96, 97; goal of, 94; and honor, 73; parental, 93–96, 123, 128, 130, 132, 136–37, 141, 163, 170, 181–82, 188–89, 197; patriarchal, 135; and power, 94, 148; relaxation of, 128; and resentment, 128; and severity, 153; tutorial, 197

aversion: to duty, 114, 176–77, 198; to learning, 175; to misery, 173; to play, 176; principle of, 99, 120; and punishment, 160, 182; to study, 176–77; to waste, 170. *See also* pain

Axtell, James L., 145, 164, 184–85, 203, 260 n.79

Bacon, Francis, 6, 87, 111, 156

Barclay, William, 23, 27, 31–33; in Locke, 62

Barker, Sir Ernest, 2

Bartolomeis, Francesco de, 108, 179, 180, 236 n.50

Bellarmine, Roberto, 11, 19, 22, 23, 27, 28, 30, 52

Blackwood, Adam, 23

blame: of children, 107; in instruction, 119; punishments of, 100, 103; sensibility to, 102; and virtue, 182. *See also* disgrace

body, 35; education of, 83, 84–86; habituation of, 85; and mind, 136; and nature, 84; politic, 35, 37, 41

breeding, good, 123–28; and civility, 193; and esteem, 195; as one part of education, 184, 193–98; and virtue, 186; and wisdom, 193

Buchanan, George, 23–24, 28, 31, 33, 52

Calvin, John, 23, 25–29, 127, 134

Chapman, Richard Allen, on Hobbes, 44, 45, 49

children: and age of discretion, 4, 55, 72; and civility, 196; and crying, 150–53; and cunning, 192; and curiosity, 172, 174; deception of, 176, 182; desires of, 46, 132, 135, 150, 174; and discipline, 114; and fright, 157; and honor, 43–45, 59; and ignorance, 172; instruction of, 43, 47, 48, 78, 80, 81, 88, 137, 198–99; and justice, 145–46; liberties of 94, 107, 134, 160; and love of dominion, 131, 150; and motivation to learn, 199; nature of, 89; and the notion of property, 146–47, 178, 206; and parental espionage, 175–76; and parental power, 11, 39, 55, 60, 75, 91, 94; and power, 150, 178–79, 199; and prayer, 186, 188; self-love in, 140; and social conceit, 170–71; and worldly wisdom, 191. *See also* duties, filial; family; obedience, filial; reason

265

esteem: and children, 102, 105, 118, 176;
and civility, 138, 194–95; concern for,
101, 111–12, 116–17, 142, 162, 190,
198; and habit, 112; and happiness, 95,
195; and hypocrisy, 139; of inferiors,
171; and learning, 199; and liberality,
141; in Lockean pedagogy, 169; love of,
101, 104; for others, 196; parental, 107,
135; and pleasure, 102, 112; and pride
95, 162; sanctions of, 169. *See also*
breeding

family: and monarchy, 28; and natural
freedom, 66–76; and parental instruction, 42–51; and patriarchalism, 11, 50,
51, 57, 58, 70, 75; in state of nature,
34–42, 53, 54. *See also* Scripture
fathers, 68; authority of, 94; and divine
right, 19; and dominion, 35, 41, 43, 75;
and natural right, 67; and political sovereignty, 11–13, 44, 57, 59, 135; in state
of nature, 38, 41. *See also* family; parents; power, parental
fault(s), 189; of deficiency, 175; of excess,
174; of lying, 181
fear(s): and authority, 97; of children,
187–88; and courage, 156, 187; and
daring, 153; of the dark, 187; of death,
37, 101; of evil, 154–55; and foolhardiness, 155–56; and honor, 43, 140; and
individual temperaments, 129–30; and
learning, 199; in Lockean pedagogy,
183; of pain, 158–59, 161; and power,
94, 128, 139, 162; and pride, 155, 163;
of punishment, 98; real, 159; and religion, 187; and state of nature, 39; to
offend, 111; utility of, 153–54; vain,
159, 161. *See also* education
Figgis, J. N., 61
Filmer, Sir Robert: and the Commandments, 11, 56, 57; and divine right, 19,
23, 28, 34, 61; and Hobbes, 16, 18, 20,
34, 37, 40, 41, 51–57; influence of, 214
n.6; and liberty, 10, 21, 23, 28, 34; in
Locke, 57–66, 78; and natural freedom,
23, 28; and natural law, 19, 53; and
natural rights, 4, 5; and property, 19,
60; and reason, 52; and scripturalism,
21, 52, 55–58, 61, 62, 64; and sovereignty, 52, 58, 59; *Directions for Obedience to Government in Dangerous or
Doubtful Times*, 15–17; *Patriarcha*, 10–66

passim. *See also* Adam; partiarchalism
freedom: and education, 73; and God, 39,
66; natural, 1, 20, 21–34, 38–40, 51–53,
58, 59, 66–76, 91; and power, 92; and
prejudice, 48; and providence, 17. *See
also* desire; liberty

gentry (gentleman): and accomplishments,
204; and desire for superfluity, 144–45;
education of, 5, 81, 90, 123–28, 184,
186, 207–8; and English law, 201; and
foreign travel, 206–7; and fortune, 170;
and good breeding, 193–98; and government, 5, 6, 166, 208; and Latin, 200;
and learning, 198–204; and liberality,
142, 145; as lover of truth, 201; and
lying, 181; and property, 5; and reason,
93, 145; and sciences, 200; and the
study of history, 164–66, 200; temperament of, 140–41; and trades, 204; and
virtue, 186; and worldly wisdom, 123–
28
God: and divine sovereignty, 37, 59; and
duty, 20, 167; and freedom, 39, 66; and
human nature, 67, 68, 109, 173; and
monarchy, 28, 29, 31–33, 49; and natural reason, 106, 168; and obedience, 25;
and original patriarchy, 13, 20, 58, 59;
and pedagogy, 111; and political providence, 9–22, 24–26, 29, 30, 32, 57, 60;
true notion of, 185–88. *See also* government, divine; power, divine
government: and authority, 141; of children, 78; divine, 187; and education, 5,
7, 72, 81, 82, 100, 122; and the family,
71; and force, 96; foreign, 207; the
foundations of, 12, 14, 15, 20, 25, 26,
28–33, 52, 65, 97, 165; and human nature, 28, 122; and individual well-being,
3, 24; instruments of, 100, 113, 114,
120, 171; limited, 24; mixed, 29; and
morality, 27; and pain, 117; and religion, 27; republican, 133; and rights, 1,
9, 23, 61; and shame, 99; and virtue, 3.
*See also* consent; liberty; power, political
gratitude, in Hobbes, 36–38, 44, 50
Grotius, Hugo, 18, 19, 22, 30, 52, 200

habit: and authority, 97; of courage, 156;
as cure for terrors, 158; and custom,
85, 89, 92, 108; in education, 46, 47,
84, 85, 89, 103, 107, 108, 111, 146,